P9-BZO-652

OUTRAGED

OUTRAGED

How Detroit and the Wall Street Car Czars Killed the American Dream

Tamara Darvish
and Lillie Guyer

iUniverse, Inc.
Bloomington

Outraged
How Detroit and the Wall Street Car Czars Killed the American Dream

iUniverse books may be ordered through booksellers or by contacting:

iUniverse
1663 Liberty Drive
Bloomington, IN 47403
www.iuniverse.com
1-800-Authors (1-800-288-4677)

ISBN: 978-1-4502-8944-3 (sc)
ISBN: 978-1-4502-8945-0 (hc)
ISBN: 978-1-4502-8946-7 (e)

Library of Congress Control Number: 2011913963

Printed in the United States of America

iUniverse rev. date: 09/29/2011

Dedicated to all the men and women
who courageously won and lost
on the battlefield of America's car wars in 2009;
and, importantly, to every entrepreneur
who believes in protecting free enterprise.

"Oh," God said to Abraham, "Kill me a son."
Abe says, "Man, you must be puttin' me on."

. . .

"Well," Abe said, "Where do you want this killin' done?"
God says, "Out on Highway 61."

—"Highway 61 Revisited," Bob Dylan

Contents

Introduction 1

The Fifth Amendment to the US Constitution 8

Chapter 1—Unraveling the War on Dealers 9

Chapter 2—The Company Hit Lists 44

Chapter 3—The Woman Who Knew Too Much 67

Chapter 4—Fast Cars and a White Cordoba 80

Chapter 5—Revving Up: Trips to the Hill 88

Chapter 6—Making a Difference on Main Street 111

Chapter 7—The Big Lie Times Two 125

Chapter 8—Outraged: Killing the American Dream 157

Chapter 9—Something Happened: Zombies and Stepford Wives 196

Chapter 10—Eat. Run. Push Congress.. 220

Chapter 11—Hometown Heroes 246

Chapter 12—Pride and Politics 276

Chapter 13—Showtime in Congress 301

Chapter 14—Who's Phoenix? 308

Chapter 15—Exile from Main Street 324

Chapter 16—Legal Eagles Take Aim 341

Epilogue: Fixing Humpty Dumpty 364

Acknowledgments 384

Appendices 387

Glossary 394

About the Authors 397

Bibliography/Index 399

Introduction

Shattered Dreams: 2009

The taking out of America's hometown car dealers is perhaps the most misunderstood or little-known story of the decade, certainly of the last few years. The collapse of the "Detroit Two" automakers (General Motors and Chrysler; Ford is the third component that makes up the so-called "Big Three," or "Detroit Three" automakers), and a temporary government group designed to rescue them set the stage for the events that transpired. The automakers saw new life. But a good portion of "Main-Street" car dealers were left to hang out to dry. Main Street and Highway 61 are used as metaphors for the rejected dealers, many of whose businesses were located on Main Streets or along highways in rural, small and midsize towns, as consultants pointed out. And dealers, as portrayed here, represent entrepreneurs everywhere, as symbols of the American Dream.

The dream goes something like this: you work hard, play by the rules, treat others well, and you too can attain the good life. It's a dream that has reinforced the hearts and minds of Americans since the pilgrims landed in Plymouth Harbor in Massachusetts to escape the tyranny of Great Britain in 1620. It was recorded in the Declaration of Independence in 1776. The dream has brought immigrants to our shores since that time. *Outraged* attempts to show the collapse of the American Dream from the perspective of dealers who won and lost on the battle lines. It's generally known that the auto industry suffered great losses from 2008 to 2009. Of all businesses, car dealers suffered perhaps the greatest fall. As of this writing, many are still fighting to get their businesses back or are awaiting some restitution from court proceedings. Most believed their constitutional rights were violated, particularly their Fifth Amendment rights. As recently as February and March 2011, dealers filed class-action suits against the US government for the unconstitutional taking of their businesses without compensation, as you will see in the legal chapter.

This story is mine to tell. As an affected auto dealer in the Maryland-Washington DC area, I joined the Committee to Restore Dealer Rights (CRDR). We vowed to reverse the dealer closures and became committed to positive action, carried out in a nonviolent way. My life has never been the same. My father, who founded DARCARS Automotive, lost three dealerships. After wins and losses, DARCARS still operates thirty-four franchises in three states and in Washington DC.

As you will see, the story shifts to third person as we start out Chapter 1. The narrative was developed by Lillie Guyer, an automotive journalist and coauthor of the book.

At its heart, this story represents the thousands who had their lives shattered and dreams destroyed. On a larger scale, it portrays the power of people who stand up for what they believe is right, or its reverse. What happens when you feel powerless and betrayed? Do you lie down and cower? Or do you stand up, raise your voice to the power players, and say, "This is not right. We're not going to take it anymore."

I like to think this is an important story for people in America, the country all Americans love. It's about people who get up every day, go to a job, and then come home to their families, if they are lucky enough to have both. Maybe they pull out a can of beer, switch on the TV, watch a ball game, help their kids with homework, or just vegetate. After a hard day's work, this is what they want—this is what they deserve.

But thousands of US car dealers didn't have that choice. In May and June of that fatal year 2009, they were stripped of their life's work and property. In some cases, four generations of a family's work were gone with an impersonal one-page form letter. Two automakers—Chrysler LLC and General Motors—essentially told them they were history, that their businesses were no longer needed. They were strangers to the party, outsiders, often after decades of doing business, breaking bread, and raising glasses together.

The rupture is much like a divorce, but in some ways it's worse. It's the death of a relationship and means of income, the killing of the dream. Blame the economy, blame corporate restructuring, blame the credit crisis. On and on the excuses came, if dealers were lucky enough to talk to a live person when they asked the simple question: Why? Most of us never got a response, verbal or written.

We look most closely at GM and Chrysler and the decisions they made to needlessly cut out a huge chunk of their retail sales force. These domestic yet global automakers crashed in the economic tailspin of 2009. And we look at how their crashes set in motion the demise of "Main-Street" car dealers. We also look at the role of the auto task force, who came along and added insult to injury as they steered the action in Washington DC and Detroit.

During May 13–14, 2009, Chrysler sent out tersely phrased termination letters, ordering dealers to shut down their businesses. They were given three weeks until total annihilation. "Have a nice day, dealer." Days later, GM lengthened the noose, giving dealers about eighteen months to "wind down," as the company put it. But the net effect again was termination—of a business, a long-term relationship. It began the process of lives spinning out of control.

Termination. It's an ugly word. It smacks of insects being squashed underneath one's foot. It's unkind. It's un-American. It smacks of repressive societies and their suppression of innocents. It suggests people being put down, often for no reason other than some higher power wanted them gone.

Major media used words like "terminated," "culled," "axed," "rejected," "whacked," and "cut" to describe the key action in getting rid of the dealers. Dealers thought of it as murder, robbery, theft, or a mugging. It was that personal.

"It can't happen here, not in the United States," the victims, often small-business owners, told each other. "It can't be true," their spouses, children, and significant others said tearfully. Does this mean good-bye to college, good-bye house on the hill, and good-bye nice meals out? Even worse, does this mean starvation?

Let me tell you about the Jim Painter family, a four-generation business owner in St. George, Utah, who thought they lost everything. Let me tell you about Yale King in Colorado, Richard and Jackie Mealey in Michigan, Frank Blankenbeckler in Texas, Mark Calisi in New York, Jim Tarbox in Rhode Island, Lee and Karen Carlson in Minnesota, Mike Comiskey in Louisiana, and Gus Russo and his daughter Gina Russo in Michigan. There are hundreds of others whose faces I still see, whose words echo in my ears.

Some of their stories are detailed here, although we can't do justice and cover them all. Their stories are poignant because they are true. This book is about their journey, our journey. We tried to right some undeniable wrongs by setting forth facts, feelings, and events. Dealers and their families, lawyers, Congress members, and a host of others became willing sources for our work.

In 2005, hurricanes Katrina and Rita wiped out three states—Louisiana, Mississippi, and Alabama—and affected countless others. These were natural disasters, and most Americans took note. Hurricanes Chrysler and GM blew by, sometimes unnoticed, affecting every state in the nation.

But we rose from victimhood. We came together in groups—sometimes small ones—to say to the power structure: "This is wrong." And if something is wrong—a law is broken, the Constitution is trampled, people's lives are destroyed for no reason—change things, we said. "We the people" still have power. Silly me, I still believe in the notion of "and justice for all." I still believe in the founding principles of our great nation.

In July of 2009, I spoke at a press conference at a dealer rally on Capitol Hill in Washington DC. I wanted to address the plight of the US car dealer. Moments before, I was shaking in my shoes. But I did it because I knew what had happened was wrong, and I believed the dealers could be vindicated. I brought my two children, then ages twelve and fourteen. I wanted them to see that when you believe in your heart something is wrong, you speak out. You take action.

The backstory: In 2009, GM and Chrysler announced they would shut down about 2,200 dealers, affecting nearly 170,000 jobs in small, medium, and large cities across the country. Among insinuations of personal vendattas or paybacks, lists were created in corporate offices, maybe in social settings as martinis were sipped, backs slapped. Targets must be met, after all. And in the private offices, and stored in computers of two of the world's most powerful corporations, names were supplied, anecdotes related, lists constructed. This is further detailed in the book.

Much of what we write in this book describes how dealers, as part of CRDR, engaged Congress in the process of restoring dealers. Later, almost every member of Congress said rejected dealers should be restored. They asked, "Why this person, this group, why that one?" But the criteria for selecting who stayed and who went was slippery and illusive. The terms sometimes changed after the fact. Congress and an investigative group would find what the rejected dealers knew: the cuts had been unnecessary.

We addressed the outright lies made to US court judges, Congress, subcommittees, and in public forums by the automakers, their minions who stepped in line, and, in complicity, the government. The media jumped on the dealer rights story, rendering good and bad accounts. But often fair enough.

But the American public—numb from a deep recession, their own jobs sometimes in peril, unemployment spiraling in an economy the worst since the Great Depression—often couldn't deal with another American tragedy—the killing of the Main-Street car dealer, which will be detailed throughout the book. Perhaps Americans didn't realize what was happening. They didn't think about the dealership-related jobs in communities and among suppliers that would be lost, along with the millions of dollars in charitable contributions made by dealers to their communities, from Little League teams to sports and charity sponsorships. Perhaps they didn't care. From parenting to holding down demanding jobs, they were immersed in a world of their own.

Yes, the affected dealers are outraged. Many are still shocked and heartbroken over their unbearable losses. Even those who can't bear to talk about their pain still feel it. *It's like I'm being punished every day, but I don't know what I did wrong.* That kind of feeling permeated the dealer groups I know.

But the lesson for all is that it can—did—happen here and could happen again. Every private citizen in America—especially entrepreneurs—should be concerned about what happened to dealers.

Another reason I had to put this story on paper—this is personal. I simply refuse to let John Darvish, my father, go down being called "a poor performer," or "a reject." I refuse to let the reputations of thousands of men and women connected to this fine industry be cast in that negative light too. I know many personally. Poor performers, rejects, deficient, underachievers—those were the labels created for them in the corporate backrooms. They are mostly convenient excuses and are not true. In *Outraged*, several successful dealers relate their stories of being victims of personal vendettas or of having to watch as their businesses were handed over, often to favored "third-party" dealers.

This is not intended to be a polemic on left or right, Democrats or Republicans, or the emerging Tea Party. It's meant to be nonpartisan. Most of the action takes place primarily over eight months in 2009, unless noted, and then jumps to a time period called "arbitration" as dealer lawyers argued cases of the terminated dealers before supposedly neutral arbiters.

Inside, we try to offer answers, not just anger. If failing to always do so, it's a human failing. We hope to set out some facts, some truths. Let the cards fall where they will.

Sometimes our own tears, and fears, are too much. I'm a woman, and I get emotional. Just ask GM or Chrysler; ask Congress and bodies like the auto task force, many of whom likely can't be located these days. Ask the dealer auto associations. They should know me as a passionate believer in human rights, not always quiet or willing to shut up when I believe wrong is being done. Like the corporate leaders I often encountered, I wouldn't—couldn't—back down.

We want to bring you inside the process. Take you on the journey with us. Shine the spotlight on America's power structures, so you, too, can be a truth seeker. Brave people, braver than I, showed me the way, enabled me with every step I took. You, too, can stand up if it ever happens to you or those you care about. Stand up to the powers that be. They are mere mortals, like all of us.

The word "committee" is used often here to refer to the CRDR (Committee to Restore Dealer Rights) group run by Alan Spitzer, Jack Fitzgerald, and me. Although my given name is Tamara, most people know me as Tammy. Otherwise, there is a glossary at the back that defines some industry terms and acronyms not commonly known to many readers.

We've attempted to share some interpretation and insights on the events that led to the war on dealers. And there are some positives on the scales of justice as our fight became history. Our varied sources included hundreds of dealers, their employees, family, members of Congress, lawyers, consultants, analysts and government officials, as well as thousands of pages of documents and memos. "We live in the greatest country the world has ever known. What makes this country so great and so wonderful is our divinely inspired Constitution and our unconditional love for individual liberty. Car dealers are the ultimate example of capitalism and the American Dream." That is the beginning of a letter I wrote on September 3, 2009, to Congress and others. It's part of our narrative herein.

This is the car dealers' story, as best as we can portray it. It could be America's story. We must guard that it doesn't happen again.

Respectfully,
Tammy Darvish,
US car dealer, as told to Lillie Guyer

The Constitution of the United States of America

The Fifth Amendment of the United States Constitution states:

"No person shall be held to answer for a capital, or otherwise infamous crime, unless on a presentment or indictment of a Grand Jury, except in cases arising in the land or naval forces, or in the Militia, when in actual service in time of War or public danger; nor shall any person be subject for the same offense to be twice put in jeopardy of life or limb; nor shall be compelled in any criminal case to be a witness against himself, nor be deprived of life, liberty, or property without due process of law; nor shall private property be taken for public use, without just compensation."

Chapter 1—Unraveling the War on Dealers

If you abide by the law you should be protected by it; if you adhere to our common values you should be treated no different than anyone else.
—President Barack Obama's 2010 State of the Union Speech

A lasting image in America's collective mind is that day, November 18, 2008, when three chief executives of the Detroit Three flew into Washington DC aboard their corporate jets. The stories instantly made national broadcast news and major headlines.

General Motors CEO Richard Wagoner debarked from the company's Gulfstream IV jet, and ABC TV showed the descent in living color. Ford Motor Company CEO Alan Mulally, and Robert Nardelli, CEO at Chrysler LLC, also flew in on company jets, the media reported.

Broadcast stations were all over it after *ABC News* broke the news. The next day, in a story headlined "Shocker: Fat cat CEOs fly on private jets!" *Reuters* reported the story that was soon "heard around the world." Rick Wagoner told media he took a company jet because he's a busy guy. Ford's Mulally, who didn't say much, seemed to be following Henry Ford's motto of "don't complain, don't explain." Robert Nardelli tried to stay out of the limelight at the time as well.

While America watched, the CEOs had arrived to ask for a twenty-five-billion dollar lifeline, a taxpayer bailout, to keep their companies running. Their timing was atrocious. The "B-word" was becoming a dirty word in consumers' minds. Of the more than $700 billion in Troubled Asset Relief Program (TARP) funds available to rescue failing companies, the majority had been doled out to the financial institutions and Wall Street entities.

The automakers kept saying their request was a conditional *loan*, not a bailout. But that distinction was lost on many Americans. And they would ask for more in the coming months.

The executives took heat for the private jets and later changed to other transportation modes, as if just discovering them. Top-dog Wagoner tooled around DC in the new production model Chevrolet Volt, a combined electric and gas extended-range car that debuted in November 2010. The other leaders originally flew in on private jets but seemed to get less flack.

Big PR splashes were later orchestrated to show the execs arriving on commercial jets or driving more fuel-efficient company vehicles as they pressed for public funds. But the damage had been done. The earlier images of corporate excess were difficult to erase.

What "Joe and Josephine America" remembered was that executives earning millions of dollars a year and fat perks were asking for taxpayer-funded assistance, a new form of "corporate welfare." In a time when many Americans had to tighten belts and live more frugally, the execs were traveling on luxury jets on trips that cost upward of $20,000 to fly from Detroit to Chicago alone, a shorter distance than to DC, *ABC News* reported. In the public eye, it was like watching a welfare recipient buy tons of caviar and vodka with food stamps.

"This is a difficult time for a free-market person. Under ordinary circumstances, failed entities, failing entities, should be allowed to fail. I have concluded that these are not ordinary circumstances," President George W. Bush said on December 18, about a month before he departed office. Bush did not want to leave office knowing that the American car industry had gone down under his watch. The funding spigot was turned on then.

In exiting, the Bush administration punted the auto-rescue problem to the incoming Democrats. It was all tied to the huge money pot called TARP (Troubled Asset Relief Program) that was used to prop up banking, financial, and now the auto industries. But it came with strings attached. Money always does.

Fast forward to the Barack Obama White House in January. With the new president installed, the auto executives were asking for more money. Since their earlier November meetings with Bush officials, the auto leaders had one mission in mind: secure a massive infusion of cash to save their fragile, bleeding companies.

Earlier, the Bush Treasury, headed by Hank Paulson, had approved loans of $17.6 billion for GM and Chrysler. As it turned out, Ford backed out and said it would not ask for federal loans, saying it would go it alone by relying on private credit lines of financing and selling off assets. By the time GM and Chrysler asked for emergency loans, Ford had already tapped into its remaining credit lines—luckily well before credit markets froze nationwide.

In 2008, Ford had its worst year in its recorded history but was able to bring its cash reserves up to $24 billion by January, CEO Alan Mulally later said. They would tough out the lousy economy without the emergency federal loans, Ford leaders said Ford had borrowed about $24 billion in late 2006 right after Mulally arrived, coming from Boeing Company. The automaker also put up its major assets and began austere cost-cutting measures.

In the Bush White House, Paulson was a big proponent of saving the auto industry, as would Larry Summers, who served then as President Obama's chief economic advisor. He was joined by Timothy Geithner, the US Treasury Secretary who drove the bus that would lead to restructuring the auto dynasty known as General Motors and Chrysler LLC, the nation's third-largest automaker, then owned primarily by Cerberus Capital Management.

Ironically, Summers, a former Harvard University dean and true believer in capitalism and free markets, expressed his distaste for government interference in business. Yet that was exactly what his fledgling auto group that was charged with rescuing the automotive industry went on to do.

On February 15, not quite a month into office, Obama announced a new interagency group called the "auto task force." It was this temporary group that would take on the complex assignment of restructuring the automakers and making the calls on key stakeholders such as the United Auto Workers, creditors groups, suppliers, and dealers.

Why was it important to save these automakers in this industry? At stake was the nation's industrial manufacturing might and history. Manufacturing has always been a major engine for the economy; it's also an industry important to national defense. Some estimates were that one in nine jobs rely on the auto industry, directly or indirectly affecting everyone from dealerships to department stores, barbershops, restaurants, and other businesses.

Also at stake was GM, the US kingpin and the largest auto manufacturer in the world until 2008, when Toyota Motor Manufacturing replaced it; and Chrysler, the underdog company which had struggled over the decades to compete and remain solvent, was important to the economy and keeping people working. Shut down Chrysler alone and watch three hundred thousand jobs disappear, the auto task force said.

And economists feared the declining economy could not withstand a Detroit implosion. President Obama claimed he inherited a $1.3 trillion budget deficit from the Republicans and should not be judged so harshly on his efforts to save the automotive industry. The new president had his share of critics in funding yet more failing companies. After beginning his term on January 21, he spoke about shared sacrifice. That's what ordinary citizens and companies need to do in extraordinary times, he said. Take the bitter medicine and pull together for the greater good.

White House Press Secretary Robert Gibbs said, "It is clear that going forward, more will be required from everyone involved—creditors, suppliers, dealers, labor and auto executives themselves—to ensure the viability of these companies going forward." It was the genesis of Obama's "shared sacrifice" pitch to the country.

Following the bailouts (the "B-word") of the banks and Wall Street, the two automakers, their finance arms, and their suppliers could apply for the bulk of available TARP funds for auto—about $82 billion in conditional loans to be paid back with interest.

By now, Americans were getting sick of the B-word and watched as corporate giants were rescued but Main Street went empty-handed. It led to a new rage brewing across the country.

The whole restructuring was history in the making. A new chapter of the American car wars was being written. Rather than fighting against the foreign rivals on US shores, the war had become domestic.

It was these government and automaker-controlled scenarios that set up a chain of events that would cause the collapse of car dealers, who would be cut en masse about four months later. The unraveling of the American free-enterprise system in auto retail was set in motion. There were no street signals as the collision course between automakers, the government oversight group, and auto dealers was paved.

All systems were "Go," following the task force involvement.

Two iconic automakers, GM and Chrysler, became part of a rescue operation that would lead to the demise of a good portion of car dealers, considered among America's original entrepreneurs, who were all independent business people. Dealers were often among the highest taxpayers and bigger employers in their communities, a factor that went largely ignored by the power players.

The competition was fierce between the three domestics and between domestics and imports (also called "transplant automakers") with US factories. There was even competition between the brands in the various companies. It had come down to every customer, every deal, counted.

Fueling the controversy, some auto critics erroneously believed that the imports sent their profits back to the mother country, such as Japan. Automakers such as Toyota maintain that a majority of their US profits are reinvested in the US and North America, with US investments standing at about $18 billion, according to company spokespersons and the media website. Toyota, for example, says it has thirteen US plants, with a new one to open in Mississippi, and counts more than two hundred thousand American jobs; even more if dealers and suppliers are factored in.

Dealers Tighten the Reins

While the auto rescues were unfolding, the "new normal" was seen in belt tightening around the country in early 2009. Americans everywhere were feeling the pinch as jobs, savings, and benefits spiraled downward.

The John Darvish family, who ran DARCARS Automotive, was tightening the reins too, adjusting to a new and tough economy at their Maryland-headquartered dealerships in Silver Spring. They had lost two Chrysler stores and one GM dealership in the automaker cullings.

Like many dealers, the Darvishes did all the right things—taking care of customers, and trying to keep their employees working rather than laying them off in a severe economic recession. They paid huge taxes. They also contributed to or chaired major philanthropic and community events that raised more than $2 million a year, part of their corporate and personal philosophy.

Tammy Darvish, a mega-dealer's daughter, held the title of executive vice president at the dealerships. She held the title but was concerned about the lavish displays of excess she had seen with the automakers. Maybe it was her upbringing, but she tried hard to live within her means. She shopped at Kohl's, Macy's and Target like many Americans do. She often cooked at home on weekends and wore duct tape on her shoes to preserve them as she roamed the dealership grounds. Like her customers, she loved a good bargain.

"There's a great sale at Kohl's this weekend," she said in a call to her cousin, Mina Gharib, who also worked in the family dealerships. "Want to go at lunchtime?" She sometimes ran errands whenever she could grab a minute. She would often buy supplies and groceries in bulk at Costco Foods for parties and large meetings. She wasn't above trying to save money in running her dealerships and household affairs.

A lecture to her two children might be that they couldn't have the latest gadget or gizmo just because they wanted it, or because other kids had it. Her teenage years of growing up watching every penny reinforced the value of working for what you get.

Rob Smith, Darvish's colleague at Fitzgerald Auto Mall in nearby Kensington, Maryland, often commiserated with her on child care and dealership issues. Few people knew that Smith was a single father of three children, aged four, fourteen, and seventeen, who lived with him full time.

Darvish and Smith knew one another from countless industry meetings, but became friends as the dealer crisis unfolded. Together their "shared sense of humor and practical jokes would carry us through some difficult times ahead," Smith said. In an industry known for long hours where balancing family and work is already tough, it was even more so when you had to go it alone. He was also a no-frills vice president and right hand to dealer Jack Fitzgerald. "I've got the kids tonight," he'd say, rushing out to pick up a child in day care before running to a meeting at the high school for another child.

To his boss, Jack Fitzgerald, he'd say, "See you in the morning; call if you need anything," as he departed with his laptop and paperwork in his briefcase to tackle at night. The car ride home meant a recap of the day with Darvish about contacts made, any must-dos for the evening, and plans for next steps. There was often a phone call at night to check strategy.

Smith said, "I have the ability to cook, but no longer have the time." So meals often were on the run. Some nights his teens had to go it alone and put the youngest to bed if his meetings went long into the night, as they did when negotiations between dealers and automakers started. He realized at times he would have to hire two to three people to do the job of a typical at-home parent. He tried to do it all.

His work morning typically started at 6:00 a.m. as he checked news stories online about dealer activities, made calls, and handled e-mails on his home computer. After seeing his older children off to school on their 6:40 bus and driving the youngest to day care, he would arrive at work by 8:00 a.m. to prepare for meetings at work or on Capitol Hill. Dealership employees across the country were going through similar routines, tightening up, making do with less.

* * *

In 2008 and leading into January 2009, the country teetered on Depression-like economic conditions. Recall that troubled time period: the auto industry was near collapse. President Obama's new Democratic administration had inherited a huge budget deficit and a world of problems—from a banking and oil crisis to plunging real-estate prices and a credit freeze. The Iraq and Afghanistan wars were still rearing their ugly, expensive heads.

The economic crisis had gone global. Banks were drowning in debt, and the stock market had plunged. Health-care costs skyrocketed as everyday workers lost their jobs and older and younger Americans struggled to keep up. In autos, the domestic carmakers were hanging from a cliff by their fingernails. Sales had plummeted as middle-class purchasing power eroded. Small, medium, and big-time investors watched their savings, pensions, and 401Ks vanish. Once known as the "Big Three," the automakers were now called the "Detroit Three": GM, Ford, and Chrysler.

An interesting sidebar: in December, right before Bush departed, Steve Feinberg, founder and CEO of Cerberus, the private equity firm that owned most of Chrysler, wanted to sell Chrysler to the outgoing government. The asking price? One dollar. A steal. The offer was refused, laughed at in White House meetings.

Chrysler CEO Bob Nardelli could perhaps see the train coming toward him. He had been pursuing partners to merge with or take over the ailing giant. Like the unpopular boy who couldn't get a prom date, he came home alone. He had approached Rick Wagoner at GM, Alan Mulally at Ford, and the much-acclaimed Carlos Goshn at Nissan-Renault, widely recognized as perhaps the best CEO in the business. He got "no thanks" from all. He contacted creditors and tried to call in favors. The answer was always the same. No, no, no. A thousand times no.

"I love you to death, Bob, but I've got my own plan," Mulally said, one of the kinder refusals.

Finally, Nardelli turned to Sergio Marchionne, the quixotic, voluble leader of Italian carmaker Fiat SpA, who had been trying to reenter the US market it had departed about twenty-seven years earlier. That relationship would bear fruit much later.

Chrysler needed to be propped up by another partner, and Cerberus was unable to staunch the cash drain. GM was bleeding badly too. Only Ford would be able to steer around the jagged cliff called the economy after the family-owned enterprise had pared itself down to four brands—Ford, Lincoln-Mercury, Mazda, and Volvo. Instead of asking for federal funds, they mortgaged the farm to the hilt and pursued private credit lines.

Here's what else happened pivotal to the dealers' story. The fourteen-member auto task force began their work of dismantling the GM and Chrysler that the world had known for more than a hundred years. They started by imposing strict requirements as a condition of the government's multibillion-dollar loan agreements. Although it was called an auto bailout, the automakers were obligated to pay back the conditional loans, unlike the earlier Wall Street and bank bailouts that contained no strict payback conditions. A big part of the task force's job was to structure the loans and make recommendations to the Treasury and the president on what to do about GM and Chrysler.

For that, a money-manager mind-set, not an auto expert, was deemed necessary. Enter Steven Rattner, who would lead the auto makeover group. Rattner, with no experience in automotive or government, came recommended by the president's advisors. He was a Wall Street investment banker and cofounder of the Quadrangle Group, a New York private equity firm. The media dubbed him the "car czar," and to his displeasure, the label stuck. He was joined by "first lieutenant" Ronald Bloom. Bloom, the junior car czar, was a former investment banker and advisor to the United Steelworkers of America. The Steelworkers were loosely tied to automotive, unions, airlines, and other industries. Bloom used the Steelworkers affiliation to claim his "auto expertise."

"This was not a managerial job," Rattner, the task force architect, would say. "It was a private equity assignment." And that was his specialty—tearing down and rebuilding failing companies.

President Obama, in defending the bailouts to auto, talked about the shared sacrifice that would be required by all stakeholders. He often repeated the word "sacrifice" throughout his public speeches nationwide in his first year in office.

The Fast and the Furious

The special task force was quickly assembled in February 2009 and barely had time to understand the White House office layout when they learned President Obama would make an announcement on the state of the automotive industry to the country by the end of March. They dived into their tasks fervently, but apparently did not research the role of auto dealers in the automotive sales picture much. They did refer to consultants and advisors saying auto dealers needed to be reduced dramatically for the automakers to succeed.

Their deadline to act was staggering. It all happened too quickly for most people's liking. Operating in fast and furious time modes, the task force members became instant experts as they raced through automotive history documents and brushed up on GM's and Chrysler's performance over decades. None had a lick of auto experience; they'd been assembled for their financial and legal prowess. Law school was never this hard, some said.

Rattner, the most senior of the team, was also a former investment adviser at Lazard Freres and was married to Maureen White, who headed fundraising for the Democratic National Committee, raising money for Hillary Rodham Clinton's campaign when she ran for US president in 2008. Obama, of course, later named Hillary Clinton to his cabinet as Secretary of State. So the Rattner ties ran deep. Driving the train were "conductors" Larry Summers, the administration's National Economic Council advisor, and Timothy Geithner, Treasury Secretary. This task force comprised a so-called Treasury auto team that would decide on the auto restructuring plans. Rahm Emanuel, then Obama's chief of staff, had an indirect influencing role on policy and decisions in Treasury.

With Geithner preoccupied with banking and the country's deep financial crisis, Summers, a well-regarded strategist, would take the lead on autos, a natural for him. He was fascinated by automotive and didn't want to see the industry fail. But the main engineer was Wall Street money man Steve Rattner, well regarded for his finance wizardry at Quadrangle and earlier at investment firms Lazard, Lehman Brothers, and Morgan Stanley, where he had worked as an analyst. He was a *New York Times* finance reporter for eight years, polishing his investment expertise. In his task-force role, Rattner reported to Summers and Geithner.

Coming in cold, the auto task force found the manufacturing sector to be in worse disarray than they could possibly have imagined. In an October 21, 2009 article in *Fortune* magazine, penned by Rattner after he left the task force, he wrote that his group was "shocked by the stunningly poor management that we found" at Chrysler and GM.

At this point, Wall Street became firmly entrenched in the government and its restructuring of Chrysler and GM. The task force admittedly approached their job with "surgical dentistry," a precision aided by a heap of TARP money.

So what did the Rattner crew do?

They simply sprinkled "magic fairy dust" over whatever they wanted to keep. It was called taxpayer money, being printed in fresh green piles. The US Treasury was their overseer. In all, $81.8 billion in federal funds went to automotive entities, according to Rattner. The lion's share, or $50 billion, went to GM, and Chrysler received $12.1 billion. Their financial arms got a smaller portion of the huge federal pot. Suppliers, as a whole, qualified for slightly more than $5 billion; while GMAC, the finance company first owned by GM and then serving other clients, including Chrysler, got $17.7 billion; while Chrysler Financial, which was being eliminated, got $1.5 billion. A small portion went into consumer warranty- and supplier-support programs.

"Money matters, and so does management," Rattner would later say. His group went on to put public money where their mouths were. At this point, car dealers were barely a glint in the collective task force's eyes.

From the start, industry experts roundly criticized the auto task force for its lack of automotive or manufacturing experience. But that didn't seem to bother anyone in charge. The fact that the neophytes were preparing to advise the new president and top officials on auto issues didn't seem to enter the equation. They gathered several dozen other so-called fiscal experts, again without much experience in the industry they were called upon to save.

"Although this group was responsible for managing the AIFP (automotive industry financing program), none of the auto team leaders or personnel had any experience or expertise in the auto industry," according to the Special Inspector General for the Troubled Asset Relief Program (SIGTARP), the group assigned to determine if abuse of TARP funds occurred. The SIGTARP audit report came out more than a year later. "They were young, brash, and inexperienced, mostly in their twenties and early thirties, but the bigger problem in the group was arrogance," observed Jack Fitzgerald, a candidly critical Maryland-based car dealer with five decades of automotive retail under his belt. Arrogance and naiveté were subjects he would take off on, after he and Ohio-based multiline dealer Alan Spitzer sparked the US Congress to rescue auto dealers, who would bear the brunt of the automakers' scalpels. They soon involved Tammy Darvish at the huge DARCARS enterprise, and the campaign took off.

The threesome all had GM and Chrysler dealership contracts cancelled. But that wasn't their only motivation when they formed a group called the Committee to Restore Dealer Rights (CRDR). There were many confusing elements that needed to be unraveled before people in America understood what was happening, and would happen, as the automakers targeted a good portion of auto dealers, Their single-focus mission grew into a campaign to save the dealers that would be fought on Capitol Hill and across the American heartland.

What got lost in the bigger auto restructuring picture was this: dealers were independent business people who worked for themselves and made money for the automakers. Indeed, dealers have a relationship with the automakers only in that they sell and market their vehicles.

No matter what was going on in the economy, dealers, as classic entrepreneurs, would have beaten the market, left on their own, CRDR leaders said. The market would have weeded out non-performers anyway, the cancelled dealers believed. They had survived every known disaster—from economic droughts to oil crises and consumer credit freezes affecting auto sales. They would have kept employees working and earning paychecks; they would have continued to give back to communities, many interviewed dealers said.

"Dealers would have been fine if left alone to figure out the market dilemma; they would have recovered on their own," said Jack Fitzgerald, a veteran in the car wars of America since 1956 who operates Fitzgerald Auto Malls, serving the Maryland, Virginia and DC area, Pennsylvania, and Florida. Fitzgerald bristled at the claims automakers made that they would save money by closing dealerships. Considered a major dealer, Fitzgerald sold seventeen vehicle brands in fifteen locations and employed thirteen hundred "associates." He lost ten Chrysler and GM (five each) dealerships during the bloodletting.

The automakers, dealers thought, were aided and abetted by the new task force in making the closure decisions, providing them target numbers to shoot for. The auto task force included some Treasury employees. But the core team joining Steve Rattner included Ron Bloom, a former United Steelworkers adviser; Brian Deese, a thirty-one-year-old with stints in consulting think tanks; Matt Feldman, the legal brain who helped engineer a shortcut Section 363 bankruptcy; and Diana Farrell, a former consulting company expert who worked for Summers and gave the group more senior grounding. There was also Brian Osias, a thirty-one-year-old investment analyst on Wall Street, helping with GM chores. Harry Wilson, a more experienced restructuring specialist with a Harvard MBA, was appointed the chief GM negotiator; and Austan Goolsbee, a former Obama organizer in Chicago, rounded out the main restructuring teams.

Rattner himself took on the complex task of the Chrysler restructuring, UAW negotiating, and dealing with creditors, investors, and banks. He'd assumed Chrysler would be the harder nut to crack, and in some ways proved correct. It was also Rattner who made key decisions regarding personnel, which included hiring and firing automaker CEOs and board members. Surprising, since a month earlier Rattner had admitted to being "terrified" to take the task force leader job and had many qualms about his qualifications and desire to come aboard.

Assigned to do the heavy lifting on the GM side was Brian Deese, assisting Harry Wilson, the architect of dismantling GM. As he came aboard, Deese, a Yale Law School dropout, was headlined in the *New York Times* as "The Thirty-One-Year-Old in Charge of Dismantling GM." He'd also worked in Chicago on Obama's transition team before being tapped for the auto task force.

Like a proud uncle, Rattner christened his fledgling group Team Auto, desperate to shed the media-dubbed term "car czar." But that's what stuck.

Most media referred to them as the auto task force, or task force. Rattner also described part of the core group as former "Wall Street refugees," another appellation that fit.

Rattner took over in February, and the temporary group began the heavy-duty job of dismantling Detroit's two iconic automakers. By March, GM and Chrysler, then majority-owned by Cerberus Capital Management, became their adopted children. Despite their critics, the group had to become quick studies of an industry that has a unique, almost incestuous language and culture; and the groundwork is ever-changing. It takes employees steeped in automotive to understand the lay of the land. That was not the auto task force. Like Hank Paulson before him, it was chief economic advisor Larry Summers who kept the auto issue on the front burner with his team. "You are not going to let the autos fail, are you?" Summers asked them in one early meeting. They got his drift and focused even harder.

"The Democrats were moving Detroit to center stage," Rattner wrote in his book *Overhaul: An Insider's Account of the Obama Administration's Rescue of the Auto Industry*, sensing Summers' and Obama's interests.

Five months later, in July, the task force finished the overhaul job, but most of their recommendations were implemented by early April. GM was 101 years old in 2009, Chrysler eighty-four, but neither would ever be the same. But that is cycling ahead of the story here.

GM and Chrysler were the task-force targets, of course, because they came to Washington seeking federal aid to keep operating. A lifeline was thrown by President Bush, which was then tossed by President Obama to keep them afloat. It was heavy lifting all the way, with US taxpayers on the ropes.

The task force decided nothing less would do than to completely overhaul the GM and Chrysler industry players. Their goal was to build "a shiny new GM," as they called it, from the rubbles. This time it would be a true renaissance. Not the tinsel kind that existed in Detroit's Renaissance Center where about five thousand GM employees and contractors worked after much talk of moving them to the Warren suburbs (where GM's tech center complex was located).

At Chrysler, the objective was not as clear. The big problem, the task force said, was always what to do about Chrysler.

When the Obama finance wizards came in, they were told to put some conditions and structure on the automaker loans, which were to be paid back to taxpayers via the Treasury. GM and Chrysler were required to submit detailed plans to the Treasury to satisfy the government as to how they would use the federal money; the feds set payback terms based on projected profitability.

The two automakers had to provide restructuring plans in order to get federal funds. Shortly after they got them, it became abundantly clear that they did not demonstrate viability or sufficient sacrifices from their own stakeholders, Rattner said. The controls got even tighter. The neophyte group was racing to complete deadlines coming at them in late March when President Obama would face the country and report on the auto issues. Their personal and professional lives, according to written accounts, were chaotic, almost nil.

Before the stiff deadlines, the task force also restructured the Chrysler and GM boards of directors. The GM board, more unwieldy due to its vast global operations, was pretty much dismantled, and Chrysler was seeded with new names and faces.

In its review process, the auto group marveled to learn that Chrysler and GM could not get cars or trucks named as recommended buys on well-regarded *Consumer Reports* lists or on quality reports issued by J. D. Power and Associates, another credible industry barometer of quality and production. Despite vast Internet resources, consumers still relied on *Consumer Reports* to make their purchase decisions. It was a golden parachute for automakers making the grade.

Early on, the group was amazed at the mismanagement at GM and Chrysler. "Trivial issues loomed large while big ones got lost," Rattner observed. He learned that in GM's earlier days, marketing copy could not be released until CEO Roger Smith signed off on it, including, absurdly, color changes. He couldn't believe top brass were preoccupied with the *crisis du jour* that a competent mid-manager would have handled in other organizations.

In a way, Chrysler was in even more disarray than GM, the task force found. Even Cerberus, a private equity investor and a 40 percent majority owner with Bob Nardelli in place, couldn't right the wrongs of previous management decisions that seemed embedded in the culture.

By 2007, another arc was curving and veering, changing course. Relationships with dealers and suppliers of parts and components were becoming strained.

Even though automakers were pouring multibillions into customer relationship management (CRM) efforts, the concept tied more into metrics and statistics on sales and service than on improving relationships. The new order seemed focused on sales or short-term performance measures. Managers regularly got reassigned, leaving gaping holes in institutional knowledge.

"What have you done for me lately?" became the modus operandi as upper-level executives scrutinized ten- and thirty-day sales reports, using them as key decision-making indicators.

Chrysler: Stay or Go?

Chrysler was otherwise on the ropes after the task force entered the scene. The historic company came within minutes of being liquidated. The decision-making moment had arrived. The mood at the auto task force was tense, somber. Should Chrysler stay or go? Should they pour more money into a failing company? Its demise could strangle the economy, proponents said. Letting it go would put more business in GM and Ford's coffers, the other side argued.

It was mid-March, a few weeks before President Obama would deliver his auto talk to the nation. Indecision permeated the air in the room in the White House where the task force huddled. Near the end, it came down to a 4-to-3 vote (four to let go, three to keep). Steve Rattner remained undecided.

Then Larry Summers forced the vote. He pressed Rattner to make up his mind. Rattner was reluctant and unsure but seemed influenced by where he thought Summers was going. Rattner voted to keep Chrysler afloat. Tied vote. Summers intervened. He said Chrysler would stay. The group made their recommendations to Obama, noting the early split in votes.

On March 30, a Monday night, President Obama went on the air; he announced the news. The government was bailing out Chrysler on the condition that a deal with Fiat was worked out.

A similar bailout announcement came regarding GM, with one important proviso having to do with the CEO, engineered by the task force. Obama explained that by April 1, Rick Wagoner, a thirty-two-year GM veteran and loyalist, was effectively fired as CEO of GM. The shock value had worn off a little, since the news had already leaked out to the press. Still, shock and disbelief reigned from Detroit to Los Angeles. It was like a major nine-point tremor had hit, and it wasn't an earthquake. The president of the United States had just fired the chief executive of the largest auto company in the world (until it was surpassed by Toyota Motor Corporation in 2008).

A key factor in ousting Wagoner was that the company had gone bankrupt and lost about $11 billion in taxpayer money in the last three months alone while under his watch. And Wagoner had come back to DC asking for additional funds, even after the private jet PR disaster. But underneath the reasons was a more fundamental one: Wagoner strongly opposed placing GM in bankruptcy. He was going against what Rattner and the task force wanted.

Executive Shuffle at GM and Chrysler

Reportedly, Wagoner immediately vacated his office in the glass towers of GM in Detroit. A game of musical chairs, especially at the top of GM, was about to ensue. The headlines for months in papers, broadcast TV, and on the Internet pondered, "Who's in, who's out?" at the two car companies; or who's on first? The executive shuffle was on. Fritz Henderson, the former GM president and another GM lifer, immediately stepped in as CEO. He was the temporary "golden boy." Henderson brought along credentials as chief financial officer as his calling card; he also had served in various overseas positions, a customary grooming station for top executives. And GM's treasury group was known as the cradle for future GM CEOs.

Then Ed Whitacre, a selection of the task force and a disciple of legendary leader Jack Welch at General Electric, now a retired AT&T executive from Austin, Texas, was drafted to serve on the GM board of directors. That set up the succession scenario if Fritz failed. The GM board, like Chrysler's, was also restocked to the task force's liking.

Under Henderson, who knew how to use the corporate scissors, GM was scaled back to its 1902s' size, according to industry data. "This is a remarkable opportunity for us," Henderson said in his best corporate speak. "This allows us to permanently address problems we have not been able to before today." His comments appeared on June 3 in the *Los Angeles Times*, after the bankruptcy filing in New York.

So why did Rick go? It seems Wagoner refused to consider bankruptcy for GM, the company he had dedicated his life to, or thirty-two years of it. He presumed to know what was best for GM even as the company went bankrupt under his watch. Ultimately, that position proved untenable to Rattner and company. Perhaps Wagoner knew at that moment how several thousand car dealers would feel nearly a month later: bereft and thrown out like yesterday's newspapers.

The money guys were looking at spreadsheets and bottom lines, not company loyalty. By February, GM had burned through $20 billion in twelve months and was in the process of losing another $11 billion in the first quarter of 2009, which would end in March, according to the task force. That bleeding would come out of taxpayers' wallets, something the task force at least voiced concern over. Worse, GM via Wagoner said it would need still more bailout money.

Rattner, a financier at heart, couldn't see it. "Put money behind only a bankable team. To my mind, no private equity firm on the planet would have backed Rick Wagoner or GM's current board. I knew from the outset he had to go. It wasn't personal, it was business," he said later. And task force member Harry Wilson and his team, who were the ultimate architects of GM's restructuring, agreed.

With Wagoner's ousting, another major boulder was removed, and the task force whacked away at scrub brush as they continued streamlining and reshaping the corporate entities, all the while saying they weren't running the companies.

For this task force, lean and efficient trumped job preservation in the new economy.

But the changes at the top set into motion a game of musical chairs at GM and Chrysler.

Bob Nardelli's last waltz was coming too. The task force cut a deal with Cerberus to let Nardelli step aside once the new ownership structure was announced. A few months after the task force took hold, Nardelli would be replaced with Italian carmaker Fiat CEO Sergio Marchionne, who reportedly leaped at the chance to expand Fiat's empire into North America.

After the government kissed off Cerberus and Nardelli, Chrysler LLC would be called Chrysler Group LLC under a new ownership structure. And GM would revert to General Motors Company, from General Motors Holding Company. But the task force still fondly called it their "shiny new GM."

Rattner spent many days negotiating with Marchionne. He pushed him to put up money for Chrysler, figuring they were getting operating control and should be invested in outcomes. But Marchionne wouldn't budge from his "no-way" position. They were offering technology assets and management of a company on the brink. Being Sergio, he got his way. Of course, Chrysler had already devalued the company trying to sell it to the government for one dollar.

After June 1, Fiat had gained management control of Chrysler, even though it was not the majority owner. In the deal of the century, Marchionne became Chrysler's CEO at no cost to Fiat. He replaced Nardelli, who left the company and returned to private business. The Chrysler-Fiat agreement was similar to the relationship between Nissan of Japan and Renault of France, in which Carlos Goshn, who was a Renault executive, took charge of Nissan. He serves as chief executive of both companies.

At Chrysler, Tom LaSorda, another American president in charge of manufacturing, resigned as well. Jim Press survived and went through some title changes as a key exec but served at Marchionne's pleasure for a short time. The Italian-Canadian Marchionne was a flamboyant, hard-driving leader, cut out of a different mold than many auto executives. Rarely seen in a suit, he appeared in his standard black sweater (known to order them by the dozens) and dark slacks, and smoked imported Italian cigarettes, even though the company enforced no-smoking rules inside its buildings. Sergio tooled about the grounds of the vast Auburn Hills campus in a golf cart, exhaling smoke and getting air.

Splitting up the ownership pie for GM and Chrysler was another dicey matter. Here, the auto task force heads became the chief shoppers, bakers, and pie splitters. They held emergency meetings, usually in their basement offices of the White House. Many were working around the clock to meet the March 30 presidential deadline when everything needed to be wrapped up.

Meanwhile, Canada had approached the US government about doing their share to support the automakers, especially GM. They kicked in money that was roughly proportional to production in that country, so close to Detroit and so reliant on auto income. Windsor, the entry port to Canada at the southeastern end, was connected to Detroit by the Ambassador Bridge and the underwater Windsor Tunnel beginning stateside in Detroit. The two cities shared a passion for casinos, gambling, and cars.

Who Owns Who?

With the new GM stripped of its downsides, the stakeholders were well defined by early summer of 2009: the US government, or Treasury, owned the majority 60.8 percent stake. The rest was split between three stakeholders: the UAW's Voluntary Employee Beneficiary Association (VEBA), the Canadian government, and bondholders.

Much later, GM would seek to shed the government yoke by going public again through initial public offerings, or stock purchases, to investors. After the new ownership structure was announced, a *Wall Street Journal* op ed piece dubbed GM "Government Motors." The rest of the media chimed in, and the label stuck. If nothing else, it would propel GM to get out of the government-ownership business as quickly as it could.

At Chrysler, the pie was split differently, with less US and Canadian government involvement. The UAW's health-care trust for retirees, VEBA, had a majority stake of 55 percent; Fiat, 19 percent; the rest divided between the US government and the Canadian government. Fiat's stake could grow incrementally to 35 percent, once it repaid the federal government loans.

"The US will loan what it calls 'new Chrysler' an additional $4.7 billion, the final payment due in eight years. Fiat cannot take majority stake in Chrysler until the federal loans are paid off," the task force said at a final juncture as Chrysler pitched for funds. An about 15 percent stake was reserved for that time.

There were also the thousands of individuals and institutions who held automotive bonds. These were the bondholders who had originally put up funds. They, too, were left holding an empty bag. They would have to accept pennies on the dollar; not easy in a credit and fiscal crisis. They had expected a minimum of one hundred cents on the dollar, one major creditor told the task force. Appeasing bondholders and creditors, both secured and unsecured, in jeopardy would not be easy, almost impossible.

Who owns Chrysler and GM? Now the world knew.

GM Owners*
US government: 61.8 percent
VEBA: 17.5 percent
Bondholders: 10 percent
Canada: 11.7 percent

Chrysler Owners*
UAW's VEBA: 55 percent
Fiat: 19 percent
US government: 8 percent
Canadian governments : 2 percent
*Source: 2009, *Media Sources*

A Most Convenient Bankruptcy

All along, bankruptcy was the elephant in the room, stomping and snorting about, demanding its day.

The structure devised by Matt Feldman, the task force's legal expert, was called a Section 363 bankruptcy ("363"). This shortcut form of a traditional Chapter 11 had rarely been used with big industrial companies. Feldman knew that a 363 conveniently allowed a company to quickly transfer intact business units and assets to a new owner while shedding old, unwanted, "toxic" assets in bankruptcy. Despite its coming critics, it was the magician's sleight-of-hand that kept GM and Chrysler out of legal hot water and evading the coming legislation. Afterward, it proved to be their salvation.

Rattner and Feldman endorsed it as the best means to help Chrysler and GM rise above the wreckage. From this grew the idea of the "old car companies" and the "new car companies." Steered by the task force, Chrysler LLC, the designated "old car co," filed for bankruptcy protection on April 30. GM followed suit on June 1.

The *New York Times* wrote on April 30 about the Chrysler bankruptcy: "It was a stark moment, and one unseen in modern times, as the fledgling president deepened his involvement in a struggling but iconic American company. Chrysler, which Mr. Obama called 'a pillar' of the industrial economy, invented the minivan and owns the Jeep brand.

"With the filing, Chrysler became the first major American automaker to seek bankruptcy protection since Studebaker in 1933. It was a humbling moment for the nation's third-largest automaker, which recovered strongly after a near bankruptcy in 1979 with help from the Carter administration before entering its latest, dangerously fallow period under the ownership of the German auto company Daimler-Benz and, as of 2007, Cerberus Capital Management."

After the two companies declared bankruptcy and were under court protection, they set about trying to get their houses in order. All the deficits and liabilities of the former company were lumped under "old car co." And the new good assets were put under "new car co" umbrellas. Again, magic fairy dust was trickling down courtesy of the US government.

And then they went after the dealers.

The War on Dealers

The war on auto dealers was formally declared on May 14, when Chrysler and GM said they would shrink their US dealer base by at least 25 percent. They sent the dealer notices around the same time. Chrysler would close 789 dealers, leaving the company with about twenty-four hundred US "stores," as they are often called. Larger and more swollen, GM would trim about twelve hundred dealers, aiming at a size of around forty-five hundred by the end of 2010, although the original estimate was higher. GM also would discontinue the Pontiac, Saab, Saturn, and Hummer brands, which raised the number to be cut significantly above the reported numbers. Dissolving these brands was all part of the bankruptcy restructuring, although internal debates had been raging for years about which brands should go.

Chrysler dealers would be forced out by June 9. But GM suggested a less harrowing path, choosing to wind down dealers when they ran out of inventory, with a final deadline of October 31, 2010. Unlike Chrysler, GM refused to disclose its list of targeted dealers, saying it wanted to protect dealer confidentiality and that the information had to come from dealers.

This was an industry and two giant companies used to cutting and downsizing large swathes of workers, plants, suppliers, and whatever appeared to be a financial drain. Under Fritz Henderson, GM pared twenty-four thousand autoworkers and four thousand salaried workers from their lists primarily through retirement offers, according to media. They had cut out many brands and product lines over the years, affecting hundreds of thousands of workers and assembly plants. In 2004, they had eliminated the entire Oldsmobile line. They had shut down or left behind national and international business alliances and suppliers without looking back.

What were a few thousand dealers when dealing with mega-numbers? The bottom-line experts at the task force snipped away with what they called surgical precision.

Of course the automakers had reorganized their internal operations many times over the decades. GM, for example, had switched from being an engineers' company to micromanaged by fiscal operatives during CEO Roger Smith's era in the 1980s. Smith, who was lampooned in Michael Moore's 1989 documentary *Roger and Me,* was known for micromanaging daily affairs, along with GM's fiscal people.

Based on the film, though, one would think Smith had little to do besides fly from one spot to another to avoid Michael Moore and his invasive camera. Creative license was used more than liberally in the film's telling about the destruction of Flint, Michigan. The factory town is about an hour north of Detroit and was once Michigan's second largest city, one that GM built up and then deserted. Automakers often cite "competitive reasons," or economic pressures, when they pull up stakes and leave a community or region. But they usually leave for cheaper labor, downsizing, or because business conditions have changed drastically.

The dealers, whose contracts were not rejected (called "move forward" or "continuing" dealers), would fall under the "new GM" in the restructuring process; cut dealers would remain under the "old GM." At Chrysler, they were part of "old car co" (the goners), versus "new car co" (the go-forwards). So the new Chrysler emerged, christened Chrysler Group LLC. Tradition-bound GM emerged as simply General Motors Company. This division would produce two classes of dealers: those continuing and those with cancelled contracts. Both groups would operate their companies under extreme duress in a period of economic turmoil.

The cancelled dealers had to sell off a glut of inventory and parts, potentially losing billions as a group, and losing their livelihoods. Without cash flow in, they were still paying for property, mortgages, loans, insurance, and everything associated with running a modern dealership. Perhaps worse, the division would also begin to pit dealer against dealer.

Congress Gets Active

On May 20, nearly two months before resigning his post on the auto task force, Steve Rattner penned a quick letter to Rhode Island Democrat Senator Jack Reed, in his DC office. He was responding to Reed's inquiry over six Rhode Island dealers being cut by Chrysler. "Consistent with the role of the auto task force in the restructuring process, we were involved in the specific design or implementation of Chrysler's dealer consolidation plan. However, the sacrifices by the dealer community alongside those of auto workers, suppliers, creditors, and other Chrysler stakeholders are necessary for this company and this industry to succeed," Rattner wrote.

He reminded Congressman Reed that "a month ago, Chrysler faced the real prospect of liquidation, which would have eliminated all seven of the company's dealers in Rhode Island, and all 3,200 across the United States. As a result of the successful Chrysler-Fiat partnership and the backing of the task force, Chrysler was now positioned to move forward with a plan that retains the substantial majority of Chrysler dealers," he said.

In his way, Rattner was repeating the "shared sacrifice" mantra made by President Obama and Tim Geithner. Obama had talked about the sacrifices that all stakeholders needed to make if the two companies were to survive. But his "car czar" was in charge of executing such sacrifices. In his version, dealers and others would take it on the chin for the greater good. Like the American people, dealers were suddenly paying dearly for a problem not of their making.

As much as the task force wanted the dealer problem to go away, agitation was starting in the US heartland and in the halls of Congress. Bipartisan agreement on a national issue, something unseen in recent modern politics, was emerging. The debate on the necessity of dealer closures and who made the decisions was bubbling up.

On June 3, right after the GM bankruptcy announcement, the automakers were castigated by the Democrats at a hearing of the Senate Commerce Committee. Senator Jay Rockefeller, a West Virginia Democrat, called the dealer closings a "nationwide tragedy that many of us feel strongly about." Senator Kay Bailey Hutchison, a Texas Republican and one of the early objectors, was threatening to hold up a war-funding bill because of dealer closures in her state.

House majority leader Steny Hoyer and Chris Van Hollen, both Democrats in the House, and Roscoe Bartlett, a Republican from Maryland, were also getting up to speed, making phone calls to the task force and higher. Congressman Jim DeMint, a South Carolina Republican, said he was learning what "government-managed economies feel like." Ohio Republican Steve LaTourette also was crafting a bill that would float through the House.

Democrats Dan Maffei (New York) and Frank Kratovil (Maryland) were working on similar legislation.

John McEleney, chairman of the National Automobile Dealers Association (NADA), wrote: "The idea that dealer numbers should be rapidly and drastically reduced apparently comes from Wall Street advisers." NADA was speaking out clearly against the reductions and taking out full-page ads in newspapers opposing the cuts.

Congress and the task force were also hearing from the three leaders—Tammy Darvish, Jack Fitzgerald, and Alan Spitzer—of the newly formed Committee to Restore Dealer Rights. They wanted to shed light on the confusing elements that had led to the "war on dealers" and why it should never have happened to this group—or to any other in the future. To do that, they attacked the false premises and lies the shutdowns were based upon.

Despite dealer concerns, the question of why certain dealers had been chosen over others was not a primary concern for the task force. They were too busy fighting the automakers' other battles. The criteria issue for closures would not get more than lip service for months.

Richard Mealey, a prominent former Chrysler-Jeep dealer in Michigan who testified in US bankruptcy court in the May-June hearings, said, "I never got any clear criteria from Chrysler as to why I was let go. It was sealed in bankruptcy court." He thought that was true for many dealers that year as Chrysler gave vague criteria on dealers who were terminated.

State franchise laws designed to protect dealers from overencroaching manufacturers were being trampled on too. Dealers are supposedly protected by their state laws; it's why they form strong relations with state leaders. State dealers associations spoke out on the closures, but the federal-versus-state law battle would also heat up.

Pushing the Toyota Model

At one point in an update huddle with the auto task force, President Obama reportedly asked the members, "Why can't they make a Corolla?" He was speaking of the US automakers, alluding to Corolla's once-heralded quality. No one could answer that question.

The task force was promoting a Toyota dealer model for GM and Chrysler as part of their restructuring requirements. The automakers balked initially at the number of cuts but were bound to comply. Chrysler, for example, had its own "Project Genesis" dealer consolidation plan unfolding, which aimed to trim dealers more gradually. GM had long been in the process of paring down its own brands and car dealers selling them.

Genesis and Toyota were quickly adopted as the way to go. Smaller dealer networks, like Toyota's and the imports', would generally lead to more sales per dealer and more sales for the two companies, the reasoning went. There was a rah-rah commitment to the foreign model among the task-force people who were mostly East Coasters where the imports sold strongly. They viewed Chrysler and GM—especially Chrysler—as non-destination brands for buyers.

Leonard Bellavia, an attorney partner at Bellavia Gentile & Associates, LLP, in Mineola, New York, offered another theory on how Genesis and the Toyota model came to take on such importance in the minds of the task force. In earlier testimony, Jim Press, the Chrysler copresident who had earned his stripes at Toyota where he was the top American executive, spoke of Toyota's smaller, efficient dealer group to the task force, Bellavia said.

Bellavia thought Jim Press was a conduit to the task force on the Toyota dealership model. It's why he suffered such guilt later on when he saw the horror unleashed on US dealers, a group he had once defended. "Mainly he told them Toyota had far less dealers, which means higher throughput per dealer," Bellavia said. Throughput referred to the number of car units sold per dealer per store. More simply, it meant actual sales volume per dealership.

Press had responded to task-force queries on why Toyota was so successful in the US market, Bellavia said. Perhaps in meeting with them, Jim Press unwittingly provided the formula for why Toyota was dominating in sales, he said. It had to do with dealer counts in key markets. As an example, Toyota as a group had some sixteen hundred US dealers, compared to GM's six thousand-plus, and Chrysler's thirty-two hundred. Toyota said it had 1,232 US retail dealers in 2009; Lexus (its luxury division) with 227 and Scion (entry level) had 995. That totaled 1,688 for three brands. All numbers are according to most recent company records. Meanwhile, Chrysler had four brands and GM had eight at the time of the dealer terminations.

The task force jumped on the idea of "fewer dealers equals better performance" and tried to turn Chrysler and GM into Toyota by following their dealer numbers, Bellavia surmised. They concluded they could copy the Toyota model and trim down dealer counts to fit. Other import transplants, such as Honda and BMW, also were studied. They all had fewer dealers than the domestics, thus higher sales and profits per dealer, the task force believed.

Bellavia deposed Jim Press in bankruptcy court hearings in June of 2009. He observed a man tortured by guilt. "He was internally conflicted, like he knew he'd created a monster" by providing the Toyota comparisons, Bellavia said. His mannerisms also suggested that he didn't believe his own language about the need to cut dealers, Bellavia, a keen observer of body language and verbal messages, concluded. Thus, the task force adopted a false premise by mistakenly applying the Toyota model to the US automakers, Bellavia and other auto experts concluded.

Steny Hoyer Versus Steve Rattner

One other misstep: the task force seemed intent on bypassing Congress as part of making their restructuring decisions. That move—ignoring the traditional route of shaking up the country—would prove to their disadvantage in the coming months.

In an initial testy meeting with US Representative Steny Hoyer, Steve Rattner was growing irritated with the clamor arising over dealer closures. Hoyer, who ran the House of Representatives after Speaker of the House Nancy Pelosi, further pressed the case of dealers.

Hoyer brought up the issue of two Maryland dealers he knew, Tammy Darvish of DARCARS Automotive and Jack Fitzgerald of Fitzgerald Auto Malls, as among the closing stores. They ran dealerships in three states each, and they happened to be his constituents in Maryland. But it was about more than two dealer groups, even such large ones, to Hoyer.

In many areas across the country, dealers were among the biggest employers, taxpayers, and community boosters. Some experts placed automotive as responsible for almost 20 percent of overall US retail sales. According to NADA in 2009, a time when dealer cuts were escalating, as a group, dealers accounted for:

- 15 percent of total retail sales; more in stronger economies
- 1.1 million people employed
- $53.5 billion in annual employee payrolls
- $40 million-plus donated to charities, communities, and disaster effort funds

Rattner claimed to be confused as to why so much noise erupted over a few car dealers—referring to Darvish and Fitzgerald. "I was mystified that the House majority leader chose to devote so much time to this," Rattner wrote in his book *Overhaul,* published in September 2010.

"The nation was plagued by economic and financial crises; why would the second most important member of the House after Speaker Pelosi think that two car dealerships merited his personal attention?" The lesson Rattner perhaps failed to grasp is that Darvish and Fitzgerald were appealing to Congress on behalf of several thousand disenfranchised dealers and several hundred thousand US jobs. In fact, the two CRDR leaders rarely brought up their own cases of cut dealerships when speaking in public or when meeting with congressional representatives.

All along, Rattner continued to be mystified on the dealer-closings issue and why his office was suddenly flooded with hundreds of calls, e-mails, and letters about the closings they had to handle. He sensed the politicians' growing anger over the dealer issue and he and his colleagues tried to allay their concerns, he said.

"What hundreds of calls did the task force, or Rattner, respond to?" Tammy Darvish asked incredulously in a dealer memo. "The task force didn't talk to dealers. They didn't decide which dealers would go, but they surely mandated that dealers be reduced based on their willful ignorance, lack of experience, and bad information they got on how retail dealer networks work."

At the same time, the voice missing from the table before the task force did its surgical work of snipping was that of dealers. The government was there, the automakers, the UAW, the bondholders, and the credit companies. But not the dealers or their recognized representatives.

All along, Rattner dismissed the cuts of thousands of dealers, not seeing what the furor signified. To a financier, though, five thousand, two thousand, one thousand, or fifty are just numbers on a spread sheet. He or she doesn't see the human beings these numbers represent. The bigger the numbers, the more the savings, from a bean-counter perspective. Another message lost on the task force: Nearly 170,000 direct jobs in dealerships and directly related businesses would vanish if car dealers closed, and even more if their employees and the trickle-down effect on businesses in their communities were counted, the CRDR group argued. The projected job losses were based on numbers from NADA, which operates a well-regarded research group.

If dealers disappeared, it could shatter entire communities. The campaign to save dealers was also about consumers and private citizens who watched mainstay businesses being shuttered and wondered where they would buy their cars or go to get them fixed; or where they might find another good-paying job. The communities in which dealers did business depended on them for everything, from jobs and a solid tax base to charity and goodwill support. Flipping burgers in fast-food restaurants or selling sundries was not a viable means of support for most people. Rattner and crew didn't seem to factor in the clout of dealers in the task force's decisions, or maybe they didn't know it, dealers thought.

But Hoyer knew. He would not go away. He called a July 8 summit with a select House committee, the two automakers, and the task force in his cramped offices on Capitol Hill. Dealer reps were not present at that meeting; NADA was apparently invited, according to Rattner, but didn't attend. NADA was the largest dealer trade group, based in the DC area, with about eighteen thousand members. David Weaver, the senior staff advisor to Maryland Democrat Chris Van Hollen, who attended the July meeting, said the road was strewn with misunderstanding on the part of the task force on the dealer situation. After the July summit, he said, things still did not clear up as Rattner and the task force dug in their heels. They didn't understand that Congress was not anti-automakers. Their fight was pro-dealers and small business.

"At no point did Congress ever say they disagreed with the decision to bail out Chrysler and GM," Weaver said. "What they didn't get, or what it comes down to, they were acting like finance guys—forgetting everything else because a collapse of the automakers would cause a significant ripple effect on the American economy. They clearly bought into the argument manufacturers were making that they were overdealered, and dealers were part of the problem and not the solution. The only ones more arrogant than [the task force] were GM and Chrysler."

The upshot of that session was to pit Congress against the task force. The standoff didn't get better. The dealer groups saw that they needed Congress on their side, and that became a focus.

At the time, Darvish, Spitzer, and Fitzgerald began campaigning vigorously to get a bill passed in Congress that would restore dealers to levels before the restructurings, as independent businesses. Their support base grew among the lawmakers, who were largely Democrats in the beginning. Bipartisan support would build as lawmakers saw this was not a partisan issue.

The task force would say months later that they had perhaps focused "too much on restructuring and not enough on supporting auto sales and a broader industry recovery," as Steve Rattner noted in *Overhaul*.

Darvish was sorry the flash of insight came so late. She pointed this out to her dealer groups after hearing his admission "You think? How will you support sales with fewer dealers who are your only source of income? Who will sell these cars? Who will finance them and take care of customers?" she asked.

House leaders Steny Hoyer and Chris Van Hollen became major boosters and sponsors of the fight to save the closed dealers. They were gathering dealer stories, and they were listening.

But rewind the clock a bit here. Look at the playbook again.

Following the Money Trail

TARP, the Troubled Asset Relief Program, was created in October 2008 to purchase assets and equity from financial institutions. The Automotive Industry Financing Program (AIFP) followed in December as an extension of TARP and allowed the US Treasury to invest in the automakers. AIFP also created the role of chief architect for the federal government to restructure the auto industry. That would be Rattner and crew.

In essence, TARP provided the financial vehicle for the merry band called the auto task force to sidestep Congress in restructuring the automakers. And TARP was under Geithner's Treasury group who oversaw the task force, a neat package.

Treasury had already pledged more than $81 billion of TARP funds to GM and Chrysler and its allies. The first wave of TARP money flowed in December 2008, under Paulson, Bush's Treasury chief. It all came out of the bundled $700 billion in TARP money used to bail out banks and financial institutions.

That big pot of stew cooked with taxpayer dollars gave many consumers heartburn. When they heard about bank bailouts, Wall Street bailouts, and now automotive bailouts, they lumped them all together. The B-word had gained notoriety: bad. But an informed public began to latch on to one fact: the dealers were not part of the bailout or the problem. Congress got active.

Before that, Chrysler had launched Project Genesis, a plan to reduce the number of models it sells in order to consolidate its Chrysler, Dodge, and Jeep franchises under a single roof. The company also would carve out the Ram truck brand, separating it from Dodge to claim four brands. Now, in brand numbers at least, they were the same size as GM, which shed four brands.

Chrysler announced its Genesis plan on the eve of a national NADA dealer meeting in San Francisco on February 8, 2008. In a statement released on its website at the time, then Chrysler Co-President Jim Press said he and his team would discuss the plan with dealers at the convention. Asked later that day, a Friday, Press said Chrysler had no targets for the number of dealers under Genesis and the number of vehicles planned for the future. This statement came after a speech in San Francisco to a J. D. Power and Associates Automotive Roundtable.

What a difference a year makes.

On June 1, Chrysler asked a New York federal bankruptcy court to allow it to reject its dealership agreements in an effort to cut costs, boost profitability with its remaining dealerships and to help complete its pending merger with Fiat SpA. The Italian carmaker planned to take an initial 20 percent stake in Chrysler when it emerged from bankruptcy protection, adding more when it proved itself.

In bankruptcy court hearings and before Congress, Jim Press said the dealer cuts needed to be made. Bankruptcy Judge Arthur Gonzalez ruled for Chrysler and against the dealers who volunteered in large numbers to testify in their own defense. In New York, Judge Robert Gerber found for GM when GM filed for bankruptcy on June 1 in US Bankruptcy Court for the Southern District of New York. Dealers did not go up against GM as they did with Chrysler.

Chrysler's Jim Press and GM's Fritz Henderson gave damning testimony to courts and Congress that there were too many dealers who cost automakers too much to maintain. Peter Grady, Chrysler's vice president of dealer network, testified to that effect to the US bankruptcy court.

Thus the die was cast. The task force made history with the largest industrial restructuring ever. But history would be made again as the dealers took on their former manufacturing partners.

Hire a Good Consultant

You don't make multibillion-dollar structural changes without a good consulting group to back you up. In complicated sectors such as automotive, the need for consulting advice is even greater. If nothing else, you need a fall guy. "The consultants said so" comes in handy if all else fails.

The Treasury auto team hired outside consultants to advise them on restructuring GM and Chrysler and making them more financially viable. They were the Boston Consulting Group and Rothschild Inc., a Wall Street investment firm and bankruptcy specialist.

According to reliable sources, the consultants recommended that GM and Chrysler reduce the number of dealerships too; this, they reasoned, would improve sales at the remaining dealerships and make them more profitable. They, too, brought up the success of certain imports, namely Toyota. Their sales models were thought to be efficient, lean, and successful.

The task force was quickly sold on the Toyota model; its dealer plan became fait accompli.

Other outside firms that were called on to consult with the auto task force and the automakers were UBS, J. P. Morgan Chase, Deutsche Bank, and Barclays Capital. The finance and investment firms had become well entrenched in the auto industry, its supposed collapse, and its reinvention.

GM and Chrysler quickly restructured as the task force worked at lightning speed. Even GM and Chrysler, once considered slowed by corporate lethargy, sped up their normal pace. Any insider knew it wasn't so much lethargy but the lengthy time it took to make a decision and get it through layers of bureaucracy, including legal signoffs and other approvals.

* * *

More events began to unravel that would affect dealers directly. "Main Street," whether it was a local diner, tavern, repair garage, beauty shop, or car dealer, would never be the same again.

That summer, a recession-weary public was sick of bad news. Wall Street got massive bailouts of cash infusions while Main Street went empty-handed, the public thinking went. *What about the bailouts for the little guy, people like us?* they wondered.

Another little-known force was emerging that would affect dealers. Congress had requested that the Special Inspector General of the Troubled Asset Relief Program (SIGTARP) office investigate the misuse of TARP funds and the wisdom of closing GM and Chrysler dealerships during an economic crisis and bankruptcy climate. A year in the making, their report would not be available in time to help dealers much in the present crisis.

But Tammy Darvish, Jack Fitzgerald, Alan Spitzer, and other influential dealer advocates urged that the investigations move forward, and more quickly. Darvish later submitted her memo to Congress detailing the problems dealer closings represented for the country. The document became central to her theme of "it's a great country we live in—why is it being ruined this way?" was the implied and agonizing question inherent in the message.

In Detroit, as a game of executive musical chairs played out, the new leaders—Ed Whitacre and Sergio Marchionne—made their views about the dealer closures known. The old leaders had testified in bankruptcy court and to Congress: the dealers were a cost burden, and there were too many of them.

Chrysler maintained its position on reducing dealers and continued to dig in its heels. GM was resolute in restructuring and reshaping its dealer network with some modifications.

Right before Christmas 2009, Sergio Marchionne told media that reinstating dealerships would "cause havoc within Chrysler." He said that the company could challenge Congress's upcoming decisions in court. He later accused the dealers of being stubborn, as if not falling in line to be massacred was somehow stubborn and rigid.

In fact, dealers got the message from both automakers: "See you in court, guys."

Merry Christmas. Happy holidays, dealers.

***** MEMORANDUM *****

TO: All Members of Congress

DATE: September 3, 2009

RE: Car Dealers and Individual Liberty

We live in the greatest country the world has ever known. What makes us so great and so wonderful is our divinely inspired Constitution and our unconditional love for our individual Liberty. Car dealers are the ultimate example of capitalism and the American Dream.

All of us have shed a tear at the struggles our two iconic carmakers have experienced this past year. More saddening was the unnecessary terminations of thousands of family-owned dealerships across America. This action jeopardizes the well being of 170,000 employees suffering from this fallout. Dealers are the heart, soul, and fiber of their communities. The auto task force blew it when they wrongly assumed that dealers cost the factory money and that closing down their loyal business partners would help them in their own recovery.

America has never before shied away from doing what's right and just or shrunk from the call of duty to risk life and limb to uphold our freedoms. The most basic freedom is property rights. Our founding fathers knew that blessing our people with individual liberties was not only a give to our nation, but that men (and women) left to their own acts of commerce would know better than anyone else (including government) what goods and services to offer our citizenry and in the end produce the economic miracle that is the envy of the world. They knew that without economic freedoms, there would be little room for political freedoms.

The task force's mistaken intrusion into the unilateral revocation of the dealer's property rights is astonishing and uncalled for. Even more frightening is the closing of one dealership to then turn around and give his or her property right to a competitor down the street. While this may be fashionable in Cuba or Russia, Americans don't act that way.

We want GM and Chrysler to succeed. We've been their trusted business partners for decades. We want our manufacturing base to thrive and grow.

The terminated dealers want to be a part of this recovery and ultimate success. Fortunately, Congress has not only the ability, but the duty to right this wrong, and it's not too late. By enacting HR2743 and Senate Bill S1304, our leaders can allow the dealers to do what they have already proven they do best, helping our economy grow.

The American taxpayer has given GM a second chance and Chrysler a third chance. The dealers deserve their first chance back !

Please restore the dealer rights with HR2743 and Senate Bill S1304.

Most Sincerely,
Tamara C. Darvish
American Car Dealer (second generation)

Chapter 2—The Company Hit Lists

A man can be destroyed but not defeated.
—Ernest Hemingway

There was talk of a "dealer hit list" being created in Detroit.

By early May, Chrysler had declared bankruptcy and GM was next in line. As a global operation, GM's restructuring had more pieces and was infinitely more complex. It would take until June to sort out the various holdings.

Rumors of the hit list for Chrysler had circulated soon after their bankruptcy proceedings ended in late April. Then the media buzzed that Chrysler and GM would be paring their dealer counts, based on the bankruptcies that put the companies in restructuring fever. The US government had taken an ownership stake in the automakers—an unprecedented move in American history.

But the companies had reorganized hundreds of times before. This might just be business as usual, dealers thought. Chrysler dealers remembered when Lee Iacocca had borrowed $1.2 billion in loan guarantees from the federal government to help Chrysler Corporation, as it was called then, survive in the early 1980s. They'd all pulled through together and made the company stronger.

Still, this was bankruptcy. And the federal government was involved and carrying buckets of money. This time could be different. Thus, the nail-biting began in thousands of dealerships across the country. But no one believed they would be on any hit list; most dealers knew they were solid performers, even exceptional ones. Many had won Chrysler's Five-Star dealer standing, deemed the best of the best by Chrysler itself. The company, then owned by investment arm Cerberus Capital Management, was run by its handpicked chief, Bob Nardelli, a former Home Depot executive, who had left with a reported $210 million severance package from the home-improvement giant. At GM, many soon-to-be fatal dealers had won scores of dealer awards and ranked high on quarterly and annual measurements, such as sales and service and customer satisfaction index (CSI) reports. Many had outperformed their competitors.

But the rumor mill had it right again. The Chrysler hit list was out.

* * *

Tammy Darvish's cell phone kept buzzing that morning in mid-May. She and her father, John Darvish, were attending an American International Automobile Dealers Association (AIADA) spring conference in Washington DC, an annual dealer gathering.

John Darvish, normally reticent and private, was even more so now. The early Chrysler and GM bankruptcy news had been disturbing. Like other dealers, he was apprehensive.

At the meeting in the downtown St. Regis Hotel, reporters buzzed around, hoping for scoops. It was if they had one thing on their minds: filing stories about the latest news on dealers. And fast. Reporters from *Nightly Business News*, *Washington Post*, *Automotive News*, and *National Public Radio* were on hand, nosing for news at the AIADA event.

Tammy Darvish often had to leave a session to take a call. It was mostly reporters calling to track down information, squash rumors. "Hey, are you guys on the Chrysler closure list? Is there a GM list?" they would ask, as if they knew something dealers didn't. She'd developed decent working relationships with many reporters over the years and was known to be cooperative and would often provide a good quote.

That morning, all hell was about to break loose.

Initial news of the closures had been leaked online and via broadcast reports in the morning before most dealers got word themselves. News of a Chrysler hit list came first. GM never put out an official list, but questions were swirling. Some reporters tested the waters. "We see you're on [Chrysler's] list; will you talk to us, and this and that," Darvish recalled.

Meanwhile, Darvish's comptroller at their local Chrysler dealership texted her, saying they had received a notice from Chrysler by UPS delivery. They were on the list. She quietly told her father about it, and he could only nod, his worst fears confirmed.

Later that morning, her cell phone rang again. Jim Press, the Chrysler president, wanted to speak with her father. The Darvishes knew Press well from his Toyota days, and now at Chrysler. And Press knew who the go-to person was to track down John Darvish. Tammy Darvish could tell by Press's voice that this was not a "happy talk" call. She slipped back into the main meeting room. An important speaker, Republican Senator John Ensign from Nevada, was presenting at the time.

She asked her father to step out and take the Jim Press call. John Darvish and Press spoke quickly. Press's words were apologetic and full of regret. He said, "Hey, I'm really sorry, but everyone had to take a haircut on this," John Darvish said later.

"'Haircut' was becoming a new industry buzzword. Transparency, haircut, you know. And Press was saying, *you know*, everything will be okay," Tammy Darvish related, her tone implying, "No, we *don't* know that."

After talking with Press, her father became concerned about other dealers he'd talked with, not for himself. It was typical of John Darvish, a former medical student with humanitarian instincts.

"My father said, 'Tammy, can you see what you can do to help Jack?'" It seemed Chrysler had shut all his Chrysler, Jeep, and Dodge stores—five of them. Jack Fitzgerald was obviously not in a good mood. But she rushed to his side. She could see he was beside himself. She'd never seen the normally composed dealer so agitated. Fitzgerald, their colleague and friend, with stores in Maryland, Pennsylvania, and Florida, was attending the conference too. At the time, it was hard to do anything more than be supportive, Darvish knew. How could she reverse the damage done for her father, let alone Fitzgerald, whom her father had known for three decades?

That day and that week, Jim Press was calling dealers across the country. But he didn't call all 789 of them. She knew he didn't call Jack Fitzgerald, who would eventually lose ten stores between Chrysler and GM, because she was by his side, and Jack would have told her if it had happened.

The two had been loyal, committed colleagues for years and felt the same way about many issues. Fitzgerald, a dealer since 1966, could have written a book on how to run a dealership.

Later, reporters still hounded Darvish, hoping she would share what she knew about the cuts. To accommodate them, she arranged quick interviews in the bar of the St. Regis Hotel.

The call from Jim Press had come in earlier. Shortly after that, she told her father, "Listen, we've got to get over to the dealership. Employees are freaking out since the news broke. They're like, 'Am I going to have a job tomorrow, or what's going to happen here?'" Darvish knew employees were in panic mode at their Chrysler stores. Her first thought: get back and hold an all-employee meeting as soon as possible; two stores had been affected. This was an emergency like nothing they had faced. "We've got to tell people something," she told her father. "We've got to meet with people, and as soon as we can."

Nervous tension filled the conference meeting rooms. No one could concentrate on any educational topics now. She imagined other dealers got the calls too. A few days ago, she'd hoped they would ride out the turbulence at the Detroit automakers. She was an optimist but not a fool. You can hope until hope is gone. Facts become facts.

Then *Washington Post* reporter Tom Heath texted her, wanting to know what was going on. She looked about but couldn't see Heath in the crowd in the main conference area.

"Where are you?" she texted back.

"Right here." Tom Heath suddenly appeared at her side. He was anxious to talk. She told him they had to get back to the dealership right away; she'd catch him later.

Being persistent, Heath asked if he could ride to the dealership with her. She begged off, saying she had another interview to do. She was agitated herself. She knew by then they had about three weeks to shut down a very complex Chrysler business. GM was giving dealers more time than Chrysler, calling it a wind-down, but the wheels were in motion. Dealers were skidding about, flying blind.

Heath said he'd wait until she finished up her interview. Then Darvish said, "Why don't you ride over with my father?" She meant to Fairfax in nearby Virginia where the affected Chrysler store was located. She knew her father would hate the company because he was a reserved, quiet man. He wouldn't want to talk to any reporters. But she escorted the business reporter to meet her father anyway, and the two took off together. She did her interview, and because John Darvish drives slowly, and she drives too fast, she beat them to the dealership.

At the Fairfax store, they all gathered in the service department, a big area. Tammy Darvish was at her father's side to help answer questions. "My father told employees the facts. He said we didn't know exactly what was going to happen because this had never happened before in our long history with Chrysler. But he told them very clearly what he did know at the time."

Judy Darvish, John's wife, joined the meeting; she handled accounting functions at the dealerships. A few minutes later, one of Tammy Darvish's brothers, Jamie, came in. Jamie and her other brother, John, functioned as vice presidents at the DARCARS dealerships, as she did. "Our Chrysler stores are being closed between Maryland and Florida. We might have to shut our Chrysler new-car business down, but we don't really know everything yet," John Darvish told the group. He did not know about the GM business at the time.

Then John Darvish made a statement that quieted everyone. "Every single person here, 100 percent, will be guaranteed their jobs, whatever happens. There's nothing to worry about," he said, reassuringly. "We'll do something." John Darvish understood a concept that the two automakers apparently did not: employees make the business work. He was loyal to them, as they had been to him. Like many dealers, his loyalties were not divided.

The *Post* reporter was furiously scribbling notes. The next morning, a picture of John addressing employees was on the front page of the *Post*. Heath had called in a photographer. The story was bylined by Tom Heath.

By 2007, John Darvish had built a $1.1 billion revenue dealership group. He began by selling Chrysler cars in his own dealership in 1977. Later, his thirty-four-store DARCARS chain grew to include Chevrolet, Ford, Chrysler, Jeep, Dodge, Volvo, Toyota, and Nissan brands. The majority of DARCARS stores were located in Silver Spring, north of DC, Rockville, and College Park, as well as Jacksonville, Florida. In the Maryland area, DARCARS controlled the Montgomery County and Prince George County regions.

That day in May, John Darvish had been served notice that his two Chrysler stores were to close. Notice of the GM Chevrolet store cancellation came in June. The closings affected Chrysler in Fairfax, Virginia; Chevrolet in Lanham, Maryland; and Dodge in Jacksonville, Florida. For John Darvish, who began by selling Dodge cars in 1962 at another dealership, it was a day of infamy.

Dear John: "You're Fired"

Chrysler kicked off the ball by sending terse "Dear John" type letters to 789 dealers. The one-page rejection notice was overnighted to dealers by UPS for receipt May 14, paper hardly worth the expensive shipping charges.

"Imagine getting fired via UPS or Fed Ex," Tammy Darvish said, her dark curls shaking. But this was horribly true. It was like someone at Chrysler and later at GM had watched one too many episodes of Donald Trump's reality TV show, *The Apprentice.* "You're fired!" rang in her ears.

The Chrysler notice was straightforward, almost breezy, stating bare facts. "It basically said, 'Hey, by the way, effective June 9, your dealership contract is being cancelled,' like it was something other than a kiss-of-death," Darvish recalled. No explanation was given. "Just that the 'new' Chrysler will no longer be accepting your dealer agreement, and you have until June 9, less than a month, to shut down your business," she said.

"Slam, bam, thank you, ma'am and sir," seemed the tone of the notices. Nearly eight hundred dealers got the same letters.

Gallows humor hung in the air.

"The Fed Ex guys knew before we did who was being whacked. They delivered those letters in big batches everywhere," George McGuire, a rejected Chevrolet dealer in Shakopee, Minnesota, half-joked. But his tone was bitter.

"Why didn't they just go for broke and make it an even 790 or 800?" another dealer asked. As if the 789 number suggested precision, attention to detail. "Why not just send an e-mail? Faster, cheaper," said another.

* * *

The task force had it in for Cadillac, some consultants and dealers said. They wanted a slimmed-down business model, like Toyota's Lexus had. Lexus was Toyota's upscale division, a strong Cadillac competitor. All of Toyota had about fourteen hundred Toyota and Lexus dealers, compared to GM's nearly six thousand dealers and Chrysler's thirty-two hundred levels before the closures.

Why couldn't GM and Chrysler slim down, get the fat out? That's what was on task-force minds. That's when Cadillac dealers were brought to the altar to be sacrificed. Most were targeted because of their small-town locations, consultants later said. "It seems like the GM strategy has been to align Cadillac to look more like BMW, Mercedes-Benz or Lexus in terms of focusing dealerships on urban areas on the East and West coasts," Scott Watkins, a consultant at Anderson Economic Group in East Lansing, Michigan, said in news accounts.

Cadillac was one of GM's saved brands, but it made far fewer sales each year than did Chevrolet, GMC, and Buick. Buick was spared at the last minute when Fritz Henderson pleaded its case to the auto task force because of its strength overseas, especially in the China market. GMC had an important truck line, but so did Chevrolet. Apparently, the only safe group was Chevrolet, which sold about 70 percent of GM's total volume and had a growing overseas presence.

Once the task force got involved, the Toyota dealer model was hailed as one to follow. And the slicing and dicing began. But the domestics were as different from Toyota and the imports as tea is to coffee, as Toyota's manufacturing arm in Toyota City, Japan, is to Chrysler's Sterling Heights Assembly in Michigan.

"For one thing, Toyota had a car that America wants. The Camry, for example, has been the best-selling car in America for years, even now with all the recall problems they have had. We think that they're still going to come out number one in 2010," Tammy Darvish said. Her prediction proved true as Camry set the sales pace in its class.

Before the bloodletting was over, Chrysler appeared to want more cuts, going deeper into the dealer network, into the bone. But ultimately the company backed off, according to dealer sources. The Chrysler Unsecured Creditors Committee, participating in the bankruptcy hearings, played a role in holding them back.

The question many dealers and auto experts posed was: Will Chrysler survive? Some analysts and consultants weren't betting on them.

But the real questions on their minds hung in the air: Who did it, and why were certain dealers selected but others not?

Shortly after the notices arrived, on May 26, a Chrysler spokesperson told *Reuters* that the decision to cut a quarter of their dealer network was "not coming from the task force." Spokeswoman Carrie McElwee said, "Our position is that the market can't support the number of dealers that are out there. This has been our plan for more than ten years to combine Chrysler, Dodge, and Jeep under one roof."

According to Chrysler, the decision to cut dealers considered factors like location, customer satisfaction, and sales potential and actual sales, part of a complex formula called a dealer's "minimum sales responsibility" (or MSR). Nearly half of the terminated dealers also carried non-Chrysler brands, and most relied on used vehicles for the bulk of their sales, Chrysler said, as if this might justify some closure decisions.

The government task force, who many blamed put the pressure on the automakers, had asked for the high level of GM dealer cuts, but not Chrysler's, some auto expert sources said.

To dealers, these were partial answers, but not enough. At this point, there was no organized group to pull the dealers together. Not knowing who to call or what to do, they mostly relied on their own wits.

Betrayal in the Heartland

Barber's Chrysler, Dodge, and Jeep dealership in Spanish Fork, Utah, was among the dealers targeted for closure because of their low sales, Chrysler would say in bankruptcy court proceedings.

On the morning of May 15, Fred Barber in Spanish Fork, Utah, opened an overnight delivery envelope from United Parcel Service. He and his brother, Chuck Barber, who ran the Barber Brothers Inc.'s Chrysler stores, were the recipients of bad news. The Barbers are four brothers; all are in the car business. Two brothers, John and Sam, run a successful Ford store in nearby Morgan, Utah. Their Chrysler stores had recorded profits over most years, the

Barbers said. Admittedly, 2008 was a nosebleed for dealers and consumers nationwide. The credit and real-estate markets and the economy fell apart simultaneously.

"Chrysler sent a letter to all the affected dealers with no explanation as to why we were terminated. Just a cold, hard letter that said, 'You're done' after forty years in business," Fred Barber said.

Little did the Barbers know that 788 other Chrysler, Dodge, and Jeep dealers across the country—including a dozen in Utah—had received the same overnight UPS packages telling them that their dealership agreements with the automaker would be cancelled on June 9. The cuts represented about 25 percent of the old Chrysler LLC, nearly thirty-two hundred dealers.

"It's a really ruthless company," Fred Barber said, still in some disbelief eighteen months later. "And when you look at the way they took us and others dealers out—it was really low class, merciless. We couldn't believe it."

Taking out the dealers, as some put it, was like leaving them out to dry. Not drifting slowly in the wind like some cruel political moves were designed to do, but quickly and brutally in the case of Chrysler. In GM's case, it was called a wind-down, giving owners eighteen months to get their affairs in order. More humane? Practical? Just ask these sound businessmen and businesswomen.

"Why take out your distribution arm?" Barber asked. "It's the stupidest thing I ever heard of in my life. It's like cutting off your right arm."

It also didn't make sense in his Utah area, which had been growing steadily at a rate of 68 percent over five years, unlike many parts of the country. Utah is also a big country for truck sales, like the popular Hemi-powered Dodge and GM work trucks produced that sold well in the country, dealers said.

"They spent hundreds of millions to keep dealers out, including me," Barber said about Chrysler and GM. It was the worst kind of betrayal, he and his brothers thought.

Legal consultants said the automakers' costs to defend the dealer cuts were astronomical. Dealer attorneys later estimated that Chrysler, for example, spent more than $15 million in legal fees alone in arbitration procedures.

When Fred Barber told his customers and friends about the dealer closings, they looked at him in disbelief. "Are you kidding me?" they asked. Barber came to believe that "a lot of anti-Chrysler sentiment" was building in the heartland, not just among dealers but with customers who didn't want to drive sometimes a hundred miles back and forth for service to their vehicles.

Even sadder, Barber had had heart surgery a few years earlier. Dealing with termination issues and financial losses were not exactly part of the low-stress lifestyle he should have been engaging in, he knew. But the auto industry and its dynamic cycles were inherent in the life he'd carved out for himself so long ago.

Over four decades, the Barber brothers had operated as auto dealers. Among them, they'd witnessed gas rationing, skyrocketing gas prices during the 1973 oil crisis, and sales slowdowns after the crazed September 11, 2001 terrorist attacks on America. Then came four-dollars-a-gallon gas as the Iraq war built up. More recently, they'd survived the greatest economic disaster since the Great Depression. But they weren't able to survive the wrath of Chrysler.

They asked, "Why us?" The best Fred Barber can figure is that someone had it in for him at Chrysler because he had been quite vocal on product quality issues at dealer council meetings and how Chrysler tended to mistreat dealers over the years. He'd served on Chrysler's dealer council for twenty-two years, a prestigious spot. But Chrysler, an elephant with a long memory, didn't like outspoken dealers. Other dealers would testify to that too.

One saving grace was being reinstated by GM's Chevrolet group, Fred Barber said in 2010. The Barbers also had the good sense to buy a Mitsubishi store well before the Chrysler deal collapsed. The ironic thing is they had never seen themselves as "import dealers." This was true-blue Americana country. They were domestic guys.

Chevrolet's theme song "Like a Rock" by Bob Seger, followed by John Mellencamp's "This Is Our Country," played big here. It was a market the automakers seemed to be turning their backs on, even though trucks had long been their bread-and-butter market.

Fred Barber's regret is that they couldn't save all their employees, dropping from seventy to twenty-four in the three weeks it took Chrysler to shut them down. "It will take GM longer to come back, but the way they treated their dealers later has customers at least wanting to come back to them," he said.

Dealers like Barber wondered why clear criteria for closure were not readily available until dealer advocacy groups and their lawyers pushed for them. "Chrysler showed us some criteria after it was all over [in legal hearings]. It was a speed bump in time."

Then Barber paused, as if looking down the long road ahead. "You know, Ford is setting the market on fire. I never thought I'd see that." Ford, as many dealers said, was eating its rivals' lunch. Sales rose, and their quality ratings were going up.

Indeed, twenty months after the shutdowns, Ford was to record its biggest profits in ten years.

Of course Chrysler and GM argued that the closures would create stronger, leaner companies, better able to compete with their rivals, especially imports. But dealers said the automakers had long threatened to trim substantially or even eliminate their dealer base. For years there was rampant talk of the Detroit automakers buying out dealers.

Fred Barber recalled those times. "This is not a new thing. They've been talking about taking out dealers for decades." Without state franchise laws to protect them, dealers might have been terminated in large numbers sooner. The task force came along and gave them the perfect vehicle to do damage through the short-form 363 bankruptcy, dealers such as Barber contend.

Another problem surfaced: Where would the "orphaned" customers go for sales and service once their local dealerships were closed? In some outlying areas it was reported that customers would have to drive forty to one hundred miles round trip to get their vehicles serviced, or to buy the same brands. The government had guaranteed warranty work would be completed as it propped up the automakers, but who would do the work nearby dealers, who faced their customers' questions, wondered.

Steve Biegler became a cancelled Jeep dealer whose family business was rooted for more than eighty years in Aberdeen, South Dakota. He had one answer. Biegler said the chickens would still come home to roost on the closures. "Chrysler made a big mistake when it failed to realize that people get connected to the dealership more than the vehicle. It's all about personal relationships, particularly in a city like ours, which has less than twenty-six thousand people. Jeep thinks it can keep the customers that the axed dealers had. That's simply not the case. I can refer my old customers to a Jeep dealership sixty miles away, but it's more likely they'll buy a different car right here in Aberdeen, where they know the dealer," he told a *Wall Street Journal* reporter in July after the closures.

"This has definitely been a bump in the road, but the community has been supportive. I've had customers come in the store and pledge they won't buy a Jeep again.... We've continued working as hard as we always have to maintain the business (used cars and service). Like all the other dealers, we will find other things to sell and support the customers we've had in the past. We're not going away," Biegler said.

* * *

Jim Lunt, vice president of Lunt Motor Co. in Cedar City, Utah, said employees at his Chrysler dealership located in the town's Main Street were extremely anxious when the closure announcement arrived. There was little the owners could do to reassure them they'd pull through this. They themselves felt abandoned and thrown under the bus.

It was the worst kind of betrayal, because the Lunt family had remained loyal to Chrysler, not considering other brands in nearly seventy-five years in business. They had continually turned their backs on import businesses back then. They, too, were "domestic guys." It's like they chopped off your legs," Jim Lunt said. "We hadn't looked at other manufacturers. We've stuck with Chrysler through thick and thin. You kind of feel like you've been thrown overboard."

It was a custom in their Rocky Mountain region to "dance with the girl you brung," said his father, Mitch Lunt. He is the eighty-two-year-old patriarch of the dealership, starting in the business as a kid, washing floors and cars when *his* dad ran things. They had been loyal to one master, Chrysler, for more than seventy years.

Mitch Lunt said they heard about their closure on the Internet. Their parts manager was checking out inventory availability and saw it posted online. He ran into the boss's office with the startling news. "We couldn't believe what he was telling us," Lunt said.

The next day the fatal letter came. Proof of closure, if nothing else. Still no criteria were offered; these would come much later, after much infighting between all affected parties.

"It was a political thing," Mitch Lunt concluded later, as he observed old-line dealers and "ma- and-pa stores were being taken out."

* * *

Jim Tarbox once had a top-performing Chrysler Jeep store in North Kingston, Rhode Island. He was so successful that Chrysler asked to him in 2005 to open a dealership in Attleboro, Massachusetts, where they needed a presence. A classic hard-charging type A personality, Tarbox was often in the top 5 to 10 percent of all Chrysler dealers nationally. His third-generation family business began in 1935.

Tarbox never saw himself as doing anything but selling and servicing cars. When he got the termination letter that May, he tried to figure out what went wrong. His scores were great, and he truly loved the business he had grown up in.

"All I worked for, all I had built was gone within the few seconds" it took to open the letter from the Chrysler home office, he said. His first thoughts were about his family and his employees, Tarbox, the father of three young girls, said. "Everything I worked for, my businesses and my rights, were gone in seconds—and given to my competitors on a silver platter."

He called the decision to cut his stores "arbitrary and unfair, a vendetta." But it was all too true; Chrysler did not want him on the home team. That hurt all right, but he was ready to take the battle up in court, if he had to. Like he had done before when he protested in state court about Chrysler's decision to place a competing business close to his. And therein lay his demise, he realized much later. Almost two years later, everyone affected by the news remembered that day and where they were. It was a grim reminder of an event they will never forget, like combat veterans of wars.

"The problem is, they never looked to see where the carcasses were buried," dealer Jack Fitzgerald said. At the time, an idea was percolating between him and Alan Spitzer, his dealer friend in Elyria, Ohio, whose dealer chain also was decimated by Chrysler and GM.

Fitzgerald, owner of Fitzgerald Auto Malls, selling seventeen major vehicle brands and a dealer since the mid-1960s, was severely affected by the cuts. He and Spitzer would go on to develop Spitzer's brainstorm: form a cohesive dealer group with a single-minded purpose. They were passionate in their mission to represent the affected dealers and challenge the auto task force, which was muscling the automakers to make drastic changes in the dealer network. They were not going to take the blows lying down; they were not going without a fight or be defeated without a voice. Those thoughts planted the seeds for the Committee to Restore Dealer Rights, the dealer advocacy group that in a short time would stand shoulder-to-shoulder with the other established lobbying groups: the National Automobile Dealers Association, National Association of Minority Automobile Dealers, and Automobile Trade Association Executives.

CRDR's clear purpose and growing support suggested they were the right ones for the fight, attorney Mike Charapp said.

The two dealers later brought in Tammy Darvish as a coleader, knowing her father, John Darvish, and her strong organizational and people skills. They also knew of her dedication to work tirelessly for ideas she believed in passionately—and that restoring dealers' rights rated at the top with her.

GM implemented the dealer cuts differently from Chrysler. Both automakers continued to roll out their plans in their own way. GM gave dealers until October 31, 2010 to wind down their businesses. As if that would make the bitter pills easier to swallow. Not quite as cruel as Chrysler and its quick shutdown orders, but still not easy to take at the time, Darvish recalled.

"In many cases you might as well just shut those people down today, because they're not going to sell you any cars," Darvish said about the automakers. Her observation proved true for many dealers. The grand design seemed to be to cut off the product line and watch them choke, many dealers said.

For the Darvish family, it was also tough. They had recently paid several million dollars in upgrading their GM dealership. "I had just paid seven years prior on two million dollars just for the blue sky value of the Chevrolet dealership. Plus I had this crazy long lease on the building. We had just completed renovations and had just redone the entire building, finishing it sixty days before our rejection notice," Tammy Darvish said. "What lousy timing, huh?" "Blue sky" is an industry term indicating the allocated worth or value of a business above its asset value.

* * *

A long-term GM dealership manager, Scott LaRiche in Plymouth, Michigan, echoed what dealers were saying when they received the dreaded closure notices from Chevrolet in May of 2009. "We thought it was a mistake, we couldn't have been on the hit list." His store was in an affluent community about thirty miles west of economically battered Detroit, the heart of GM country.

Scott's father, Lou LaRiche, had been in business selling Chevrolet products for more than forty years. A loyal Chevrolet dealer with high performance scores, the dealership was always at the top of their game. LaRiche says they had performed near the top of all sales and customer satisfaction records for many years. A lower sales year came in 2008. But dealers across the country were hurting at the time, as a near depression took over the nation, and a severe credit freeze hampered sales everywhere. But even then, as other dealers reeled from the economic meltdown, the dealership ranked ninety-seven in sales out of about forty-six hundred Chevrolet dealers nationwide, LaRiche said.

In Troy, Michigan, Richard Mealey was another top-performer for Chrysler. "It's time for Congress to rectify this gross injustice," Mealey said about the senseless closures that left dealers saying they had been robbed of their livelihoods, reputations—and personal dignity. Mealey, who owned Birmingham Chrysler Jeep (BCJ), was one of about twenty dealers who testified against Chrysler in US bankruptcy court in New York City between May and June.

One Dealer's Protest

At ten o'clock in the morning on May 13, Longmont, Colorado, dealer Yale King and his brother and dealership partner, Rex King, were headed to a dealer event. King's cell phone rang; his wife, Shauna, was on the line, choked up with emotion. She had just heard on a radio station that King's group was being cut by Chrysler. Not the kind of news you want to start the day with.

King listened. His own feelings were in turmoil as he tried to reassure her. "The tears flowed, but our strength prevailed. It would be five more hours before we received official notice in the mail about our situation," King said later. His award-winning GM franchise was yanked the next day. Again, an unsigned letter arrived, stark words from a nameless decision maker at GM. The double whammy was aimed at the heart, he thought, when GM followed suit.

Like everyone in the country, King knew GM CEO Rick Wagoner had been fired April 1 by President Obama and the auto task force, who were calling the shots on automotive. Later, dealers would learn that Wagoner was forced to go when he opposed deep restructuring and bankruptcy proceedings for GM.

With Wagoner out, King figured the task force was setting the tone for the manufacturers' leaders to get in line, march to their drumbeat. Anybody could be next. "Whose job is safe?" King asked. You could only wonder when the top auto executive in the world goes down.

"We began checking every legal action we could to appeal the process with GM and Chrysler," King said. "We wanted to find out what legal basis the manufacturers had for doing what they did." King was part of the initial group notified. His Longmont franchises in Colorado were the first wave of GM and Chrysler dealerships to get notices. After that round, the auto task force seemed to call for more numbers; the cuts weren't deep enough, dealers heard.

King personally waged more than a year-long battle to win back the King Auto Group dealerships from Chrysler and GM. He ran the dealer group along with two partners—Mitch Pierce and his brother, Rex. As he took on the big guys, it was a period much like a cat-and-mouse game, King feeling like the mouse.

Beginning in 2009, King sent e-mails, memos, and letters to everyone he could think of at Chrysler and GM. In his letters to Jim Press, then Chrysler's co-president, he gave facts on the performance of their Chrysler-Jeep franchise in Longmont, showing why they never should have been targeted. The main reason: they posted record sales growth in the nearly four years they ran the stores. There was one down period in 2008, in the height of the recession, when most dealers lost sales, some their shirts. Indeed, King and his partners had built the business and brought Jeep back from the brink in 2005 as a renowned brand in the Longmont area, where it had nearly died a painful death. The group also recorded high customer satisfaction index (CSI) ratings in that time. Sales and customer satisfaction index scores were two critical drivers that the automakers supposedly looked at to determine did you stay or go. Their CSI was exemplary.

King took over in July that year and quickly turned things around. In one month, the group shattered records, improving sales 1,600 percent over the former owner's rates the first quarter. In a three-year period, King sold 593 vehicles and their Jeep sales averaged nearly 60 percent of their total volume, which included the GM stores. The numbers didn't seem to faze the decision makers in Detroit.

By 2009, the group was on pace to exceed their Chrysler sales goals, a remarkable achievement. He also had earned Chrysler's Five-Star rating, the top mark Chrysler itself gives high-performing dealers. That's when Chrysler pulled the plug.

With his GM dealership, it was a similar story. Great records, thank you, but no contract renewal. When he asked the GM power players why their franchise, including Buick, GMC, and Pontiac, was axed, the answers kept changing. "There was never one consistent reason. I overcame each objection raised, but it was like constantly trying to hit a moving target," he said. Pontiac later was understandable since GM eliminated the brand, but what about Buick and GMC?

Even after being cut in June, his GM dealerships generated an average of 182 percent of their sales objectives through year's end—even without receiving one new car from GM.

He kept searching for answers. Why was he cut? Did they not know his numbers? Finally, a semblance of an answer: in late June, a GM Dealer Appeal Group said he was removed because "GM wanted to take out smaller dealers and divide the market share among the bigger metro area dealers," King said.

Stunned, King tried to get a better idea of what that meant, and why. When he could not get answers, he became politically explosive. "The reason I became so politically nuclear was not only because of the national stance I took, but also because Colorado leads the way for the toughest state franchise laws in the country. Our story in this state was a key factor. Not only did we receive one state franchise law signed by the governor, but when Chrysler would not abide by it, we were able to get another state franchise law that severely changed the penalty for not abiding by the law."

He added, "We received, in most cases, full and unanimous support from both state houses and various committees. GM even ended up taking out commercials and full-page ads in Colorado to try to get the law stopped. This obviously was a large contributing factor in their position regarding my case."

The song and dance with the automakers went on and on for King and partners. After numerous contacts in the fall, King heard from GM that his closure was not about dealership performance. Instead, one e-mail said GM didn't want to be in the Longmont market. For dealers who were there, it was tough luck. "Performance was not mentioned anywhere in that e-mail."

In another memo, GM said they terminated him because he "was an unofficial dually owned dealership." Yes, he ran a joint Chrysler and GM store, but so did many small- to mid-size dealers. This puzzled him too, because Jeep had been there from the start, and GM had approved the deal. He'd also offered to separate the brands, but neither automaker took him up on it, as if they already knew his fate.

King believed unfair scoring was taking place for certain dealerships, like his. In his Chrysler store, King's performance scores were lumped in with the poor records of the former owners as "a ten-year sales history" worked to his disadvantage. How could he be responsible for ten, or six, years of sales records when he had been in business fewer than four? The formula used showed an inaccurate reflection of his score, which was artificially low because of the previous dealer's poor history, he maintained.

He continued pressing his case with executives at Chrysler but never got any resolution.

In July, 2009, Fred Diaz, the former Chrysler Denver business center manager (who became one of Chrysler's top executives with Dodge in Detroit), called King. He brought up the problem of King being "dualed" with GM and a stand-alone Jeep franchise. It went against the Genesis concept Chrysler was promoting. Diaz at least was honest and told him his case was "a tough one because you have an excellent reputation."

King asked, "Why would you cut me out after just a few years of being here at Chrysler's request to take over a failing store?" Chrysler could have exercised a "first right of refusal" instead of asking King to invest millions and then torpedo him. Diaz replied, "We should have thought about it better then."

First refusal rights spelled out that if an automaker brought the same franchise back into a market, the terminated dealer had the right to refuse the deal first or be given adequate compensation for the loss.

Another Colorado law came after Chrysler sued the Colorado Attorney General, the Colorado Department of Revenue, and the State Department of Motor Vehicles. It essentially said that every day a franchisor did not honor the franchisee's rights, a substantial financial penalty would be levied against the franchisor—in this case the automaker—on a daily basis, according to King's lawyers.

After numerous legislators inquired on King's behalf, the reasons still continued to change, King said. In fact, one of the Chrysler zone managers had said King hadn't been included in the initial round of cuts and never should have been on the list.

King struggled with many of the vagaries. The hard part was this: he'd always considered himself a team player. In 2005, he had bought the three GM brands at great personal expense because he was encouraged to do so by GM.

King pursued all his legal options to get back his businesses. Then the money ran out. "I'm tapped out. Our partnership spent hundreds of thousands of dollars on legal fees," he said. King had cashed in his IRAs and savings. "My timing has been terrible on this," he said.

But the GM discussions were not over. On the evening of October 7, King called Tammy Darvish at home. They weren't in the habit of conversing at night. They exchanged mostly e-mails that traveled across cyberspace at all hours. But that night, he was upset over a disturbing conversation he'd had that day with Brian Lee, a middle manager with GM's dealer placement group.

One thing to know about King is, he's a pious, highly principled man. He firmly believes in doing what's right and serving others. By profession, he was an auto dealer, but could have been a preacher, religion is so important to him. He'd proudly sent two sons to fight in the Middle East wars and couldn't believe what was happening on US soil to wipe out domestic car dealers.

A lot of mid-managers in Detroit were scared these days about their own jobs, dealers like King knew. But the call from Brian Lee bothered him. It was the kind of call that keeps you up at night. "I've never been talked to this way, or so rudely treated," King told Darvish. Lee basically called King a liar and told him his CSI scores "sucked." King called it "one of the most unprofessional conversations I have ever had in my career."

The call began confrontationally from the start. Lee said, "I don't know why I'm even reviewing this case," referring to the King closure decision by GM. Then he added that King's dealership "CSI sucks," claiming that his CSI score, which looks at how dealerships satisfy customers was "forty-eight," definitely a low score—if true.

But King clarified, "Our score was eighty-four at the time, and it's been even higher." To that, Lee replied he must have had "dyslexia" when he looked at the number.

Pretty easy to transpose eighty-four and forty-eight, King thought forgivingly. The next thing he knew, Lee was accusing him of lying and submitting false financial statements to GM. King was stunned, offended at the inferences of dishonesty, but he offered to resend Lee documents detailing his performance again. He was trying to keep it together. He had sent the paperwork earlier to Lee, who couldn't seem to find his records.

King then tried to explain that in 2008 the store had a sales dip when GM sent almost no inventory. More accusations followed; the exchange grew nastier. Lee proceeded to call him a liar, as if trying to break him down, King said. Lee indicated that GM had fulfilled its order obligations and that there was no way GM did not build the product that King had ordered, he recalled.

The economy was a disaster in 2009, and King knew that sales were declining for most dealers nationally. But he didn't play that card. Halfway through, King couldn't go on with the phone call. He told Brian Lee, "The accusatory tone and the unproductive environment" were leading nowhere and they would have to end the call. King later followed up with a letter to Lee on October 9, copying legislators with his twenty-four-page documentation backing up his performance.

That letter outlining the King group's sales and profit records was sent to Brian Lee but never received a reply. Lee had told him earlier, "The dealer consolidation was part of this overall plan and GM did not have the opportunity to analyze each dealership on a case-by-case basis."

King actively lobbied Congress and the state for fourteen months to restore and protect dealership franchises between the federal and state levels. He helped make changes. But after a protracted battle and passage of two Colorado State laws protecting franchise rights, his attorneys warned him that litigation against Chrysler could drag on for years and cost hundreds of thousands of dollars more in fees. By then, his partnership had been devastated. They already had spent half a million dollars, with nothing to show for it.

Chrysler and GM continued to challenge Colorado State laws as unconstitutional. For dealers such as King, It seemed another losing battle.

The events at both GM and Chrysler had shaken him. On November 1, King wrote to Neil Barofsky, the special investigator general for SIGTARP, heading the investigation of wrongdoings in the dealer closures. King supplied a chronology of events from mid-May to October 9 and what had happened with his businesses and others like his. He touched on various points, including his attempts to contact each member of the auto task force and GM to try to rectify fact from fiction. He briefly referred to the phone call with Brian Lee, which he simply termed "unprofessional."

Under protection of bankruptcy restructuring, the automakers were cleaning house, King thought. With the task force overseeing the automaker reorganizations, dealers like King were caught in the middle. "This was the auto task force's way of putting pressure on the manufacturers in a political environment to shed dealers on a cookie-cutter basis," King said. And there was enormous pressure from the task force to reduce the dealer numbers even more, even if they didn't specify the dealer names to be cut.

By the following year, King backed down from further battling the automaker giants and government, discouraged as much as angry. "I couldn't continue the legal costs against Chrysler, now a company propped up by the US government. I am a little guy."

* * *

It took many months and much elbow grease and legwork to change the political climate, especially on the part of Tammy Darvish and the leaders of the newly forming CRDR, growing out of the minds of the Maryland- and Ohio-based dealers. The leaders had to sift through a multitude of lies and innuendos, but the dealer messages would soon be carried by media nationwide and the US Congress.

Jack Fitzgerald had looked closely at the role of the auto task force, the former Wall Street money-baggers who charged in like the cavalry to rescue the two ailing auto companies. "The auto task force began tinkering with the country's viability," Fitzgerald said. "What these Wall Street guys do is come in and buy big, old overbuilt companies [distressed businesses]. Then they cut out all the fat to slim it down, while the fat spurts for a while. They're heartless. They know they will make their money on the initial public offerings that ensue when the companies sell stock."

Fitzgerald shook his head. "They had a chance of a lifetime to fix the industry, but they did horrible things. To save allegedly 75 percent of the dealers, they killed 25 percent. That's preposterous. They squandered a golden opportunity to rescue America's auto industry."

Why do dealers think that such an egregious act of wrongdoing was committed? In addition to having their property and personal investments taken away, the automakers had fed the government and the public a major myth: dealers cost them too much money and were drains on the bottom line. They had been robbed of their businesses and their reputations ruined, some said.

"Dealers don't cost the automakers a cent. We are their customers, not their creditors. We financed these manufacturers," Fitzgerald said nearly eighteen months after the ax fell on US car dealers.

But there was another fact working against the dealers. Courtesy of the auto task force, neophytes in automotive and in government, the automakers had been turned upside down in fewer than four months by the task force, a group of temporary project workers. Their leader, Rattner, had spent perhaps a day in Detroit before his group made their decisions, and their favorite part, as Steve Rattner told it, was the sparkling new terminal at Detroit Metro Airport. He had expected a lump of coal and found a diamond in the outlying Detroit airport.

Meanwhile, Peter Kitzmiller, president of the Maryland Automobile Dealers Association, said as the GM closures were about to be announced, the automaker will not "reduce expenses one dollar by shedding dealerships. This doesn't do anything to help make GM viable. In fact it does just the opposite." During the debacle, Maryland was slated to lose about fifty-eight dealers who would no longer pay taxes or employ people, according to NADA.

The CRDR team began to campaign vigorously for dealer rights. Darvish was building her "A-team," the all-star team of dealers that grew out of the advocacy group's organizing efforts. These were the few dozen natural leaders who emerged to help in the trenches.

The CRDR team sometimes had to ask whether they were shouting into the wind, not being heard. But anyone who knew them understood this group was made of sterner stuff. Their battle had just begun. Chronic underachievers, indeed. They would show otherwise.

The small group was just revving up, despite the voices of doom telling them to quit. How many times would they get the message: *The train has left the station; go back home.* But they were just starting their engines and calling all dealers aboard. Dealer Jeff Duvall in Clayton, Georgia, later wrote what could serve as their fight song in the long march ahead:

> What is that light I see way down at the end of the tunnel?
> Look, it's a train, oh yeah, I see, it's that locomotive,
> it's the little engine that could ...
> Who's the conductor? That's Tammy Darvish, Jack Fitzgerald, and Alan Spitzer I see.
> And look, they are pulling the Automobile Dealer Rights Train down the track.
> Oh yeah, I see it now; and it looks like they have thrown all the bums off the train.
> What did they just yell? Do you hear it?
> They said, "Shovel on a little more coal," we're going faster ...
> and it looks like they're coming back to get the rejected dealers.
> Oh yes, *the train has definitely come back to the station.*
> And the dealers are climbing aboard.

Chapter 3—The Woman Who Knew Too Much

Mama, Mama, there's too many of you crying... don't punish me with brutality. Tell me what's going on.

—"What's Going On?" by Marvin Gaye

"I know all the secrets. I know all the dirt. I know all the dirty games Chrysler and GM played on Capitol Hill, and well before that." That's what Tammy Darvish told her few confidantes about the closures that would shut down several thousand car dealerships during that tumultuous period in 2009. Often she would confide in her close friend, Rose Bayat, as the Committee to Restore Dealer Rights cranked up and Darvish became its voice and front person to dealers, the media, and Congress.

Darvish knew about secret e-mails between Chrysler executives that were being kept under wraps. The private e-mails detailed discussions on several dealers being cut and why. They even talked about potential problems of cutting certain dealers because their performance scores were so high. She knew about executives who were twisting the truth in courts and before Congress. She knew about giving away dealerships to favored friends before many others in the country did.

"It was powerful stuff," said Bayat, who managed customer relations at DARCARS and had known Tammy Darvish since college. Often when she heard the stories about the closing dealers or Darvish's growing involvement with Congress, the task force, and the corporate higher-ups, she cautioned Tammy to back off, tone it down. She worried more than anything about her personal safety.

Darvish knew she was working against highly paid interests and very connected lobbyists being paid millions. It could backfire. You never knew about the far reach of such powerful people, friends warned her.

"What are you going to do with it?" Bayat asked after Darvish shared a confidence that was weighing on her.

"I don't know yet." Darvish shrugged, feeling dejected at the time. Too much had happened. The thousands of personal stories, the many tragedies she was hearing from dealers, their families, and associates weighed heavily on her shoulders.

"She's driven beyond belief, always digging, making sure she's got the proper facts," Rose Bayat said about Darvish. When she sees something that's not the truth or blatant lies, "she wants the truth to come out. She will fight for that truth."

Above all, Darvish is generous, Bayat said. "She gives time and money to many charities and sits on the boards of at least ten different civic organizations and trade groups. Her list of professional awards from groups such as *Automotive News*, *Time* magazine, and *Dealer* magazine is longer than her resume. "If she had one last glass of water, she'd give it to you," Bayat said.

"Tammy Darvish for president," some of her admirers would joke, but they were half-serious.

If you ask Darvish why she got so involved, you get a simple answer. "I really believed we could save people's livelihoods and restore their rights. We could make a difference." Simple but complicated to execute, this saving of souls and businesses.

Mina Gharib, Darvish's cousin, manages a couple of DARCARS dealerships in Rockville, near Silver Spring. "That's just the way she is. She's like this with every cause she believes in," giving to charities, to dealers, and to those in need.

That's why Tammy Darvish got so involved in the dealer struggle, Gharib said. "She couldn't stand by and see the injustices being done and do nothing. She had to right the wrongs." Gharib recalled how Darvish took her under her wing as a child when her mother died. "I was a kid and she helped me with everything. We pretty much grew up together," she said.

That's what many others say of Darvish. Yale King, a Colorado dealer who worked closely with her to restore dealer rights, said, "She's a selfless leader."

* * *

These were troubled times in Washington DC, in Detroit, and at dealerships around the country. The two automakers were restructuring under a shortcut bankruptcy protection law, but 25 percent of dealers had already borne the brunt of their scalpels. The middle class was reeling from economic shockwaves after a year of deep recession.

In her role as coleader of the committee, Darvish had become everything from rumor control to confidante for dealers, their families, and employees—even customers—over the course of a few months. The CRDR website, which Darvish and her team built and managed, grew to include dealers, members of Congress, congressional aides, and later, investigators for SIGTARP. She was also the key fact finder and sender, including many thousands of e-mails to anyone with questions and concerns, including the media. If they asked a question, Darvish would answer.

But she wondered about Rose's cautionary advice. Should she back down? Take it less seriously? There was enough work at her father's dealership chain to occupy more than two full-time jobs for one person. The stacks piling up on her desk and in her office told her that. She should get focused on that. Something told her to push on, get the truth out. This story was not over. An inner compass told her so much more was yet to unfold.

Like Jimmy Stewart in the classic Alfred Hitchcock thriller *The Man Who Knew Too Much,* she heard all the secrets, lies, and innuendos. But how could she, one woman, make a difference in a system set up to block her and others who spoke out against power? How could she speak for thousands who had no voice with the powers that be?

In meetings with Congress and other power brokers, she would sometimes become a fly on the wall, often soft-spoken and inconspicuous. Or she became an assertive voice on the phone, or in e-mails, talking about the grave injustice done, the injustice that was committed in the private meeting rooms and gleaming structures of corporate America. She knew almost intuitively what she had to do: mobilize the dealers who had been disenfranchised and had no voice. Help them speak out.

Easier said than done.

* * *

Sitting in New York bankruptcy court in early June, Tammy Darvish didn't think she could stand it a moment longer. She was here on an official mission, as a representative on the Unsecured Creditors Committee for Chrysler. She had been listening to dealer testimony in hearings on the Chrysler bankruptcy appeal. In one case, a Michigan dealer talked about the abrupt shutdown of his Jeep and Chrysler store in less than a month and how it affected employees and his family—how it hurt a community he had long supported, and a state battered by unemployment.

She knew him. It was Richard Mealey, who had enjoyed many award trips and outings with her father. He had been a top Chrysler dealer, and his business had dropped from more than one hundred employees to just a few, and then none, with one letter from Chrysler.

Richard Mealey spoke candidly before a roomful of strangers and a somber judge. He talked about his proven performance year after year before the closure of his store in a suburban Detroit location. He cited statistics and customer-satisfaction testimonials.

Many times in the courtroom dealers like Mealey were overcome with emotion. Darvish imagined them thinking about their years of hard work and the dedication of their families and employees in helping run their dealerships.

Afterward, Tammy Darvish rushed to find a bathroom, unable to hold back tears. She couldn't bear it when these established dealership owners couldn't hold it together in the courtroom. Later she thought about a dealer she had heard testify that day. A broken Jim Tarbox, who set sales records in his Chrysler-Jeep stores in Rhode Island and Massachusetts, said on the stand, "They've taken everything from me. What more can they take?"

One after another, the dealers related stories of feeling robbed of their life's work and betrayed by the automakers. Darvish heard stories of devastated dealers, families, and communities; she felt their pain. Friends often worried that she perhaps overidentified with loss. But Darvish took this shock that dealers personally experienced to heart. She thought especially of her quietly stubborn father, suffering from Parkinson's disease, and under even greater stress now. She saw him thinking about the rejection letter from Chrysler; and then his gaze filled with sorrow, wondering if his thirty-two-year history with Chrysler as an owner had gone up in smoke.

The Darvishes had lost two Chrysler stores and a GM-Chevrolet store. After the rejection letters came, she noticed her father, ever the risk-taker, being more cautious. When he heard about her actions on the dealer front and taking on the auto giants, he warned her, "You've gotta be careful. You've got to worry about your future now. It's not like you can alienate these people, you know. You might need them again someday." It was practical advice, but she would worry about it later.

She worried about him too. That spring, she had convinced him to move his office to the main store in Silver Spring. Her office was there and she wanted to work closer to him, to help out more directly in all phases of the business, rather than by constant phone calls back and forth to his location. She wanted to continue learning the business from him. But secretly she knew she wanted to make sure he was eating right, taking care of himself.

When pressure hit, she tended toward the philosophical. You manage. You try to make do with what you have. But then there were her daughter and son, Nadia and Nima. Their childhood years seemed to be slipping by too quickly. Her obsession with the dealer struggle wasn't exactly helping in the parenting category. There was no flex time in her twenty-four-hour schedule.

* * *

The television set in her son's bedroom was broken. At thirteen, Nima was old enough to complain about the world's injustices and was adamant about wanting a new TV set. "Come on, Mom. It's only fair," he said. His sister, Nadia, after all, has a TV in her room.

"I'm not going to fix it; I'm not going to get you a new TV," Tammy Darvish responded, trying to be the firm mom. They would be moving into a new home shortly and the timing was bad. She had told him this many times and wondered why he didn't get it.

He's just upset because he can't play his videos, or whatever. He'll get over it. That's what she tried telling herself.

But Nima persisted. "Come on, Mom, please."

She told him again that they were moving soon and he didn't need a TV. Maybe later, not now, she said, giving in slightly.

The family indeed was moving to a new larger house in Potomac shortly, and this was no time to be acquiring more possessions. More toys. Large, expensive ones like TVs. *Besides, kids today are a little spoiled anyway,* she thought.

Shortly after that episode, she came home from work one night to find Nima in a sleeping bag on the floor in her bedroom.

"What are you doing here?" she asked.

He glanced up sleepily, mumbling, "I'm watching TV."

"Let's go; you're going to bed right now."

"No, I'm not," he said, standing his ground.

"So why are you here? What's the deal anyway?" She was tired and in no mood to humor anyone, least of all her stubborn son.

Nima gave her a resolute look. "Mom, you're the one who said that if something is going on that you don't like, you have to stand up and take responsibility for it yourself. Or you have no right to complain about the consequences later," he said, just as firmly as his mother would.

Tammy Darvish swallowed hard, hearing her own words, her own lessons coming from Nima's mouth. She had told her son enough times that the televisions would be moved soon. But what he remembered was her actions at critical times.

Is this called a teachable moment? She would often ask herself this kind of question where her children were concerned. What parent doesn't want to teach her or his children important life lessons? Make sure they absorb mostly the good, not the bad. But why did it have to be at a time she was waging the greatest battle of her life, trying to restore the dealers? Life just wasn't fair at times.

She remembered how she told others too about how important it was to teach your children to stand up for what you believe in; she tried to model that behavior more than anything.

Then she recalled her daughter, Nadia, a busy and pretty fifteen-year-old, looking at her regretfully some days. "Mom, we haven't been doing much lately," Nadia said.

She vowed to pay more attention to Nadia too, watch TV with her, make popcorn, listen to her gossip about boys and problems with girlfriends. Bake cookies and cakes with her. Like she used to do. Before the madness hit. The one little luxury she permitted herself with Nadia was when the two would get mani-pedis at a local spa. But even that she'd put off now and then. Her work with the dealer struggle was all-encompassing.

She'd taken her kids to see *Precious*, the intense urban teen drama that had won many Academy Awards. At least she'd done that. Generally Tammy Darvish liked dramas. She danced, in her mind mostly, to Motown music from the seventies and eighties. Give her The Supremes, Marvin Gaye, and Donna Summer tunes and she was happy. And a good read for her was a Jodi Picoult or John Grisham crime novel. She often recorded *All My Children* and episodes from the *E* network. But she was behind on all that too.

Escapism suited her just fine at times. The business world, and this anguish with dealers, was crazy enough real-life drama. It was the story of her life, often taking more than one hundred hours a week. She was a runner but found no time to run these days. *One of these days, I will start de-stressing. I will start taking care of myself and mine.* Those were promises she hoped to keep. *One day soon.*

On a Saturday night, she and Nadia were watching a TV show. Despite their age difference, they liked many of the same programs. In the middle of Nadia's sentence Darvish drifted off to sleep, exhausted from her workweek. But still that nagging voice in her head, every working mother's guilt trip, said she wasn't spending enough "quality" time with her kids. She wasn't there for them enough. And what about Hamid, her husband—how could she ever make it up to him?

Hamid said he loved her, like always. But the nagging inner voice wouldn't quit. Sometimes she spent more time with her business associates—Rob Smith, Jack Fitzgerald, Rose Bayat, Courtney Wallin, and others—than with him.

When she traveled on business, she brought the kids along whenever possible. But she couldn't exactly stuff Hamid in a suitcase and bring him along. She'd been living the life of a high-powered dealership exec a little too long. It was so unlike the lives their relatives in Iran lived, the life her family here avoided. She remembered having to cover the few times she'd visited relatives for family occasions in the Middle East. But there was too much at stake to turn back the clock now. She was born in the United States, and her life had always been here and now.

* * *

In July of 2009, Nadia and Nima accompanied their mother to DC, where she was handling press conferences on the dealer rights issue before Congress. The kids knew this was big, important. Their mother had been preparing for this event for days, although it had been cooked up pretty fast. Now there were camera bulbs flashing, dozens of microphones in her face, people thronging Triangle Square by Capitol Hill, and reporters firing off questions. The Darvish kids knew their mother was in charge.

"This doesn't happen in America, the seizure of your property by government and corporations," Tammy Darvish told the press, members of Congress, and their aides. "Maybe in the Soviet Union or Cuba. But not in the United States of America."

By July, dealers were still reeling, stunned from the news of their closures by Chrysler and GM. For Tammy Darvish and her supporters, it was a constitutional issue hinging on the illegal seizure of property and trampling on basic human rights.

Nima and Nadia didn't exactly understand all the issues, but they were beginning to understand why their mother was so passionate about this "dealer thing." The kids were impressed with all the activity and commotion, but that's not what Darvish had intended. Her lesson to them was something different. "When you believe strongly that something is wrong, you do something about it. " Sometimes you have to take a stand on the important things; or you will stand for nothing. That's what she wanted them to understand.

Her belief was that children learn by example. *You try to teach your children that you've got to stand up for what you believe in,* she thought, but this was a way they could see it in action.

Several hundred dealers and other supporters had shown up for the dealer rally, and so much work had gone into organizing it. But privately, Darvish was a little disappointed. Where were the massive protests, the screaming in the streets at the injustices? Where were the hundreds of thousands and millions who came for something like the Million Man March, women's rights, human rights, or antiwar protests of the past?

What could she do to energize people more? No matter how hard she worked, it felt like she wasn't doing enough. She even had a hard time telling people what she did for a living. "Well, I'm no soccer mom," she told a reporter who was quizzing her about her career and personal life. Neither was she just a rich car dealer's daughter. She tried to give back to society as much as possible. Still, the nagging inner voice would not be quiet.

"They've Taken My Honor"

In her characteristic fashion, Tammy Darvish walked hurriedly into her father's office. She was not sure why she'd been summoned. She had piles of work to do. It was a sun-drenched morning in May, the air fresh and alive in the throes of annual rebirth. In Washington DC and its environs, such as nearby Maryland and Virginia, the cherry blossoms were ending their season in full bloom, saying good-bye for yet another year. The annual cherry tree festival, beginning in late March, was ebbing like the cold winter nights.

In Silver Spring, Maryland, where the DARCARS auto group has its headquarters, the warmth outside was suddenly a stark contrast to the turmoil going on inside the president's office. Tammy Darvish saw something she'd never seen before. John Darvish, an automotive icon, sat slumped in his chair, his face ashen and eyes downcast. He was distraught.

Tammy had never seen her father so upset. And she'd worked in the stores since graduating high school, only taking time away for college. "Dad, what's wrong?" The worry in her voice was unmistakable.

The letter from Chrysler was on his mind. The Chrysler Group in Auburn Hills, Michigan, the company's corporate headquarters, had delivered the letter the day the Darvishes were attending a dealer conference in DC.

"I just can't believe this is happening," he finally said, eyes averted.

Tammy Darvish watched her father's face for a few moments. What she saw was a host of feelings: sadness, anger, fear, but mostly resignation. It was like the bad news was just sinking in. In his own way, he was problem-solving the situation. Even after he'd reassured employees and his family that things would be all right, he was still assuring himself.

Moments later, in his positive way of dealing with life's setbacks, he said, "Oh well, I suppose we will get through this, and everything will be okay."

Then he sat back and stared ahead reflectively, but with a very sad, faraway look in his eyes. It was a moment she'd think about many times in the year ahead. She, too, had to look away. Her father had tears in his eyes.

"They've taken my honor," he said, glancing away. But his daughter, his confidante, saw and felt his pain. It was then she knew she had to act, even if he would or could not.

John Darvish had started the Chrysler dealership in 1977, building it into a thirty-four-franchise empire with many leading brands. By then, he was a multi-dealer, to use the industry lingo. But Chrysler, his first dealership, was always close to his heart.

* * *

A Chicago-area manager, Marni McClennan wrote Tammy Darvish a note on June 20, a little more than a month after the Chrysler closures. Darvish understood the irony and pain in her comments. McClennan signed her e-mail, "The last remaining manager at Richard Auto Center." Their St. Charles Chrysler, Jeep, and Dodge store near Chicago had been operating for thirty years, with strong performance records. That's what kept people in business, McClennan thought, their performance. The company had never shirked in sales or taking care of their customers.

By this time, Darvish had gone into overdrive, was highly active in CRDR, building the nonprofit group into a meaningful dealer advocacy. McClennan's was a story Darvish and her group would hear many times from Chrysler and GM dealers.

"We're in a prime location on dealer row in a rather affluent suburb of Chicago," McClennan wrote. They had high performance scores, she related. "It just didn't make sense."

Richard Auto's owner, Rocco Massarelli, was being "continually terrorized by Chrysler financial because Chrysler just didn't want us to stay open," McClennan said. "We were starved of product and money."

Financial hardship was a common refrain from countless other owners who contacted the committee. Many dealers said they had been targeted for personal reasons. The automakers didn't want them to stay open and would fight it at any cost, perhaps forgetting that public money was being used to shut down other taxpaying private businesses.

Darvish added McClennan to her contacts and kept her updated on progress made on legislation. In fact, she added anyone who wanted to be informed. It didn't matter that they didn't have money to contribute to the cause that some in the CRDR group insisted on.

Thus, Darvish's network grew with each day. Soon CRDR had an active e-mail list of several thousand names, members or not. It was not NADA, the national dealer lobbying arm, with more than sixteen thousand members. But NADA was shrinking and CRDR was quickly growing with the unmet dealer needs.

* * *

Christine Rupert is another example of thousands of affected dealers Darvish personally heard from. Rupert had inherited the role of running a Jeep dealership when her husband, fifty-one-year-old Bill Van Burkleo, died of cancer in 2005. She was Christine Van Burkleo before she remarried after his death. She had worked in marketing positions, supporting her husband's role in the business. That was before she became a widow.

Suddenly she found herself transformed into "the dealer," responsible for running the complex family business in McAllen, a southern Texas town nestled in the Rio Grande Valley. Barely prepared for the job, she felt compelled to keep up her husband's dream, a promise she had made. "We have four children, and Bill asked me to try to keep the stores if I could so that our children could one day come into the business," if they chose, Rupert said in her note to Darvish. She wanted to protect her husband's wish for their children.

She worked hard to keep the business going but was not ready for what lay ahead—the collapse of the domestic auto industry. "I was really only getting my footing when the economy took its devastating downturn in September [2008]." The business was hurting badly, and she felt compelled to "make my exit as quickly as possible."

She almost succeeded in selling the Jeep store and had signed a lucrative contract with a buyer. Then suddenly, Chrysler declared bankruptcy, and the world changed even more. Chrysler had cut her store as well as the potential buyer's, who she described as "the most successful Chrysler, Jeep, and Dodge dealer in our south Texas area—well capitalized and profitable." That business was out too.

"I lost my [financed inventory] with Chrysler Financial, and I lost my profit. At the same time, I lost my opportunity to sell my business that had been in our family for forty-six years," she said. Those losses came after being certified as a Five-Star Chrysler dealership, the highest award Chrysler bestows on dealers. Suddenly they were being called nonperformers, has-beens.

And then, in late 2009, the new Chrysler group was up to the old Chrysler tricks, Rupert said. "The final insult" came in early September when she saw that Chrysler had drafted $31,700 from her dealership bank account without her approval to pay for inventory and other debts.

"This is unconscionable. They have become trolls," she said in disgust. "They were out there looking to see who is naïve enough to give them the opportunity to steal from [dealers] further."

Rupert couldn't believe Jim Press's actions. Of Chrysler's past president, Rupert said, "He's a liar. He sat before the Senate subcommittee and outright lied. Every person who I've explained this to is shocked and literally frightened that this can be happening in America."

Rupert apologized profusely for her sometimes harsh language, saying, "This has been so incredibly painful for me, my children, and family."

Darvish understood completely where Christine Rupert was coming from. She'd been in the same boat many times herself, using even worse language to describe her outrage. But right now Darvish had a bigger kettle of fish steaming on the front burner. She felt compelled to tell the world what had happened to America's car dealers and what it signified for the country. She would get Congress's collective ears. That was another promise she made to herself. Unlike the one to take better care of herself, this was one she would keep.

She thought about all the other owners and employees whose confidence she was gaining. It would take Congress and President Obama until December to act on the "dealer economic rights" bills. But in a few months, Darvish was hearing all the stories of personal ruin, their pain, and the brutal truth. It was as though she had punctured a vein and the blood was spilling forth.

By June, the battle lines were drawn by Tammy Darvish and her A-team, the all-star team emerging from CRDR. They had launched their campaign to "save the dealers," and the train was leaving the station. Still running on hope, they thought they were ready to confront the obstacles that lay ahead. But time was not exactly on their side.

Chapter 4—Fast Cars and a White Cordoba

It takes a whole village to raise a child.

—African proverb

Who Is Tammy Darvish? Why did she take on the cause for dealer rights, human rights, Constitutional rights, when she stood to gain nothing? Maybe stood to lose everything herself.

She's a wife, a mother, a daughter, a crusader, and a fiercely loyal friend say those who know her best. A close business colleague and confidante, Jackie Mealey, described her this way: "She's a friend, loyal, righteous, a leader, and focused, so focused. She is truly the measure of a woman." Mealey got to know Darvish well through their work on CRDR and became an instant admirer.

Colleague Alan Spitzer, the coleader of CRDR, described her this way: "She's a 220-volt energizer bunny on steroids."

When Darvish was unpacking after her family moved into a new house, she found an autographed Washington Wizards Michael Jordan jersey in a box. Asked what she was going to do with it, she said she wanted to donate it. In a celebrity auction such a shirt might fetch thousands of dollars for charities. Her family looked at her incredulously. After all, her then nearly teenaged son, Nima, a sports fanatic, would have loved it.

* * *

Tammy Darvish hates minute-rice. She believes in cooking from scratch, even for a crowd. On Sundays, she usually cooks at home. She's been known to prepare filet mignon for a hundred guests. Her kitchen and home in Potomac, Maryland, often becomes a community center where friends, relatives, and colleagues drop in. They often come unannounced because it was always open house at the Darvish home.

But in many ways, family life would no longer be the same after the dealer-rights campaign kicked in. Like many mothers, she worried she wasn't spending the time she should with either of her children. She worried sometimes she couldn't be the soccer mom many of their friends' mothers were. But then she also worried about spoiling them materially, so unlike her own childhood.

Privately, she worried about her marriage to Hamid Fallahi, a busy construction engineer. They had been together for nearly eighteen years, but could it withstand all the pressure that had descended on her and her family in the last year? She could only hope that Hamid understood what was going on and would in his own quiet, usually patient way forgive her.

She and Hamid became better acquainted when she needed a date for a dinner event and couldn't get one of her brothers to go. Hamid was no stranger. They'd known each other for several years then; he was related to a general manager at the Darvish dealerships. Five years later, they were married. The fact that she ran a mega-dealer family business and was caught up in the dealer-rights struggle complicated things at times.

On a busy weekday, between meetings and tending to customer concerns and employees at work, Darvish fielded texts from her assistant, Courtney Wallin, reminding her about their son's award event that afternoon at school. Hamid would meet her there, Wallin said. That day she was running from one meeting to another and in the normal pressure cooker at work. She showed up a little late at the school, where her family was waiting, not so patiently. For business meetings, she made it a point to arrive early, but family, she realized, sometimes got left on the back burner.

"It's not that I forget about them. It's just that I lose track of time, there's always too much going on. I hate being late, but sometimes I can't help it," Darvish told her friends. As always, there was too much on all the burners. Her mind was always in overdrive, working on the next problem, the next fix to whatever problem she encountered.

* * *

Tammy Darvish wasn't raised in the lap of luxury. Even now she's somewhat frugal, a habit from her childhood years. Cook in big batches, freeze it, make it last. She still does that.

John and Bonnie Darvish divorced when their twin daughters were four.

Tammy Darvish grew up in Chicago with her mother and twin sister, Terri. Their mother, Bonnie, a sometimes stressed woman of Italian descent, held two jobs to make ends meet. She clerked in a tool-and-die shop during the day and at night kept books at a local food mart. Her at-home time with the girls consisted of some weekends. The two sisters learned to fend for themselves.

Darvish's father, a well-off businessman in Maryland and Virginia, was more distant to her in those years, but mainly because of geography. Like many children of divorce, she saw him during some holidays and summer breaks. Her father, originally from Iran, had come to the United States to study medicine and never returned. He was often tied up in business and had three children from his second marriage to Judy Darvish.

Of those early Chicago days, Darvish recalled a tough, fairly unsupervised existence. Money was something you earned; it was not necessarily given to you. Bonnie Darvish's family wasn't poverty-stricken, but money was always tight.

Tammy Darvish was often hungry in those days. Her mother got paid every other week, so that meant they would buy groceries every second Friday. That's when they went to town buying as much as the meager budget allowed. Then they cooked up big batches of food at home to last for days.

Her sister Terri now lives near Boca Raton, Florida. They still talk about those early years now and then, laughing. But it wasn't so funny back then. They ate a lot of eggs, cereal, bread, and noodles—things that stretched and lasted a while. They cooked big pots of spaghetti sauce and froze it in plastic storage containers. Their refrigerator was always full of frozen containers. Pop it in boiling water, throw in the pasta, and presto, a meal.

At age thirteen, Tammy Darvish started working in a laundromat, washing laundry by the bundle. She had said she was fifteen at the time so she could get a work permit that year. For this job, she sometimes earned fifty dollars a week.

She worked nearly every day after school and on Saturdays, finally leaving for home around nine o'clock, long after dark, thinking about her unfinished homework. Mostly she and Terri were on their own on school days, both working to bring in extra money.

"We were latchkey kids. We didn't have babysitters. We had babysitters until we were in second grade. We would let ourselves in; but we had chores every day and made dinner. We did our own laundry; we did everything ourselves," Tammy Darvish said. The money she earned didn't go toward buying designer jeans or nice shoes. It helped pay the family bills.

Her father was not an uncaring man, the problem being more geography since he lived so far away. He often bought his daughters better things than their mother could afford.

Darvish learned her first lesson in social economics in those days, like how unjust things could be for those without money, often single or divorced mothers like hers. She just couldn't see it then. "When you get older you realize it really makes your mom sad to not be able to do that much for you."

When she was seventeen and a normal, rebellious teen, she decided to live with her father in Maryland, three states from Illinois, even further from Florida. Her mother had moved them to Ft. Lauderdale when she was a senior in high school, and she didn't like her daughter's decision to move one bit. Until then, Maryland had seemed a world away. But living with her father was always something she'd wanted to do, the teen realized. It would be a hugely different experience, but one she was ready to pursue.

That was the year Darvish fell in love with fast cars. She zipped around Silver Spring in her 1981 white Chrysler Cordoba. The two-door coupe Cordoba was a hit when introduced in the 1970s, helping rescue Chrysler as it faced an earlier period of bankruptcy. *This is it; ain't life grand?* Darvish thought she was living the high life back then. But she never forgot those early years of doing without. She would never be a rich kid trying to get over. Something inside told her that.

She didn't know it then, but her new fast-lane lifestyle was preparing her to take bigger, monumental steps in the future where car dealers are concerned.

* * *

Life can change in a New York minute. That was one thing Tammy Darvish was learning every day. One day you're walking around, a mostly happy college kid, not always into studying, but having a great time. You're walking down the street thinking what you might do that night. Party or study? Go out with friends? See a movie? The dilemma of most college kids. The next minute you're lying in a hospital bed with two broken legs and a concussion. Plenty sore. Plenty scared.

Only the city isn't New York or Washington DC or Chicago. It's Midland, Michigan. Smack in the middle of Michigan, heading up north, as they say there. Home of Dow Chemical, the city's largest employer. It's also home of Northwood University, where Tammy Darvish went to college to study business administration, focusing on automotive marketing. She wasn't especially studious. This college move was more to please her father, who insisted she get a degree in an automotive area. It would be good for business, for her future. Back then, she doubted it.

Walking back home from classes that unforgettable hot day, she saw a friend driving his van on campus. He had stopped and was waving to her to cross the street. Suddenly he swerved and rammed into her with all the power of the conversion van. He ran over both her legs. It was lights out until Darvish woke up in the ambulance on the way to the hospital.

That day, she didn't tell her father about the accident. He learned through a friend when he called her dorm that she was in the hospital. He called all the right people—police, doctors, school officials—to make sure she would be all right. He wasn't satisfied until he talked to her himself. He learned something about his stubborn daughter that day. She would always learn to make do.

Darvish spent much of the summer term on crutches and healing but still made it to classes. In a hurry to get into the real world, she took extra heavy class loads and graduated in two years, not four. The natural path after that was helping in the family business.

At that time, John Darvish owned three dealerships and was in need of extra sales help. He saw his daughter as a natural in sales. He put her in the sales group as a junior salesperson. But maybe one day, if she earned her stripes, she'd move up the ladder. No promises, he told her. Nothing in his business happens until a car is sold, he often said. In a male-dominated environment, she would find it beneficial to earn her stripes. Kind of like the military, as he saw it. You paid your dues to get ranking. Employees respected you more that way too. Especially the guys.

Still, jumping from college right into a multi-line dealership business was not exactly the future Tammy Darvish, college graduate who wanted to roam the world or save it, envisioned. "I was upset. I was very offended by it," she said. "What do you mean, sell cars? I'm a college graduate now." She threw it in her father's face. In the end, she gave in, and it was that forced decision that altered the path her life was to take.

For years, she worked in sales at the same Chrysler dealership, the one where her father dutifully reported every day, beginning in 1977, the business he loved. She tried stints in other departments—service, body shop, and parts. But her path landed her in the upper levels of sales management, where her father wanted her.

Now she tells those who inquire, like reporters, about what she does: "I'm just a salesperson."

* * *

Tammy Darvish is known to patch the bottom of her shoes with duct tape. Constantly in motion, she can be heard rushing throughout the dealership departments because of the scraping sound her shoes make as she hurries about from sales to service and body repair shops. Then she returns to her cramped, small office where stacks of file folders and messages await her.

True, she liked to muck around with grease in the service and body shops and get her hands dirty. But duct tape on her shoes?

The truth is, she has no time to run around and buy new shoes. That was one job she couldn't entrust to Courtney Wallin, her assistant and right hand. It was Courtney, after all, who had helped with most of the work getting their new house together and the old one packed up while all the dealer commotion, hearings, and negotiations were going on.

"They were moving, and it was all so crazy. Tammy didn't even have time to do that, packing and all. So of course I helped," said Wallin. She had worked as a personal assistant to Darvish since being hired as the Darvish children's nanny while in college, nearly fourteen years ago. She accompanied Darvish to many CRDR-related meetings and events and was likely to be the one shuttling important packages to Congress, the post office, or Federal Express during the intense dealer campaign months.

Some days, Tammy Darvish felt like she couldn't make a move without consulting Wallin first. Even all her high tech gadgets—from BlackBerrys to electronic calendars—didn't help. Wallin, like good assistants, kept track of everything from her schedule to whether she remembered to have lunch that day to making sure she didn't forget the kids' dentist appointments and school meetings. Not to mention her flight plans to one city or another, which grew increasingly complex.

* * *

In Hillary Clinton's classic book *It Takes a Village,* the once presidential hopeful described her view of the world. Clinton's book was published in 1996, well before she was considering running for the presidency or became President Obama's Secretary of State in 2009. In *It Takes a Village,* she talks about the fact that children are raised not just by their parents but by all the people in the society around them. Therefore, Clinton notes, the building blocks of society—schools, government, and businesses—have to consider how what they do affects children and society at large.

That book's central theme aptly describes Tammy Darvish's humanitarian life-view too. "We're all in it together," Tammy would say. Like Clinton, her belief was "the more people who stand behind us, the more powerful we are." She believed in the power of unity. She would help create it in her dealer world where it seemed things were falling apart. The dealers could be a small village of support for each other.

When the chips are down, most people just need a break, someone to show they care, to help lift them up, Darvish thought. They, the dealers, marched on Washington as a large united group in July. They could do it again. They would do what they had to do to overturn an outrageous practice of the Detroit automakers—the closing—the seizure for no discernible reason of privately owned businesses.

"Our strength in Washington is unity. We have to work together, to help each other, as a people, as a society. We can't do it alone. It truly takes a village." Those were the words Tammy Darvish told others when they asked her why she was taking this huge leap from the safety net of running her father's dealerships to organizing dealers nationally. Why take a major risk at the moment when things could only turn bleaker? The power brokers could take more away from dealers who appeared to oppose them. It was a time when many dealers were afraid to speak out, afraid to lose more than they already had. Many stayed quiet on the sidelines, waiting.

Tammy Darvish and the CRDR leaders understood their reluctance. They became the voice for the voiceless, the ones who couldn't, or wouldn't, speak out more. They vowed to protect the interests and livelihoods of those who couldn't afford expensive lobbyists or take on more legal debt.

Chapter 5—Revving Up: Trips to the Hill

It is error alone which needs the support of government.
Truth can stand by itself.
—Thomas Jefferson, *Notes on Virginia*

Tammy Darvish was going to Capitol Hill again. Later she would take hundreds of auto dealers with her. But now she was on her own. She would sometimes meet Rob Smith or Jack Fitzgerald there, or both. Alan Spitzer came in at times, but he was further away, in Ohio. Fitzgerald and Darvish were based in Maryland, so their proximity to DC made it easier for them to handle the frequent personal contacts with members of Congress on Capitol Hill.

The drive from Silver Spring, where DARCARS is located to DC takes nearly thirty-five minutes, more if she had to circle around to find parking. She tried to travel light for these trips. Her Lexus 350 was equipped with a GPS, displaying map and directions. She rarely got lost. Her BlackBerry functioned as her phone and computer, with data and desktop functionality on the road.

Darvish liked to drive along the winding George Washington Parkway, a scenic, calming route. She tried to avoid I-495, the Capitol Beltway; the freeway system made non-locals crazy since it looped in circles so it was hard to tell which direction you were going in. By the time she approached downtown DC, traffic was often a bitch. So was finding parking. She would aim for the NADA parking garage near the Capitol. Sometimes it took a lot of ingenuity—and a small cash bribe—to get in there.

In May and June, the automakers had told the closing dealers to hit the road. The dealer response: It's time to rev up and hit the Hill. In that long uphill climb, they unknowingly would make history.

Capitol Hill, known as the Hill, is the seat of the country's political power, if not industrial power. Near the White House, it is home to the two houses of US Congress, the House of Representatives and the Senate. It's chiefly the lawmaking arm, created to ensure checks and balances of other branches, namely the White House. The third arm of the triangle, of course, is judicial, a separate enforcer of the law, located in the Hill complex.

The Hill campus is bound on the east by the grayish-green Anacostia River. The west side is dominated by a sprawling old residential area, also called Capitol Hill. North lies the H Street corridor with its alphabet soup street letter names and famed Georgetown shopping district; and the west also leads to the city's business district.

* * *

On May 18, CRDR leader Jack Fitzgerald appeared on *C-Span* to talk about the dealer dilemma. That was four days after the Chrysler closure letters hit dealers, and three days after GM's first wave of terse notices arrived. Even earlier, he'd worked with NADA on the myth of "too many car dealers." They charted statistics and grouped the country's dealers by "blue" and "red" states, for starters. In this case, blue states represented the domestic penetration and dealer cuts, not Democratic leanings. Red states showed the import's dominance, not Republican strongholds. Fitzgerald's group gathered laborious research that eventually found its way to lawmakers and the media. Later that month, Darvish was summoned to the country's capitol. She felt the call internally and externally. It was time to drop the polite gloves and happy talk. It was time to be heard.

Dealers, at this point, began pinning their hopes on Congress. A legislative process could perhaps restore their rights—and get their businesses back. If they wanted help, Darvish and her A-team saw, they would have to approach Capitol Hill. Clear signals were coming from the Treasury's auto task force that their interest lay with the welfare of the two carmakers, not the dealers.

Soon CRDR became ultra-focused on one thing: restoring the cancelled dealers.

"CRDR decided we have to fight back," Darvish said, and use nonpartisan political tactics for leverage. But first they must grease the skids—build momentum in communities and in the media. There were enemies in their new world; they needed the news media to help tell the story of the injustices done. Her marketing sense told her that much. They needed to make friends and influence people in high places. Mostly in Congress. And quickly.

Even though Darvish worked and lived in the DC area, like many busy people, she rarely had visited Capitol Hill or the White House nearly a mile away. Sometimes her family took in the Smithsonian or the National Monument and other sightseeing points.

Feelings of self-doubt began to change earlier in May when she got the wake-up call from the CRDR leaders. It was time to devote her energies to something bigger than herself and DARCARS Automotive.

She was about to become a regular on Capitol Hill.

* * *

Before her forays to the Hill, Darvish spent several weeks in the US bankruptcy court in New York, listening to the Chrysler bankruptcy hearings, which pitted rejected dealers against Chrysler LLC, the "old" Chrysler that existed before the bankruptcy restructuring. In late May and early June, she witnessed her first pivotal courtroom drama. She was attending as a member of Chrysler's Unsecured Creditors Committee and was a new NADA member. In fact, a NADA official had called to inform her there was a dealer spot open on the creditors committee, but it required an intense, almost twenty-four-hour turnaround on completing a complicated application. The average person would have said "no way." But Darvish applied, interviewed immediately with the group trustee, and was appointed, beating out hundreds of applicants.

Among the Chrysler creditors, unsecured creditors fell behind secured ones in getting paybacks. At the top of the heap, senior secured creditors who have collateral get preferred treatment in a bankruptcy situation. Unsecured creditors—suppliers, injured workers, union groups, or others—who say they are owed money may think they are owed money, but they typically divide whatever is left after Chrysler's secured creditors get their portions.

The Unsecured Creditors Committee she served on consisted of major suppliers, UAW, and dealer groups who were Chrysler debtors hoping for paybacks. She attended the bankruptcy hearings as a dealer representative along with several other Chrysler group dealership owners.

In a way, she felt she was on the wrong team. She'd feel better if she were representing dealers alone. But she took her task seriously and slogged through the hearings. She was amazed at what she saw and heard.

US Bankruptcy Judge Arthur J. Gonzalez, a tough veteran in the Southern District of New York, presided over the Manhattan-based bankruptcy court, the site for the Chrysler bankruptcy hearing as well as the unsecured creditors hearing. It was the dealers' first chance to see the famed judge in action. In addition to Chrysler's case, he had handled two of the largest and thorniest bankruptcies in corporate history: Enron and WorldCom.

During the court proceedings, Darvish found herself between an uncomfortable rock and a hard place. One of her worst nightmares was coming true. As a member of the Unsecured Creditors Committee, she was being called on to make a decision that could swing the vote toward Chrysler. New York dealer Rick Zanetti, a "continuing" dealer (meaning he was not cancelled) with Chrysler also served on the Unsecured Creditors Committee in the same capacity as Darvish. At one point, he told her Chrysler's fate and the potential deal with Fiat was in her hands. It happened when a tied vote stared her in the face. She had not voted yet, and Zanetti's words tugged at her conscience. She wanted to abstain from voting, but it was not an option. During a recess, she ran to the restroom, sick to her stomach. She was panicking. She quickly called her father on his cell phone, praying he would be there. She needed his advice.

Luckily he answered. Her words gushed forth. "So many people can get hurt, Dad. I don't know what to do. I really don't. I'm torn up here."

John Darvish listened to his anguished daughter. He knew she wanted him to tell her exactly which way to vote, be the decisive father when she could not be rational. He didn't do that. He said he couldn't help her decide or talk about it because of the confidentiality terms she was under. But then he gave her some parting words, advice of a kind. "Someone's going to lose here," he said. "Pick the side that will hurt the least amount of people."

She returned to the courtroom, walking slowly. She decided to go with her gut feelings. She cast her vote. The dealers were her peers. Thousands of people could be hurt. She couldn't live with that. She sided with the dealers. Later, the dealers would have their say. Around eighty-five dealers had signed up to testify against Chrysler, and about twenty were selected to serve as live witnesses. They packed the courtroom, along with a gaggle of lawyers, interns, dealer colleagues, and other interested observers. The dealers would be able to present their cases as needed, to tell their stories of success and loss after the creditors committee completed their work. So they were testifying on their own behalf as much as anything.

The affected dealers had been branded as poor performers, but many had brought documentation to show otherwise. So far, they believed objective criteria had not surfaced as to why they had been terminated. It had taken a great deal of courage for them to come forth in a public forum such as a courtroom. Understandably, it was an intense, emotional time for all.

* * *

Meanwhile, Jackie Mealey was getting up-to-speed on the dealer issues. She sorted through mountains of e-mails, news articles, and correspondence from diverse sources—from media to CRDR.

"If this could happen to us, it could happen to anyone's business. Even my hairdresser said if they (the task force) think there are too many dealers today, maybe tomorrow it will be too many hairdressers, or too many pizza outlets, or other entrepreneurial businesses," she told her husband and family.

Small businesses around once-comfortable towns in the Detroit environs were already feeling the pinch from the ongoing recession. The bad news kept piling on as barbershops, tire stores, taverns, grocers, and other small businesses faced dim prospects. "The only ones expanding here these days seem to be Starbucks and some chain-style stores," said a friend of the Mealeys.

Jackie Mealey's husband, Richard, owner of a now-shuttered Chrysler dealership in Troy, Michigan, was testifying at the end of May in bankruptcy court. She recalled that their dentist, hearing of the closures, asked her one day, "What did Richard do to upset Chrysler so much?"

Dealers, she noted were "getting a bum rap, and it was so wrong."

Public perception that the dealers must have done something horribly wrong to be let go was growing. They were "underperformers," according to the automakers' PR spin. How could that be when many were "five-star dealers" where Chrysler was concerned? Wasn't that the top award the company gave to dealers with superior performance in all categories—including customer service? Weren't many of these "underperformers" adept at selling cars and trucks?

Those were the kinds of questions dealers would ask. Darvish knew that Detroit car honchos Rick Wagoner of GM and Alan Mulally had roared into town aboard their private jets last November. The press noted their bad timing on public displays of lavish excess, suggesting insensitivity to the country's deepening economic crisis. On top of that, the automakers were asking for huge public dole-outs—or taxpayer dollars—to keep them afloat.

Three months later, Wagoner was forced out. It was not because he flew in private jets, but because of his position when he came up against the empowered auto task force, a group that was single-handedly dismantling almost two hundred years of auto history and Yankee ingenuity between the two automakers. Wagoner, a good soldier at GM for more than thirty years, began his career in GM's finance groups. His problem? He resisted change by openly opposing the GM bankruptcy restructuring; that pissed off the task force. Steve Rattner, its head, details much of Rick Wagoner's stance in *Overhaul.* Right behind him, in April, Bob Nardelli would follow suit, exiting Chrysler. The only true survivor was Mulally at Ford, who resisted the federal bailout.

Stopping the Dealer Train Wreck

Dealers Alan Spitzer and Jack Fitzgerald were creating a new template for the fledgling Committee to Restore Dealer Rights. Of the two leaders, Fitzgerald, who ran businesses in three states, was the key facts-and-numbers guy. His group tracked everything from states where imports and domestics dominated to economic profiles of dealers in dollars and cents, including taxes paid, payroll, and community impact. Spitzer had the pulse on membership and handled administrative and treasury functions. He also updated members frequently with guidance on the issues troubling dealers.

When it came to the dealer cuts, Fitzgerald, like Spitzer, showed his passionate side. Not long after the AIADA May meeting in DC, Spitzer, credited as the CRDR founder with franchises near Cleveland, and Fitzgerald decided it was time to stop the dealer train wreck. Spitzer also did business in three states.

It began on the night of May 20. Spitzer dialed Fitzgerald at work, hoping to catch him in the office. Fitzgerald answered. Fitzgerald had lost ten stores and Spitzer had an equal number closed, seven with Chrysler brands. The two dealers had known each other since the 1960s, both having served on various dealer committees and councils.

The two commiserated for a few moments and then got to the point. They were in the mood to take on the big guys, Chrysler and GM. Spitzer wanted to put together a dealer group that would act independently of NADA, which he saw as being more concerned with active dealers, called "go forwards." But the closed dealers seemed to have no real voice. No one represented only them. That conversation was the birth of CRDR.

Both men firmly believed the wrongs done to dealers needed to be righted. And quickly. Congress, they saw, was the path to getting the problem fixed. Both were well-known at the local and state political levels.

Shortly after a soft launch, the two realized they needed someone with marketing and people skills to be a front person. Tammy Darvish nicely fit the bill. She was known as a natural organizer and problem solver. She intuitively knew which buttons to push and when. And she had the proper fighting spirit and believed as they did in the dealer cause, the two leaders observed.

Skeptics told them it would take a miracle to reverse the dealer terminations, to move Congress to create a new law. To even get such a law passed was unthinkable. But when you put people with the right chemistry together, sometimes miracles can happen. The link between these three, at this time time in history? Passion, yes, fervor, for the dealer rights cause.

Sometimes timing is everything, although they didn't know it at the time. Darvish and Alan Spitzer ended up at the Chrysler bankruptcy hearings in New York. They were staying in the same hotel, and Spitzer invited her to dinner with him and his lawyer. He wanted to discuss the simmering powder keg of dealer rights and his idea for the dealer advocacy group that would restore the terminated dealers. By that time, great minds were thinking alike, and the idea had taken off. Fitzgerald, who knew Darvish and her father well, had planted the seeds with her earlier. She was in.

In the beginning, the fledgling group had no paid staff or funds. In fact, they needed to raise money; they needed a membership drive and were poorer than a charity. So far, the two dealers had funded everything themselves and did whatever they couldn't delegate to their assistants—Rob Smith for Fitzgerald, and Alison Spitzer, who worked for her father, Alan. At a later point, the three leaders figured they had sunk nearly $500,000 of their own funds into lobbying and carrying out the dealer campaign. By late 2009, lobbying expenses mounted to about $1 million, Spitzer figured.

Not long after the New York encounter between Spitzer and Darvish, the deal was struck. Thus, the Committee to Restore Dealer Rights (CRDR) was born.

The duo swept Darvish in and gave her the title of coleader, immediately empowering her. The CRDR group suddenly grew wings. And Tammy Darvish's work and personal life would never be the same. Little did the two dealers know that Tammy Darvish was committed before either had said a word to her. They soon became known as the "big three" of CRDR.

Jack Fitzgerald became her mentor and sounding board as she began an intense e-mail campaign targeting potential CRDR supporters, key congressional aides, and media.

In early June, Fitzgerald and the prestigious DC law firm Arent Fox were drawing up initial language on legislation that could reverse the dealer closures. Dan Renberg, chief legal partner at Arent, and Mary Jo Dowd, a partner in the firm, were greasing the wheels with Congress. They were the lobbying experts, along with Darvish's attorney Michael Charapp of Charapp & Weiss LLC, in McLean, Virginia, who later handled arbitrations and other legal chores.

Their combined efforts got the committee some traction in DC with the lawmakers and media.

* * *

By early June, the serendipity of natural forces took over.

For Darvish, June turned into an exhausting month of mobilizing supporters and meeting with lawmakers and their executive staff. She became a wheel in motion, energizing her base and building even stronger dealer ties and contacts. Her A-team, the several-dozen volunteers growing out of CRDR, would help in the trenches, like soldiers at the ready.

Darvish and her dealership staff compiled thousands of e-mail names on lists to share primarily among their dealer groups; they copied relevant congressional staffers on their progress. In the coming months, they would videotape key dealer cameos and their stories of loss and perseverance to be shared at large.

Tammy Darvish had signed on to the more than full-time job of organizing the CRDR troops and serving as the at-large media person. What started as a personal quest for retribution became a passion to save the dealers. She found herself driving to Capitol Hill about four days a week, sometimes spending all day. Certain members of Congress were starting to pay attention to the closed dealer dilemma, and priming the pump was essential.

She gathered her courage and patrolled the long corridors of congressional offices. She was seeking lawmakers' ears to tell them about the wrongful doings by the automakers, supposedly icons of the industry. She told them about her group, CRDR, and of their goal to restore the rights of thousands of dealers whose businesses had been abruptly terminated.

Darvish roamed the quiet hallways of Congress, a little reserved at first, and often inconspicuous. Dressed in business attire and nicely groomed, she fit in to the casual observer. There were lots of professional, pretty women working in DC and its environs. In fact, DC was considered an ideal place for young workers, with slightly more than 50 percent of government employees being women.

She got to know the high-up aides to Congress members personally. She knew they liked to put "executive" before their titles. She got to know all the shops, bathrooms, parking spots, and fast takeouts ringing the Capitol. Survivor skills 101 in the nation's Capitol.

Inside lawmakers' offices, she found the legislators often welcomed a friendly visitor in their days full of faceless phone calls, polls, and e-mails. Some of them—such as David Weaver (then Democratic Rep. Chris Van Hollen's chief of staff), and John Hughes (with Steny Hoyer), Ben Abrams (for Representative Kratovil), and Michelle Stockwell (who was with Hoyer and Hughes' boss)—were especially attentive and helpful to Darvish.

She would go in and introduce herself; some remembered her from e-mails, but others didn't know her at all. She didn't arrive with slick PowerPoint presentations or a sheaf of manuscripts like the auto execs did in DC. She simply used her own wits. She'd give a quick summary of herself as an orphan dealer and then quickly launch into the plight of dealers nationwide, the thousands she was representing.

With an informal, off-the-cuff style, she didn't rely on prepared notes or scripts. At most, she'd leave behind a fact sheet the committee had constructed. She reminded the Congress members' aides that they had already received CRDR economic-impact packets. If they needed them again, she would send them. No problem.

In a few months, she personally had visited at least one hundred legislators to plead the dealers' cause, throwing out tidbits from examples she received nonstop. In these visits, she never went to plead her own lost dealership cases, or give them a hard-luck story. Instead, she brought up all the other closed dealers, citing numbers, examples, names, and the sudden community impact when a dealership shuts down.

As part of the committee, she e-mailed and wrote thousands of letters, notes, and updates. She wondered if the House and Senate members even bought their own cars; maybe they were like the upper-level auto execs whose vehicles were arranged for them. Many execs didn't walk into dealerships for sales or service. They had employees who did their bidding.

What surprised her most was how little Congress knew about the ABCs of automotive. A: about the auto industry; B: about how dealerships worked; and C: how dealers were not part of the automakers' business. They were independent businesspeople totally reliant on their own resources and earnings.

For some this struck a nerve. Certain lawmakers dismissed it out of hand, putting dealers in the same bucket as the automakers and Wall Street, saying they wanted a bailout. These legislators claimed they were on the record as against any form of public bailouts. Many were succumbing to the pressure of the growing "Tea Party" movement, which wanted to strip down government to its bare bones.

But nothing could be further from such erroneous thinking. Restoring dealer businesses would not cost the carmakers a thing, despite claims being made in federal and state courts. That was CRDR's position. Dealers would add money and jobs to the economy and local communities. Jobs that were now lost.

Suddenly on June 8, a pair of Democratic freshmen—Representatives Dan Maffei (New York) and Frank Kratovil (Maryland)—introduced the first House bill (HR2743) that aimed to restore dealer franchises terminated by GM and Chrysler in the bankruptcy process. The bill was called the Dealer Economic Rights Restoration Act and was proposed largely at the urging of Steny Hoyer and Chris Van Hollen. The backbone of the bill was carefully crafted by CRDR lawyers and Jack Fitzgerald for the CRDR group.

At the same time, Steve LaTourette, a respected Ohio Republican, submitted a similar dealer rights bill (HR2750) to restore all the dealers in whole, indicating bipartisan support. Ohio was the hardest hit state in dealer closures, according to NADA data. The legislators had been listening and doing their homework. Maffei and Kratovil had heard some of the tragic stories by this time. Their chiefs of staff, Jill Murray (Maffei's) and Ben Abrams (Kratovil's) kept them up-to-speed on well-documented contacts from Darvish and her group; also from NADA, ATAE, and NAMAD, the other key lobbying groups. The personal stories of distress and tragedy spilled forth like water breaking through dams.

About ten days later, Sen. Chuck Grassley (R-Iowa) introduced a Senate bill similar to the House versions. Most compelling to the two bodies of Congress were the facts that more jobs were being lost in communities already riddled by the economic meltdown—and that the dealers were shut down for no apparent good reason. And they heard something few people in the country understood: The dealers were independent business people. Like a 7-Eleven store or a pizza outlet, they put money into the economy, but on a bigger level. They were distributors of vehicles made by the auto companies. And they were not part of the auto bailouts.

Yes, they were stakeholders in automotive, but separate and equal. They wanted to see the auto industry survive, because their businesses depended on it. But the way the automakers were going about it by slashing dealers was not only wrong but would hurt the domestics and help the imports, CRDR leaders concluded.

The ugly specter of constitutional rights being trampled on was surfacing. It had to do with illegal seizure of property and destroying livelihoods without benefit of due process and adequate compensation. Dealers and their attorneys were raising the issue more and more. Surely this bore more study, more consideration, the lawmakers surmised. This was about people's Fifth Amendment rights, something every lawmaker took seriously.

* * *

Congress also had a private bone to pick with the new White House administration. Or, more precisely, with its automotive task force. This group, new to Washington and its ways, had not consulted Congress before making the decisions to overturn the automotive sector and cut dealers. This did not sit well with many bipartisan members of the two houses who believed in rules of advise and consent, and the traditions of centuries-old political processes, lobbying experts thought. The task force was pushing an agenda that was incompatible with American traditions and values, they thought.

In the first week of July, the twin bills gathered steam, mostly in the House, where it had 205 supporters, and ten in the Senate, which was just revving up but presented a bigger challenge. Shortly after this, the lawmakers were able to get more than 240 members to cosponsor the bill, well more than half the House.

Some opponents became more vocal. Yet another stakeholder wanting a handout, these congress members concluded. Of course everyone was entitled to an opinion. But this one wasn't based on facts or goodwill toward the disenfranchised dealers.

On balance, it was a good start with the lawmakers in the House, the CRDR leaders figured. They had nowhere to go but up, if they could keep the momentum going. Would they sail on to final victory? The odds makers still wouldn't bet on them.

Even a well-regarded executive editor at *Automotive News* in Detroit and as well versed on dealer issues as anyone in the country, said in the beginning he didn't think the CRDR group had a fighting chance of success. There was no way the CRDR leaders could get Congress to pass the bills, and it was unlikely President Obama would sign them, he thought. Time and money were not on their side. In the first few months, Darvish was chasing down rumors that flew with wild abandon. Most were related to how the group was handling the automakers and Congress in negotiations over the closures. The majority were progress questions on the bills in the House (HR2743) and in the Senate (S1304) and just how each bill could potentially affect real people. Individual people, voters and citizens, who were losing their jobs and their futures.

"I have ninety souls who depend on me," Frank Blankenbeckler, the Texas dealer who stood to lose his Chevrolet and Chrysler dealerships, said. He was speaking of his employees, their families in the community, and his own. Many dealers felt as he did.

Another particularly bothersome issue cropped up late in July. The rumor mill was spinning a bizarre story. This one said CRDR was in "settlement talks" with Chrysler and GM. It made it appear they were backing down on dealer rights, taking a softer line, perhaps appeasing the automakers. That's what the auto guys were used to—their "opponents" caving in, crying "uncle," the committee thought.

There was a need to sort fact from fiction, lies from innuendos. Darvish fired off a barrage of e-mails, mostly to dealers. "We have no intention of engaging in settlement talks at this time as we feel we have not reached our peak in movement on the Hill and have too much at stake now," she wrote. They obsessively worked the phones, computer keyboards, and BlackBerrys, contacting dealers and Congress.

It was possible that letters sent to Ron Bloom, who was the new task force leader after Steve Rattner left might be causing confusion. She had sent the same letter to GM and Chrysler requesting they meet with CRDR leaders, and those could have "been misinterpreted by some as our desire to negotiate or settle. But that's not true," she asserted. "We are not backing down." They were still asking for reinstatement of dealers to their status before the bankruptcies, she wrote. The committee wanted full reinstatement, not a compromise.

By that point, GM leaders notified Jack Fitzgerald to say they wouldn't negotiate with CRDR. The larger, established NADA group was more official in their eyes, and NADA was taking a middle stance, preferring to use the original automakers' criteria. Chrysler remained mum on the request to talk.

But the grassroots movement of the CRDR and its A-team grew legs quicker than many thought. It was a movement that had found a home. The negotiations stalled, then cranked up.

Internal Grassroots Support

Sometimes your support system kicks in unexpectedly. When that happens, it's like a breath of fresh air. And it's those times that make you want to rejoice, Darvish found.

On June 8, Michelle Primm, who headed up a group of women dealers east of the Mississippi River, sent NADA leaders a message following a dealer conference call. "At-Large Women East of Mississippi votes for the Fitzgerald bill, which stands up for dealer rights and not just accepts a compromise of a softer landing. Sometimes in a car deal, you have to scrape the customer off the ceiling to get their attention," Primm wrote.

"My point is that when negotiating, we need to be willing to walk away from the deal. It's time to take a stand. I believe with our grassroots efforts we can get this [bill] passed. Then it's up to Obama to say no. The whole deal stinks of payback redistribution, and dealers are the victims. Who is next after car dealers?" she asked pointedly. It was exactly the point Tammy Darvish and her A-team had been making all along. Primm, managing partner of the Cascade Auto Group in Cuyahoga Falls, Ohio, was well-known. At the time, she was an at-large director on NADA's board. She represented a vocal segment of dealers east of the Mississippi River, hence the name of her group.

Closer to home in Maryland, Rob Smith, Jack Fitzgerald's right-hand man, turned into a "Tammy Darvish disciple," her partner in energy, commitment, and knowledge on how to make things work on the Hill. In many ways, they were cut from the same cloth, only he was better at minding the p's and q's, or old-fashioned political protocol. An ever-present referee and advisor, he counseled on how to approach everything and everyone from the dealer advocacy groups to the corporate entities—political correctness moves that might evade Darvish. She liked to be a straight-shooter and "tell it like it is" when she felt strongly about an issue, especially on dealer and human rights.

With his wry sense of humor and as fired up as Darvish to make ripples, he helped lighten things up. Smith, the father of young children—two girls and a boy—was a good antidote to the intense political drama surrounding and sometimes drowning the fledgling group.

"Stop using big words such as 'epiphany.' You will only confuse them," he said tongue-in-cheek about a misunderstanding between Darvish and NADA over the numbers of dealers who wanted their franchises back. In her informal surveys and talks with dealers, Darvish found that nearly 100 percent wanted their stores back. NADA put the number closer to 10 percent, she said. The gap was ridiculous, she noted.

One day she was crafting a touchy memo to the NADA board asking for their support for CRDR. She ran her ideas by Smith. He coached, "Remember you get more results with honey than with vinegar—make them feel good or important, not guilty or embarrassed."

Since Darvish was inclined to do everything for everybody, he cautioned her to back off from giving legal or other advice she shouldn't give. "Not your job," he penned, reminding her she wasn't qualified to practice law.

"Chill," he'd suggest at other times. "Take a breather from all this," urging her to take a little family time, which she rarely did. Sometimes he tried following his own advice. Three kids raised by any single parent tend to focus you on their priorities.

* * *

With their franchises endangered, Darvish knew it was time to tell the former Chrysler and GM dealers' stories to Congress. Who better to do that than her, Jack, and Alan?

Darvish often took time to share their stories of despair and loss with her contacts in Congress and her support base. These personal stories of tragedy kept pouring in. She couldn't keep them to herself. It was like thousands of screaming souls in her mind. With each one, Darvish was more determined to shake things up with the automakers and the auto task force.

Did she and CRDR have enough evidence, enough proof that the needs were real out there? How much more "proof" did they need anyway? Then another e-mail from people pushed to the brink and needing help would arrive.

A Cape Cod, Massachusetts, dealer's wife wrote that summer to say that their family business had been decimated. Marilyn Stagg related that her dealership was down to seven employees and a lot full of cars they couldn't sell since losing their Chevrolet and Chrysler stores. Their bank, now a foreign entity (wanting out of the dealer floor-plan business), shut off the Staggs' financing plan, making it impossible to buy cars and do business. They were no longer deemed credit-worthy. Their employees, from accounting to sales, were quitting daily.

"My husband and son are trying to do it all … and we're here with all the parts and special tools Chrysler and GM stuck us with, along with new vehicles we can't sell as new because we're not a franchise any longer and Chrysler won't take them back," Stagg wrote.

It was worse than a catch-22. The mental and physical stress, not to mention financial hardship, was wearing them down, Stagg said. They'd been working days and nights and weekends with little compensation—"With no office personnel but me, we're exhausted, frustrated, and financially strapped." To make matters worse, Stagg said, "Chrysler took our customer list from our computer and gave it to our competitor, along with our franchise."

Darvish offered support and told her that CRDR would like to share her story as they pushed Congress to reverse the closures. Dealers banding together had some clout, she said, even when things looked their bleakest.

An Omen: Early Votes

Then a flash of brightness emerged from behind the dark clouds. The frustrated dealer groups were trying to help people like the Staggs and take on two of the world's largest and most powerful auto companies. They were plowing new turf here with scant resources.

The cold war in business, as some called it, was heating up. By July, Darvish's CRDR start-up group was almost two months old. They were losing some skirmishes but were determined to win the war. There was much bandying back and forth on the dealer rights legislation.

Dealers who might not have watched proceedings on bills moving through Congress in the past became enthusiastic spectators for good reason.

On June 18, a Senate bill (S1304) came out, including language very similar to LaTourette's on dealer economic rights.On July 6, 2009, a US House panel voted to require GM and Chrysler to restore dealer franchise agreements. That bipartisan vote came despite the automakers' dire financial straits since asking President Obama for public bailout funds to keep operating after December 2008. But the panel vote was not final.

Shortly after that, an amended House bill with careful but similar language was tucked into a larger appropriations bill pushed by LaTourette, the Ohio Republican who spoke from the industrial heartland. The Ohioan had been busy hustling amended bills since early June that would grease the skids for much of the action on the Hill that rolled into the summer, fall, and winter months. Ohio, like Michigan and Illinois, had been particularly decimated by the auto crises sweeping the country, and dealers were hard hit in "rustbelt" states. The LaTourette Amendment formed the basis of much future legislation bandied about between the two bodies of Congress, the House and Senate. Still, the July House vote was a turning point, a signal that the voices of the rejected dealers now were truly being heard on the Hill. But that panel's earlier action and a subsequent dealer bill were to change course over the next few months. It's not over until it's over, Darvish's A-team reminded each other. They were in it for the long haul.

With the legislation likely headed to the floor in final resolutions, a spokesman for the House Appropriations Committee said that David Obey, the Wisconsin Democrat who chairs the Appropriations panel, was likely to keep the car dealer provision in the House spending bill, another good sign.

Still, CRDR knew support was dragging on the Senate side. Early on, the Senate bill to restore dealer rights had only twenty cosponsors. They needed a firm majority of the one hundred senators, or those voting.

At a press conference in mid-July, Senator Harry Reid, the Democratic majority leader from Nevada, gave lukewarm encouragement to the cut dealers. Reid said summarily, "When you have a bankruptcy, there are winners and losers." Some senators were prone to listen to constituents bound to big business and other economic crises plaguing the country. He seemed to be one of those.

Reid added that the dealer issue was not "on the top of the agenda in the Senate at this time." The Senate, he said, was grappling with larger economic and health-care issues tearing the country apart. He was right and wrong, many dealers believed. The closures fed right into the economic disaster plaguing the country.

It was another of those letdown moments for those who wanted to restore the dealers. Harry Reid, a friend to presidents and lawmakers, held powerful sway. They knew the Senate could quash their entire campaign almost overnight. *Whoever told you life is supposed to be fair must have been the joker in a deck of cards.* Sometimes the dark side had to come out in Darvish's internal thinking.

The mood among dealers she heard from wasn't exactly light and breezy, and the storm clouds hovering overhead still looked threatening. But these were thoughts she tended to keep to herself at the time, shared with only those she trusted to the core.

By mid-July, the dealer groups would turn a corner. Legislation to save the dealers was gaining powerful backers in more parts of Congress. Majority leader Democrat Steny Hoyer on the House side, and Jay Rockefeller in the Senate. Hoyer had taken on Rattner's task force and was holding his ground, like a one-man gladiator fighting off enemy attacks. Barney Frank, the Massachusetts Democrat and chair of the House Financial Services Committee was blasting the automakers, particularly GM, about job losses in his state.

Democratic Senator Jay Rockefeller from West Virginia had an influential presence as chairman of the Senate Committee on Commerce, Science, and Transportation. On July 23, he came onboard as a sponsor of the Senate bill to restore dealers, helping to change the tide.

Darvish e-mailed news of his support with a "this is big" announcement to her lists. It was Rockefeller who called for an investigation into the dismissed dealers by the SIGTARP group as they probed the use of public TARP money for that purpose. Rockefeller was aiming at the whole enchilada, wanting to know what led to the dealer shutdowns in the first place. "Taxpayers deserve a thorough review of these decisions," Rockefeller said.

Democrat David Obey, chairing the well-oiled Appropriations fiscal arm, joined Rockefeller in calling for the investigation, signaling even wider support on the dealer issues.

Those actions suggested a break for their side, CRDR leaders thought. Surely, the fact finders would get to the truth: the unfair termination of dealers, who ran independent businesses. The fight to save dealers looked like it was not going away, buried in politics as usual. With Steve LaTourette, the Republican still steering action in the House, significant bipartisan support seemed to grow. These nonpartisan moves alone, by US Democratic Senator Rockefeller and Republican Representative LaTourette seemed unprecedented at a time when Democrats and Republicans were engaged in heated partisan battles on everything from health care to the economy.

At last, the dealer issue seemed to draw both parties together like nothing else. The outrage of the rejected dealers and cries from the heartland shook the walls of Congress.

Jack Fitzgerald told his supporters that such bipartisan agreement on big votes was rare, occurring in fewer than 1 percent of cases. But this was about jobs, taxpayer funds being used, and constitutional rights of businesses, he said. Members of Congress were listening.

Yet Michigan, the heart of auto country and big unions, was an especially hard nut to crack. The state had around 20 percent unemployment in hard-hit industrial pockets like factory towns of Flint, Detroit, and Pontiac; overall, state unemployment was nearly 16 percent in 2009. It was a big UAW state. How could they add more to the jobless rolls? Darvish wondered. Again, it did not compute.

Although hugely disappointed, Darvish took comfort where she could. One good sign: Van Hollen's chief of staff, David Weaver, was becoming a staunch advocate and a close advisor on the Hill. He kept the congressman up to speed on the latest dealer developments.

Darvish trusted Weaver implicitly. She had mentally added him to her A-team, even if he wasn't in the auto industry.

As the weeks rolled into months, Weaver helped guide the CRDR leaders through the intricacies of the lawmaking process and political ways of Washington DC. Early on, Darvish well understood how essential he was to their ultimate journey.

"Congressman Van Hollen got personally involved, and the fact that it was a priority for him made it a priority for me," Weaver humbly said about his role. Van Hollen took part in meetings and phone conferences with CRDR and dealer advocates that sometimes lasted for more than an hour, he said. Those meetings began in late May and continued into several seasons, and well before the Rattner task force wondered why Congress was getting steamed about "a few dealers."

Weaver, for one, believed the system was working the way it was supposed to work. "A segment of our communities—significant business leaders—felt wronged and aggrieved and sought legislative redress," he noted. And leaders such as Van Hollen and Hoyer responded responsibly and were concerned.

Weaver's view found the dealer closure issue a fascinating one to be involved in from a congressional standpoint. "On the surface it seemed straightforward that dealers had a strong case. Taxpayer money had [bailed out] the manufacturers and should not have resulted in innocent bystanders being hurt. The question was how to correct the problem" at the dealer end, he said.

And John Hughes, executive chief of staff to Steny Hoyer, also was shaping the action in Congress, on behalf of the dealer fight. Another good guy, Darvish added him to the A-list too. More House Democrats had joined their forces, including Democratic Congresswoman Gabrielle Giffords of Arizona and Betty Sutton of Ohio.

US Representative Giffords was an original cosponsor of the June dealer legislation in the House. She made national news after she received a gunshot wound to the head in January 2011 while holding an open meeting with members of her constituency in a supermarket parking lot near Tucson, along with others. Giffords had challenged the task force in July and questioned automakers repeatedly on the need to terminate certain dealers. She was credited with helping reinstate dealerships in her state.

And in LaTourette's home state of Ohio, Betty Sutton, a Democrat representative, also got on board early and pushed for dealer rights legislation through the end as she organized numerous state hearings and press meetings to spotlight the issue in Ohio and nationally.

Otherwise, some proactive dealers called LaTourette "a bridge builder" between the political parties. This was a human issue, a jobs issue, not a party issue, they said. And leaders such as LaTourette, with campaign offices in a town appropriately called Painesville, recognized that. Overall, Darvish began seeing the increasingly bipartisan support from Congress as a positive omen, a sign they were getting through to the lawmakers with each step. They might lose some battles, but the dealer advocates were determined to win the war.

The wheels of justice do *grind exceedingly slow*, Darvish thought at times. But she and her A-team had little time for old platitudes. If a law is wrong, change it. If a community is asleep on an issue they should know about, wake them up. If a group has been wronged, killed in a sort of public hanging, tell the story.

This A-team, a collection of aggrieved dealers, was almost devout in their mission. They were propelled by three single-minded leaders who never dropped the gauntlet. All great causes are won because of a fervent belief of their leaders and followers. But was it enough this time?

Growing a Grassroots Movement

The CRDR group needed volunteers. They needed money. They couldn't keep up the pace with the slim number of recruits on hand, and the three leaders, and their staff assistants. Darvish tried to end most of her group e-mails by doing "the ask." But she made the appeal soft, knowing many dealers were strapped and dipping into their savings for grocery money, mortgages, and kids' college payments.

It was not a member-based group with dues like NADA which charges its members annual fees, depending on sales volume. CRDR was asking for contributions primarily through e-mail campaigns. Five dollars, twenty dollars, fifty, anything a supporter could contribute, they'd take. Compared to other large campaign-type contributions, it was "chump change," but badly needed chump change.

They had attracted about five hundred dealer members by the end of 2009; many others were supporters. The affected dealers sent in checks ranging from $200 to $20,000 (rarely), Spitzer said. Sometimes they sent what they could—$20, $50, whatever—with messages such as "sorry" and "wish I could do more."

Face it, many of these dealers were barely scraping by financially, Darvish reminded the committee's leaders. She thought they should be carried and kept in the info loop. So she kept the communication lines open, the information flowing. Even dealers who were broke stayed on her list—Darvish would turn away no one. The committee had nothing like the coffers of NADA with bigger annual budgets. NADA dues started at about $1,000 annually and went up, depending on dealer sales volumes.

Even NAMAD, the minority dealer trade group founded in 1980, was able to charge qualifying ethnic members from five hundred dollars to five thousand dollars in membership fees. Their minority base was smaller and had to cough up more. But NADA still controlled the action where dealer memberships were concerned nationwide. Some dealers knew that much of the early CRDR activity was being financed privately by Darvish, Fitzgerald, and Spitzer, even though their own coffers were strained after fighting the closures of their dealerships and lobbying Congress. These had been closed for good (in Chrysler's case) or were winding down with fewer and fewer cars and trucks to sell on their lots, in GM's case.

The biggest drain would come from hiring lawyers to lobby lawmakers and, if it came to it, handling upcoming arbitrations and negotiations with automakers. Trade paper *Automotive News* in late December (2009) would report CRDR had spent nearly $1 million lobbying Congress alone.

Alan Spitzer, who kept the CRDR books, later clarified that the $1 million was really the total group expenses in the 2009 timeframe. But support seemed to pour through the walls via e-mails and calls, and checks came from here and there. The network was spreading the word from dealer to dealer, almost house to house.

Alan Spitzer helped the group keep focus, identifying the enemy. He wrote countless memos, giving the CRDR slant. "The number-one culprit should be the failed management [of GM and Chrysler]. The arbitrary, capricious, and vindictive manner in which they carried out the terminations is clear-cut and proof of their shortsighted perspective," he wrote. "The auto task force was inexperienced and they unwittingly trusted management to use good business judgment when their lack of the same is why they went bankrupt in the first place."

One common misperception was that the rejected dealers were against saving the automakers with bailout funds. The question was not whether the automakers should be saved. They should, CRDR leaders pointed out. The problem was with the shortsighted methodology in cutting off the marketing force of capable dealers.

Darvish tried to explain their position further to GM, Chrysler, and the task force. "We all want Chrysler and General Motors to succeed. There is no alternate agenda for us. Dealers are part of the solution, not the problem," she wrote in a statement in July. Dealers across the country echoed Darvish's thoughts on rescuing the dealers. Nearly twenty-three hundred dealers were either slated for closure or had been closed as a result of the restructurings. Like the committee, most thought the reckless policies of the task force and automakers were at fault.

In Atoka, Oklahoma, Bob Sullins, a former dealer at the Chrysler and GM Crossroads Superstore, which had been shut down, said, "We just want to be restored to where we were before the bankruptcies."

His Crossroads partner and co-owner, Jack Haigh, said, "The carmakers have been talking about a more homogenized dealer base for years. They had a once-in-a-lifetime opportunity with the bankruptcy restructurings, and they took advantage of it. It's really sad for a lot of communities and people who rely on dealer goodwill. They too are suffering here."

* * *

In early July, Tammy Darvish and her group scrambled to contact everyone they could on their lists to update them on what was happening next. "This is big," Darvish promised the dealers, mimicking the style of *NBC News* personality Tim Russert, who died of a heart attack in 2008. By mid-July they were going for bigger stakes. They were marching on Washington and would bring bigger numbers of dealers with them. After all, they wanted bigger results.

They were preparing for the ultimate battle: securing the votes in Congress on the dealer rights bills to win back their businesses. The once buttoned-down dealers, as some media portrayed them, were becoming outright activists for their cause. It was called future survival.

Spring 2009: Significant Events in Congress

May 14—Chrysler announces termination of dealers

May 15—GM announces first round of expected dealer closures

June 3—Maryland dealer Jack Fitzgerald and Arent Fox law firm create legislation to reverse closures

June 3—Hearing with Senator Rockefeller and commerce committee; draft legislation presented to key NADA staff

June 8—Rep. Dan Maffei and Rep. Frank Kratovil introduce bill to restore franchises

June 8—Rep. Steve LaTourette announces broad dealer bill to return closed businesses to the dealers

June 10—Capitol Hill press conference with Steny Hoyer; NADA also meets on Capitol Hill

June 18—Sen. Charles Grassley introduces bill in Senate that is similar to the House version

June 20—CRDR continues to recruit and mobilize members to lobby Congress

Chapter 6—Making a Difference on Main Street

Our lives begin to end the day we become silent about things that matter.
—Dr. Martin Luther King Jr.

For fifty years, Bruno Bogdewic lived the American dream. He did pretty well for an immigrant's son from Warsaw, Poland, Bogdewic figured. He built a damned profitable business and took care of the family and community around him. Mostly, he took care of customers who rewarded him with loyal repeat business.

B. Bogdewic Chevrolet, located at 401 Main Street in Bentleyville, Pennsylvania, is about thirty miles outside Pittsburgh. Bogdevic started the family business in 1958 after purchasing it from Don Yenko Chevrolet. His slogan was the "home of the little guy." What he meant was they weren't a big corporate entity or a dealer chain. They just wanted to take care of customers and give them personal attention, the small-town way of doing business. That view brought business from far and wide.

The store celebrated fifty years as a Chevrolet dealer in 2008, their website boasted. Two years later, they were taking the banners and signs down. People in Bentleyville are still stunned. There had been a car dealer at the Main Street site for nearly ninety years, well before the Bogdewics started up.

A customer had given Bogdewic six handmade wooden picnic tables as down payment on a truck some twenty years ago. The tables became fixtures at the store, although a few went to family members. On customer-appreciation days, employee barbeques, and holiday or birthday parties, the tables were put to good use. Several times the picnic tables were put away for repairs, or whatever reason, and customers complained. They were used to sipping a cup of coffee, having a sandwich, and pondering a deal on those tables.

It was not a big-city way of doing business. It was the Bogdewic way: personal and customer-focused.

Bogdewic's son, Chip, came into the business as a car-wash kid and then joined the family business after getting an education degree at Wheeling University in 1974. Chip, born Bruno Bogdewic Jr., never used his dad's name. His favorite aunt exclaimed, "That's Chip!" as in "a chip off the old block."

He stepped into his father's shoes, though, rising to the top-dealer spot after ascending the ladder from service worker to floor sales to management. His dad then retired, confident his son would be fine operating the family business.

On October 30, 2010, Chip Bogdewic was the one overseeing the closure of their half-century Chevrolet business. The signs were all coming down. The GM deadline for closure was the next day. None of their interventions had worked. "I can't let my dad be here for that," the younger Bogdewic said. "It would kill him."

In March of that year his mother died of cancer.

Chip Bogdewic knows all about disaster—and health problems. That year, 2009, was devastating for him and his family. A month before the GM-Chevrolet rejection notice, his health had been failing and sidelined him for a while.

"We kind of knew that GM was closing us down," he said. Then, in April, Chip Bogdewic suffered a heart attack. In May they got the grim news from GM telling them they would be closed. By the fall, he had his second heart attack. "Were my health problems stress-related?" he repeats a bit incredulously when asked. "I would say so. I lost my mom, my health, and my livelihood all in one year."

Despite his personal misfortunes, he blamed himself for not being there to fully take care of the business that year. It was also the second year of straight economic decline for America's dealers and businesses, families and individuals. They were suffering together.

When Bogdewic explained the family health problems to his Chevrolet field contacts, they seemed to have little sympathy or time. He was not making excuses, just stating facts, he said. The corporate reaction at a time when businesses were crumbling and sales were plunging nationwide was, "What have you done for me lately?"

In some corners, the thinking was: this is an economic war, and there are many casualties. The Bogdewics were among the dealer casualties.

The Main-Street Shuffle

When it came to the dealer closures on "Main Street, USA," the issue didn't divide the nation the way health care, bank bailouts, the economic meltdown, and credit freezes did. But it should have, the dealer advocates said. Somehow, Main-Street dealers got lost in the economic shuffle as Americans faced their own economic struggles.

As business owners, dealers were being stripped of their possessions and livelihoods. The rejected dealers were being treated like common criminals, the A-team believed. It was as though a crime had been committed against society. But how many people knew the real story behind their rejection? No one, it seemed in those days, was being made to answer for it.

The power brokers were looking at bottom-line factors and slimming down for the new economy. Just look at Toyota and Honda, the task force said. Smaller, leaner, and more agile companies with fewer dealers. They were profitable role models worth emulating. Human suffering somehow didn't fit into profit-loss statements, or the new math in which failing mega-corporations reap the rewards and provide huge executive bonuses.

Another myth played into the hands of the restructuring advisors. Some people still thought of dealers as "rip-off artists" out to make a buck—a perception that dies hard. The misconceptions were fed anew by negative spins coming from automakers and the task force, who talked about "overdealering" (too many) and "cost to the factory" (too much). They also spread the idea that the closing store owners were non-performers and unprofitable.

But times have changed and dealers are more attuned to customer concerns and needs. Dealers talk about exceeding customer expectations in dealer councils and staff meetings. They spend billions of dollars, as a group, to train staffers on customer-relations management. And their efforts are measured by automakers in the CSI surveys. Many dealers heard about the distrust of auto dealers. A customer told Jack Fitzgerald when he spoke about the closings of hundreds of dealers in his state that she didn't care about car dealers; they were "just out to make a buck."

Fitzgerald doesn't get into arguments or debates with people who hold views like that. He likes to lead by example, showing that not all dealers are alike, that many care deeply about customers and the industry. "They do care; that's why they're in the business of serving customers." He stressed the word "serving."

Fitzgerald, in fact, had built his reputation on fair pricing, advertising vehicle prices on line, and building a community of customers. Those moves alone motivated many a competitor to follow suit. The dealer statistics on serving communities, paying taxes, and the trickle-down effect on employment were there, he said. NADA kept them, so did CRDR and other dealer advocacy groups.

But when all else failed, Fitzgerald would deliver one of his famous "Jack zingers": "I've been your age but you ain't been mine, so you better be quiet." That line from the elder statesman with decades of dealership and life experience was often a conversation stopper.

Still, perception often lags reality. Many people still lump dealers into the same basket as the automakers, thinking the dealers were part of the carmakers, or owned by them. So they believed dealers too had benefited from the government TARP funds used to rescue auto. But the auto bailout funds propped up the automakers, suppliers, and lending arms such as GMAC, now called Ally Bank. Car dealers didn't cash in. They didn't get a cent; instead they became the disenfranchised—outcasts, on their own.

Jack Fitzgerald, the firebrand for CRDR, explained to those souls who might need enlightening that dealers are the automakers' customers—just as consumers who visit a "store," or dealership, or go to their online websites are the dealers' customers.

In turn, the car dealer became the voice of the customer to the automakers. That's true if you buy or lease from the world's largest auto dealers like Auto Nation, Group One, the Penske group, or Enterprise and Hertz car sales, Fitzgerald said. The automakers do their own customer surveys, but it's dealers who are likely to get the scoop in the customer's own words, in the heat of the moment, when a transaction sails or busts.

Top automotive execs often don't know much about how car dealerships work. They rely on their "field people," staffers assigned to various marketing regions, to oversee those functions. Execs review the bottom-line fiscal reports, which are neatly summarized for them by financial people. For many, working in automotive is an ivory-tower existence. They might remember dealers they like or don't like from national meetings or special events. The twenty to thirty upper-echelon execs usually don't service their own vehicles. To walk into a car dealership would be a humbling experience or might waste their expensive time. Their staffers do that, reporting through the ranks.

Indeed, one popular anecdote was that Chrysler CEO Sergio Marchionne grew angry when a Chrysler driver passed him on the freeway going to the airport. Apparently, Marchionne had chosen to drive a new Dodge truck as a try-out on his way to catch a flight. The driver was supposed to meet him at the terminal to return the vehicle. The driver was waiting there, ahead of schedule. Later, the mercurial Marchionne had him fired, so the story goes, as related by a former Chrysler executive.

The firing seemed characteristic of Marchionne, a passionate leader who was known to make on-the-spot decisions. Seemingly he thought a driver passing the boss on a highway was poor for the image, bad PR, if the word got out. Marchionne was becoming well-recognized in the Detroit environs, always on TV in some interview or other photo op in his customary black sweater.

Fixing the Economy

In mid-October of 2010, Americans were glued to their TV screens as the last Chilean miners were rescued. It was the story of the day. Americans are compassionate, caring people, the stories suggest. Especially when natural disaster strikes. The last miner was brought up from the dark caves while the world cheered. Somehow the presence of TV cameras and crews still seemed to make an event legitimate in the public eye.

News of dealer shutdowns made headlines, but often in local papers and the automotive press, overlooked by a mainstream audience.

But where was national television when the car dealers were decimated, when the last dealerships closed? When Main-Street car dealers and rural dealers were being destroyed? When GM refused to reinstate the last 500 dealers—such as Chip Bogdewic and 499 others—that remained open until the final wind-down date of October 31? There were anecdotal national reports of suicides and many health issues related to the dealer cuts. Where were the camera crews then? Darvish and other dealers wondered. How did some of the worst economic news of the new century escape some people's attention?

Fixing the automotive industry was the job of the auto task force; indirectly, it meant helping fix the economy. Some media outlets trumpeted Steve Rattner's book *Overhaul,* about the overhaul of the car industry, granting him celebrity status. One chapter in particular, called "F**k the UAW," gained instant notoriety as Rahm Emanuel put down the UAW and GM power-plays. At the time, Ron Bloom had warned the task force that doing nothing to save Chrysler—an option on the table—would cost hundreds of thousands of jobs, mostly line (assembly) workers. According to Rattner, Emanuel, an advisor to the task force, replied forcefully with the expletive that gave him his chapter title.

Some industry insiders called the revival of automotive the most significant event in President Obama's young presidency—and later hailed it as one of his successes. The dismantling of car dealers was also significant, yet it was often overlooked.

* * *

In recent history, Bill Clinton ran an entire presidential campaign based on the theme, "It's the economy, stupid."

In 2008, Barack Obama used a centrist theme that "together we can" change history. When he runs again, and most likely will, maybe the theme needs to be, "It's about jobs, stupid," or his Republican opponents will beat him to the punch. The midterm elections in 2010 would be a reminder of people's anger, their economic discontent brewing like the tempest in the teapot for nearly a decade.

Many domestic dealers and industry experts knew the problems automakers faced were product-related and not with dealers. But dealers never got a place at the table when the government was tearing down GM and Chrysler, or rebuilding them. And as the old saying goes, if you're not at the table, you could be on the menu.

Fitzgerald, a numbers man, was well aware of a surprising statistic. On the East Cost, in a well-educated, affluent areas such as Bethesda in Montgomery

County (Maryland), where he did business, 92 percent of cars on the road were imports, according to R. L. Polk data, he said. And they (imports) were gaining ground, not losing it. In such areas, dealers were forced to pick up import franchises or risk losing their businesses. Yet here were Chrysler and GM giving away more business by shutting down their sales arm—many high-performing dealers in regions where the domestics tend to do well.

* * *

In 2009, while America was worrying about jobs, finances, the real-estate crash, and the credit freeze, carmakers were slashing hundreds of thousands of jobs. Jobs and the economy still weighed heavily on people's minds even after the rescuing of the auto companies by the federal government. Yet jobs were being cut left and right.

Tammy Darvish thought it ironic that the task force took credit for saving millions of jobs. But the automakers were cutting back suppliers, employees, production, and factory shifts. Most alarmingly, they were cutting at least 25 percent of dealers who sold the automakers' vehicles and took care of their customers. Dealers and suppliers, however, don't "belong" to the automakers. How do you sell more cars when you're slashing a quarter of the sales force? It did not add up.

GM was decreasing in a year from more than six thousand retail outlets to about four thousand. (Later they would revise that count to nearly forty-five hundred, after their leaders wisely reconsidered the impact of more drastic cuts.) Chrysler was paring eight hundred or so from its ranks of roughly thirty-two hundred dealers. Earlier there was talk of two hundred more, but the Unsecured Creditors Committee held sway there. GM's reversal on the numbers came nearly a year later after political pressure was exerted by dealer lobbyists, lawyers, Congress, and select media. The one thing huge corporations hate is negative publicity. They have "crisis communications" teams in place to put out fires.

Tammy-in-Distress Calls

On a particularly bleak day, Tammy Darvish called Jack Fitzgerald. Fitzgerald had grown into one of her closest confidantes, and sometimes she leaned on him heavily. Her frustration would boil over and she had to vent. She also turned to Rose Bayat in her office; Courtney Wallin, her personal assistant;

and her cousin, Mina Gharib, who managed the DARCARS Volvo and Nissan stores nearby. But she couldn't dump on them all the time. And she was supposed to be the boss, the listener. Besides, Mina was always too sympathetic. A typical Darvish workday started at six in the morning and ended at twelve at night, Gharib said.

"Mr. Fitzgerald, how can this be happening?" Darvish asked after the dealer closures were a reality. She often addressed people, especially authority or important figures, more formally this way. Respectful. Not wanting to overstep her own boundaries. But inside, she was trying to hold back the feelings about to burst like water from a weak levee. Trying to stay in control, something she'd learned long ago from her dealer father. "I just don't know if I'm doing enough—if we're doing enough." She recalled the tension she was feeling as a new NADA director for the Washington DC area. She thought back to the horrific dealer stories at the US bankruptcy hearings for Chrysler only a month earlier. About the broken dealers she had seen there.

The wise dealer veteran shook his head when he got the "Tammy-in-distress" calls. Sometimes they came two or three times a day. He listened patiently. At these times, he never told her he was too busy to talk or hear her out. He'd been in the business too long—running his own show since 1966 and selling cars and trucks since 1956 in the greater-DC area, including DC, Maryland, and Virginia.

For his part, Fitzgerald wanted to make sure everything they presented on the Hill and to the task force was factual and accurate, that they weren't blowing smoke. "We tried to be careful of what we said and were meticulous to the government about the data and its accuracy," he would explain. Later, the SIGTARP report backed up their claims.

"Tammy, I need you to focus," Fitzgerald said when she got emotional. More complex tasks were staring them in the face. They couldn't react like the proverbial deer caught in the headlights. They couldn't panic or run. The stakes were too high. Dealers were depending on them.

In his five decades in the car business, Fitzgerald had been in many tough spots, although never quite like this one, having ten dealerships yanked out from under him. This was history in the making. When times were tough, he knew it was better to compartmentalize and focus. It was how you got through disaster and hard times and was something he could help Tammy Darvish and his younger colleagues with.

Tammy Darvish was not only truly sickened by what she was seeing and hearing in the dealer ranks, she was morally wounded. Jack Fitzgerald, a principled and disciplined man, knew this. He didn't feel much better himself. In fact he was livid. But his strategy was, "Don't get mad, get even."

But his words helped as she took a deep breath, centered, and then pivoted to fight another day. She began to focus, remembering Jack's words. She made more back-channel calls to people who could help their cause: Barney Frank; Steny Hoyer; Chris Van Hollen; Roscoe Barlett; David Weaver; John Hughes; Lee Iacocca; Bob Dilmore; Tom Pappert; Betty Sutton; and others. These were powerful people who would offer advice and open doors, she hoped.

She organized one instrumental meeting with Congress after another. She lobbied those she could. She mobilized her supporters. Why should people care about auto dealers? Darvish was often asked that question, and her response was generally along these lines: "The move to strip dealers of their rights is unprecedented in our history. Today it's the dealers, tomorrow it could be your business, your livelihood. What then?"

The Sounds of Screaming Souls

On one of those soul-searching nights during a long grueling work week, Darvish sat down at her desk. She was taking stock—like she did when she needed to reflect on what she was doing and why. Most people want to believe they can make a difference in life. But other people tend to confine what they do to their immediate small circles of family and friends, maybe the church of choice, a volunteer activity here or there, a political campaign.

That's all good. It's enough. She tried to talk herself into that notion many times.

But it wasn't. That was why she was taking this fight as far as she could. She was being pounded down at times. There was certainly no money in it—not that she cared about that; she never really had. She'd always been a people-first person. She knew she was lucky to have what she did. Her father had worked himself to the bone trying to grow the business, so the kids would have something to fall back on, a decent lifestyle. Her brothers, Jamie and John, and her other siblings weren't hurting either.

Why couldn't she leave well enough alone? family and friends would ask. She asked herself that a little too often these days. Like this night, when NADA and their support of the closed dealers weighed heavily on her mind. The dealer crisis and her role in it were all a little too much to handle at times. But the sounds of screaming souls haunted her. She heard and saw them in their letters, phone calls, e-mails, in bankruptcy court, in meetings, and in her travels.

To the three committee leaders, by mid-June, it seemed they had wasted time in moving the dealer rights campaign along. With all of NADA's resources, if they all had agreed from the get-go instead of enduring the squabbling between them, they could have done much more quickly, Darvish thought. When she went to him, her father urged her to be careful, not offend the wrong people. Like the concerned father he was, she knew he meant well. But she hadn't been raised to be timid or back down from a challenge. She kept the dark-side details of her mission to herself, only sharing the high points. "Gotta go to New York; bankruptcy hearings there this week; call you later," she said already on the run. Or "Big meeting tomorrow with NADA and Congress leaders;" again, she was stingy with details. Why trouble him? He was already carrying the weight of the remaining dealerships on him.

Darvish knew she was in hot water half the time with many of the powers-that-be in Detroit or DC. Especially when she brought up the cases of terminated dealers who should be reinstated.

"Dealers who weren't affected by the terminations wouldn't be interested in a federal law that said you had to go to arbitration, would they?" some dealers asked. Why should the continuing dealers care about those being let go? Less competition for them was better.

Darvish would point out the short-term thinking of that position. "While you might make a few more dollars today because your neighbor is out of business, what happens next year when other manufacturers decide to shut down more dealers? And it's not just the car business; it can happen in any industry, any business," she said. "Any entrepreneur or business owner should be worried."

Sometimes her peers, other dealers, would remind her how much she and her group had done for them. Witness the availability of about eighty-five dealers for New York bankruptcy court to testify against Chrysler as witnesses for the galvanized dealer group in early June.

Witness that a bill to bring back dealers was in the works and getting serious attention in Congress. Witness that powerful members of Congress lined up to speak out on the "dealer problem," trying to reverse the closures. Witness that more dealers were jumping aboard (in record time) the train whose engine CRDR had stoked.

Slowly at first, and then like a meteor shower, small notes of appreciation hit her computer, her mailbox, her ears. Soon there would be a thousand points of light or more as a result of these messages alone. George H. W. Bush had been right about those "points of light"; *We need them,* she thought. And when she was bone tired, wanting to stop the world, it was the words of dealers that kept her going. Along the way she had drawn admirers and volunteers from a wide stretch of dealerships nationwide, legal groups, media, and even other competitors' stores.

The affected dealers were increasingly recognizing the power of what the small group called CRDR was accomplishing with its singular focus and purpose.

"Tammy, most dealers are clueless as to all you are doing for us. THANK YOU! What a difference maker you are," wrote Mark Sims, an affected Chevrolet dealer from the Cleveland area who had lost his business. Sims came along to help the cause later in 2009. "You rock, you positively rock," he said, watching her efforts. Dealers like Sims apologized at times that they were not doing enough either, that they had failed to snag this congressman or that one.

"She's an angel" in the dealer world, said Massachusetts dealer Steve LaBelle, saying dealers had benefited in untold ways from her interactions with the automakers and even their legal staffs.

But failure was not to be in this dealer script. That's what dealers also told her.

Debbie Young, a dealer manager from Vero Beach, Florida, wondered when "the Tammy movie would be made." She said more than once, "This dealer saga belongs in a movie. You're an unsung hero, Tammy. And it should be about how the automakers and government ruined thousands of lives for no reason. It's worse than death for many dealers."

The Youngs lost their Chrysler dealership, Dependable Dodge, although the GM store was reinstated. They turned Chrysler into a used-car operation and were getting by, but things weren't great, Young said more than a year later.

Yale King in Longmont, Colorado, who had lost two brands, penned almost daily cheery notes and "attagirl" praise. He would add words that he felt deeply.

"I know that with every passing day I would not have gotten this far if it wasn't for your relentless pursuit of righteousness." That was a common theme in the letters and notes Darvish, Fitzgerald, Spitzer, and others received.

Elaine Vorberg, a private-practice attorney who fought to restore her father's GM, Buick, and Pontiac dealerships in Chicago, also marveled at the difference being linked to the CRDR group made in dealers' lives. She said the unity and bonding between dealers was an astonishing sight. "It took all the dealers banding together through CRDR to make this happen." More importantly, Vorberg added, "Tammy and her group kicked it all off. They were very invigorating from the start. They kept us all going."

Another couple, Lee and Karen Carlson in Anoka, Minnesota, were going through a long and tortuous year. Their GM, Cadillac, and Chevrolet dealership, Main Motors, had been in the Carlson family for ninety-one years when they were notified they would close. The Carlsons were gratified when they learned about CRDR; when they joined up they saw what Darvish especially was doing for all dealers. "I can't say enough about that woman. This whole thing was not just about the auto business. It should never have happened to any business. Tammy saw a wrong and was determined to make it right. There are no words to thank her enough," Karen Carlson said.

The Carlsons blamed the automakers for what transpired. "There were so many years at GM of mismanagement. If they had done what a responsible corporation would have, this would never have happened," Karen Carlson said. No matter what kind of praise the task force later received, the problem became magnified by their role in the dealer disaster, she said. "These people were completely unqualified for the job they were given."

Lee Carlson, her husband and co-dealer, said, "I never thought I'd have to fight so hard for something that belongs to me."

Karen Carlson, for one, couldn't help but give high praise to the three CRDR leaders who made a difference to all the cancelled dealers. They didn't have to take on the dealer fight, she reminded others; they could have continued to run their own businesses and been millionaires. "The fact that they did it speaks to their character," she said.

And then there were the chance encounters in dealer meetings and at airports nationally. By July, strangers were starting to recognize Darvish by face.

She asked her friends, how weird is that? She was becoming known outside her own dealer communities and DC market area where she had shot TV commercials for the DARCARS group and was fairly visible.

Nai Nan Ko, an Asian dealer in the Boston area, also had his Chrysler stores shut down. He remembered Darvish from a dealer meeting and her photo in news stories. His e-mail message is quoted here, without edits: "Even though it was a short encounter, I truly believe we both felt we share the same values and believe the same economic principles," Ko wrote. In an airport in Las Vegas, he saw her. He couldn't help but stop her and say hello. He spoke in slightly broken English. He kept thanking her. They exchanged business cards. Later, back on home turf, he sent her an e-mail. "What you have done deserves the ultimate respect. I thank you from the bottom of my heart. Your father must be very proud of you. You must be from a great family. What expired recently will be judged by a history book," he said, attempting lavish praise in his adopted language.

Then Nai Nan Ko briefly shared the story of his personal misfortune in his own broken sentences. "I am a first-generation immigrant. I love this country. Where I am today is not an accident, it is what this country is all about. When I was a Jeep-Chrysler dealer, I use my Toyota earning (sic) to support them. We keep all our employees working and waited for a 'turn around' which never came. It is you who pass the message on Capitol Hill. When you spoke, you spoke for all of us. Your voice is ours. Thank you. We could sit down and talk all day. To simply put it, we do what we believe is right because we love our country."

Here was a man, a stranger, in effect, treating her like she had made a difference already. Or like she was *somebody* in his world. Only days before, they had been perfect strangers. She couldn't bear it, but she read Ko's heartfelt words over and again.

What made it harder for Darvish was knowing that many private business owners, like Nai Nan Ko, had lost much in their struggle to get their lives back. Yet they always looked for the silver lining, and cared about each other's suffering. *That was the power of unity*, she thought—the power of the bond these dealers had created with one another.

* * *

There were those who didn't join in the struggle, or bailed at the end. Some refused to be interviewed. Many feared more repercussions from the automakers. Why take the risk? Were they the ones who punched the pillow at three in the morning, not able to sleep? Did they repress the inner voice that haunted them; did they tell themselves to just forget about the wrongs done to them, to move on? If only they could.

Darvish didn't blame any of them. She would do the same, if she could. But she had joined up with CRDR, like a marriage, for better or worse. She was in it for the long haul.

When Darvish, Fitzgerald, and Spitzer first geared up their CRDR advocacy group in May, the oddsmakers wouldn't bet a dime on them. The message was to quit while you're ahead. That's a good rule for people who aren't risk takers. Here they were, the new kids on the block, barely organized, and with little operating cash in a climate when cash was king.

The dealer movement was founded on a simple, game-changing principle. As a grassroots group they could influence the outcome of dealer closures. They could bring the alienated dealers together and reach lawmakers. The CRDR leaders were in it because "divided we fail," they thought. And for this group, failure had never been an option. Of the advocacy groups, "CRDR had a clear purpose; that's why they were the right ones for the fight ahead," said Mike Charapp, the DC-area lawyer who advised Darvish and others from the start.

There would be plenty of doubters to come. Top media people wondered at their brashness. Reporters remarked on it, including terms like "against all odds" in their write-ups. But this group, at least, didn't listen to naysayers. They pressed on regardless. Not always a safe course, but without this fight as their compass, they would be lost anyway.

Chapter 7—The Big Lie Times Two

It is true that you may fool all of the people some of the time; you can even fool some of the people all of the time; but you can't fool all of the people all of the time.

—Abraham Lincoln

It's time for GM to admit finally its two-billion-dollar lie.

—*Automotive News,* November 9, 2009

Follow the money, the saying goes. Funny numbers. Funny money. They somehow go together.

"Figures never lie, but liars often figure." Mark Calisi cited Mark Twain's adage about liars, comparing it to the automakers and their exaggeration of the cost of dealers to run their businesses. A rejected Chrysler dealer in Riverhead, New York, Calisi owns Eagle Auto Mall on the eastern end of Long Island where customers can select from multi-brands, including Chevrolet, Mazda, Volvo, and Kia. He formerly sold Chrysler and Jeep brands, but that stopped once Chrysler closed his operation in their bankruptcy restructuring.

Calisi is on-tap to sell the new Chrysler GEM electric vehicle golf-cart style car, which he's happy about. What he finds puzzling is that one part of the company (old Chrysler) shut him down, while another renewed his contract with GEM. He's still the same dealer. Calisi loves selling and servicing vehicles. His main gripe was with Chrysler's treatment of him and other dealers. He had met and often exceeded Chrysler's performance targets and over time spent about $9 million upgrading his facilities; still, he was cut in favor of a Dodge dealer in an older and less desirable space. "We were well-capitalized and profitable. It was not a performance issue," he said about his Chrysler and Jeep store closure.

Eventually, he won his Chrysler-Jeep store back but was pressing the case against Chrysler further in federal court. Before that, he said, "I've never sued anyone. The Chrysler requirements to get back in business were cost-prohibitive and impossible to meet," Calisi said. He was advised by his attorneys to not sign the agreements, as were other dealers.

There was a need to continue to expose the big lies told about the dealer closure decisions. In many cases, lies were stacked upon lies, dealers said. The news media increasingly was reporting on the significant savings GM and Chrysler were claiming to achieve by closing down dealers. They made the claims during court proceedings and before Congress often in sworn testimony.

In June 2009, Fritz Henderson, GM's CEO and former chief financial officer, testified in Washington about the closings. He claimed that the battered company could save about $2.3 billion, plus $415 million in support costs, such as advertising, training, and information needs. They could do this by simply closing 1,350 targeted dealerships. Henderson also said that by getting their network to thirty-six hundred dealers in 2010, including presumably the closed brands, GM would recoup big savings. Operating dealerships, he said, cost the company money. In addition, they could save costs spent on incentives paid to dealers, floor-plan support, and 1 percent in market support paid per vehicle per dealer.

At this time, Henderson had been handpicked by the auto task force to replace Rick Wagoner as GM's CEO when Wagoner was forced out at the end of March. The auto task force members liked Henderson because he was amenable to the idea of restructuring the failing giant. GM had been bleeding money to the tune of billions a month, and Henderson's job was to staunch the flow. In 2008, GM posted a $15.5 billion quarterly loss under Wagoner, the task force said.

When it came to cutting dealers, GM had conveniently included in their calculations money they said would be saved by not paying for gas fill-ups when buyers drove their cars off the lot. Dealers countered that those numbers assumed the vehicles would be sold, a sleight of the mathematics hand. Later, dealers and lawyers said they saw the savings calculated as a convenient lie, like others told under oath.

Industry paper *Automotive News* wrote in a November editorial (which represented the paper's official viewpoint so no author was cited, according to editors), "It's time for GM to admit its two-billion-dollar lie": "Eliminating 1,350 US (GM) dealerships—or even 2,500 if you include stores that have sold the discarded Saturn, Saab, Hummer, and Pontiac brands—will not cut anywhere near $2 billion in costs. GM executives must know that. And so should the Treasury officials on the auto task force if they have done their homework … but as many outraged dealers have noted, most of those are variable costs that depend on the number of vehicles sold—not the number of dealerships selling vehicles. Or, in many cases, they are expenses for which the dealer ultimately is billed. To claim otherwise is disingenuous and the worst kind of new math."

"Dealers Cry Liar, Liar," *Ward's Dealer Business* headlined in a story on April 1, depicting dealers refuting the two automakers' claims about how they cost the two automakers money—the multibillion-dollar lie.

"Dealers don't cost the manufacturers a thing—or next to nothing. If you did a cost analysis, you would see the manufacturers make money on dealers. Dealers are a profit center for the carmakers before they buy their first car," insisted Alan Spitzer, a vocal leader of CRDR. He was known as the "fiscal guy" of the group and did his own analysis plus compiled data from other credible industry sources.

"Fritz Henderson's claimed savings are laughable—e.g., saving by not prepping cars or filling tanks," Jack Fitzgerald said, citing CRDR research reports. In one instance, GM claimed it could save $120 million by cutting on dealers' fuel-filling expenses on new cars. The only way to save this amount is by not selling those cars, Fitzgerald and CRDR argued.

"The fact is, dealers cost automakers nothing, zero, so there are no savings. GM and Chrysler may be risking everything for nothing," Fitzgerald said. The "big lie" was the high cost of dealers to both automakers that so many people believed, he said. And that's what he and the committee kept hammering at, trying to expose the untruths inherent in the claims by GM and Chrysler.

Fitzgerald, a veteran in the car wars of America since 1956, said that the numbers from the two automakers and their internal experts were manufactured to justify the closings. Fitzgerald operates Fitzgerald Auto Malls in Maryland, Pennsylvania, and Florida. Like other CRDR dealers he was hard hit with the closures. "The fact is we make money for the manufacturers; that somehow got lost in the equation," Fitzgerald said, bristling at the automakers' savings claims.

GM and Chrysler won the right to terminate dealers in US bankruptcy court in 2009, but they did it by twisting the facts to judges and to Congress, Fitzgerald and others said. Chrysler, when it came up to bat in New York bankruptcy court in May, said it could save more than $33 million annually, plus extra money in advertising support and other related costs by cutting the dealers.

And Chrysler Vice President Peter Grady, who headed dealer network development, posted in his July corporate blog that the company spends $150 million yearly in advertising and marketing costs to support the rejected dealers. He also testified to the dealer costs in court. Grady said it cost the company $1.4 billion over four years "to develop and engineer overlapping sister vehicles for the dealers representing different brands."

Alan Spitzer couldn't believe what he heard coming from Pete Grady regarding dealer costs to manufacturers. "I'm not sure where he comes up with the $150 million in advertising costs. Each dealer pays an advertising charge of several hundred dollars for every car purchased. It's another myth," Spitzer said. "And Pete wins the prize for the biggest con of all by claiming $450 million for building sister vehicles [on platform concepts]. Even GM, which also builds a large number of vehicles on platforms, didn't have the audacity to claim these huge incremental costs. Because it ain't so," he said. "Anyone who's ever walked down an assembly line knows how ludicrous this claim is."

He pointed out that *automakers* decide whether to build car models, and where and on what platforms, not the dealers. The carmakers build a number of vehicles on common "sister" platforms. "All manufacturers do the same thing—because it's cheaper for them," Spitzer countered.

Hearing the Chrysler savings claims in court, dealer Mark Calisi said in an "uh-oh" tone, "Pete Grady is a man with a noose around his neck. He lied big time."

The trouble is the automakers came to believe their own spin. When you say something enough times, it takes on a false veracity. And many people behave the way power wants them to behave. "Yes, the emperor is wearing splendid clothes" becomes truth if enough people say it about the naked emperor, as any reader of childhood fables might remember.

"It's true, even if it didn't happen," American novelist Ken Kesey said in his novel *One Flew Over the Cuckoo's Nest.* If enough people say it, even if it's untrue, it becomes part of the conversation. But the automakers never claimed to be spinning tales of fiction. Chrysler CEO Marchionne, who preferred to not discuss the dealer closings, finally said, "The decision that we made, I think it was made with diligence, it was made equitably, and I think it was done fairly. What I cannot do is unwind the last seven months of history, during which Chrysler went on and started rebuilding a distribution network on the assumption that the ruling of the bankruptcy judge was final." He added, "My conscience is clear."

After Pete Grady posted his argument on his corporate blog about why dealers should be closed, readers could see it was all about dollars and cents, purported savings. His mid-July 2009 post immediately drew many reader responses, mostly negative.

One of them, from "confused," hit the nail on the head: "We have one Chrysler dealer in Charlotte, North Carolina, with a population of more than 600,000 in the city limits and 930,000 in Mecklenburg County. People live in a city for convenience. One dealer cannot meet the need of this many consumers. The dealership on South Blvd. that is being closed was just built last year. It is on one of the busiest roads in this city, which is free advertising for Chrysler. This dealership's sales needed restructuring, but it should not be closed. Please look at the whole dealership, not just sales. There is service, retail, and wholesale. If Chrysler wants to grow in this city, it would be a mistake to lose this location. There are three Chevrolet, three Ford and two of each of the imports but only one Chrysler dealer. In a city this size on South Boulevard alone there is a Chevrolet, Ford, Toyota, Hyundai, Kia, Honda, Saturn, and Mitsubishi dealer. What will the next car or truck purchase be for all those potential customers that drive that road every day?"

Most casual observers are not that well informed about the industry, perhaps until something happens in their town, like the writer above, or to someone they know. Former dealers such as Steve LaBelle can certainly confirm that.

The Ted Kennedy Letter

Steve LaBelle, a rejected Chevrolet dealer in Bridgewater, Massachusetts, couldn't believe how little Congress, or everyday people, knew about the workings of the auto industry. He'd been knocking on doors and working the phones tirelessly in his campaign to restore dealer rights. People didn't understand basics like who owns what brand and who owns which company, he found. Very few people knew GM owned part of Saab until they spun them off as part of the bankruptcy restructuring. No wonder the spin worked, he said.

LaBelle was shocked to learn in his talks with politicians and people not connected to automotive the paucity of knowledge about auto dealers specifically. Most of what people believed was based more on myths or secondhand talk than reality. "I found it amazing that they thought GM and Chrysler gave cars on a consignment basis to dealers. Many thought the automakers owned the dealerships. And they didn't know dealerships are a separate business and we were on the hook for all that money (inventory, mortgages, parts, etc.). We were on the hook and took a big beating," he said. "We got screwed."

To the uninitiated, LaBelle would simply say, "It's individual store owners' money that is spent on cars and everything related to running a dealership." People did not realize that basic fact, he said.

Thus, dealers constantly found themselves educating people on basics, telling audiences:

- "We're independent businesspeople and we don't work for the auto companies."
- "We buy vehicles and parts directly from manufacturers; that's why floor-plan credit and financing are vital."
- "We pay for our own marketing, advertising, and training, even if manufacturers are involved."
- "We pay for our own land, facilities, and all inventory and parts in the dealership."

Frustrated with his own situation and what he saw happening to others, LaBelle got US Representative Barney Frank, the Democrat from Massachusetts, to enlist Senator Ted Kennedy's support. Kennedy, on his deathbed that summer of 2009, made calls and wrote to GM leaders and others about rethinking their position on closing the dealers. He also interceded on LaBelle's behalf at the highest levels of GM.

In a letter on July 22, 2009, Kennedy wrote to Fritz Henderson: "Mr. LaBelle exceeded the [GM] dealer standard for working capital by 200 percent. I urge you to reconsider the decision. The closure is obviously a serious issue for the dealership, but it is also a serious issue for the surrounding community." He signed it simply, "Ted Kennedy." (See appendix A) That letter was sent nearly a month before Kennedy, known as the lion of the Senate, died of cancer on August 25.

LaBelle, as a GM dealer, didn't work with Jim Press at Chrysler, co-president along with Tom LaSorda at the time. But he criticized Press, who had built industry credibility in his thirty-seven years at Toyota, for betraying dealers who trusted him. "He should have had more backbone, more guts, in those behind closed-door meetings at Chrysler. He should have spoken up earlier," he said. But he didn't. Instead, Press spun the corporate tale of too many dealers.

Press said in testifying to the bankruptcy court that the dealers needed to be closed for Chrysler to be competitive. His former standing as president of Toyota USA gave him instant credibility. He later refuted the claim about dealers needing to be cut, but it was too late to help the fallen dealers much. Tammy Darvish recalled when Jim Press was one of the good guys and a force at Toyota. "He was amazing," she said. She and her father had worked with Press through their Toyota and Lexus franchises. "What a difference a year made for Press, and for us dealers."

The rejected dealers grew more and more incensed as so-called experts, such as Press, Grady, Henderson, and Nardelli, testified in the courts or before Congress. They were especially appalled when Jim Press got up and swore that a good percentage of dealers needed to go.

In an interesting sidebar, Press was asked publicly by Congress members whether Fiat, the future owner of Chrysler, required the dealer cuts. Press at least truthfully replied at the time, "No, they did not."

"So Fiat never requested that Chrysler cut the dealers in order to get the alliance with them?" The question was repeated several times. The answer was always the same. "*No, they did not.*" Yet during Chrysler's forty-two-day bankruptcy filing in the spring of 2009, Press oversaw the closure of 789 dealers, 25 percent of its total network.

Dealer attorney Len Bellavia in New York, who deposed Press in US bankruptcy court in June, saw a man uncomfortable in his own skin. He later believed Jim Press was giving nonverbal cues in court that he was not leveling with him. "It was like he was signaling, 'I'm telling the opposite of what the truth is,'" Bellavia said. "Jim Press felt internally conflicted, and it showed."

He thought Press had given the auto task force "bits and pieces" of information that led them to try to remake Chrysler, and to a lesser extent GM, into a Toyota sales model. "Trying to remake Chrysler into a Toyota just doesn't work," Bellavia said. "It was a false premise to begin with. Chrysler needs more of a market presence—more dealers, not less."

Press's nearly two-year tenure at Chrysler was between 2007 and 2009. It proved to be one of Chrysler's more turbulent periods as sales went south and the industry declined. When he left as deputy CEO, after having several title changes in his short tenure, it was not with the same head-held-high he had going in. In fact he appeared shrunken and walked with a stoop, some witnesses observed. He looked defeated, a hero fallen from grace.

Florida-based dealer consultant Tommy Gibbs said that Press unfortunately came to Chrysler at the wrong time for him and the company. He had been a hero at Toyota, but look what happened, Gibbs said. Like others, he had hoped Press would make more of a difference at Chrysler.

Rejected dealers and certain DC lawmakers may have blamed Press and other Chrysler execs, but Press defended the action as necessary though painful. At one point he claimed that cutting the dealers was "the most difficult business action I have personally ever had to take." He also called his resignation from Toyota after thirty-seven years, "The most difficult decision I have made."

Carl Galeana, a continuing dealer (he survived the bloodletting), owns Chrysler dealerships in Florida, Michigan, and South Carolina. Galeana gave Press a free pass, saying that even though he didn't live up to the hype that greeted his much-heralded arrival at Chrysler, Chrysler's slide was not his fault. The economy was a disaster and Chrysler's cupboard was bare after the Germans (Daimler) departed in 2007. "He came in at a time when there wasn't a lot of upside," Galeana told local media. "All of a sudden everything came crashing down, and from that point on it was all survival mode" for the automakers. Debbie Young was a manager at Dependable Dodge in Vero Beach, Florida. Their store closed, but she is still miffed at another lie that upper-echelon leaders kept feeding the media: "We are getting rid of our unprofitable dealers." Even friends in Europe repeated that story, she said. The news floating across the Atlantic was that US dealers were being cut because they were performing poorly.

The Young family owned Dependable Dodge and had been doing business in Vero Beach since 1963. They experienced a few months of slow sales during the financial crisis all dealers faced nationwide in 2009, Young said. But who didn't? "I feel that we have been slandered. And Chrysler was telling our customers we are not viable and profitable," she said. The perception created was that the closed dealers were not viable, hence not worth doing business with any longer, Young said. Now the store is selling used cars and service as Dependable Sales and Service. The Youngs still considered themselves "dependable," as did their customers, even if Chrysler did not.

Some consultants believe Chrysler may still fail after receiving $12.1 billion in cash infusions from the federal government to avoid liquidation. Some also question Chrysler's long-term viability due to lack of an internal captive finance company. Plus, their former finance company, Chrysler Financial, was eligible for an additional $1.5 billion, but wasn't sustainable. A captive finance company is usually wholly owned by the parent company. Ford has Ford Motor Credit Company, for example. GM once owned GMAC (General Motors Acceptance Corporation). The loss of a captive at GM and Chrysler has hurt their competitiveness—and dealers' ability to finance more customers, dealers and consultants contend.

Bob Dilmore, a former GM fleet sales-executive-turned-consultant, thinks GM will survive in the future, unless legal battles prove even more crippling. For better or worse, GM shed four brands and focused on its stronger family: Chevrolet (constituting about 70 percent of its volume), Buick (the "China killer"), Cadillac (the luxury marque), and GMC (popular for its solid truck line).

It's Chrysler Dilmore was worried about, at least in 2010. "They could be totally overextended. And Marchionne, the quick-tempered Italian leader of Fiat, does not understand the American market," he said.

Other issues were equally distorted as more mixed messages flew about in the dealers' upside-down world. Inventory or product deliveries to dealers were precariously low, preventing sales. But Chrysler did little to buy back the parts and special tools dealers purchased to repair vehicles. The service area props up sales when the economy is down, often accounting for more than 50 percent of profits. "Sales sells the first car, service the second one," is a familiar adage in the dealer world, and most service departments are expensively stocked.

Jeff Duvall, who owned Duvall Chrysler-Dodge-Jeep in Clayton, Georgia, explained to a reporter that lack of inventory—cars and trucks to sell—wasn't the only real problem for dealers whose product pipeline was being shut down.

Parts buybacks were also a major problem. "Inventory is scarce and very easy to move now," he said. The real problem was that parts and special tools dealers had invested millions of dollars in, not to mention single-use facility investments such as body shops. "Chrysler has done little more than give lip service with their redistribution program, and Congress thinks [Chrysler] have repurchased [parts and tools] from dealers. But we are left holding a near worthless asset that we have hundreds of thousands of dollars tied up in," Duvall said in August of the crisis year, 2009.

Why so much misunderstanding on the dealer and cost issues? Duvall is asked that a lot. A titanic-style shipwreck was going on, and no one was paying attention to the facts, to the plight of the sinking dealers, he said.

Apparently, on July 21, Ron Bloom of the auto task force told a House Judiciary Committee hearing that "Chrysler has made provisions and already agreed that it will buy and has purchased in fact the cars from its terminated dealers." Bloom also said, "Chrysler has agreed to purchase the parts and tools from all its dealers and they are in the process of doing that."

Incensed, Duvall said, "Nothing could be further from the truth. [The task force and Chrysler] continue to lie to Congress, and Congress continues to delay passage of the bills to restore franchised dealers' rights. And the dealers continue to go out of business," and profits spiral downward. "Like victims of a shipwreck floating at sea, tired and thirsty, one by one they give up and go under, or the sharks eat them first," he said. "I, for one, will not give up until this bill is brought to a vote. Mr. Bloom is either lying, been lied to, or is very misinformed and unprepared on the dealer question. In any case, his testimony to the House committee should cause great concern."

"Concern" is putting it mildly, according to many dealers. How about huge protests on the streets, protests in front of the White House, on the Hill, and before the corporate entities? Those didn't happen and wouldn't happen because of the misperceptions about dealers and their role in the automakers' decline.

Actually, Duvall considers himself one of the lucky ones. He didn't get eaten alive by the human-eating sharks swarming about. At the last minute, after he'd considered investing even more money into the dealership slated to go away, things turned his way. He was offered reinstatement by Chrysler before the arbitrations kicked in. But that was in the late innings of the game.

For many dealers, though, the problems only worsened as the closures took hold and the financial strain worsened.

Is Anybody Listening?

The year was 2009. It was a sad time in history for dealers and for the American public. People in the country were sick of bailouts, sick of Washington infighting, and sick of seeing their savings and assets crumble or get wiped out entirely. Numb with their own problems, the general public seemed to pay scant attention to the dealer problems surfacing now and then in the news. Most were not students of trade papers such as *Automotive News*, which followed the issues religiously. When they heard broadcasters announce "More dealer cuts made" on TV, perhaps many hit the remote. For them, it was just another business going down as victims of a poor economy.

Was anybody listening to the stories of dealers, related businesses, and suppliers in distress?

The automakers wanted a non-legislative solution to their dealer-closure problem. But as the noise increased from dealer advocates such as CRDR, members of Congress began showing dogged interest in the dealer closures. They could see communities being ripped apart, stores closed across the country. After that, Chrysler and GM were forced to respond to dealer concerns.

On July 9, David Weaver, chief of staff to Congressman Chris Van Hollen from Maryland, confided to Darvish and others in CRDR that GM sales chief Mark LaNeve and Chrysler execs had paid a visit to the congressman that month. So far, Van Hollen stood with the closing dealers. But Weaver was struck by the GM executives' mannerisms. "They're getting desperate," he observed—as if they suddenly saw the train wreck ahead. Still, they were not publicly admitting anything.

"Houston, we have a problem," wasn't coming from these executives' lips in June or in July as GM and Chrysler emerged from bankruptcy. Corporate execs might bear understanding and repeating it much sooner—to one another when crisis-type problems first surface. Ford Motor certainly did.

When it came to Chrysler, it was the flipside of the coin, Weaver observed. The corporation struck some lawmakers and dealers as swaggering with confidence. "With Chrysler, it was like they were on another planet, acting like none of this has anything to do with them. While GM recognized they are on a track and the train is coming toward them," Weaver said.

And that simple fact—GM saw the train lights and Chrysler didn't—spelled the difference to come. Congress was trying to negotiate concessions with the automakers at the time. David Weaver recommended that CRDR keep the heat on "real hot" in Congress at this critical juncture. The leaders intended to do just.

* * *

In Dearborn, Michigan, Alan Mulally understood he would be turning around a stalled company when he walked into the portals of Ford country, in 2006. "Everything is on the table," or negotiable for cutting, he soon learned. There were no sacred cows in a crisis. He, too, faced a huge deficit and financial headaches. Ford was bleeding red ink and recording massive losses after the 108-year-old company was nearly disintegrated under CEO Jacques Nasser's turn at the top (1999–2001). Now, Mulally, a former Boeing Aircraft exec, was installed as Ford Motor CEO and was calling the shots. He was willing to shake things up, with chairman Bill Ford Jr.'s blessing, of course. He began slashing jobs internally and cutting brands that had swollen the company immensely after a merger-and-acquisition frenzy with foreign brands. "Ford was not as near to the edge of the cliff as the other Detroit rivals when Mulally arrived," said David Cole, auto analyst at CAR, an Ann Arbor auto think tank. Ford's rescue came when it "got a line of credit because finance companies thought they were in such deep trouble" after Nasser ran it down, Cole added. The junior Ford, Bill Ford, great-grandson of company founder Henry Ford, in 2006 admitted he needed help to upright the sinking ship. Oftentimes, admitting you have the problem is the first step. Ask any support group in the country and they will tell you that. He brought in Mulally.

At Ford, a slower winnowing of the dealer ranks was part of the grand design, and Ford didn't force quick dealer reductions in the same way Chrysler and GM did. And that seemed to make a difference for the then-ailing company. Ford, in its bold-moves initiative, made the boldest move of all—shaking up the top layers. This trend actually began with the ouster of Nasser in 2001, who served as CEO for only two years but had been with the company for thirty-three years.

In the crisis period, to raise cash, Ford sold off its European luxury brands of Jaguar, Land Rover, Aston Martin, and finally, Volvo. Ford had always prided itself on developing marketing slogans such as a "better idea" and "bold moves" so started its deep restructuring earlier than GM and Chrysler. Was this a template for the other automakers to follow later? It's not uncommon for copycat moves and stealing big ideas at the automakers.

Alan Mulally also kept a close eye on the proceedings at GM and Chrysler, the government intervention, and requirements. He applied the lessons to Ford Motor Company without going through bankruptcy or costing the US taxpayers a thing. It was his "Cliff Notes" version to a successful turnaround.

By 2010, Ford was eating Chrysler's and GM's lunch. Smart guy, that Mulally, industry analysts would say. Lucky Ford. That year, Mulally placed second in *Fortune* magazine's 2010 "Businessperson of the Year" awards. He was the only automaker to place in the top forty. First place went to Reed Hastings, the Netflix CEO who had reinvented the company. Sergio Marchionne placed forty-fifth out of fifty in the rankings.

* * *

Watching the action unfold between Detroit and DC, the CRDR group saw that the misperceptions and innuendos swirling about needed to be clarified quickly.

"Congress, the White House, and the American people have been misled by GM and Chrysler," CRDR wrote in its media releases. "There is misguided logic behind the decision to terminate nearly 3,400 dealers around the United States, putting at risk the jobs of more than 169,000 Americans. Dealer terminations will be counterproductive. GM and Chrysler vastly exaggerated possible savings and underestimated the adverse impact of closing dealerships and ceding market share."

And: "It is time to end the big lie perpetrated by GM and Chrysler. Dealers are not an economic liability for an auto manufacturer. Dealers are the robust economic engine that permits auto manufacturers to sell their products and for customers to receive quality service and parts."

Then Darvish and her A-team blasted another message that hit lawmakers where it hurts. These are, after all, elected officials who don't want to be blamed by voters for cutting jobs. "Dealers are the backbone of product support at the local level, with 1.1 million employees and $234 billion invested" in businesses. The committee cited expert sources such as NADA, R.L Polk, and J. D. Power and Associates for its data.

Let these economic dollars talk, they figured.

CRDR leaders also were puzzled when Bob Nardelli, soon-to-be former Chrysler CEO, fired away at dealers in his testimony to Congress, again pleading the money thing. But he didn't seem to have his facts straight.

In fact, Darvish was astonished at Nardelli's sworn testimony in bankruptcy court. He didn't know answers to basic FAQs (frequently asked questions). "How many dealers does Chrysler have?" he was asked. He did not know; maybe he could get back with them on that one.

Darvish wanted to slip him the answer: "Hey, around 3,184 before the cuts, round it off to thirty-two hundred, if that's easier for you." And those cuts were the well-known 789.

He also professed not to know that dealers—not Chrysler—pick up the costs related to running their entire operations, including marketing and advertising. Did he really not know? Or was he pretending to be so out of the loop? Darvish and CRDR leaders could only wonder. Was it acceptable that the CEO of Chrysler does not know that dealers pay for training, brochures, advertising, all the tools used, and even the products we sell? Darvish mused. It all seemed too incredible.

Nardelli had eighteen months to turn Chrysler around before being replaced by Fiat's Marchionne. Although more mild-mannered and affable than his successor, Nardelli did very little to forge a relationship with his biggest and only customers, car dealers.

"Is this someone who should be in a position to destroy hundreds of thousands of lives and jobs because he said so, or someone else in power asked him to?" she asked her press and dealer contacts later. But who was above him? Only the chief of Cerberus Capital Management's Steve Feinberg, and he left the running of auto pretty much up to Nardelli.

Puzzled, dealers asked each other and their legal consultants more than once: Is it acceptable that no one can challenge the lies that were going on in the dealer drama? No one seemed to be paying attention to constitutional issues. This was a very big deal, in their eyes. For the present, no one was addressing it.

* * *

Meanwhile, Chrysler and GM were slashing dealerships right and left that kept their production lines going, their union employees and managers working. It was a double-edged sword. If the country wasn't working, neither were the factories or dealers.

It was more than a tune-up or "a haircut," as Jim Press had suggested to John Darvish, in that tense call in May at the international dealer meeting. Darvish said that to affected dealers, it was a massacre, a mugging of epic proportions. And totally unnecessary.

Even Lee Iacocca, former Chrysler CEO and president, offered a letter of support to CRDR when Darvish called on him. Iacocca, who brought Chrysler back from the brink in the early 1980s, said, "I am unaware of the dealers costing manufacturers money and decision makers should look very closely prior to altering for good what is the fabric of America." The fabric of America Iacocca was referring to was auto dealers as part of the big entrepreneurial picture. (See appendix B) It must have pained the wily auto veteran when he heard that Cerberus, the capital management firm that owned majority stake in his old company, Chrysler, later wanted to cut bait and sell the automaker to the government for one dollar.

* * *

Meanwhile, rumors and innuendoes still flew wildly about the dealer-closure problem, especially on Internet blogs and in chat rooms. Why had the dealers been cut, and who cut them? As with any major political scandal, rumors of a conspiracy theory surfaced on the Internet mostly. The online community dubbed it "Dealergate," saying dealers were being taken out by Democrats because of their political affiliations and contributions to the Republican party.

According to factcheck.org (http://www.factcheck.org/2009/06/dealergate-mistaking-anecdotes-for-data/), the name "Dealergate" came up as blogsters suggested that dealers who tend to contribute more heavily to Republican candidates were being singled out for closure. But the conspiracy theorists weren't able to produce the data or solid evidence to back up their claims, the national fact-check group said. Instead, they offered tiny samples and anecdotal "evidence" or "metrics" that led them to jump to conclusions.

Lawyers for dealers also denied claims that dealers contribute mainly to one party and would be targeted. "I strongly doubt that any dealer contributes to only one political party; it doesn't make sense," said attorney Len Bellavia. He has represented hundreds of dealers and believes they have too much at stake to support only one party.

Bellavia also grew up in a dealer family. His father, Joe Bellavia Sr., ran Talley Motors Lincoln-Mercury, Buick, Chevrolet, and Hyundai franchises for fifty years (adding Hyundai later) in the New York area until 2003. Young Len worked in the family business through his teens and then to put himself through law school. His affinity for dealer concerns thus comes naturally.

For the record, White House Press Secretary Robert Gibbs said at a White House briefing on May 28 that the Obama administration, namely Treasury and the auto task force, were not "involved in picking which dealerships stay open and which are to close." This was three months after the task force started overhauling the two key players in the domestic auto industry.

"The president's task force on autos did not pick individual dealerships. It hasn't—it isn't involved in picking which plants may or may not be closed. That's not the job of the president's auto task force. That's the job of the individual car company. They've got to figure out in their newly restructured world, based on the market, what their central supply chain is. And I think those are the decisions that they made," Gibbs said in a statement.

When a *Fox News* reporter asked about "concern in the blogosphere" about political influence in cutting dealers, Gibbs said, "Let me reiterate that we don't make those decisions, okay? Chrysler makes those decisions."

Steve Rattner in *Overhaul* stated more than once that the task force had nothing to do with selecting dealers for closure. Chrysler and GM did that. Some dealers and consultants went further laying the decisions at the feet of mid-level and upper managers in the field at GM and Chrysler, in tandem with certain executives in Detroit who signed off on the deals.

And how does one explain that the preponderance of support for the ongoing legislation to restore dealers to their businesses was coming from the Democrats in Congress? Those are facts, not lies, realists will say.

But still, people sometimes believe what they want to believe. Lies can easily become truth. The naked emperor can be "seen" wearing finely woven suits as he parades in streets paved with gold, as the ancient tale, *The Emperor's New Clothes*, goes.

In that fable, it's a child who finally cries out, "But the emperor has nothing on at all!"

Closed dealerships, such as Mark Sims' Chevrolet store in Lyndhurst, Ohio, got national attention during the midterm elections in 2010 as politicians descended on one of the states with the most dealer closures. *(Photo: Getty Images)*

Dealer Jack Fitzgerald appears at a House hearing on the automakers' plan to close massive numbers of dealer franchises in the country. *(Photo: Fitzgerald Auto Malls)*

Sergio Marchionne of Fiat took over as CEO of Chrysler Group LLC after the bankruptcy hearings in 2009. *(Photo: Chrysler LLC)*

The Jim Painter family's Chrysler-Jeep-Dodge dealership in St. George, Utah, was gifted to a nearby dealer who combined it under one roof with a Nissan store after the transaction completed. *(Photo courtesy Painter dealerships)*

Steven Rattner led the government's auto task force in 2009 as the group restructured the Detroit Two automakers within months *(Photo: Getty Images)*

George McGuire, owner of Shakopee Chevrolet in Minnesota, through the legislative efforts of CRDR, reopened his GM store but couldn't forget the painful experience he and employees went through. *(Photo: Shakopee Chevrolet)*

General Motors CEO Rick Wagoner, left, Chrysler co-president Jim Press; Ford Motor Company CEO Alan Mullaly; and Chrysler co-president Tom LaSorda appeared in Washington DC seeking federal bailout funds. Ford later declined the federal funding. *(Photo: Getty Images)*

House majority leader and US Representative Steny Hoyer (right) speaks at a news conference outside Capitol Hill on the need to restore dealer businesses. CRDR leaders Tammy Darvish (left), Jack Fitzgerald, and Alan Spitzer (behind Fitzgerald) listen. *(Photo: Joe McCary, Photoresponse)*

Jack Fitzgerald, owner of Fitzgerald Auto Malls, headquartered in Maryland, helped spearhead the committee that fought for dealer rights. *(Photo: Fitzgerald Auto Malls)*

Gina Russo (from left) and Gus Russo and Lochmoor Chrysler-Jeep employees in Detroit watch President Obama's announcement on the bankruptcy and government rescue of the Detroit auto industry. *(Photo AP)*

Richard Mealey, former dealer at Birmingham Chrysler-Jeep in Troy, Michigan, was instrumental in testifying for dealers in US bankruptcy court in May 2009. *(Photo: Jim Casper)*

Jackie Mealey, wife of Richard Mealey, wrote to members of Congress, the auto task force, and even President Obama to alert them to the dealer struggle. *(Personal photo)*

Sign of the times: a deserted Nashville Chrysler dealership showroom shows the aftermath of the closures. *(Photo: Bloomberg News/Getty Images)*

Mike Comiskey's busy Orleans Dodge in New Orleans, Louisiana, before it was shut down. (*Photo:courtesy of Mike Comiskey)*

Mark Calisi in Riverhead, New York, was one of the early dealers who won in arbitration against Chrysler but decided the conditions offered to return were too expensive and prohibitive. *(Photo: courtesy of Mark Calisi)*

Yale King, first row, former dealer principal of the King Auto Group in Longmont, Colorado, waged a long battle to win back his GM and Chrysler businesses. His two sons, Yale Blake King, upper right, and Rex King (left), are serving in the US Army. His two younger sons pictured are Sebastian King (left) and Remington King (right). *(King personal photos)*

Long before the fall: James Painter in 2007 in Utah with his prized 1968 Plymouth GTX. The Painters ran dealerships in the St. George, Utah, area for sixty-five years before being shut down. *(Personal photo: Painter dealerships)*

United Dodge in Las Vegas, Nevada, is one of the 789 dealerships Chrysler opted to close in 2009. *(Photo: YouTube dealer videos)*

Renaissance Center, home of General Motors Company, in Detroit, Michigan. *(Publicity photo)*

The US Capitol building on Capitol Hill in Washington DC *(Publicity photo)*

Steve LaBelle, former Chevrolet dealer in Bridgewater, Massachusetts, enlisted the support of influential lawmakers, such as Senator Ted Kennedy and US Representative Barney Frank in his home state to reverse dealer closures. *(Photo courtesy Steve LaBelle)*

Rob Smith, a major player in the legislative effort to pass the Dealer Economic Rights bills, oversees operations at Fitzgerald Auto Malls in the Maryland-DC area. *(Photo courtesy Rob Smith)*

Jeff Duvall and his son, Louie Duvall, campaigned hard for the economic rights of small businesses even after their Clayton, Georgia, dealerships were restored. *(Photo courtesy Jeff Duvall)*

Tammy Darvish and her father, John Darvish, in his dealership office in Lanham, Maryland. *(Personal photo)*

Maryland US Representative Chris Van Hollen, a Democrat, appears among dozens of congressional staffers at the July 14 dealer fly-in to Washington DC organized by CRDR leaders. Dealer-closure issues were at the heart of the two-day talks. *(Photo: Joe McCary, PhotoResponse)*

Chapter 8—Outraged: Killing the American Dream

When you're going through hell, just keep on going.
—Winston Churchill, during the darkest days of World War II

If they can do this to car dealers, they can do it to anyone in America. That's why this fight is so important to the entire country.
—Elaine Vorberg, Chicago attorney

A fight was brewing.

It began in the hearts and minds of dealers like Tammy Darvish, Jack Fitzgerald, and Alan Spitzer. It spread to the several thousand US car dealers who had learned their fates at the hands of Chrysler and General Motors in harsh ways.

It actually began the day Chrysler and GM announced they were cutting about 25 percent of their dealer networks in the name of efficiency and competition. At one point, the projections were for 25 to 40 percent cuts, if counting the four discontinued GM brands. The dealer rejection letters began arriving in mid-May from Chrysler and a few days later from GM.

Adding insult to injury, many of the termination letters were unsigned. "It doesn't get any more faceless than this," Doug Hawkinson, general manager at Koronis Motors in Paynesville, Minnesota, told local media. Minnesota was a hard-hit state for dealer cuts, and more than 4,250 dealership jobs stood to be lost in the state, according to NADA's projected job losses by state. (See state map in appendix C.)

The hastily assembled auto task force had delivered a clear message to GM and Chrysler: pare down the dealer base to resemble the imports' leaner sales models. Toyota was cited as the one to emulate. If automakers didn't trim down and restructure, federal money would be withheld.

If that wasn't a call to action, or a veiled threat, what was? Tammy Darvish wondered.

Some analysts estimated the closings at more than three thousand dealerships with the elimination of the GM brands Pontiac, Saturn, Saab, and Hummer. The automakers filed a Section 363 Chapter 11, a shortcut form of bankruptcy, orchestrated by the auto task force. That meant automakers could get in and out in record times, all conveniently arranged by financial wizards on the task force. Chrysler filed at the end of April and GM on June 1 in New York federal bankruptcy court. They then used the bankruptcy cover to justify consolidating their dealer networks.

It was a hatchet job, experts said, looking at what occurred at the automakers.

"GM will be trimmed down in almost every respect. And they're not using scissors. They're using a hatchet," Michael Robinet, a vice president with CSM Worldwide, an auto research firm in Northville, Michigan, that merged in 2010 with IHS Automotive, told the media.

The rejected auto dealers, many in smaller towns, in rural and metro regions, were outraged at the cuts and lack of verifiable facts behind them. Many were financially at the breaking point. Many long-term relationships were instantly severed at Chrysler, more slowly at GM. Feelings of outrage and betrayal swept the dealer group after being cast aside by their supposed business partners. They did what they were asked to do, often spending millions of dollars to upgrade their showrooms, buying vehicles when they didn't need them, performing above expectations.

Outraged. It was a word Tammy Darvish and other dealers would use repeatedly in describing their reactions, their feelings during a time of great upheaval. It wasn't the best of times or the worst of times. It was the worst possible time they could imagine. Dealer outrage came up frequently in conversations and e-mail outpourings between dealers.

Darvish said dealers felt outraged, betrayed, up to and even after the vote in Congress in December. In her many "call-to-action" memos and updates to her base she would remind the troops to keep up the fight. Keep calling, blogging, writing Congress, their supporters and their media contacts.

Jack Fitzgerald called the decision to kill a large percentage of dealers in the hope of possibly improving the fortunes of the rest "preposterous." He said the auto task force also blew it when ordering dealer cuts. "The task force squandered the opportunity of a lifetime to fix the country's problem. They are tinkering with the country's viability. Our country's competitive position in the world is at stake here."

Alan Spitzer was even more graphic in his assessment. He called the cuts "death by lethal injection by GM and hanging by guillotine by Chrysler. Either way, you're dead."

Only AutoNation, the largest publicly traded dealership group in the country, lost as many dealerships as Spitzer did, according to media reports. Later, Spitzer's Dodge and Jeep stores in two Cleveland area locations settled in arbitration, and he combined the franchises in one location, promising to be one of the biggest stores in the state. He also was able to work out settlements for his three GM stores, which did not reopen under his name.

What's Loyalty Got to Do with It?

Elaine Vorberg is a Chicago attorney who dedicated part of her law practice to fight for the rights of her father's GM dealership and for other dealers who were losing their businesses.

"No one was paying me $700 an hour to take this on," she said, contrasting herself to the corporate attorneys she dared to challenge. She did it because her father's reputation was on the line, and because it was the right thing to do. Like many, she believed all small businesses and their employees were at risk if the cuts were allowed to stand.

"If they can do this to car dealers, they can do it to anyone in America," Vorberg said, looking at the bigger picture. "That's why [Tammy and her group's] fight is so important to the entire country."

Nicholas D'Andrea, her father, formerly owned D'Andrea Buick-Pontiac-GMC on Chicago's south side. Before buying the Buick dealership, D'Andrea had worked his way up through sales and management positions since 1979. In late 2008, he took on additional debt to satisfy GM's requirements by purchasing nearby Pontiac and GMC dealerships. In the litany of closed dealerships, beginning in 2009, his was another profitable store—just a few months earlier the favorite to handle additional GM model lines—that was slashed, Vorberg said.

* * *

In Michigan, after Chrysler shut him down, Richard Mealey began investing his own money into a pre-owned certified used car business and service center for all makes and models. He would hang on for several months after opening. But the state of the economy and high overhead expenses of operating a huge facility proved an obstacle as he tried to make a go of the business.

To cut down on expenses even more, he and his wife, Jackie, put their home on the market. The former Chrysler dealership had been their main source of income. "The unfairness of all this was such an emotional blow that it was hard for us to function," Jackie Mealey said. During the 2009 holidays, they did not put up a Christmas tree, one of the joys in their lives.

In many ways, rejected car dealers like Richard Mealey had been loyal to the companies whose products they ordered, marketed, and sold. Mealey, for one, served Chrysler for forty-three years, a single-point dealer, meaning he did not acquire other franchises. Some dealers had run businesses in the family for two, three, and more generations. Some hoped to pass on the legacies to their family members, as did the Mealeys. According to media reports, GM and Chrysler were eliminating around twenty-one hundred dealers, more if the brands GM was discontinuing as part of their restructurings were counted.

Another of those closures was Jim Painter's Sun Country Chrysler, Dodge, and Jeep franchise in St. George, Utah, operating as a dealer entity for sixty-five years. The Painters sold Chrysler and GM products in southern Utah. In fact, they had always been loyal to the domestic makers, not seeing themselves as import sellers.

But what's loyalty got to do with it?

When Phil Painter in St. George thinks about that question, he too is outraged. So are thousands of other dealers like him who lost not only their own businesses as independent franchise owners but their reputations when they were branded as nonperformers and underachievers. Many had decades-long relationships with the automakers and saw them tossed aside in a day.

In the wide-open spaces of Utah, people often feel forgotten by the corporate interests of big business. Utah is known as the "industry state" and is famous for beekeeping. It's also the adopted home of Hollywood icon actor-director Robert Redford, who helped popularize the local arts with efforts such as the Sundance Film Festival in upscale Park City, where many new talented filmmakers and actors get their starts. Redford founded Sundance in 1978.

A total of eleven dealers were originally slated to shut down in Utah. Three belonged to the Painter family, known as local legends in their home town of St. George. The town is known for its outdoor lifestyle—skiing, camping, sports—and respect for family values.

In a dealership video, Phil Painter is wearing a black sports shirt and khaki shorts as he strides across the street to the franchises owned by a competitor. The other owner now carries the Chrysler, Dodge, and Jeep brands in its signage, a new addition to the import logos. "The total distance is sixty-five feet," Painter tells the camera. You can tell he's worked up. He's not just getting his daily exercise. He hopes to make a point. His family-run business had been around for sixty-five years. They had always been loyal to Chrysler—and the notion of American-made cars and trucks.

"After sixty-five years, wouldn't you want someone with that experience selling your products rather than some [newer guy] sixty-five feet away?" he asks. The video, Painter's idea, was shot right after Chrysler gave their family franchise to a neighboring dealer. Yet the Painters said they did everything Chrysler asked of them and still lost their dealerships.

The Painter family history of selling cars in southern Utah actually goes back to 1935 when a Painter opened the first GMC truck dealership in Utah. All three of the family's dealerships—the Chrysler store that three generations of Painters ran since 1945, the Chevrolet-Buick store nearby, and the Chrysler store that Jim Painter opened two hundred miles away at Chrysler's request—were closed over the course of two days in May. The Painters claimed the businesses had been profitable and financially stable.

In more modern times, Jim Painter, the current patriarch, is rather a local hero. The family had built strong community ties and donated to every cause in and around their towns. After decades of serving customers and his community, Jim Painter said, "What Chrysler did to us is certainly not the way things should work in America."

It was Phil Painter's idea to create the roughly two-minute video of his dealership and distribute it to likely places including media outlets, online, and Congress. Then Tammy Darvish took the idea further, extending it to all dealers who wanted to tell their stories. Her daughter, Nadia, and her cousin Shyon came up with the idea to create dealer YouTube videos as they sat around the kitchen table one morning. Then Darvish's assistant, Courtney Wallin, posted the links, while later Wallin and Rob Smith at Fitzgerald's group maintained the YouTube site.

The dealer videos, for example, on youtube.com/rejecteddealers featured cancelled dealers and garnered nearly sixty thousand hits by the end of 2010. That's as much as the readership of a mid-size newspaper, but these were at least direct hits by interested viewers. The videos were released in September 2009.

Phil's brother, Patrick Painter, who is a Republican Utah state representative, ran Painter's GM store in Nephi until it was slated to shut down. "This doesn't happen in the United States. It has all been a devastating, horrible mistake," Patrick Painter said when they were notified of the closures. On his congressional profile, he proudly lists "dealership owner" as his occupation. The Nephi store sold Chevrolets and Buicks, two of GM's surviving brands after they slashed half their other brands during the restructuring.

They lost their stores, but even more was at stake for the Painters—their reputation. "They've taken everything we own," said Painter, the Utah lawmaker. "After what happened to us, I feel like I live in North Korea or Nazi Germany, not the United States of America."

An emotional Patrick Painter added, "My mom and dad want their honor back, as much as anything. It's the ultimate showing of disloyalty, after all the years we've been loyal to them; for them to take our stores is unbelievable."

Gifting: Dealer versus Dealer

As the events of the year unfolded, dealers believed they had been given bitter pills that choked going down. The battle intensified, and it wasn't just the rejected dealers versus GM and Chrysler. The divide-and-conquer game was on.

Here's the rub. Many of the rejected dealers suddenly became pitted against other dealers. Chrysler predominantly, but GM too, began a practice of giving closed franchises to other dealers, as if they were worth nothing. The idea of "gifting" was born. But it was more dirty pool in the rejected dealers' eyes.

The betrayal goes even deeper, in Phil Painter's eyes. "Chrysler said they wouldn't reassign our dealership. But then they turned around to give it to this dealer across the street. This is happening all over America," he said, describing the practice of giving a business to favored "third parties," as Chrysler referred to them.

Some had heard that Chrysler CEO Nardelli had offered to sell the struggling automaker to the Bush administration for one dollar in late 2008, but that offer was not taken seriously, even scoffed at. So why should they be angered to learn that their franchises were being given away free in some cases?

Because they had spent their lives investing in their businesses, or preserving ones their families had built. Because they hoped to have something to pass on to their children and future generations. It's what business people do. It's part of the American Dream. It was like watching a thief steal everything you've built up for years. What's more, the practice was condoned, even initiated, by the power players in Detroit.

It went against the argument that the automakers were heavily burdened by having too many dealers and that these dealers cost them money. Darvish thought about the perplexing set of circumstances. On the one hand there were "too many dealerships," and on the other, they would close one and open another in its place. It was fuzzy logic, and it was unreal—but it was happening.

The idea of gifting was like salt rubbed in a fresh wound.

The practice angered Phil Painter and his nine siblings, who ran the family-owned car businesses. The closure was a triple whammy for dealerships like theirs. Not only were their stores closed, the automaker turned around and gave their businesses away while sticking them with the costs. They still had to pay for remaining inventory (cars and trucks), parts, building costs, tools, taxes, mortgages or leases, and supplier bills. Not to mention costs for upgrading their facilities, which they had invested in for years, even decades.

Some were stuck with millions of dollars in unpaid bills, the Painters said. Dealers felt bad because they were not able to pay their suppliers or even their employees at the end.

"It makes no sense," Phil Painter said. "You can't take property rights away from one person and give them to someone else. This is not right. This is not done in America."

"It makes no sense" was a common refrain among dealers, industry experts, and government officials. So was the "not in America" theme. But it had happened here, and many dealers did not fully know their rights until the nonprofit CRDR group formed to represent their interests.

Suspicion, hurt, and anger loomed large in the minds of the affected dealers. The year 2009 would stand out as a nightmare for them, one that would continue for who knew how long.

* * *

Rob Engel owned a profitable Chrysler-Jeep franchise in Tenafly, New Jersey, until the Mayday alarm sounded. He and his brother, Rich, had acquired Chrysler and Jeep franchises in Tenafly and Wyckoff. Both were shut down.

The business his father, Peter Engel, built in the 1960s was over in minutes. By the end of May, a visitor could walk into their former showroom and see nothing but space. Vast space. It looked like a ghost town. The family was facing financial ruin, as were sixty-five employees who were let go, said Engel. "It was a very sad, upsetting day. This was not a political issue, not Democratic or Republican. It's an American issue," he said about the closures.

"Something like this should not happen in America. If Wall Street can be bailed out, then Main Street can be helped out. People are in desperate straits, not just me. The money given to Wall Street or the automakers is not going to trickle down to Main Street," he said in a video documenting his experience.

Engel, like other dealers, feared that the lessons being taught to future generations were dangerous ones. "We're teaching the next generation of young people that hard work for a generation or more is for naught."

Healthy businesses that were making money were randomly and arbitrarily closed. The culprit, Engel said, was a small clause in the bankruptcy code that set aside the service contracts for petitioners of the bankruptcy. That opened the floodgates so established, successful businesses—some in business sixty-plus years—had their contracts abruptly cancelled.

Playing "Pinkie Swear"

George McGuire, who ran Shakopee Chevrolet in Shakopee, Minnesota, knew one thing. He couldn't bear letting his thirty-five employees go. They had stuck with him through it all, even as GM delivered the obscure wind-down notice telling him to close in the coming year.

The childhood game of "Pinkie Swear" came to McGuire's mind when he thought of what the auto task force and automakers had done to the car dealers. In Pinkie Swear, the participants give an "I promise" oath to stick together as they enjoin little fingers (pinkies), no matter what.

According to McGuire, "If the sky is blue, why not say it's something else? No matter what makes sense, stick to the program." That concept underlies Pinkie Swear. And GM and Chrysler stuck to it as they "had to justify the unjustifiable," he said.

At one point after his closure, he asked GM, "You guys got a second chance; did you give dealers a second chance?" He didn't get a real answer. But he hadn't expected one.

Dealers who were "single point," meaning they own one franchise (often one brand such as Chevrolet or Chrysler) fared the worst. That's why, when McGuire got the cancellation notice from GM, he was in total shock. To him, it was a horrific dream you couldn't wake up from, and then a shock you can't sleep off. "It was a state of panic—this is my entire life," McGuire, a father of three, told local media. "I don't have another dealership, I don't have another business."

McGuire stressed that his is not inherited wealth. He can relate to working-class values and people. "We were profitable and well-capitalized. But I'm not a guy whose father gave him the business." Like many of the axed dealers, McGuire was no legacy dealer. He'd worked his way up from dealer sales in another store; he sold Chrysler and Dodge brands beginning in 1984. He hired in as a manager at the Shakopee Chevrolet store in 1996. In 2000, a new decade and century, he thought he had achieved the American Dream. He bought out the dealership that year, becoming the owner, not the worker.

Many of his employees had worked at the dealership before he did and did fine with McGuire now as their boss. And he felt responsible for them, like he did for his own family. Like other free-enterprisers, McGuire touted the idea of a neutral marketplace as the key decider. "The true measure of profitability is, do you stay in business over time," he said. "Dealers are essentially a cost-free distribution point for automakers. In many ways this was a settling of scores. Once they were in bankruptcy protection, it was a chance to clear the deck and get rid of anyone you wanted to get rid of." They went crazy, he said.

Not every dealer who would remain open favored closing down potential competitors. "Some continuing dealers are absolutely appalled by what happened and the overall process," McGuire said. One dealer told him, "I don't mind winning as long as it's on a level playing field of battle." This was not the case as some dealers took over the businesses of the fallen dealers, gratis. But savvy or conscientious dealers looking at the situation might understand it could happen to them next.

Another continuing dealer wouldn't play the game GM and Chrysler set in motion. He flat out told GM he didn't want to get a store for free. Then he went to DC in the summer and shared his experience with a Senate group. He spoke about the wrongful actions of the automakers. In McGuire's eyes, such dealers are unsung heroes. "He was so appalled at the process he had to speak up," McGuire said.

And in Maryland, Peter Kitzmiller, who heads the state dealers association, said the Maryland dealers on his board of directors overwhelmingly supported the cancelled dealers. "Even though they were not impacted by the terminations themselves, they said, 'We've got to fight this,' and they jumped on the issue in defense of the affected dealers," Kitzmiller said.

Looking back at how things evolved, with forces such as the bankruptcy courts and government's "team auto" lined up like some huge fraternity, McGuire, like others, was dismayed. "I truly don't know how they sleep at night," he said of the judges, executives, and government officials who took out the dealers.

Then a strange thing happened in McGuire's shop. His ordeal was overwhelming, but none of his employees deserted him during the hard times. Rather, he noticed they were working even harder. "I am still in awe of that today. It is a very humbling thing as an owner." Loyalty to good people was still alive in Shakopee, Minnesota.

McGuire was eventually reinstated. But that brought mixed blessings. On the downside, he was constrained by lack of inventory. Chevrolet was not sending the new cars and trucks he needed. "We did not have new cars from June through about a week ago," he said in late October 2010. That meant nearly sixteen months in which they had to figure out how to survive the storm, selling used vehicles and doing service work while keeping people working.

"Since I've been reinstated, our relationship with GM has been fine. I'm not here to throw rocks. But it was very hard on me and my family. Emotionally, it was a tremendous strain." He still can't stop talking about the period when he lived in fear, trying to survive by selling used vehicles. "It was so destructive for me and my family and employees. Every single one of my employees stayed with us, and they worked even harder than ever. It was so cool to watch the process here."

That at least was one bright side to an otherwise overwhelming situation. At the automakers' end, "They didn't realize that for dealers, employees create the business," he said.

Chrysler was more ruthless in its treatment of dealers, McGuire observed. GM at least doled out settlement money to some dealers to ease the pain of closing. Chrysler was cheaper, he said, just like its leader had been in acquiring the up-for-grabs company.

CEO Sergio Marchionne didn't pay a dime for nearly a 20 percent stake in Chrysler. Fiat told the task force its contribution was in sharing its technology and management of the failing automaker. "But he still got 19 to 20 percent of something for nothing," McGuire said.

Personal Vendettas or Criteria?

In early June 2009, Chrysler was emerging from bankruptcy court and GM was going in, with the task force overseeing both. Many dealers said they didn't know why they were picked, or who picked them, for closure. Steve Rattner, who headed the task force in its first five months, often said his group did not select the dealers; the manufacturers did.

But dealers (and their lawyers) suspected they got cut because they were not playing the ball game the way the automakers wanted. The reasons, they figured, ranged from taking legal action when a rival dealer or brand moved into their territory, to not always singing to the corporate hymnbook. And when the dealers tried to get answers, or real criteria from the automakers, they were often stonewalled.

The conclusion many high-performing dealers reached was that at some point, they had not played along with the carmakers. They weren't "Stepford wives," or "yes"-men and -women. They marched to their own drummers. They weren't playing Pinkie Swear.

Some dealers and legal experts believed the acts were vendettas, motivated by internal politics at the automakers' corporate and field offices. Some would prove their cases.

Their attorneys agreed. "It was personal and a vendetta," Len Bellavia, a New York lawyer with Bellavia Gentile & Associates, argued for dealers he represented in court, such as Jim Tarbox and Mark Calisi. Bellavia forced the hand of Federal Judge Arthur Gonzalez to release secret e-mails since the companies were pursuing arbitration against the automakers. "The release of the private e-mails later proved a substantial victory for the two dealers," Bellavia said.

Jim Tarbox testified before the House Judiciary Committee on July 22, saying he was stripped of his right to sell the Chrysler-Jeep brand due to a personal vendetta on the automaker's part. His North Kingston, Rhode Island, dealership had a sales volume that was 450 percent above Chrysler's plan or requirements, he said. He was so successful that Chrysler asked him to buy a dealership in Attleboro, Massachusetts, which he did. He was in the top 5 to 10 percent of all Chrysler dealers nationally and was a third-generation owner. The family business had begun in 1935.

When he was shut down, his first thoughts were about his family and his employees. How would his young girls go to college? How would they make their payments on still owed-on inventory, buildings, and property? "Everything I worked for, my businesses and my rights, were gone in the seconds it took me to open the letter from Chrysler—and given to my competitors on a silver platter."

He added, in pleas to Congress at the time, "If my dealership is not restored, we will lose everything, including college savings for my children and our home. I am at a loss as to how a small businessperson like me found himself in this position."

The difference between Tarbox and others is that he later found out why he had been cut, and it had nothing to do with performance, as he claimed. During a hearing in Chrysler bankruptcy court in June, a witness revealed the internal e-mails about Tarbox and Calisi, a New York dealer. The e-mails bounced around the Internet between Chrysler executives, almost like office chitchat. In Tarbox's case these executives called him "a belligerent and combative dealer," he found out later in court.

Chrysler's VP of dealer affairs, Pete Grady, said in the e-mail exchange with Phil Scroggin, the northeast Chrysler staff manager who was accusing Tarbox. "This is going to be tough—his dealerships are performing fine and with good scorecards."

The "belligerent" rap came about because Tarbox had opposed Chrysler in state court to stop another Jeep store being opened within a few miles of his facility in Rhode Island, as stipulated in state franchise laws. He figured he was standing up for his rights under state franchise laws then too. Chrysler manager Phil Scroggin wrote in a reply e-mail to VP Grady: "He's a belligerent, combative dealer who litigates and protests any new Jeep franchise in the Providence area. Management made a decision to cut him. He has not operated in good faith," Tarbox related.

In their testimony, Chrysler officials claimed Tarbox was closed for being a standalone Jeep dealer, which no longer fit into their Genesis model aiming to consolidate the Chrysler brands—Jeep, Chrysler, Dodge, and Ram—under single dealer locations.

But Tarbox argued otherwise. "It seems closure was decided based on personality and relationships, not performance. This is not a fair or sound business practice. This is not in the best interest of the taxpayer who suddenly has a stake. And this company is playing with our lives," he told Congress. Tarbox had worked in the auto industry all his life, buying out his father's business in 2001.

Mark Calisi is one of many dealers who likes to look at numbers and facts for proof positive. A multi-line dealer in Riverhead, New York (on eastern Long Island), he sells four different brands; and earlier, he also sold Chrysler and Jeep vehicles. Calisi was caught up with Jim Tarbox in the Chrysler campaign to discredit them in corporate e-mail slurs.

The e-mails between a dealer placement executive and field staffer referred to Calisi as "litigious" and "acerbic." Unlike Tarbox, Calisi had not sued Chrysler at the time. "I've never sued anyone," he said, but this time he was fueled by outrage, feeling singled out. He, too, thought the vendetta was personal. And he was angered by the dealer closures nationwide. "This was wrong on every scale imaginable; some dealers lost everything. That's why I had to get involved and try to make things right," he said of his stepped-up role with CRDR.

A Chrysler spokesperson dismissed claims that dealers were singled out for retribution. "This wasn't easy for anybody, but it wasn't personal," Kathy Graham, a Chrysler spokeswoman, said in media reports.

Calisi said a special investigator's report on TARP funds later refuted the claims Chrysler made about saving money by closing the dealers. "It was more sound-bites than anything else. No one connected the matrix or proved that this is how they came up with the numbers on savings. It was just the opposite," he said. "No one knows where they [automakers] got the numbers. Hey, maybe they pulled them out of thin air. My position? If the numbers are real, show me," he said.

Chrysler had testified that dealers represented a cost barrier and needed to be trimmed for the group to be competitive. Calisi was surprised when he and other dealers testified or presented affidavits to the contrary in bankruptcy court, but it fell on the deaf ears of Judge Gonzalez. He knew then the decision had already been made. The judge found for Chrysler against the dealers.

Calisi wrote to Jim Press on June 28, 2009, hoping to clarify misleading information about his dealership closure and that of a so-called "facing Dodge dealer" Chrysler wanted to replace him with. That dealer was actually in a different area and didn't want the business, he pointed out. He reminded Press that he had sunk almost $11 million into upgrading his properties at Chrysler's request over the years, while the favored "facing" dealer had not done so and had a less desirable facility and location.

"Due to recent dealer terminations, many lives have been ruined, businesses destroyed, and families torn apart, and because of the circumstances surrounding my termination, no one, including you, lawmakers, or I can just stand by and do nothing," he wrote. "After e-mails and testimony become public, it's going to be very difficult for many people including yourself and other executives to ignore the fact that part of the termination process was retaliation and not data-driven, as stated in testimony by Chrysler employees."

Calisi got no response but hadn't expected one. But he did call Jim Press shortly after he left Chrysler in November. When he explained who he was, Press remembered him, possibly from earlier e-mails, his letter, and by reputation. In that call, "Press apologized and said he knew I got a raw deal. I felt better at least knowing someone had a little remorse," Calisi said.

Later, Calisi and other dealers wondered how Chrysler could commit injustices on a massive scale against dealers and get a free pass in the courts. It just fueled dealers' outrage more.

What was hurting Chrysler was that their products lacked appeal and weren't selling in big numbers in certain market areas, dealers often said. The two automakers, Chrysler more so, did poorly on the coasts, where imports were strong. That's what dealers told CRDR and other groups who cared to listen. In the middle and outlying areas, where the domestics made most of their dealer cuts, they were stronger.

* * *

Mitch Lunt, an eighty-two-year-old Chrysler dealer, still can't believe that loyalty has gone out the door with the automakers. His Dodge-Chrysler franchise had been in the family for seventy-five years when it was slashed. He now runs a used-car operation with his son, Jim, on his Main Street property in Cedar City, Utah. That May, he was among the 789 who got word that Chrysler wanted to cut them out of the action. Good-bye seventy-five years of history and loyalty where he started as a shop floor worker at Lunt, his father's enterprise.

Good-bye to excellent relationships with customers. There was no gold watch, dinner, or fond farewells at stores like his. "I think there were fishy things going on under the table [at Chrysler]. They picked dealers to cut who did not say 'yes' to them. What you did for them earlier didn't count," said Mitch

Lunt about Chrysler's motivation. So it was the yes-men who stayed after all. It was a common refrain being sung at the slashed dealerships.

Lunt felt great sorrow at seeing history come to an end in his rural community, where everyone knew everyone else, especially the Lunt name. Even so, Lunt said the hard part was telling his longtime loyal customers he was closing and didn't know why.

But what's loyalty got to do with it? Everything to dealers such as Mitch and Jim Lunt. Customers complained of having to drive great distances to buy or take care of their cars. "Some of my customers say they won't drive one hundred miles round trip to get their cars serviced. They tell me they'll buy used here or they may go to the imports," Mitch Lunt said. Such was the anti-Chrysler sentiment spreading in the heartland, he said.

Chrysler also lost a major presence in outlying areas that support truck and minivan sales. It's Ford and GM who will come out the winners, Mitch Lunt thinks. Ford because they took care of their business privately, and GM, who at least had the sense to modify their originally rigid posture. They brought back hundreds of dealers without bitter, expensive arbitration or court battles, he said. It was that easy.

* * *

"Chaos, Pure Chaos"

In New Orleans, Louisiana, Chrysler dealer Mike Comiskey read the headlines on Chrysler's closures in May. He knew the warning shot had been fired, but that didn't prepare him for news about his own dealership closing. Comiskey's Orleans Dodge-Chrysler-Jeep store in New Orleans East would join another fifteen to close across Louisiana's legendary bayou country. With two dealerships going down in his area, that left no Chrysler dealers in all of New Orleans.

"I'm not giving up, but I know it's an uphill battle," Comiskey said. He doubted Chrysler had really given the closure in his case a lot of thought. He was a profitable dealer. He was insulted but mostly torn up inside.

Starting in high school as a mechanic, Comiskey held service-management positions at Chrysler dealerships before becoming the dealer/operator of Orleans Dodge-Chrysler-Jeep. He bought the location on the Interstate 10

Service Road in April 2005, along with several investors. To supplement new car sales in the New Orleans market, which was severely damaged following Hurricane Katrina in August 2005, his franchise pushed successfully to make strong fleet and municipal sales, Comiskey said.

From April to December 2005, his dealership sold 1,167 new and used cars and trucks and brought in almost $25 million, he said; an excellent record. From 2006 to 2008, despite losing half his employees and customer base after Katrina, sales increased each year, reaching a total of more than five thousand new and used cars and trucks for a three-year period, considered high in the battered market region.

In early 2009, the dealership had brought in almost $5 million, but it was behind sales rates of previous years. Comiskey's dealership comptroller Angela Shroyer said it was difficult for the dealership to purchase cars because of Chrysler's scheduled plant shutdowns and dealer litigations. At the time, dealers were hurting all over the country because of the credit freeze and economic meltdown.

Comiskey said he might have been in a better position if he had received payments owed by his Chrysler insurer for his Katrina storm-damaged cars. In August of 2007, the dealership sued the insurance company who told him they could not verify that Comiskey lost as many cars as he claimed, possibly putting a checkmark by his name. To the best of his knowledge, this had not happened at any other Chrysler dealership in his area post-Katrina.

After Comiskey rebuilt the facility with the help of his partners and employees, his modernized dealership was set on a three-acre lot. Timing is everything; but sometimes it works against you. It was then he got the closure notice. He tried to keep going by selling used cars and reducing staff to thirty-seven employees from sixty-eight. As the countdown came, the mood was somber inside the dealership. Although he could not sell new vehicles under the Chrysler, Dodge, and Jeep brands, he had planned to stay at his current location as long as he could and sell used cars. But he found he couldn't make a living at it, or meet the high cost of running a new-car dealership. He took a day job.

He looked back at the dealer rights struggle as destructive and working against the known order of things. "In the business world, many times we make decisions based on franchise laws. Remove these laws, then what do you have? Chaos, pure chaos. All of this was way bigger than me or anything I ever expected to be part of. It was the civics and legal lesson of a lifetime—powered by Google, YouTube, and the automakers," Comiskey said reflectively nearly two years later.

The destruction also spread to human lives. One of his partners suffered a heart attack after the closure, despite having no history of previous illness. He asked not to give his name, as did other health-afflicted dealers and employees across the country.

But the overall experience of joining the ranks of shuttered dealerships was not one Comiskey would wish on his enemies. "With what Chrysler did, there was no way I could protect myself. They say adversity makes everyone stronger. If that's true, I'm going to be King Kong."

* * *

Jeff Duvall became a second-generation dealer in 1983, a young man coming of age, building a comfortable lifestyle. He bought out his father and then began expanding his small empire. His father had started out in 1956 when he bought a Ford franchise. It was located on Main Street in downtown Clayton, Georgia, in a storefront building where his dad operated until 1965. That year the state opened up a new highway that bypassed the downtown area. His father purchased property there and was the first business to relocate to the new road.

Duvall continued operating in the original building, which received several upgrades. Being a natural entrepreneur, in 2003 Duvall bought a local Chevrolet-Pontiac store which had been around since 1960 near their original Ford dealership. He relocated the Chevrolet store next door to the Ford facility on the new highway, developing a campus of sorts.

In 2006, he acquired "a failing Chrysler-Dodge-Jeep dealership in Toccoa," he said, about thirty miles from Clayton. That's what dealers did in those days, before the restructurings. Buy-sell was heating up as natural forces and attrition forced dealers to get out of the market and others to gobble them up. Later, Duvall closed the Toccoa facility at Chrysler's request and agreed to build separate facilities for all his brands (Ford, Chevrolet, and Chrysler) in Clayton, where he could open up the Chrysler franchise after construction was complete. He was a committed domestic dealer, covering his bases.

Luck seemed to be on his side. He was beginning construction on the new Chrysler complex when he read the tea leaves. The economy was weakening, and Chrysler was suffering in sales. Duvall postponed new construction; that was in 2009, the first quarter. It was a good decision. Shortly after that, the ax fell. "With the weak economy and the apparent bankruptcies, I decided there was no way I was going to spend the amount of money it was going to cost to build the three new facilities. Plus I already owned the forty-five-thousand-square-foot building in a great location that I could spend one-fourth the money on and have a better set-up than I would have with the three stand-alone buildings," he explained later.

"I suspected that we probably would be terminated by Chrysler and possibly Chevrolet as well, but I knew we would be selling something, even if it was only Ford and used cars." He held on.

"After Judge Gonzalez threw us out with the garbage in New York bankruptcy court, I received an e-mail from Alan Spitzer's daughter about the dealer meeting, a rally, in Washington in July. I did not hesitate, we signed on, and my son Louie and I made plans to go to DC."

He joined the movement to help other dealers who were being cut unnecessarily. He would stand up to the agenda that he thought was wrong for the industry and hurt so many dealers and customers. He threw his weight—and money—behind the CRDR group, pledging to do whatever he could. He knew what was going on around him was wrong, and he'd always been the kind to make waves.

After his three Chrysler brand dealerships were targeted, he wrote Ramsey "Bub" Way, the Georgia auto dealers association director, to say he was considering dropping his longstanding NADA membership. He had been a member since 1983, and his father was one before him. He didn't like some of the internal practices, such as the support of gifted dealers. "Our family has long supported NADA and its mission to protect the dealer franchise system and communicate dealers' views within the government system. However, for the first time I question my continued support and involvement. My NADA renewal letter arrived recently, and I am weighing the potential benefits of my ongoing membership," he wrote.

His comments appeared publicly on the Jim Painter website.

* * *

Jack Haigh at Crossroads Superstore in Oklahoma found having his contracts cancelled by GM and Chrysler a "surreal" experience, more than unsettling. "I always wanted to be a GM dealer, from the time I was a little kid. I wasn't rich. I worked very hard to build a business," he said, always thinking he was going to live the American Dream. He had saved for fifteen years, living frugally until he could buy into Crossroads with business partner Bob Sullins. "I paid almost one million dollars for Crossroads and then worked another ten years to make it profitable."

The short version is that the auto industry tanked and along came the auto task force. "Many profitable dealers' businesses were destroyed. So much for my American Dream," Haigh said, after losing his holdings. "Even if I get back in, somehow, I'm years away from where I was when all this happened."

In their termination rationale, the only negative Chrysler could pin on them was lower figures "on working capital, which is totally bogus because we had $900,000 in cash in a Chrysler cash management account," he said. He and his partner, Sullins, think they were flat-out terminated because they were dualed GM and Chrysler dealers. Even after offering to separate the facilities, they were left out of the action.

Constitutional Issues at Stake

Many dealers brought up the issue of constitutional rights being at the heart of the dealer closures. In Texas, Frank Blankenbeckler III became an outspoken leader for closed dealers, equating the dealer closures to a violation of the Constitution. He operated Carlisle Chevrolet-Cadillac and Chrysler-Jeep franchise in Waxahachie, a midsize town in metro Dallas. Blankenbeckler took action, not willing to be silenced or coerced into cowardice. He got a double whammy from Chrysler and GM within twenty-four hours. He received "an unsigned letter from our former business partner saying you are no longer part of the team." Carlisle was thus notified they were part of the rejected dealer group.

"It's a violation of my constitutional rights. This is an illegal taking of my property. Our country is in grave danger if this is allowed to happen," he said in a video segment sent to Congress. Like an unlawful seizure, he believed the closure "violates individual property rights and individual liberty."

Blankenbeckler got choked up when he testified before a House Energy and Commerce subcommittee that his Jeep-Chevrolet-Cadillac dealership in

Waxahachie was on the chopping block. He recalled how his grandparents and his father had worked to pay off the dealerships decades ago. It was their generations who had fought to preserve democracy for people today. That's what was on his mind when he went up against the corporations and a government that ignored what private businesses did for their country and communities.

"I am glad my father is not alive to witness this terrible injustice. To have risked his life for a country to do what they are doing would have destroyed him," he told local media. His father had a bronze star, which Blankenbeckler proudly wore on his jacket when he spoke publicly.

He believed Chrysler and GM were using federal bankruptcy to bypass state franchise laws and violate dealers' constitutional rights. His family had been contributing to the Texas community for nearly one hundred years, he said. The economic impact on smaller towns such as Waxahachie would be severe. The company was a substantial employer in town. In 2008 he paid $1.3 million in salaries and paid higher taxes than most businesses in his metro area. "Ninety souls depend on my business," he said about his employees. "Nearly six generations of Carlisle customers will be hurt and inconvenienced by my closures." The community would be hurt, he knew.

A few deletions appear, but his dealership website declared: "Carlisle Chevrolet—serving the residents of Waxahachie and Ellis County in Texas for over eighty years. We started in 1926 with the Chevrolet brand; Carlisle is also a full-service dealer for Cadillac. Carlisle Chevrolet's sales and service departments have received outstanding recognition over the decades. In recent years, Carlisle has been honored with the GM Mark of Excellence which is presented only to 'Our finest dealers who have committed themselves to unsurpassed performance and customer satisfaction,'" according to GM.

Blankenbeckler's Chevrolet dealership was restored by GM, but the hurt is hard to forget.

* * *

Bill Sowles, owner of a Jeep store in Brunswick, Maine, also got the notice to shut down in three weeks a business he had built up and invested in for twenty-five years. He also was bothered by the constitutional issues involved in the taking of private property from private businesses.

Chrysler later told him they would not buy back any inventory (unsold cars), tools, parts, or anything else connected to their operation—despite what top brass were saying publicly. It was a tough-luck message. Like others, he was enraged by the idea of giving another owner what dealers had built up for years.

"I equate this to the government coming in and taking your home and giving it outright to your neighbor. I invested in this business, my employees, and property for twenty-five years. It's my investment but the neighbor [dealer] is reaping the rewards," he said, trying to explain his anger. "I know it's wrong. It's absolutely wrong," he managed to say.

* * *

Tammy Darvish continued to be astounded that the wrongs being done to dealers could be swept under the rug and cloaked in vague terms such as competitiveness and marketplace performance. People's constitutional rights were being sandblasted away. One of the key issues buried under all the hype was the illegal nature of property seizures. Dealers and their lawyers kept hammering on it. But besides Congress, was anyone listening?

Her heart ached for old-line dealers like Blankenbeckler, the Painters, Bill Wallace, and the Lunts. She knew they were solid citizens, concerned about their families, communities, and customers. They were everyday people like her friends, relatives, and neighbors. To her, they were America.

She knew Florida dealer Bill Wallace had deep regrets about losing his businesses and seeing seven of ten Chrysler outlets in his area go down. A ridiculous irony was that in his Florida market area, several of the dealers who were not rejected, considered "continuing" dealers, were filing bankruptcy at the time viable dealers faced cancelled contracts, Darvish pointed out.

"Are GM, Chrysler, and the auto task force exempt from complying with the basic rights of the US Constitution?" she asked Congress pointedly in one meeting. "Aside from the obvious greed and arrogance of the [gifted] dealers, how can this be happening in America? Why should dealers be stripped of everything they own and have their generational legacies, or their years of hard work, taken away and handed to a third party for free?" These were the questions of the year. No one could answer them.

But Darvish persisted. She could be stubborn too. "Right now, in Michigan, a Lexus dealer that was awarded a free Chrysler-Jeep franchise is selling that franchise for millions of dollars—around five million," she specified in 2009, citing the growing practice of gifting. "Congress not only has the ability but the duty to right this wrong. By supporting, cosponsoring, and enacting HR2743 and S1304, our leaders can allow the dealers to do what they have already proven they do best—helping our economy grow," by selling and servicing vehicles, she bluntly told Congress.

* * *

Fred Barber, the Spanish Fork, Utah, dealer was stunned to hear what Chrysler would say about him in the coming arbitration hearings. "What they said about me in discovery was crazy; I was shocked. Let's say they were less than forthright," he said about Chrysler and their lawyers. He was too nice to say he heard some outright lies, or exaggerations.

Dealers were often overpowered by Chrysler in arbitration, with five or six corporate lawyers appearing to the dealers' one, or none. "They were going against dealers losing $50,000 to $100,000 a month trying to keep their doors open, trying to stay alive," Barber observed.

Nearly twenty months later he did not know of one happy dealer out there, even among the survivors. After two years, he'd heard of maybe one Chrysler dealer back in business. The Barbers' costs to go after the company were financially crippling, he said. "It was brutal. I easily spent $100,000 fighting them."

The Barbers were slowly building up but squandered "massive resources" in trying to get back up to speed, Barber said. Chevrolet's arrangement put him in a temporary dealer pattern where he could sell their products but had to meet very stiff targets to survive. "It's called a performance agreement and requires us to hit a quota of sales, have certain CSI scores, working capital requirements, and install their 'image' program in the store." The so-called image program called for steep facility investments.

Originally, the Barbers had placed their Mitsubishi franchise in the more upscale Provo-Oren market. But after the Chrysler and GM closures, the banks terminated their floor-plan funding lines and called all of their building loans due, meaning they had to close the Orem location too. The Barbers decided to move their active Mitsubishi franchise to Spanish Fork in the vacant Chrysler building, close to their GM store. They were just trying to generate enough revenue to stay alive. "We're still clawing our way back," Fred Barber said two years after the Chrysler and GM closures.

Spanish Fork was still a small enough town (population around thirty-one thousand) that businesses such as car dealerships live or die by their reputations and good deeds with customers.

As a longtime community contributor, Barber had to cut back on his philanthropic efforts. "We used to give to everything that happened here," Barber noted. "It's really hard on me that after twenty-seven years, I have to tell people who call or come in for community support, 'No, we can't do it right now.'" Barber's car business also dropped from seventy to twenty-five employees after being cancelled.

That was one of the bitterest pills for him to swallow.

* * *

Chevrolet dealer Steve LaBelle knew what dealers were talking about when they said they were being "product starved." Many so-called restored dealers also complained of this problem in many parts of the country, so it seemed it was not a regional or isolated issue. They couldn't sell products they couldn't get.

"It's criminal how the auto task force, not knowing the industry, could make these swift decisions about it. I think the whole thing was criminal," said LaBelle, in Bridgewater, Massachusetts, whose GM store had been cancelled, despite good performance scores.

"I was in the second wave of wind-down dealers. In February, after arbitration passed as part of the new law, I applied for arbitration. While I was waiting, GM put another dealer in my primary market area, in fact in the very building I'd asked for a year earlier."

Congress had asked the automakers not to do that while negotiations were going on between dealers and the automakers, LaBelle said. Indeed, the automakers said they were putting a moratorium on dealer placements or assigning them to "third parties," for a certain time period, but dealers doubted that they honored it.

GM argued in negotiations that LaBelle's DPS (dealer performance scores) were low, "But that's not true," he said. He showed them his sales and service records and well proved his point. LaBelle understood how some low-performing dealers could be terminated, but these were usually the exceptions, not the rule. "With someone selling ten new cars a year out of their house or gas station, it may be justified, but dealers who relied on selling cars and had a full-fledged dealership were axed—and this was their primary source of income," he said.

These were not "Craig'sList sellers" or often small-lot "we tote-the-note" (where dealers hold on to [or "tote"] the car note, and the buyer pays the dealer directly, rather than a bank or other financing service) dealers. There are other confusing terms traditional sellers use, such as "buy here, pay here," "in-house financing," "no one refused credit," "guaranteed credit approval," or some combination of these terms. The internal lingo can confuse customers. By buying a vehicle at a buy-here, pay-here store, customers simply finance their purchase through the dealer instead of a bank or other financing service. In doing so, payments go straight to the dealer.

The terminated group often included well-established dealers who produced the numbers, LaBelle noted, no matter what type of financing methods they used. He worked with CRDR in their efforts to reinstate all dealers unilaterally. That was their hope anyway. Or they would keep pushing and agitating for change. *It had a lot to do with why I had a target on my back,* he later thought.

* * *

In one shining, hopeful moment, Senator Ted Kennedy called Mark LaNeve, the GM sales and marketing chief, and asked him to come up with another plan to save money, something other than axing the dealers. Senator Kennedy could barely speak, LaBelle recalled. He was on his deathbed when Barney Frank brought up the dealer problem to him. Long a fighter against injustice, Kennedy took the side of the rejected dealers, LaBelle said.

Kennedy also wrote to Fritz Henderson at GM and pleaded with him to reinstate LaBelle because of his excellent performance. If Kennedy hadn't died in August 2009, who knows how much traction the "save-the-dealers" campaign would have gained early on, dealers like LaBelle wondered. Kennedy reportedly had sway with Obama. It was Kennedy, after all, who gave the Obamas their first pet in the White House, a Portuguese water dog.

LaBelle raised another point that some overlooked. "Dealers pay taxes and form a substantial base of local employment. If the politicians had helped immediately when we were begging earlier, we could have got up and running sooner. We really got screwed." Not by Congress, he said, but by the other powers that be—the corporate execs and the auto task force.

Dealers also fund numerous community activities and charities—from kids' baseball, soccer, and hockey teams to various youth groups to March of Dimes and cancer fund-raising drives, LaBelle said. One closed dealer who employed at least one hundred people in the Midwest said his annual donations to charities ran more than $25,000. That didn't include fund-raising drives for organizations he belonged to. All that dried up when he was shut down.

From May to September, some dealers at Chevrolet stores received no cars—or very few—from the factory. LaBelle was one of those. "We're still not getting inventory," he said in October of 2010, long after things should have been resolved and he had been reinstated. "I received a total of twelve cars in four months."

Even some dealers with agreement letters to return weren't getting products, he said. "It's like we have no history with them." By pulling back on products, he thought automakers were saying, "We're going to force you out anyway." During one forlorn period, he told himself: "They don't want me on the team." Some GM officials, however, explained they were cutting back on production and closing plants or cutting shifts around the country, and that accounted for the product shortages. Hard times were everywhere. They were not singling out certain dealers, GM said.

In mid-October, Steve LaBelle, a once-prominent Chevrolet dealer, closed up shop and had to let most of his employees go. He said later, "I couldn't survive selling parts and service." Especially in the new economy. He opened a "pre-owned" (used car) operation but was seeing a slow start-up.

The good times were memories of yesteryear.

When Dealers Wept

Nationwide, the statistics were alarming. In metro Detroit, an area severely battered by the economy, nine rejected dealers alone employed nearly a thousand people; many were proven performers. They paid $7.7 million combined in federal income taxes and nearly $1 million in state property taxes in 2008. This data came from the dealers who compiled it themselves to show lawmakers and courts the economic impact of their closures in a once-vital area of the country.

Richard Mealey was one of those high-performing dealers. He had paid good wages in fairly affluent Troy, Michigan, and ran a nearly seventy-million-dollar Chrysler-Jeep operation, Birmingham Chrysler Jeep (BCJ). It was his family's sole franchise. After winning numerous Chrysler awards and serving as the Detroit area dealers association president, he never thought he'd be out in the cold. Like others, he'd paid his dues. Now he found himself thrown under the bus by Chrysler.

Chrysler shut down Mealey's forty-three-year business after he had invested more than $9 million into the facilities to promote and upgrade them. The stores ran smoothly with family members and dedicated employees at the helm. His sons-in-law, Jim Casper and Paul Konkal, and his nephew, Jonathan DeWindt, later had to find jobs elsewhere after being groomed for years to run the family business. They planned that their children would one day be fourth-generation successors to the business.

After four decades as a Chrysler dealer, he had three weeks to close shop and dispose of parts, a body shop, and an inventory of three hundred-plus cars. Soon after that, his franchise was gifted to a mega-dealer down the street. He could see that dealer's building from his office windows.

Mealey's successful dealership operation was located in a once-expanding high-tech region. His dealership was on Maple Road, a main artery connecting the northern suburbs of Detroit, in a desirable location called the Troy Motor Mall.

Richard Mealey appeared in New York bankruptcy court to try to defend his rights in late May. Before that appearance, he submitted a five-page document and backup materials to the Manhattan court where he testified. It outlined his position and included operating data and financial information on BCJ that might sway an objective or dispassionate judge. But that's not what happened with Judge Arthur Gonzalez, the judge hearing the automaker bankruptcy case.

Mealey succinctly described the state of the slashed dealers. "Bankruptcy has conveniently usurped all of our rights according to franchise laws. Despite our many years of success, profitability, and community contributions, we [rejected dealers] have been given no golden parachute as executives receive, no buyout packages as line workers received, no bailouts as the factory received, and no viable options or rights as business owners," he wrote.

Some dealers related they had their life-insurance policies—which they had paid into with Prudential Insurance through Chrysler—mysteriously cancelled.

Mealey also said, "BCJ meets or exceeds all of Chrysler's stated criteria for choosing one dealership over another. The manufacturer's lack of judgment, unfairness, and seeming randomness in its decision to terminate Birmingham Chrysler Jeep is clearly demonstrated by analyzing BCJ's past and current performance." His performance record, he showed, was more than outstanding.

As one example of thousands of dealers, Mealey's annual payroll for about one hundred employees was about $5 million, including benefits, in 2008. And his combined tax bill was at least $1.6 million a year. His annual payout to local suppliers was nearly $1.9 million. Those people all frequented local shops, restaurants, taverns, dry cleaners, gas stations, and so on. That pipeline was shut down with the cutting of one major employer, a single car dealer in devastated southeastern Michigan.

He had prepared volumes of materials for his court presentation. What he wasn't prepared for were his own emotions as he talked about letting his employees go, losing his franchise, and telling his family there were no jobs for them. Halfway through their testimonies, Richard Mealey and several other dealers found it hard to continue, even though it was on their own behalf. Their emotions were still raw. There were many emotional moments as dealers testified during the bankruptcy hearings, attendees recall. Some wept in front of strangers. Observers in the courtroom, such as Tammy Darvish, choked up too.

Jim Tarbox, another Chrysler dealer who was shuttered, was one of about twenty dealers sworn in in early June. The Rhode Island dealer fought back emotions as he told about the moment he learned that the franchises for his pair of dealerships were part of the Chrysler termination list. "I thought there must be a mistake," he said. However, he acknowledged he had posted a loss for 2008, like many dealers across the nation in a severe economic downturn.

He also said he had won awards for both sales and service in other recent years Chrysler was considering.

That public bankruptcy hearing ended up a "kangaroo court," as some dealers and observers put it. There were no tender mercies rendered in the cold light of that court. But the written records of their testimonies are public and told the story long after they left the witness stand.

In June, Judge Gonzalez ruled in favor of Chrysler. And hundreds of dealers were left outside the system, holding the empty bag. Main Street car dealers were going by the wayside, and most didn't know what they had done wrong. As one consultant noted, the death of the old boulevard, or Main Street, dealer was in play across the nation.

Meanwhile, anti-Chrysler and -GM sentiment was building in places other than dealerships. Customers, employees, suppliers, and other small businesses were being adversely affected in every town where dealers did business. Some spoke out.

One example is Tim Kersenbaum, who owns Tricsity Computer Solutions in Troy, Michigan. Supplier firms are the ones businesses hire to keep their own operations going. Technology supposedly is a safe business to be in, Kersenbaum thought some years ago. He supplied tech services to dealerships and other businesses. His was one of the thousands of smaller businesses nationwide to lose their contracts and substantial income when the rejected dealers scaled back or shut down.

Kersenbaum wrote to Richard Mealey after his store closed, expressing his sheer disbelief. "I could give ugly examples describing the devastating impact the closing of the dealership caused its ownership and employees, but I would like to point out that there are many others who were crushed," he said. Like himself. Kersenbaum lost much of his income at the same time his wife lost her job. What's more, he couldn't believe there was no longer a Chrysler-Jeep store on the main strip in Troy leading to Birmingham, part of the affluent Troy Motor Mall and home to dealerships in a dealer-row concept.

He had seen for himself that Mealey's store once had many happy employees and customers. He said it was one of the most friendly work environments he'd ever been in. That he attributed to Richard Mealey and his wife, their genuine fondness for the business, and for people. The move by Chrysler to cut good dealers has brought "nothing but devastation to many, many families," Kersenbaum said.

Jackie Mealey couldn't help thinking that small-business owners had become victims of corporate cronyism. "The very tax dollars dealers and private citizens have paid in have been used to take away, to confiscate their property," she said of the nationwide closures.

"At the very moment we were closed, all of our income stopped. We still owned the dealership property and buildings, and paid taxes, the mortgage, and loans on it, as well as a state-of-the-art collision shop where we also ran our Mopar parts operation," said Mealey. They had ninety employees at BCJ, earlier 114, and had to let them all go. Mealey's dealership also was the second-largest parts distributor in Michigan—with its own body and collision shops—and among the top fifteen parts and Mopar dealers in the nation. But those kind of numbers did not register with bean counters doing radical surgery on US car dealers.

Nearly eighteen months after the closures, Jackie Mealey could finally talk about the sense of anguish that overwhelmed her husband and other dealers. "We all felt so betrayed at how the whole matter was handled. The dealers were Chrysler's best customers, and yet with all the money they spent trying to fight us, they could have done the ethically and morally right thing. They could have at least paid us what we were worth to close down," she said. "It's simply outrageous what they did to the car dealers of America."

After spending more than $20,000 fighting the closure, the Mealeys stopped the legal wrangling and got a minimal settlement. Richard Mealey said it didn't cover their shutdown costs, let alone their nine-million-dollar investment in the business over at least eight years.

When Chrysler cut Mealey's BCJ franchise it was clearly outperforming the nearest Dodge dealer six miles away, the Mealeys said. But instead of allowing BCJ to assume the Dodge franchise, Chrysler arranged for a third-party mega dealer to purchase Dodge, then gifted Mealey's dealership to another mega dealer one-quarter mile away, they said.

Gifting, of course, usually meant it was given to them free.

"This was just another devastating aspect of this whole closing situation," Jackie Mealey said.

Nearly twenty months later, Richard Mealey was able to express his frustration. "It's excruciating to see all your assets gifted to another dealer. Every day you wonder what has happened to morals, ethics, and conscience in our country. We pray that someday this American tragedy will all be investigated," he said.

Jackie Mealey was happy about one thing. Her husband's health was holding up. She knew of many stories of dealers and employees who suffered major health problems, even a number of suicides, connected to the closures. It's the other side of the dealer problem no one wants to talk about. There's apparently no real data yet on the mental and physical health issues that resulted from the dealer debacle. But the anecdotal evidence shouts it loud and clear. It perhaps will be the focus of future research.

Emotional stress and health risks are related to business closures and unemployment. Yet, it's not something the bean counters care to think about when they are slashing away and calculating numbers on a spread sheet. It's not part of the bottom line. Those items after all are about numbers, not people.

* * *

While GM was tough on dealers, they at least allowed eighteen months to wind down operations, thinking this was a saner approach to ultimately cutting out their former business partners, many dealers said.

Chrysler, meanwhile, took a harder stance. There was little wiggle room for Chrysler dealers on the chopping block. When the 789 Chrysler dealers (Chrysler, Jeep, Dodge) got cancellation notices, they had less than a month to close down. Never mind the emotional adjustment needed to handle a great shock. Tell that to your shrink. There was no bereavement time at these funerals, dealers were reminded.

Auto insiders and dealer lawyers remarked that Chrysler brought down the ax swift and fast. And the two company's approaches to handling the same problem were vastly different.

"Chrysler rolled a bomb into dealerships and blew them away. GM took a more cautious approach, giving them time to wind down and then offering negotiating room," said David Cole, industry analyst at the Center for Automotive Research in Michigan. He thought the GM approach was ultimately saner.

Some GM dealers also struggled and had difficulty staying afloat for long. The franchise owners in wind-down status often found themselves in limbo. They tried to stay in business selling used cars, or buying new cars from other dealers to sell. But many could not keep up the expense of running the business on shoestrings, or as used car centers.

So why were dealers taken out in such a cruel way? They still ask one another that question. Most were loyal and produced the numbers. It was like looking at a math problem and getting the same answer each time, yet the answer was rejected by some authority. And the common refrain, the dealers' answer, was always the same: "It does not make sense!"

Attorney Len Bellavia in New York said most of the thirty-nine dealers he represented later in hearings had been profitable and loyal, even if not subservient to the automakers.

Like many of his peers, Ron Marhofer of Marhofer Chevrolet in Stow, Ohio, never thought his would be among the shuttered dealerships. The dealership had been doing well and received no explanation for the non-renewal. "The answer I was given when I specifically asked was, 'We can't tell you,'" he told local media.

Marhofer, president of the Ron Marhofer Auto Family, was devastated. He appealed to GM without success. He was left with an empty storefront, one of several dealerships owned by the family. In two years through June, Marhofer's dealership had sold more Chevrolets in the county than any other Chevrolet dealer. Like other dealers whose contracts were pulled, he was left wondering why—part of the dealer puzzle.

* * *

"We still live in America. People may think this can't happen to them, but if it happened to us, it can happen to anyone," Gina Russo said of the closures. Russo had worked in her father's Detroit-based dealership, Lochmoor Chrysler Jeep, since high school. Gus Russo had opened the store in 1979.

On that fatal day in May they, too, got the burn notice from Chrysler. Actually, they first got the news earlier since it was being blasted on news and Internet sites everywhere, including YouTube. The Russos had been attending a family wedding in Florida and rushed back immediately. Their employees were in turmoil. "It was devastating; it had to be a mistake," Gina Russo recalled thinking at the time.

The Russos lost their prominent Chrysler facility bordering Detroit and Grosse Pointe. It had been Gus Russo's store for thirty years, boasting several upgrades. Grosse Pointe signals the beginning of the upscale area on the eastern side where Detroit ends and Grosse Pointe kicks in. But their dealership property was in Detroit, reeling from nearly 20 percent unemployment, a retail housing crisis, and reported crimes in ex-Mayor Kwame Kilpatrick's office.

Gus Russo tried writing to Chrysler CEO Sergio Marchionne after he took the CEO office. Russo wanted to explain his long-term loyal relationship with Chrysler, going back thirty years. He'd also been among the top-selling Chrysler dealers in the nation for many years, earning every award the manufacturer bestowed on dealers, Gina Russo said.

Sure, he was hoping for a reprieve. Anyone in his shoes would have.

Gina Russo wrote letters too, sending them to anyone she could think of. She even fired off e-mails and made calls to Dave Bing's office. Bing, a former superstar with the Detroit Pistons and in the Basketball Hall of Fame, became mayor of Detroit in 2009 in a special election. Former Mayor Kwame Kilpatrick was ousted for various crimes, including an indictment on nineteen federal fraud charges and a conviction on obstruction of justice and parole violation, according to the *Detroit Free Press*. The former mayor also was caught up in a texting sex scandal with a former employee, uncovered by the *Detroit Free Press*.

His replacement, Dave Bing, was an auto-parts supplier in the city, and Russo figured he would understand the auto business. She heard nothing as a result of her appeals. To them, she was just another businessperson writing to complain. Another Detroiter with a problem. What was new?

On Jefferson Avenue, about six miles south of the Russos, former longtime GM dealer Dalgleish Cadillac also was shuttered. It was the last remaining Cadillac store in the city limits of Detroit.

"They were leaving us to hang out and dry," Gina Russo said. "There were no apologies coming from Chrysler or anyone. We have five-and-a-half acres and empty buildings in the city of Detroit, in a depressed economy. You can't sell it, so what are you going to do with it?"

What Gus Russo got in response to his Marchionne appeal was in some ways even more disturbing than hearing nothing at all. It was a "cease-and-desist" letter from Chrysler lawyers forbidding him to contact the CEO or anyone in the organization again.

It didn't seem to matter that theirs was the only Chrysler-Jeep store in Detroit and would now go to a competitor who had never sold the Chrysler-Jeep brands. It didn't matter that they had been loyal business partners to Chrysler for decades. What hurt most was that some months after the new dealer got their store, that owner made plans to sell it, for a cool $5 million or so.

"He is trying to sell my franchise!" Gus Russo erupted when he heard about it. "Now they're cutting us off at the knees."

Like many other dealers, Gus Russo, a child of Italian immigrants, had signed up for the American free-enterprise system long ago. "If the bankruptcies of Chrysler and GM had happened or not, the free market would have taken care of noncompetitive dealers. They would have closed or you'd see a lot of 'buy-sells' as other more profitable businesses scooped up failing stores," he said.

How was it accomplished, then, this killing of long-term dealers? Attorney Elaine Vorberg in Chicago has a theory. "The manufacturers' strategy was to shuffle everyone around. All kinds of relationships were killed. So there was no sentiment, nothing you could hold on to anymore." The new players barely knew the old players. It appeared in retrospect it was all part of the grand design early on, she said.

By reassigning field people, cutting staff, and making sweeping changes, Chrysler and GM, in a sense, were altering institutional memory, wiping out relationships built on years of service and working together. Nobody knew "who was on first" anymore. The game of musical chairs that ensued at Chrysler and GM with the bankruptcy filings assured that confusion and uncertainty were paramount.

Gus Russo shook his head when he thought about the auto task force, wanting to dismiss the hastily assembled group as quickly as they dismissed the auto dealers. "These are finance guys who have never signed the front of a check, only the back of a check," he said. "They've never met payroll. Wall-Street money is not something tangible," but speculative, he said. It's all speculation, and so was the big squeeze on dealers, he thought.

Russo believed the corporate guys enjoyed the process of taking out the dealers, the cherry-picking. "They could now say 'we can get rid of you, you, and you.' They couldn't wait to get rid of us." He added, "Did they get rid of the underachievers? Is anyone really looking at the numbers?" Gus Russo had his doubts.

The combination of the "money guys" suddenly running government with a desperate GM and Chrysler proved to be a toxic cocktail. That's what many dealers who discussed the subject among themselves believed.

To add insult to injury, near the end of October, before they closed shop entirely, Gina Russo sent a driver to pick up a part from the new Chrysler, Jeep, and Dodge dealer down the street, who had taken their franchise. But the dealer wouldn't take her fourteen-dollar check, so the driver returned empty handed. She had to send cash.

Some dealers and their families compared the dealership takings to a death in the family. Some compared it more to a murder, a mugging, and then being stripped of all your rights.

Will the last Cadillac dealer in town please turn off the lights?

On November 20, 2010, Dalgleish Cadillac was the last Cadillac dealership in the Detroit city limits to shut its doors. Although it closed officially on October 31, as part of the final wind-downs, the owners stayed open a few weeks longer, trying to take care of their customers, feeling responsible to them.

The dealership was run by the Dalgleish family: Charles Jr., Douglas, and Doug's two sons, Doug Jr. and Keith. The older brothers recall better times; Doug Sr. had served as president of the Detroit Auto Dealers Association, and its many fund-raisers benefited charities throughout the city and state.

"We put sixty people in the unemployment line—including us. And this happened to us when we still had people on the payroll," said Doug Dalgleish Jr. in a November 2010 *Detroit Free Press* article. He locked the door to the fifty-five-year-old dealership himself that last day. These were good-paying jobs in a city that was hard-pressed to find them.

"It's been like a death here," Keith Dalgleish told NBC-WDIV TV in Detroit. With Dalgleish's demise, Cadillac, as Detroit knew it, is a ghost now.

The rise and fall of Dalgleish Cadillac is a classic Detroit story of a four-generation family business. For decades, it meshed with the American Dream. It's now a classic tale of the demise of the American Dream. There were several thousand of these stories. Most were never told.

Minority Dealers Take Stock

Minority dealers also took big hits with the dealer cuts. Many minority dealers had an uphill climb. In the country where they had made slow gains in the last forty years or so, it seemed they took one step forward but three steps back.

Minority groups lost significant ground, especially at GM, in 2009. How bad was it? In the General Motors Minority Dealers Association network, estimates from GMMDA were that more than 30 percent of dealers were targeted for closure when GM restructured.

"This is destroying people's lives. We need dealer support from government and the auto task force to make GM and Chrysler do the right thing," said Marjorie Staten, executive director of the GMMDA in Detroit, at the height of the battle to restore dealers to their businesses.

"I am terribly disappointed that that GM has put forth a plan that does not appear to sufficiently provide a reasonable opportunity for reinstatement, additional compensation, or other appropriate relief for the minority GM wind-down and Saturn dealers," she told Detroit media after the closures.

"It's a heck of a quandary. It's a dilemma," said Desmond Roberts, about the closure of several hundred minority dealerships in a *Ward's Auto* story. Roberts, a Chicago-area Chevrolet and Chrysler dealer, was a former chairman of NAMAD, which had become highly proactive on minority dealership closure issues. His stores survived the debacle, but he spoke out for other dealers. "My responsibility is to minority dealers. We're a viable part of society—no longer a voice that can be silenced. There are too many minorities in the general population not to be represented in auto dealerships."

If the shakeups at Chrysler and GM were any warning, a disproportionate amount of black-owned franchises were closing by 2010, minority leaders warned. Of nineteen thousand new automobile dealerships, fewer than twelve hundred, or 5 percent, were owned by ethnic minorities, said Damon Lester, NAMAD president, when he testified before the House Judiciary Committee in May of 2009. Chrysler's termination of about eight hundred dealer contracts that month condensed ethnic dealerships by 25 percent, he said.

The domestic industry was slated to cut some three thousand dealers by 2010, including the brands cut. Some reports estimated 240 minority dealers would be closed among all brands in 2009, according to NAMAD statistics. That may seem a small number, but the pool of minority owners is much smaller than their non-minority counterparts who were targeted.

Minority-dealership owners such as Greg Williams faced their own bitter struggle. After he lost his New York–based dealership, former New York–based Huntington Chevrolet owner Williams waged his personal fight for survival at a political level by urging Congress to restore dealership rights. At the same time he was fighting against GM and its financial arms, GMAC and Motors Holding, GM's investment arm, alleged debts of more than $5 million they said he owed. When they added in inventory and loan balances, the tally was several million dollars higher.

"I'm fighting to keep my store. I'm still calling Congress and meeting with my congressional reps. It's our only hope," Williams said at the time. He was asking for relief in what he believed were unfair debts in the wake of GM's bankruptcy. The finance arms were talking millions here, but he had no income. He finally got a settlement from GM and the old GMAC but could not disclose the amount because he had signed a confidentiality agreement.

His story is all the much harder because he fell from such a high place. In 2003, he was a GM "dealer of the year" and served as former chairman of the GM Minority Dealer Advisory Council, both prestigious honors. He was one of only 110 dealers of nearly six thousand to receive the honor in 2003, according to a congratulatory letter from then CEO Rick Wagoner.

Williams whittled down his debts slightly but was again told some time later that he owed more than $5 million, he said in several media accounts. Tell that to a drowning man who is offered water to drink. At this writing, Williams was no longer in the dealership business and had retired to Atlanta.

* * *

In 2009, the Obama administration poured billions into bailing out GM and Chrysler with public money, on top of billions from the Bush era. Many dealers believed that actions in Congress were their last hope for surviving the debacle.

Steve Rattner and crew generally saw Congress as interfering with the restructuring of the Detroit Two and tried to bypass them in making decisions, as Rattner related in *Overhaul*. "The auto rescue succeeded in no small part because we did not have to deal with Congress," he wrote. In his *Overhaul* book, he also criticized the SIGTARP report as "ludicrous" when it said the task force "erred in pushing GM and Chrysler to accelerate the pace of dealer closings."

Hearing of the report's findings, he muttered, "Dealers again!" as if exasperated.

Dealers, meanwhile, saw Congress as a hope for pardon from the guillotine.

* * *

Nicholas D'Andrea, a former Chicago GM dealer, and his daughter, Elaine Vorberg, were attending the mid-July dealer rally in Washington DC, put together by the CRDR group. This occurred the morning after the group learned that Steve Rattner had resigned as the car czar.

The two were eating breakfast and the local news was in the background. As the news anchors went to commercial, Aretha Franklin's anthem song "R-E-S-P-E-C-T" began playing, immediately catching Vorberg's attention.

Alarmed that the news program might have been honoring the queen of Soul (a Detroit native) posthumously, Vorberg turned to her father, asking, "Did something happen to Aretha Franklin?"

"No. Maybe she's the new car czar," he quipped. Her father had operated the once-profitable D'Andrea Buick-Pontiac-GMC until its closing. He remembered when Aretha sang for America in her glittering head regalia at the Obama inaugural in January, seven months earlier.

It was a small happy moment for them, Vorberg recalled. Vorberg saw that her father could still draw on his old sense of humor even though he was bitter about the hurt done to himself and car dealers across the nation. In late October, the votes on dealer reinstatement dragged in Congress, and dealers were growing discouraged.

Tammy Darvish was trying to ease the ongoing tension that prevailed when she asked Rob Smith, "So where will these people go if there really is no hell?" She further asked, "And why should we move our businesses that are already established? Chrysler refuses to show their criteria to us." Smith couldn't help but smile at her comments. In one of their many informal exchanges, he knew Darvish only wanted to make a dire situation seem humorous, if not tolerable.

Dealers still had not seen objective termination criteria from Chrysler, and trusting the automakers to fulfill any pledges was coming hard. Smith, who was a top leader in CRDR, knew that too.

At that time, Chrysler had put another offer on the table. The company proposed to give dealers the ability to get up to 103 open points (new dealer locations) across the country. But many of those open points were being assigned to other chosen dealers. The rejected ones, the ones left out of the party, viewed this as another betrayal. Another outrage.

Chapter 9—Something Happened: Zombies and Stepford Wives

Those who cannot remember the past are condemned to repeat it.
—Philosopher George Santayana, *The Life of Reason or the Phases of Human Progress*

Drive along major highways such as Telegraph Road and Jefferson and Mack Avenue in metro Detroit, or Wisconsin Avenue (Route 355) in the DC–Maryland–Virginia area, or the 1-10 service highway on the east side of New Orleans, home of the parish districts and concentrations of small businesses once underwater after Hurricane Katrina. Or take Main Street winding through St. George, Utah, and small towns in Ohio, Illinois, Pennsylvania, Tennessee, or elsewhere. Among still-vibrant businesses, shuttered dealerships and closed businesses assault the eyes.

Copping Chevrolet's old theme song, "See the USA in Your Chevrolet," it's not a pretty picture.

Seven months elapsed between the closure announcements from Chrysler and GM in May to the action on dealer rights in Congress in December. The journey was fraught with both hope and mind-numbing disappointment. Many of the more than two thousand affected dealers would connect in one way or another through the group representing only them, CRDR.

"A lot was done on the manufacturing side that gave the automakers the opportunity to prune out the dealers they wanted to get rid of. Steve Rattner and others on the auto task force demanded the cuts be made but didn't specify the dealers to be cut," said Bob Dilmore, former GM fleet sales vice president, now an automotive consultant in Richmond Hills, Georgia. He also formerly managed a group of dealerships and owned four dealerships.

"The old boulevard-style dealer, the Main-Street dealer, is going by the wayside with the closure actions of GM and Chrysler. They want to move more toward a mall concept in cities where they can get tax breaks and presumably reach more people," Dilmore said after the cuts were made. "And dealers today need to have more than one brand to survive."

Dilmore believed the damage done to dealers was irrevocable in many ways. "GM and Chrysler, along with the whiz kids from the Treasury Department, have effectively destroyed the value of dealer franchises. They have also put a giant crack in the overall automotive franchise system. On average, a dealer today has at least ten million dollars in assets, plus land and buildings. Who, in the future, will take the risk of one day losing it all because a greedy manufacturer couldn't manage their business?" he asked.

Who indeed? Many of the entrepreneurial, risk-taking generations of dealers have been wiped out. The oppressive darkness of shuttered buildings and decimated dealers was getting even more ominous along the boulevards of broken dreams.

* * *

Colleen McDonald is one of several thousand Chrysler and GM dealers whose stores were cut in the rush to judgment in 2009. McDonald and her husband, David, owned and operated the family businesses in Livonia-based Livonia Chrysler Jeep Inc., Taylor-based Century Dodge Inc., and Farmington Hills–based Holiday Chevrolet Inc., all in Michigan. "[Automakers] lied to the courts, to the public, and to lawmakers. It's all a big train wreck," she said. And the dealers who are part of what Chrysler calls Project Genesis mostly have still not upgraded their facilities, which Chrysler said was a requirement for any of the cut or returning dealers, she pointed out.

Rather than see her closed Chrysler dealerships add to the blight, she and her husband kept them open as long as possible, selling used cars and doing service work. But they couldn't afford that for long.

McDonald's Chrysler-Jeep franchise in Livonia was located in a moderately affluent suburb of Detroit, and run by her husband, while she ran the GM

Chevrolet store in Farmington Hills. The McDonalds also had a Dodge store on Telegraph Road in Taylor, the far western corridor of an area called "downriver."

Business partner Chris Marinos helped oversee that store. Now, a sore spot in a community battered by economic woes, the store was a victim of looting after it closed. Before all three stores were listed for closure during the automaker bankruptcy proceedings, the McDonalds' group, Holiday Automotive, reported more than $115 million in 2008 revenue companywide, and had around 170 employees. Those numbers soon went down to zero.

McDonald's stores were part of the dealerships targeted for closure during the Chrysler bankruptcy. The automaker's troubles did not exactly go away with federal loans and alliance with Fiat. Then GM, in the throes of bankruptcy reorganization, informed dealers it would not renew their franchises. But GM was giving them until October 31, 2010, when their contracts expired, to wind down. It was a new definition of life on the line, dangling in despair.

Colleen McDonald is still livid about the closures. "In sales, you don't cut your arms off. GM realized later they made a mistake when its sales went down. Taking away your customers didn't make sense. They didn't have to terminate dealers to go forward with the reorganization plan in bankruptcy. They were losing sales already; you can't reduce dealers by another 25 percent [the targeted cuts] and expect to win in the marketplace," she said.

Like other dealers, she thought that GM's and Chrysler's customer approval ratings might "go sideways" as things played out. Of course she worried about her family's livelihood too.

Dealers took a big hit, but the impact on customers and communities also was devastating. McDonald said her customers were forced to drive farther away and switch to stores too busy to deal with them properly. "My customers would call and say something like, 'I don't get treated like I used to with you … I don't like it at all,'" after she had referred them to other dealerships, she said.

* * *

In testimony before Congress in June, top executives from Chrysler and GM, which emerged from bankruptcy in June, said that the closures were necessary to create competitive, leaner companies.

In Washington DC, the auto task force made quick decisions with the ease of finance experts, the bean counters who evaluate strictly on whatever the current bottom line tells them. Facing deadline pressures, they applied dentistry surgical techniques to excise the waste. Too many dealers were toxic assets, they determined.

Dealers themselves estimate that perhaps 10 percent of those cut were underperformers, as the automakers labeled them. The free-enterprise system would have taken them out on its own—without a penny spent by taxpayers or automakers, dealer advocates argued.

Closer to Detroit, Jim Press was the bad-news bearer to DC and New York. He talked about the need to close dealers for competitive reasons. Press later would recant his statements about the value of closing the dealerships, saying he never personally agreed with the plan.

At GM a variety of execs sang the same tune of excess dealers. But when it mattered most, the company minions sang to the corporate chorus: the dealer network is too large; dealers cost the company money; they must be cut if the companies are to be profitable and compete in a changing marketplace.

Stepford Wives and Zombies

By 2009, the country was in deep recession. Some leaders called it another Great Depression, especially in small towns and large urban cities. During the major dealer bloodbath that followed the corporate bankruptcies, even those in affluent communities felt the pinch. Major cities with high numbers of unemployed residents were in crisis. "Will work for food," said hand-scrawled cardboard signs held up by unemployed workers, looking more like beggars, on major street corners of cities, such as Chicago, Detroit, Indianapolis, and Oakland, California. A sign of the times (pun intended): the messages had changed from "give me money" to "give me work."

Unemployment had truly hit the working class, once the breadwinners and producers of America.

"They had dumbed down the UAW and the middle class," Detroit area dealer Richard Mealey said of the reckless policies of automakers and government, even before Obama. UAW workers, once among the highest paid in the world, were asked to take part in the "shared sacrifice" and surrender wages, benefits, and jobs in some cases. The Obama administration complained that they had inherited the problem from the Bush people, who they said drove up a huge deficit before departing in January 2009. Obama ran on a pledge of restoring the middle class, but that wasn't being seen as the war on dealers and high nationwide unemployment unfolded at the same time.

For years, GM cascaded messages down through their channels asking that everyone sing from the same hymnbook. To many, it seemed more of an order than a sincere desire for change and improvement.

Tammy Darvish called these corporate players "Stepford Wives," people who resemble zombies or lost souls. It wasn't that they were all bad people, but many had mortgaged their souls for a big paycheck, she thought. Many thought they were just doing their jobs, following orders, like good soldiers.

In some corporate cultures where employees are controlled by fear, or are overly concerned about moving up the corporate ladder, it is difficult for people to think for themselves and raise their voices to power. In instances where a fear culture pervades, too many leaders surround themselves with sycophants who are deferential to power and a paycheck.

At the corporations, they are often order takers and yes-men and women, who won't venture their own opinions or go against the grain. They may fear for their jobs or promotion possibilities if they speak out. It is hard for innovation to take root in such risk-averse cultures, consultants say.

Gone were the John DeLoreans and Lee Iacoccas, the former risk-taking leaders of GM and Chrysler, respectively. Bob Lutz, who spurred GM into changing direction, was relegated mostly to the product side of the house. He was GM's colorful recent product czar, brought out of retirement to wake up the automaker and freshen its offerings. He wasn't afraid to speak out and earned respect for it.

This is not to say everyone should rail against the company mantra—that's a sure way to get fired, risky for workers at lower corporate levels, especially those who are not represented by unions. But when something is wrong, when something is rotten in Denmark, somebody has to stand up and say so. That at least was the thinking at CRDR when the automakers and former Wall Street financiers took charge of excising the dealers from the sales picture.

Sales reports often showed the imports were thriving sales-wise in the country. But here were the automakers handing over more market turf by shutting down a huge chunk of their dealerships nationwide. Admittedly, it's hard to tell your bosses they might be wrong, but it's also hard to believe that no one dared to question these leaders to their faces, Darvish and other CRDR members thought.

In Rockville, an affluent Maryland suburb of Washington DC, about twenty miles northwest of the White House, the import factor is strong. Toyota, Honda, BMW, Mercedes-Benz, Nissan, Hyundai, and Kia cars and SUVs dominate the highways, freeways, and driveways of residents. The same is true for Bethesda, Maryland, about ten miles north of the White House.

These weren't future trends. These were current trends. Driving along Route 355, which snakes from DC to Maryland as it changes names from Wisconsin Avenue to Rockville Pike, and then Frederick Road and Urbana Pike, it hits you full force, like the setting sun glaring in your eyes. After the dealer closures in 2009, forty-five import-brand dealers were doing business on this US main highway, compared to seven Detroit domestic brands, according to CRDR data.

Where once sixty-four dealerships clustered along Route 355, the imports outnumbered domestics in 2009 by a ratio of six to one. That's not an example of market forces at work. That's an example of domestic dealers being taken out, one by one, and in huge numbers, dealers believed. And of course there was the shifting taste of consumers, who believed the domestic automakers couldn't build quality products.

In Maryland, fifty-eight Chrysler and GM dealerships were targeted to close, according to NADA and Auto Exec data. Ohio, Pennsylvania, Illinois, California, Michigan, and Texas were among the highest in dealership closures, NADA reported.

In Belvidere, Illinois, GM dealer Amy Wilcox ran Jack Wolf Pontiac-Cadillac-GMC Inc. She recorded outstanding performance and sales results. But in the end, it didn't matter.

Wilcox, like others, was totally perplexed. She had posted GM DART (Dealer Analysis and Reporting Tool) scores of around 150 (100 is tops) for each of the three years GM was looking at; and her store was 200 percent sales effective.

Those were superstar numbers, above all the minimums GM testified that they required. She met with the big names at GM then—Mark LaNeve, Jim Bunnell, and Brian Sweeny—in Detroit in late July. The leaders told her she was indeed a good dealer and that getting the wind-down notice had nothing to do with her performance.

Any sane person would have said, "So what gives?" and she did. "We were in the second phase of dealer cuts [by GM]. Since there was no performance issue, why on earth terminate us?" No one seemed able to answer her question.

She hated to think what she was thinking. "Could it be because I'm a female dealer?" Or was it because in 1997 she had pursued a lawsuit against GM to protest a competing dealer put in her market area? That seemed to be a common trend among the dealers closed who had excellent performance ratings.

Wilcox gave a detailed description of her dealership performance records on a complex spreadsheet. DART was supposedly the key measure GM was using to decide on who to close. The problem is that DART requirements kept changing and weren't applied consistently, dealers said.

"DART changed again with the round-two GM dealers," said Yale King, a closed Chevrolet and Chrysler dealer in Colorado. And his reasons for being shut down kept changing too, King said.

GM was still the largest domestic automaker but by 2008 was second in sales to Toyota globally. Once called Generous Motors, since it generously rewarded employees and key stakeholders, GM was bleeding red ink by 2008. The company had lost billions in profits that year, and the first half of 2009 was a shambles. GM was in housecleaning mood, dealers could see. It was harder to see, or understand, why dealers took the fall.

The US economy was still on life support after a massive infusion of federal cash. Automakers were on the cliff in early 2009.

In a famous scene in Paddy Chayefsky's *Network*, the Howard Beale character screams at the top of his lungs, "I'm as mad as hell, and I'm not going to take it anymore!" Beale, an emotionally distressed television anchorman, implores his onlookers: "Stick your head out and yell.... You've got to say, 'I'm as mad as hell, and I'm not going to take this anymore!' Then we'll figure out what to do about the depression and the inflation and the oil crisis. But first get up out of your chairs, open the window, stick your head out, and yell, and say it." Beale struck a national nerve in the oil embargo and inflation-weary mid-seventies.

The movie has an eerie relevance to the present day. Beale could have added the dealer, auto, and credit-housing crises to his "mad-as-hell" list, along with the financial bailouts of Wall Street.

The point is, change doesn't happen until people are conscious of it and act on their insights—even their outrage.

Despite more than $700 billion in TARP (Troubled Asset Relief Program) funds for the big corporations, Main Street was in trouble. Of that staggering sum, GM and Chrysler and its captive finance companies and suppliers were eligible for almost $82 billion in dedicated funds. Yes, in taxpayer dollars. And wasn't it these taxpayer dollars that were funding everything from the franchise closures to related job losses? And weren't taxpayer dollars placing new dealers in the former owners' markets; and these new dealers in many cases got the businesses virtually free? These were among the questions dealers asked themselves and Congress.

It was as if the axed dealers were paying for the companies' former excesses and management failures. As Richard Mealey said, "The corporations went bankrupt, not the dealers. But it was the dealers who took the biggest fall." The corporations got saved by government—using taxpayer dollars, of course.

There were many other signals that the automakers and the task force made hasty decisions on the dealer issues. The federal investigative report, called SIGTARP, came out too late in 2010 to do the closed dealers much good as they protested the massive cuts. But SIGTARP, headed by special investigator Neil Barofsky, concluded that the task force got it wrong when it came to shuttering dealers. The report led to even more speculation and actions by the lawyers and dealers who became increasingly involved and agitated. SIGTARP would take other legal twists and turns in the coming year.

Barofsky testified that the report looked at the accelerated dealer closures and found there was insufficient task force consideration and analysis of the cost of thousands of lost dealership jobs and how that contributed to the automakers' liability, not viability. Again, the words "it didn't make sense" surfaced on dealer closures.

When Tammy Darvish's group surveyed the closed dealers in the summer months, they found that dealers were adamant about getting their businesses back. As hard as the choice might be, it was better than no business. And it was a chance to rejoin the dealer networks, to do what they knew how to do—sell vehicles, fix cars, and serve customers. That was before the fighting became vicious.

The unpleasant facts were beginning to emerge even before SIGTARP, and some leaders would have to engage in "CYA," or "cover-your-ass" tactics. Power players such as Jim Press and Ed Whitacre reneged publicly on earlier statements made about dealer cuts being necessary.

The Darvish A-team was looking for supporters to their cause. A natural was Lee Iacocca, former chief of Chrysler Corporation when it was a success story. Iacocca would send a letter of support saying the dealers to his knowledge didn't cost the manufacturers money to support, as Chrysler claimed. It's what the dealer advocates had been saying all along.

After leaving Chrysler, Brian Schnurr, a former field manager, backpedaled too, saying privately to some dealers, "I wasn't the only one who made the decisions." Names were surfacing throughout the industry, including Steve Landry, Jim Press, Jack Gannon, and Bill Doucette for Chrysler. And of course Fritz Henderson, who ran GM for a few months, and his henchmen, got busy delivering what the government wanted: a leaner dealer body.

Attorney Mike Charapp in DC believed the automakers used bankruptcy as a quick and convenient tool to reject dealer agreements. But this kind of bankruptcy is a rare and unusual event, he said. The culling was hardly done precisely and scientifically, Charapp observed. The automakers were able to use the rejection process as a sword to forge their way ahead. "It gave them the opportunity to cut dealers, either because it didn't like their facilities, or they felt they weren't doing the volume job they wanted to see done, or because some [automaker] employees or executives simply did not like the dealer," Charapp said.

It's erroneous to think "the rejections in the Chrysler case and the wind-down agreements in the GM case were determined with some excruciating deliberation using scientific precision. In the end, they came down to the local offices saying who they wanted to keep and who they did *not* want to keep, with a rubber stamp from Detroit for the most part," Charapp said.

As several dealers intoned, "Corporate cronyism was alive and well in Detroit."

Enlarging the picture, Bob Dilmore said that under Chrysler's Genesis concept, the idea was to group the four Chrysler brands together in new facilities for the sake of image. Former GM executive Dilmore had served as expert witness in a number of termination and arbitration cases. During arbitrations, it came out that "at some point in time there was a real disagreement between the dealer and the factory [the automaker, in industry parlance] in every case involved in arbitration," Dilmore noted. This comment is significant because it comes from a veteran industry observer who once held a high-level sales position when GM was the top automaker in the world.

In some cases, the cut dealers were "dualed," meaning they operated another competing franchise on the premises, say a Chevrolet or a Ford store. "A Virginia Beach dealer did a remarkable job for Chrysler, and there was no reason to terminate him; but he was dualed with Mercedes-Benz on the same campus," Dilmore added.

How Mercedes-Benz, the premium German Daimler division, can be considered a competitor to Chrysler is anyone's guess. But apparently Chrysler thought so.

What led to all the drama in the heartland involving the dealers? How did this become a wedge issue, joining conservative and liberal forces? Barney Frank, Steny Hoyer, Ted Kennedy, Steve LaTourette, and Chuck Grassley linking arms in unity with the disenfranchised dealers? How did it overcome the partisan politics otherwise dividing the nation? Perhaps it was because it was a human issue, one that could affect any citizen who dared open a business and work hard, and then saw it pulled out from under him or her, the CRDR leaders said. This was a nonpartisan issue that any entrepreneur in the country should be concerned about, they maintained.

Tammy Darvish saw it as a violation of human rights and taking of property without warning or compensation. "This issue affects every entrepreneur in America who believes in protecting free enterprise as a fundamental way of operating a business," she said.

At the task-force level, the group was infatuated with the US Toyota model and foisted that on the restructuring carmakers. Toyota had many fewer dealers and was considered efficient and just more effective than the Americans in product manufacturing, design, and sales.

Corolla was one of Toyota's best-selling entry-level models in America and until the early 2010 recalls had a sterling reputation for bulletproof quality. Its Camry sedan was a perennial top seller, poised beside the Honda Accord, another top-selling sedan. The two often raced neck-in-neck. In 2008, the Chevrolet Malibu broke into the race and was cited as the Motor Trend Car of the Year. Ford Motor would later crack the code with its midline sedans reaping quality awards and surpassing many imports, as did the nimbly moving Hyundai Motor America, the Korean automaker.

But the real question was: Where have all the domestic buyers gone? If you're exporting US jobs, closing factories, diluting your product line, and laying workers off en masse, maybe the answer lies therein. Workers couldn't afford to buy new cars, and maybe their loyalty was slipping a tad. Jobs were to be had in the import sector, many observed.

At GM, they tended to make mistakes on the product side, analysts said. Even bringing in product guru Bob Lutz, an industry icon who had rotated through BMW, Ford, and Chrysler, didn't do the trick. And once the task force got hold of the auto business, in an effort to streamline and stem the tide of spending, more mishaps occurred.

"The elimination of Pontiac as a brand was a huge mistake for GM," Bob Dilmore said. Many of those buyers moved into the import market. GM had hoped they would turn to Chevrolets, or in some cases Buicks or GMCs, the surviving brands. They likely wouldn't go to Cadillac, the fourth and most expensive GM product line, unless they had big bucks.

In Massachusetts, dealer Steve LaBelle wrote to GM leader Mark Reuss after his closure and an unproven dealer had been moved into his market location. "After witnessing it firsthand, GM is losing market share by gross numbers as a result of reducing the dealer body. The customer, as we track it, is not going to the Chevrolet dealer down the road but to Ford or the import brands."

Chrysler, GM, and the task force got it wrong when they focused on dealers as the problem, LaBelle said.

At Chrysler, the problems were also management and product-driven, consultants such as Dilmore and Jim Wangers believed. Wangers was a California-based advertising pro who advised GM on product marketing decisions in the Pontiac era of muscle cars and image building. Wangers believed that GM's top marketers had lost their way in the 1980s and ushered in three decades of product failures.

By 2009, instead of looking internally at some bad management moves, the manufacturers blamed the dealers—and the competitive climate and erratic oil prices in a poor economy of stalled sales, the consultants thought.

Under the cover of federal bankruptcy, with Italy's Fiat CEO in control of Chrysler and 61 percent of government ownership in GM, the dealers took the greatest fall at that time. But it was a new day for the Detroit Two. They had a lifeline courtesy of the federal government.

State franchise laws were designed to protect dealers from many mishaps, like cutting them out arbitrarily, so the automakers were unable to ax the dealers earlier. Under bankruptcy protection, they saw their chance and seized it. "They saw a golden opportunity to prune out people who stood up and said 'you're wrong' to them," Bob Dilmore observed. Like many companies, Chrysler did not like confrontation, especially in courts and public forums such as media.

Bob Dilmore, like many others, defended the government's decision to bail out the automakers. Dealers also supported the auto bailouts. The auto bailouts were considerably different than those with Wall Street, which got a free pass. "Unfortunately, if the auto bailout had not occurred, I don't know what economic situation we would be in today. If GM and Chrysler were allowed to fail, it would have had a terrible effect on the country. What was wrong was rushing in and taking out the independent businesses," Dilmore said.

What happened in the 2009 dealer debacle should be a warning sign to all dealers, Dilmore noted. "Be careful who you franchise with and get all the bases covered, including documentation. Most dealers did not have great documentation when it came to the court process."

The fact is that eliminating dealers did not solve the long-term problems of the two automakers. Chrysler held out and got Fiat and was setting up dealers to sign separate franchise agreements to sell the small-car brand in the United States. "It's just more carrot dangling," Dilmore noted. He added that Chrysler took a tougher stand against dealers because the company felt it would have failed if forced to take back the 789 dealers.

Consultants noted that Ford was doing well in sales due to consumer confidence providing some market bounce—and because in certain parts of the country a good percentage of people do want to buy American products. Many consultants thought that Ford made the right decision in not pursuing bankruptcy and not accepting government bailouts. "Alan Mulally is proving to be one of the strongest industry leaders," Bob Dilmore said. For an ex-GM exec to say that is quite remarkable.

There was ample evidence to suggest that many Americans support the domestics and want to buy quality American-made products. Proof is what happened to Ford, which suddenly appeared on *Consumer Reports'* recommended buyer lists and guides. By 2010, Ford would clean up in new car and truck retail sales as GM and Chrysler stumbled.

Following the closure announcements, the state of mind among dealers was a state of total shock, as Dilmore described it. They couldn't believe it was happening, especially not to *them*. Later, they were not as furious with GM, who tried to soften their deals with monetary settlements and offers to bring back a good portion of dealers. But the Chrysler dealers remained enraged.

"They were urged to buy products and rebuild their stores and then were terminated. GM began to see how the closures affected Chrysler's sales and began settling cases, backing down here and there. They were more generous to the franchises they brought back and offered to pay them off in some cases," Dilmore said. All that helped GM, public-relations wise, he and some dealers who took settlements noted.

What about Those Criteria?

Proof. In the long run, dealers wanted incontrovertible proof that the automakers were using fair criteria to dismiss them. Most of them knew they couldn't be hung on performance. Their scorecards were solid, for the most part. One dealer estimated that fewer than 10 percent of dealers could be said to be poor performers.

But that proof would be a long time coming, especially for Chrysler franchise owners. Many had to wait to see if CRDR's battles on Capitol Hill would lead to legislation being passed; it was their last hope. Dealer groups such as NADA, NAMAD, GMMDA, and ATAE were also waging the fight for their constituents of dealers, but CRDR was engaged fully on all closed dealers' behalf.

Even Alfredo Altavilla, who headed Fiat's powertrain technology group, had testified in bankruptcy court that Fiat did not require Chrysler to reject dealers as a condition of the sale, dealers recalled. There was, however, much testimony showing there was no formula or scorecard in determining who would be rejected. But there were cases of personal vindictiveness, Darvish and other dealers said.

A Chrysler spokesperson said that the company measured areas such as sales, market region performance, customer and service satisfaction, and whether a dealer sold all three brands at the time or competitors' vehicles, as a dualed dealer. These were similar to GM's alleged criteria, but dealer advocates found them lacking specifics.

Much later, GM said it used criteria such as working capital, dealer performance, and customer satisfaction to select the 660 dealers to be reinstated. Other dealers could ask to be considered for financial settlements.

As much as anyone, Tim Doran, who headed the ATAE dealer group of executives, continued to push for clear criteria as to closure decisions. "We need specific criteria as we go through the process," Doran told Chrysler and GM officials more than once.

The evidence began mounting everywhere, from auto experts, analysts, internal executives, and the dealers themselves. Later, almost too late, a special government investigative report would confirm it. Some decisions had been arbitrary and unfair.

Colorado dealer Yale King, who lost Chrysler and GM franchises, said that Chrysler never had a "scoring system" per se, mostly relying on a rating called MSR, or minimum sales responsibility. GM used a number of factors, including DART scores, which seemed to change midstream, as more dealers were added to the lists.

King believed one of the most compelling observations to come out after the SIGTARP probe was the randomly applied criteria the automakers used. "I fought for this with Congress for months and believed I was the only dealer asked to come back to Detroit to meet with GM prior to arbitration hearings.

It did not do much good then as I wanted to have any and all criteria used—not the select criteria that GM had chosen."

In Massachusetts, Steve LaBelle, another warrior on Tammy Darvish's A-team, continually challenged GM and Chevrolet about criteria used to let him and other dealers go. LaBelle, who studied the dealer-closings issue every which way, believed the cuts using different criteria were applied at GM "because US Treasury told them they had to cut deeper after the original cuts, so they had to set a much higher bar to find a way to cut more dealers. Treasury didn't tell them what to use for a grade just that they must cut deeper," with different levels of criteria applied to the two levels of cuts at GM, at least.

Between July and September of the fatal year of the cuts, LaBelle pushed the corporate folks to reveal their rationale. Finally, a peeved GM zone manager outlined the criteria which he claimed to have shared all along with the courts and public. The criteria, of course, changed depending on which wave of dealers you were in, dealers believed.

Since LaBelle was in "wave two" of the cuts, he learned that GM required a dealer performance summary (DPS) rating of eighty or higher. That number was raised from the seventy points the wave-one dealers had to meet. No one was able to explain why satisfactorily, he said. Maybe it was one of those "oops" moments for GM deciders. Or they had to use tougher criteria to round up more dealers, as he thought. The companies usually refused to explain their rationale for the decisions.

But LaBelle said he met all the performance criteria known. "My DPS score was 88.9 (eighty was required), and I showed the required three years of profitability," even in the tough 2008 period, he said. The minimum score required during the first round was seventy, he said. His high scores, on whatever measure GM chose, didn't seem to matter. Disillusioned, he began lining up with the side that said some dealers were closed arbitrarily and vindictively.

Meanwhile, noted industry analysts were also taking a stand on the dealer-closing issue. In *Ward's Auto* magazine, analyst David Cole said he could not in good conscience watch the eroding of domestic market share as the industry crumbled. "I could not just sit and watch what looks like the dismantling of the US auto industry, at least where General Motors and Chrysler are concerned."

Cole became a strong advocate for dealer rights and restoring the closed franchises, petitioning Congress and the SIGTARP group. Dealer consulting is not an area in which he normally gets involved as chairman of the Center for Automotive Research, an industry think tank in Ann Arbor, Michigan. As the son of the late Ed Cole, a former GM president, he is well-known in Detroit automaker circles. It's easy to say about him that he tends to have GM gasoline in his veins.

"When I looked at [the automakers'] plans to reduce dealers, it didn't have any common sense to it," he said. He was especially concerned about the closings of mid-size and rural dealers and the impact this would have on sales and market share. Cole said faulty logic was applied in shuttering GM's retail sales force and a significant portion of Chrysler dealers. "Brand elimination and dealer elimination will both prove to be negatives in keeping or growing market share," he said. Hit by steep domestic industry losses, Cole believed GM and Chrysler were losing focus on smaller, rural and mid-size markets, "and that would haunt them in years to come by eroding market share even further," he told *Ward's* magazine.

But bailing out the automakers never was a big issue for CRDR. They were for it, the committee members said. They wanted to see GM and Chrysler succeed. And the auto bailouts were considerably different than those concerning Wall Street, which got a free pass. Automakers received terms to repay the taxpayer-funded loans, with strict deadlines.

What Happened to Jim Press?

Opinions differ about what happened with Deputy CEO Jim Press after he left Chrysler that fall of 2009. In cases like this, the truth is rarely revealed. But by summer, word had leaked that Press was soon to be a goner. In vague corporate-speak, he "went on to pursue other opportunities."

His story is almost as interesting as what happened to kill the Chrysler business, auto insiders believe. To his credit, Jim Press made a mistake on the dealers and later admitted it. But a big PR mess resulted, and some customers may not want to buy Chrysler products again as a result, consultant Dilmore noted.

"We had the utmost respect for him," Darvish said. She and her father had worked with Press through four of their Toyota and Lexus facilities in his earlier years with Toyota. "I couldn't believe he would leave that prestigious job to go to Chrysler and get into all that trouble. Why would someone do that, and risk their whole career?" Almost two years later, Darvish was still perplexed by what happened to Jim Press. "I just think that desperate people do desperate things in desperate times, and he was probably promised a whole lot of money to move to Chrysler."

Jim Press visited the Darvish dealership in Maryland in November 2009. At the time, he confessed a few things to Tammy Darvish, but he didn't answer the question as to why he left Chrysler. He hinted at problems with Sergio Marchionne. Mostly he apologized to Darvish for what happened with the Chrysler store closings. He said he'd always liked the Darvish family when he worked at Toyota and wanted no hard feelings between them.

Before that visit, the media had reported by that summer that Press would be leaving Chrysler; media reports claimed he and Marchionne didn't see eye-to-eye. It's no secret that in the world of corporate politics there is only one true leader. In this case, Sergio was king, and he was bringing in his own group of loyal executives when the power shift from Nardelli occurred. The Italian automaker brought with him his own cadre of top executives—so co-president Tom Lasorda, formerly a GM manufacturing superstar hired by Chrysler, and Press had to go.

For his part, Marchionne was trying to separate the new Chrysler Group LLC from the old (old car co, as it was called in bankruptcy language). He needed to shed baggage from the past. He probably would have done that with or without pressure from Washington, auto insiders suggest.

So what happened to Jim Press? When he visited her dealership, Darvish tried to talk him into setting up a meeting with Congress and telling his story, exonerating the dealers. She also suggested a meeting with Congressman John Conyers' office, which was holding hearings at the time.

"Nah, it won't matter. They don't care," Press told her.

Tommy Gibbs, a former dealer-turned-consultant in Treasure Island, Florida, also a former Jim Press fan, couldn't believe the depths he had fallen to. One of the tragic footnotes and perhaps ironies in the auto collapse is the story of Press, once a revered exec with Toyota, whose life began to resemble a jigsaw puzzle at Chrysler, consultants such as Gibbs said.

Gibbs believed Press was in the wrong company at the wrong time at Chrysler. And Gibbs was sorely disappointed in Press's actions at Chrysler. "I'm furious that he didn't do more while at Chrysler," for the dealers and the company, he said.

Press, a superstar while at Toyota and its highest non-Asian ranking exec, seemed to fall apart after Chrysler lured him away for megabucks in the fall of 2007. Or he simply lost control at the company, which didn't listen to his views, especially on dealers. The thirty-seven-year veteran at Toyota occupied a top post at Toyota's North American operations, including the United States, Canada, and Mexico. The media later reported that Press was leaving Chrysler and owed almost $1 million in back taxes and was being sued by his credit union for defaulting on a $609,000 loan. News also broke that Press's problems were mixed up with women, money, and divorce. What's new in the big leagues? one might ask.

A *Fortune* magazine article ran in October, detailing Press's marital troubles. A week or so after that story, Press's wife, Linda, filed for divorce, and the rest was part of automotive history: Press testifying against dealers in bankruptcy court and Congress and then being pretty much sidelined in June at Chrysler with the arrival of Marchionne, the new CEO from Fiat.

Nardelli hired Press at Chrysler, where his Toyota experience obviously was considered valuable. Like his boss, he lasted there fewer than two years, a blink of an eye for top-level auto execs. As *Fortune* magazine said, "The first move [joining Chrysler] may have contributed to the second, and both have proved costly." *Fortune* magazine also wrote on October 1, 2009, that court records showed that Press's Chrysler salary was $2.4 million annually, plus a three-million-dollar signing bonus. "His overall compensation package when he went to Chrysler was reported as high as $50 million, but the value of any equity stake in Chrysler has plummeted after the automaker's trip through bankruptcy," *Fortune* said.

After exiting Chrysler, Jim Press joined the Renault SA-Nissan Motor Co. alliance as a consultant in global sales and marketing in July 2010. He had worked for Renault-Nissan for about four months, when Simon Sproule, a spokesperson for the alliance, made the announcement. But that position ended before its time.

Given Chrysler's reportedly tough stance on dealers during the bailout era, one is left to wonder: Did these guys not understand that Chrysler, as an American car company, an icon, came within minutes of being totally dissolved by the auto task force? What saved them was a simple vote by one task force overseer: Larry Summers, the president's chief economic advisor, had pressed the undecided Rattner to vote. Rattner threw in his cards, voting to save them, he admits in *Overhaul*. Then Larry Summers broke a tie. Chrysler survived by one vote. They couldn't be sold for a dollar, and one vote saved their necks. Go figure.

Collision Course: Divided Camps

In the long hot summer months ahead, the tension between NADA and CRDR festered and grew. But the committee became a well-oiled and energetic machine, if not well-financed. In the early stages, most of the operating money came from several hundred dealer members of CRDR and from its leaders, Alan, Jack, and Tammy.

NADA, at the time, had its own issues to contend with, including dwindling membership in an upside-down economy and a tendency to support the automakers' agenda. Closed dealers were not the group's only focus, Darvish knew. But in this case, it was doubly difficult to serve more than one master.

It appeared the trade group had its own systemic problems stemming from marketplace changes and internal priorities. When the time came to determine what position to take and what resources they could use on fighting the battle for rejected dealers, they were not able to lobby fully on their behalf. Only CRDR was in the position of being totally dedicated to waging the war for cancelled dealers, to taking on a single-minded mission, dealer lawyers observed.

While many continuing dealers supported their fallen peers, not everyone agreed that's where NADA resources should be directed. Some dealers stood to benefit from less competition while some had nothing to gain or lose. Others did not share CRDR's views on helping reinstate all the closed dealers. That issue was tearing closed and continuing dealers apart. It was as if they sat on opposite banks of the river, firing shots.

When a gifted dealer in Troy, Michigan, was asked how he could accept the offer of a free dealership from Chrysler, he replied without blinking, "Because I was willing, and I was able."

Another example came from Chuck Eddy Jr., a NADA director from Ohio, who ran an active Dodge dealership in Youngstown—meaning he was continuing with the automaker. Eddy heard other continuing dealers in his region complain about NADA's future direction. "They think NADA is spending too much time working on the rejected dealer issue," Eddy said in media reports. The continuing dealers, who paid the NADA tab with their membership dues, also needed help. With the economy in near depression, these were tough times for them too, said dealers such as Eddy.

"NADA is between a rock and a hard place on this," he said in an *Automotive News* report. "There is pressure from all sides. In my opinion, NADA needs to stay neutral on this [dealer-rejection issue]."

* * *

Back in Silver Spring, Maryland, Tammy Darvish bristled, stung by a recent rebuke from the top brass of the group she represented. She served as a NADA director from the Washington DC dealers association. She was known for her excellent reputation in her nearly twenty-five years in the auto business. Now she was facing another test: she was working passionately to restore dealers' economic rights and had met up with a blockade, a force called NADA.

Sipping her third Diet Coke of the morning, Darvish was thinking fast. She hadn't slept well since receiving the hurtful letter from Ed Tonkin, NADA's chairman. The rebukes from the NADA officer's treatment of her still stung. The night before, she felt like she'd swallowed a bitter pill, and sleep wouldn't come.

She still questioned NADA's tacit support of the manufacturers before their own dealers, even if they were cancelled dealers like CRDR's base. Many owned other franchises and were still supporting NADA, whose membership base had dwindled over the years as the country's harshest recession since WWII loomed. A number of dealers had suffered economic hardships, especially with the GM and Chrysler losses.

It was not an outcome anyone in the leadership ranks of CRDR expected when the fight to reinstate rejected dealerships began. But it happened. The Detroit Two automakers declared bankruptcy and restructured as part of the infusion of federal funds to their coffers. Money talks and they had listened. And now CRDR and NADA were at odds with each other. It was like a gift to the automakers, Darvish thought, to divide and conquer the dealer groups.

For NADA's part, they didn't understand the fire—and what could seem like brashness that came from Darvish's singular focus—and near obsession with restoring the cancelled dealers. Darvish, Fitzgerald, and Spitzer lived, breathed, and owned the dealer cause, supporters said. Still, NADA's criticism of Darvish stung deeply. She remembered her father's words. "Be careful what you're doing. You don't want to alienate them." He was talking about the power players at the automakers, but it applied as well to their own camp: the dealer advocates, it seemed.

Darvish had placed herself squarely in NADA's sights when she sent a memo to their top officer, raising a conflict-of-interest issue that she and CRDR thought was important. She also was reminding them it was at the heart of the struggle she and CRDR leaders believed in passionately: help those who need it most, the rejected dealers. And if it wasn't the Painters and several thousand dealers today, it could be others at some future point.

"NADA cannot favor one constituency at the expense of another and purport to speak objectively when it is conflicted," Darvish wrote on August 8 to NADA President Phil Brady. She then pointed out the deal in which a competitor was given outright the Phil Painter dealership in Utah. All the NADA higher-up officers were former or current dealers, and she hoped they would understand the point here: having your dealership gifted outright to another owner. Plus, she was doing her job, reporting to NADA and standing up for dealers. At least that's what she thought as she sat down to write.

After one tense meeting with NADA, she confided in Patrick Painter, one of her dealer listening posts, "You know, it's taking all I have to not get up and tell them to go f*ck off and just walk out. I feel like I'm in *The Stepford Wives* movie, and I need to run for my life." But she didn't run for her life. She continued running into the eye of the storm. She couldn't be a Stepford wife.

At the time, NADA had its own issues to contend with. Membership was declining due to a sour economy and the gradual winnowing of dealerships nationwide. Closed dealers were not its only problem, Darvish knew. But in this case it was doubly difficult to serve more than one master. Plus, when asked, or begged was more like it, they wouldn't support CRDR financially.

Following the closures and subsequent automaker actions, major media began taking note of the conflict. Dealers "split into two bitterly divided camps," reported *Automotive News*. An August 24, 2009, headline declared: "Dealership closings turn NADA into battleground."

What was troubling to Darvish is that they were all supposed to be on the same side: pushing for dealer rights, protecting their own, standing up to the automakers and task force. All along, the new government-automaker allies had shouted: too many dealers; they cost too much money. Close the dealers. That's what they were fighting against. There was no turning back now.

How her role with NADA and the conflict-of-interest issue would resolve itself was anybody's guess, but CRDR was not backing down from protecting the rights of closed dealers. She knew that much.

* * *

After the announced closures, besides the human casualties and emotional toll on dealers, most visible were the hulks of remaining buildings of those dealers who couldn't sell or dispose of them.

The hard part was finding much good in the catastrophe of shut-down dealers. The dealers no longer invited to the party were left to their own devices—what to do with their lost businesses—and, in some cases, their empty lives. Their identities had been tied up in their businesses. So another robbery could be added to the list: identity theft.

Still, in some cases, dealers' entrepreneurial spirits seemed to emerge, Bob Dilmore noted. "They're smarter and more resilient, these dealers. They're the last of the rugged individuals we will see."

A few months after being shut down by Chrysler, Richard Mealey, for example, started up Troy Auto World, a pre-owned certified dealership that also performed service work. He was one of the first dealers in the country to open a combined outlet in his former facility. He was able to sell multiple brands in a "franchise" concept. The difference is, these were gently used cars, he said. But the cost of purchasing his own inventory, the high overhead on a huge facility, and paying for unused property for his collision shop, plus the fact he no longer could perform warranty work, cost him dearly.

The Century Motor Corp. owners in Wentzville, Missouri, fought for their closed dealership and managed against great odds to win against Chrysler in the courts. The Mock family, including dealer Frank Mock, and John Mock, his brother and co-dealer, invested about $4 million in their facilities, loyal Chrysler dealers since 1983. In all, fourteen family members were involved in the privately owned family business.

The Mocks filed a landmark lawsuit and finally won against Chrysler Group, reopening two years after their closure. The dealers claimed that the Letter of Intent they received violated the federal dealer arbitration law, *Automotive News* reported on June 21, 2010. The Mocks argued that dealerships seeking reinstatement had to meet conditions not required of the thousands of Chrysler dealerships that were never terminated.

"We were outraged by the Letter of Intent," Kevin Mock, Century's general manager, said in *Automotive News*. "We have twenty years and millions and millions of dollars invested in this franchise, and we couldn't just sit back and wait for something to happen."

Kevin Mock also told *Ward's* magazine, "We were in the top 10 percent of sales of Chrysler dealers nationally—and in one of the fastest-growing markets in the country. As a business person, when the economy is down, you look to your biggest and best dealers to get through it. Why did they cut us loose?"

For its part, Chrysler said it had been all along "following the letter of the law regarding the federal dealer arbitration statute by providing Century Motor and other arbitrating dealers who have prevailed in the arbitration process with the company's standard and usual LOI."

In Pennsylvania, Chip Bogdewic opened a new tire center in his old Chevrolet facility. He'd had enough of the stress of dealing with an automaker that didn't want older legacy dealers on their side. "Thank you very much, this is much better for me," he wanted to tell GM, who he knew wasn't listening. Why would they now, when they hadn't in the past?

Bob Dilmore, for one, couldn't stand seeing how dealers who had worked their whole lives to build a business or to preserve family foundations, like those detailed throughout this story, were forced to give up their livelihoods, in the name of a vague notion called "sacrifice" and streamlining the automakers to presumably compete with foreign rivals in what many dealers and auto experts called a flawed premise.

"I felt deeply obligated to get involved and help all we could," Dilmore said. At the same time, he expressed dismay, as if still recalling the damage, the carnage before his eyes. "I didn't like it at all—the things Chrysler brought up in the courts about dealers. It was immoral and unjust. I would say that to my dying day."

Chapter 10—Eat. Run. Push Congress.

The knowledge that one is to be hanged in a fortnight wonderfully concentrates the mind.

—Oscar Wilde

One minute to 6:00 p.m. It was the eve of the dealer rally, July 13, 2009. The site was Washington DC's Renaissance Hotel.

That morning had rolled in with stifling heat and humidity. By night it was worse, and participants rushed in to take advantage of the hotel's air-conditioned comfort.

Dealers drove or flew into DC to take part in the two-day event organized by CRDR that would culminate on July 14 with meetings in the chambers of Congress. It was designed to bond the dealers and corral the straggling legislators, if Tammy Darvish had planned it correctly. So far, the dealer rights legislation was gaining favor in the House but straggling in the Senate. The event also was a motivational rally for dealers rejected by Chrysler and GM across the country.

As they grabbed appetizers off plates of hors d'oeuvres, dealers sat at tables waiting for the speakers to start. At the earlier meet-and-greet, they milled about and could see they were not alone as dealers. Still, this was not exactly a group they might choose to bond with—dealers rejected by the Detroit automakers. Even though they were dealers much like themselves. But the mood among the attendees was understandably somber, even a little wary. Many had lost their shirts in the bloodbath, and, though apprehensive, had come here to get information, maybe some answers.

So far, many liked what they'd seen and heard of CRDR. But what could one small, recently formed group do for the larger group of culled dealers, some skeptics wondered. Unlike NADA, who everyone in the dealer community knew, they had little clout, were not a household name in the automotive world. But tonight there were speakers from most of the organized advocacy groups.

It was seven o'clock. Sixteen hours before the official fly-in event would start up on Triangle Square near the Capitol the next morning. Less, if you counted the early morning sign-ins and meetings. The speakers for that night were getting assembled.

The pep rally–style reception looked well organized, even if Tammy Darvish, with Alison Spitzer and Rob Smith, her chief allies, were scribbling the night's agenda on cocktail napkins as they moved about. There had been little time to organize the event, so there were many loose strings dangling as they moved about, preparing a few of the last-minute speakers, making sure there were no questions.

Darvish thought about how they'd had only a few days' notice from the congressional staffers who were helping with facility arrangements and Congress members' appointments the next day. That seemed to be the way the politicians operated—on the fly, getting prepped on issues as they went along. "We did the best we could," Darvish explained if anyone asked her how they'd managed to pull it off so quickly. Of course, she worried that the event might look thrown together—because it was.

But Jack Fitzgerald was his fiery best that night, decked out in a suit and dress shirt, unusual for the homespun dealer who spoke in Lincoln-esque tones. He hailed from the DC area and swore he wasn't named after the thirty-fifth US president, John Fitzgerald Kennedy—even though his first name was John too and he went by the nickname "Jack." For one thing, he was a young man when JFK was in office. As history books tell it, JFK died in 1963, felled by an assassin's bullet in Dallas. And Jack Fitzgerald sure didn't have JFK's money or heritage behind him. He wasn't a legacy dealer, either—someone handed the keys to the kingdom. He'd worked his way to the top. His father had been an office worker with Trailways Bus Company in the DC area, and he himself had sold fire alarms door-to-door before cars. As a kid, he'd lived on Capitol Street in downtown DC, so he was no stranger to the area, or the political environment.

Yet, none of the CRDR leaders had much experience schmoozing Congress. Like others, Jack Fitzgerald was well-known at the state level. Dealers knew their state legislators but didn't know how to "work the Hill." Their forte was selling cars and trucks, not big political concepts like "save the dealers."

"We had two and a half strikes against us going in," said Alan Spitzer of winning the support of Congress. Spitzer, one of the three CRDR leaders and its founder, had pulled in Jack Fitzgerald and Tammy Darvish.

Outside, steaming humid air pressed at the windows. The sun was setting. Inside, several hundred people were glad to be in air-conditioned comfort in a decent hotel. But emotions ran high and hot. Tomorrow would be another story as they were spending a lot of time outdoors and then in meetings, listening to speeches, holding interviews, networking, and gathering facts.

At first, Jack Fitzgerald was pleased to hear that the NADA group had pledged to fund the reception night. Their men, Ed Tonkin and David Regan, were speaking, along with himself and Spitzer for CRDR, and Dan Renberg, their DC-based legislative lawyer. Also on the stage were Tim Doran, then president of the ATAE, the automobile trade association executives group, and Gerry Murphy, who headed the Washington area dealers association.

Doran, who also ran the Ohio state dealers association, had long been pushing for facts and specific criteria the automakers used to reject dealers. He thought those facts should be shared with affected dealers and the advocacy groups. But that would happen much later in the legal court processes.

Tammy Darvish, the chief organizer, dashed about making sure people's questions were answered and they knew what the game plan was. She would learn later that NADA was not providing funding for the reception, so her company footed the bill.

Fitzgerald knew Darvish practically lived on the Hill these days. So did he and Rob Smith. From having been scared to talk to the lawmakers a month ago, he thought Darvish had come a long way. She could no longer afford to be the backseat dealer from Silver Spring, Maryland, well-known in smaller circles in the DC area. Serving on the Unsecured Creditors Committee, a NADA director, and now getting involved in CRDR had polished her "political street cred." It seemed history had forced her onto a bigger stage. She played her role quite well, he thought. And now everything was at stake for several thousand dealers and even more automotive stakeholders.

On the makeshift stage, it was an impassioned Fitzgerald who people remembered later. In his deep baritone voice, he spoke about the loss of dealer rights and how they all had to stand together to have a chance at reversing the course of action that had led to their downfall. He defined the enemy. The government's auto task force he believed had strong-armed the carmakers into obedience with a threat of withholding federal dollars—billions of dollars. There was some talk of Chrysler trimming the dealer network anyway with its Genesis project, but who knew which came first. It was the old chicken-and-egg question.

The companies had declared bankruptcy in the first place as a condition of getting the federal funds that gave them a chance at survival. Fitzgerald guessed he couldn't blame them. He might do the same thing in their shoes. He had told GM as much. Death and survival do strange things to concentrate the mind. When you're at the abyss staring into the depths, who knows what you will do or say to stay alive. Who knows who you might betray.

But Fitzgerald would not have cut the dealers, being in the automakers' shoes. It wasn't because he had "skin in the game," as some suggested. It was because he knew dealers made money for automakers—and were an economic stimulus in their own right—a point lost on the task force.

"The auto task force under Steve Rattner enforced the dealer cuts," he said, even if they didn't supply the dealer names. The story Rattner repeated everywhere was that the task force didn't make the dealer cuts. The government left that to the automakers' management. Maybe so. But Rattner never understood what the furor over car dealers was about either, Fitzgerald said.

David Weaver, chief of staff for Representative Chris Van Hollen, did understand. He hit it on the head when he said, "Every member of Congress knew the dealers in their towns." They were major sources of tax revenue, jobs, and community funds. Not to mention campaign contributions. There were lingering misperceptions about bad dealers, almost an oral history going back to car dealerships' early days. Still, most people would say, sure there are bad eggs out there, "But not my car dealer," Weaver said.

Jack Fitzgerald had started his first dealership in 1966 in Maryland, the Rockville Pike store. Before that he sold cars for other dealers, including Ford brands, for ten years; he'd even been a door-to-door salesman in his youth. Selling indoors would be easier, he figured. He and John Darvish, Tammy's father, went way back. John Darvish had even worked for him at one time, so that relationship ran long and deep. He'd known Tammy since she was cutting her teeth in sales and service coming out of college at the Darvish dealerships. He'd known Alan Spitzer even longer, the two having served on many dealer councils and associations together since the late sixties.

Fitzgerald and Spitzer, in launching CRDR two months earlier, had concluded that their best hope to stop the closures was through federal legislation. Politicians run for reelection. And the politicians who assailed GM and Chrysler for failing to cut costs represent states and districts in which car dealers are a major force. They make campaign contributions to both parties. They vote with their wallets. The fledgling committee also would incorporate and educate the media, although softly, in their dealer campaign.

It was as if Jack, Al, and Tammy were running for public office; their campaign to save dealers nationwide became that well-oiled and smooth in less than two months, their supporters said. Surveying his industry, Jack Fitzgerald never thought he'd see the day when Ford Motor would be eating GM's lunch. It was against the natural order of things in the auto world. GM had always been numero uno, the kingpin. But GM slowly lost market share, beginning in the mismanaged 1980s. And then in 2008, Toyota displaced them as the world sales leader; and suddenly, the US and global economies were running amok.

Not because of Toyota, but because the domestics had taken their collective eyes off the ball, Fitzgerald thought. The product ball. They'd sacrificed quality for quantity—a lesson Toyota had yet to learn.

Now all hell was breaking loose. Cash was king and customers were holding on tight to their money. The credit crisis remained just that—a crisis. The customer mood was apprehensive; people were scared to make sudden financial moves and risk even more losses. And vehicles, the second biggest purchase a consumer might make, were stalled nationwide in sales.

In the new economy, Ford turned the corner to become the number-one domestic automaker. Ford had played it smart though; they learned GM's and Chrysler's tactics but never asked for federal aid. They got private lines of credit and raised cash by selling off brands and mortgaging the company assets.

That first night in DC, dealers congregated and talked at the pre-rally. Fitzgerald gave an impassioned speech, one that people talked about for more than a year later. Mostly, he spoke about their cause being just and how they now had a good chance on the Hill to reverse the dealer travesty. Congress was listening.

Jeff Duvall, a cancelled Chrysler dealer from northern Georgia, gave a rather balanced recap of that evening. "We had a late afternoon flight on Monday [July 13] and arrived on time. We caught the subway over to the Renaissance Hotel and went directly downstairs to the ballroom with our luggage. I gave a big sigh of relief, because it was perfect timing. The meeting had not started yet," he recalled.

Duvall spotted Tammy Darvish and recognized her from a recent picture in *Automotive News*. He introduced Louie, his son, and himself. "Tammy was in high gear, which is, as I have learned, the only gear she has. She was helping some of the Washington auto dealer group get settled in."

If he had doubts about CRDR that night, he was won over.

"Tammy, Jack, and Alan all spoke, but I distinctly remember Jack's speech," he said. Later he recalled thinking, " My God, this little man with his deep baritone voice brought me back to my days playing high-school football and the coach giving us his pre-game pep talk. When Jack got through, I was ready to go to Auburn Hills [Michigan] and kick some ass."

Some dealer networking took place after the talks. Duvall and others got the game plan for the next day, including their appointments with Congress. "I could hardly sleep that night I was so pumped," Duvall said. "I knew that what I had just witnessed and become a part of was something special, something bigger than a few dealers. It was like nothing I had ever experienced before in the car business."

"The focus, the intensity, and the energy that night was incredible; and the genuine caring and selflessness of Alan, Jack, and Tammy was a shock to me, especially coming from dealers of their stature. Jack, the field general with that booming voice; Alan, the distinguished colonel; and Tammy, the tough-as-nails ranger-sniper. All three smart as hell and about five thoughts ahead of everyone else. Getting to know these three people truly has been a life-changing experience for me," Duvall said in his forthright manner.

To accomplish what seemed a small feat, he and his son, Louie, and dealership staff, had worked with their state dealers associations, the CRDR, and NADA reps. Now they were stepping it up, going national, for bigger stakes.

"We had already been working our Georgia senators and reps. With the help of our state association, President Bill Morie, we got all but two on board—Democrat Jim Marshall, who I spoke with on the phone and could not sway, and Tom Price, a Republican, who, per his staffer, was too busy with health care to spend any time on the dealer rights issue," Duvall explained.

Dealers received suggested formats to use in their briefings with Congress. They could customize these short scripts to their own situations. It helped to have structure, know that they were well-scripted, and wouldn't fumble in the meetings, Darvish thought.

By the time they got to DC for the big rally, dealers were no strangers to the politicians. Darvish, her staff, and Alison Spitzer had helped coordinate the sessions for them and provided backgrounders to the Congress members. Things went smoothly enough, despite the early hiccups. A small army of fighters had descended on Capitol Hill, at first disconnected and alone. At first it seemed as if they were in the outsiders' club, one they had never asked to join: terminated dealers. Later it was the group they found strength and purpose in.

With meetings, letters, e-mails, texting, and answering cell phone calls, Darvish was everywhere that first night. Equipped with headphones and an ear bud, she was constantly texting, Googling, and checking in with her support base and congressional lead people. The gods were in the details, even up to eleventh hour, and she was staying on top of them.

The next day, dealers went to their appointments, even if some were reluctant. Each had five or so members of Congress and their aides to meet. They made the rounds. They shook hands; they told their stories. They began to change hearts and minds. Even their own.

The Hothouse Rally

Tuesday. Rally day. Early morning, a seven- to eight-o'clock sign-in on the Hill.

Summertime. The sky overhead had lightened by the time the morning types rose, wandering the grounds, wondering what the day had in store, sensing it would be momentous. Many had never met with US congresspeople on a personal basis before.

Coffee and blissfully cold water bottles were available. The bigger meeting was in the Sam Rayburn Building later that morning and was open to the media. At least twelve members of Congress and dealer reps were speaking or part of the day's events.

The historic Rayburn House Office Building was named after legendary Democrat House leader Sam Rayburn and seemed appropriate to the occasion. Outside, masses of hot air pressed on the crowd gathered on Capitol Hill's Triangle Square. The heat hit them like a bullet. Perspiration streamed down faces and necks, although to observers the speakers looked composed enough. Most were in business attire. The blistering heat had soaked men's shirts and suits; and the women weren't much better off, wearing mostly jackets and skirts or dresses and pantyhose.

The speakers in the main area took extra heat, literally, as camera lights flashed, and they jammed the manufactured speaking area, standing shoulder-to-shoulder.

The children present, including Darvish's, fanned themselves and looked like they hadn't slept well. *I thought this was supposed to be summer vacation*, their looks said.

Hoyer's Three Zeroes

That day, House Majority Leader Steny Hoyer's presence was indomitable. The supersized Hoyer, who's around six feet four, stood holding up a huge sign with 0-0-0 on it. The three zeroes emphasized the point that dealers cost the manufacturers nothing—zero, nada, zip. Hoyer's self-appointed role was to keep the legislation moving down the field, not let the support for the bills in Congress die. He didn't disappoint that day or afterward. Without Hoyer, and Steve LaTourette with his bill-pushing crusade, there might not be any legislation, the A-team thought.

In the background that Tuesday, a huge red-and-blue map in varied hues showed where the domestics and imports fared strongest, and where the cuts had been made. Noticeably, imports dominated the coasts although the domestics covered more land areas. The data was supplied by R. L. Polk, a leading researcher of vehicle sales data in the country. It made sense, Jack Fitzgerald would say, that in those market areas where GM and Chrysler were cutting, you needed more domestic dealers to cover the huge land space and more cars on the road, not fewer.

Drilling down, Maryland would be a red state (controlled by the domestics) if it weren't for Montgomery County where 93 percent of owners in affluent cities like Bethesda drove imports, CRDR leaders pointed out. Maryland lost fifty-eight GM and Chrysler dealers with the terminations, hardly numbers it could afford to lose with such high import penetration.

Well before the fly-in, to make sure House leaders like Hoyer and Van Hollen kept up the momentum, Fitzgerald, Smith, and Darvish practically lived on Capitol Hill, holding meetings all day with Congress members on both sides of the aisle. Their colleague Spitzer showed up when he wasn't lobbying from afar.

"Profitable dealerships that were closed for possibly unfair reasons deserve the opportunity to hear why they were closed and discuss the merits of reopening with an independent arbitrator who can make a binding decision," Hoyer said to media afterward. He was second to Nancy Pelosi in the House of Representatives' power structure. Not a bad guy to have on your side.

At this point, very few dealers had heard the stories of Hoyer's shabby treatment by Rattner and his auto task force only a week earlier, shortly before Rattner resigned his position on July 13. Even the media and the automotive press hadn't feasted entirely on that story yet. Hoyer, the new lion of the House, roared back, and everyone would soon know that Capitol Hill couldn't be kept in the dark or quiet on the dealer issues. In fact, they were now in the forefront, fighting a battle no one had expected them to engage in so willingly: restore dealer rights in America. Some congressional insiders were surprised the dealer legislation got legs so quickly. "You must crawl before you walk" had lost purchase power with this group of advocates. They started out trotting and then raced to the finish line.

Lawmakers are constantly barraged with hundreds of competing issues that they must act on instantly. "To keep up with it all they surround themselves with very bright people who work crazy hours," said Rob Smith. In the dealer rights battle, the wheels of justice grind exceedingly fast. He knew the CRDR group had to run to keep up with them.

To keep Congress members even busier, the committee supplied grist for the mill and progress updates. They informed them when critical issues arose, or when a conflict or resolution presented itself, such as the struggle between the advocacy groups themselves on who should represent the culled dealers.

* * *

Rob Smith was a vice president in Jack Fitzgerald's dealerships in Maryland and the greater DC area. He and Darvish formed a cohesive team to send the message of restoring dealers nationwide. Later it became a modern "shot heard around the world" as major media picked up the stories.

Smith had come aboard at Fitzgerald Auto Mall in the late 1980s. "It's a very process-oriented dealership," he observed. He liked that. Carrying major car brands, including Chevrolet, Cadillac, GMC, Subaru, Chrysler, Toyota, Mazda, Nissan, and Volkswagen, it was a busy operation. His boss, Jack, was a numbers-and-data man. Rob Smith made his job that much easier. He clarified issues and related facts to those who cared to know them, from media to dealers, Congress members and their staffers.

"Want a chart, a statistic, a backgrounder? Call Rob Smith," Tammy Darvish would say.

A car dealership is about more than sales. It also takes care of vehicles and in many cases serves as a community center for customers. Customer cafes and coffee centers had become part of dealership design over the last decade or so. As much as anything, it was a relationship business and had changed greatly over the decades to reflect that change, Smith said. He believed if they had left the dealers in place, things would have worked themselves out.

"Natural market forces have occurred over the years to eliminate dealers who weren't up to expectations," Smith said. For many, it was like dying a natural death. If you can't stand the heat, get out of the kitchen, the popular thinking went.

"More than a decade ago, there were about forty thousand US dealers to sell and service fifty million cars on the road; now there are under twenty thousand dealers to service one hundred fifty million cars on the road. So there are less than half of the dealers with three times the number of cars on the road," Smith observed. With imports it was the opposite, imports had fewer vehicles on the roads (eighty-seven million) and fewer dealers, so now you had more import dealers than domestics to service those cars, he explained. Those were numbers the automakers didn't factor in before the cuts. They didn't get it, he said.

But many of the members of Congress *did* get it, and after this rally, they would get it even more, Rob Smith thought.

The introduction of the House bills in early June started the process of enlightenment. "The introduction of dealer bills by Democrats Dan Maffei and Frank Kratovil gave us leverage. It looked like we had the lawmakers on our side," at least considering the early support they were getting, Smith said.

Now the dealer rally was another stepping stone. Maybe it wouldn't cement the deal. But it would bring dealers face-to-face with Congress. Dealers had paid their own freight to get here. They would get out of it what they could. That day on the Hill, they made their voices heard.

Pushing Congress for Votes

Jeff Duvall, for one, could see how Darvish and her small legion of supporters were pressing Congress hard for action on the dealer legislation. This was all leading up to final votes in both houses of Congress. He could see the dealers' collective role in the process. "We bombarded the lawmakers," Duvall said, "We were for it." He signed on early to become a pivotal member of Darvish's A-team.

July had been a wild month. Now the payoff could be seen in the collective energy of the crowd—mostly dealers and related staff and media thronging the central square around the Hill. It was not a gathering for mere curiosity seekers; many were here for information and motivation.

The rally served as their pre-show, before the votes in Congress would come. With their franchises as an endangered species, the dealers had descended on Capitol Hill in larger numbers. They had not known what to expect. But once there, they saw they could personally state their cases for continuing their businesses. Or they could just mill around, make contacts, see what was happening. There was no pressure, except for internal. It was up to them.

The committed dealers would seek out the lawmakers. Shake hands, tell them your story, they were advised. Let them see that these tragedies happened to real people, human beings, not just numbers on a spreadsheet.

Dealers on the Hill didn't disappoint, that day or later.

Darvish and her existing A-team had been pressing Congress hard on the bills all summer. They wanted votes on the bills sooner, not later. As a call to action, she and Alison Spitzer organized the pivotal rally. At least two hundred auto dealers looked around, saw there were dealers here just like them. They could offer the lawmakers insights as to how the auto and dealer businesses work together, but as separate entities.

The lawmakers had the stats to show economic impact of the dealer losses in packets prepared by CRDR. Local and national jobs were at stake. And the communities dealers did business in were at risk. At one point NADA estimated that nearly 170,000 direct jobs would be lost by closing all the affected dealers. That number could inflate quickly if one took into account the collateral damage—suppliers, businesses in their communities, charities, and others could lose out after the cuts swept through the nation. The local and national economy already had stalled. The meltdown was spreading globally. The economy could not take another big hit like this one threatening to erupt.

Adrenaline pumping, Darvish took the outdoor stage that morning at a press conference on Triangle Square. She saw her two children standing to her side. They looked—what—proud, a little scared, overwhelmed? Hot, for sure. Darvish forced a smile, catching their eyes. She felt better, even energized.

She had a rough idea of what she wanted to say, but it mostly came to her when she started to speak. "You can never take no for an answer when something is not right. That's why I'm here, and that's why I brought my children today," Darvish said to the group of onlookers. Then she talked about why they were all there as heads nodded and eyes teared up.

Later she roamed the grounds outside the Hill like a nervous mother hen, taking stock. "What did you think?" she asked several dealers. They nodded, gave her smiles, a few thumbs-up in the air. But who knew what they were really thinking? The proof would be in the pudding. She'd wait for the media reviews—and the political pundits taking aim. The automakers were probably ignoring the event even happened, publicly at least, she thought. But privately they had to be taking note. And the final votes in Congress would be the real test.

Rob Smith, a student of politics in the best sense, looked at the pivotal events that moved the needle in the campaign to save the dealers. Namely:

- The bills were introduced in Congress in June in the first place by two House representatives.
- The LaTourette Amendment kept the issue alive and tied the dealer effort to an overall spending bill that Congress had to act on or lose it all. The lobbying effort continued at high levels, or the government would go out of business before the new year rang in.
- The dealer rally was the single-most important event that bonded the dealers and gave CRDR leverage and momentum as they raced to get legislation passed.

Not once did the committee believe they could coast to victory on the issue. Not once did they rest during the long desultory summer or as fall and winter came and the vote was not yet there. If anything, they ran that much harder.

* * *

In those forays to Congress, Darvish turned into a human dynamo. She was everywhere. Her self-elected job was to push Congress further and faster. She would grab a quick takeout lunch, when there was time; if not, cold tea and Diet Coke provided the fuel. Her usual healthy diet and exercise were being replaced by new bad habits. After a day-long effort—including rushing back to the dealerships—she would work into the wee hours to make her back-channel calls, send off a flurry of e-mails, and respond to voice mails. There was no personal time.

"What's happening?" She texted Rob Smith whenever she thought that deadlines for votes could drew nearer.

Same story, different day, Smith might say. It was still hurry-up-and-wait in the corridors of Congress. In Detroit, at the automakers' offices, political diagrams underlined the strategy: fight the dealers at all costs. There was public money in the coffers now partly being used to shut down dealers. The dealer groups had no written commitment that the automakers were willing to work with them. They still didn't even know the real reasons they had been shut down. So far, automakers stuck to terms like "market sales" and "profit figures," "performance scores," and "customer-satisfaction ratings."

Not knowing was not good.

Even before the dealer rally, by July 9, bipartisan support in Congress was building for restoring dealers in some shape or form. Many attributed it to the grassroots efforts of the dealer advocate groups. The committee took stock. A majority of the US House of Representatives, 222 members, had signed on as sponsors.

That at least was a good sign. They were being heard.

To announce the dealer rally in the little time they had, CRDR had sent out a press release to media, giving a somewhat optimistic update. It underlined the growing awareness by Congress that the dealers had been wronged. Congress members, now from both parties, "recognize what is clear to the American people: the leadership of GM and Chrysler made a horrible mistake by their arbitrary termination of profitable dealerships. Detroit and the auto task force's flawed business plan will lead to the direct loss of more than 169,000 good jobs and cripple the US auto industry's ability to come back from bankruptcy," the release said.

"The tens of thousands of families and communities hurt by this reckless strategy cannot afford to wait any longer. We call on all members of Congress, on both sides of the aisle, to listen to their constituents and pass this job-saving legislation. A taxpayer bailout that fails Main Street and actually *costs* hundreds of thousands of jobs is misguided, irresponsible—and in need of an immediate tune-up," CRDR wrote.

As Darvish and crew continued to lobby Congress after the rally, Darvish especially was gaining valuable skills as a political insider. She was meeting the right people, getting the word out. But at times, the universe was telling her to slow down again.

"You need a break, take the family and get a few days off if you can," Rob Smith said, reading her intensity level as maxed out. He would tell her when he was taking a rare weekend off and taking his kids to the cottage.

Her new friend, Mark Sims, a Chevrolet dealer in the Cleveland area, had invited her to use his vacation home on the Eastern shore as a getaway. Her friends and father told her to slow down, take it easier.

But there was no rest for the wicked, Darvish told herself, or no rest *because* of the wicked. *You're getting sooo good at living out the clichés of life.* That little voice inside wouldn't keep quiet.

Even her father shook his head when she announced she was off to another meeting, one state or another, all on the dealer-closure business. She traveled light, often with only essentials and no luggage in hand. Many of her trips were overnighters and she could buy what she needed, or the staff would send it, she figured.

In the DC environs, she dashed about in her car, driving fast from one appointment to another. She was supporting the local economy with speeding tickets, she joked as Courtney Wallin assessed the damage.

Sipping her countless Diet Cokes, Darvish kept one eye out for DC's finest, going from DC and then back to Silver Spring, home to the dealership. These days, the road was her home, as was Congress. A typical work week was sometimes around one hundred hours.

Give it up?

Her inner compass said something else: America is endangered. We can look the other way, hope someone else does *something*, or we can act for change ourselves. She opted for the latter. She had little idea when she started with CRDR that "change agent" was her natural calling.

Insulting a Chrysler Executive

By mid-July, the heat was intense, in more ways than one. Local legend had it that the DC district had been built on swampland. The old tale was a myth, but the scorched, steamy summer still made people wonder what was bubbling beneath the ground they stood on.

On the front lines, Darvish reminded dealers to keep up the pressure on Congress. This was no time to let their guard down. "While we're living with the losses every day, my estimation is that a high percentage of people we meet with on Capitol Hill are unaware of the suffering out there. It's not because they don't care, but there are too many issues coming at them at once. Dealers need to continue to be heard," she said in memos.

Suddenly, the universe seemed to be paying attention, at least in DC. It was an *ah-ha* moment, the time when an idea of great power sinks in. On July 16, two days after the rally, the House passed legislation to reverse the dealer closures. The proposal was attached to a spending bill as part of an amended bill, kept alive in the LaTourette Amendment. It was this bill that would grease the skids for other bills on dealer economic rights that would pass through the House and Senate.

For Darvish and her A-team, it was a victory of sorts. They were in the home stretch and CRDR had earned its stripes with Congress, at least in the House. Time will tell the real story, Darvish told the A-team. She had hoped for larger numbers at the rally; but they needed more time to get better results. They had the rally; votes were swinging to their side; but it could be better in the Senate. *Sometimes two out of three ain't bad* she thought as she drove along DC's clogged streets and highways that seemed to rival Los Angeles and Boston for congestion.

In late July, committee members spent three more intense days on Capitol Hill. The life of the lawmakers was becoming their life. Dash, dash, dash. Meetings upon meetings. Arm-twisting and cajoling. It was not part of their natural order of running a modern car dealership. Customer care would be easy after this.

"I'm just a salesperson," Darvish would say many times. But could she sell this, the biggest crisis to hit her peer group in automotive history: the push to reverse the dealer closures?

Then, at the end of the month, Darvish pulled a small coup. She had arranged for a former Chrysler vice president, E. Tom Pappert, to hold separate meetings with Congress groups, CRDR staff, and the auto task force. They were slated for late July. Pappert had thirty years of experience at Chrysler, including nineteen years in positions such as VP of sales and marketing. He was the point man in helping return Chrysler from the jaws of death in the early 1980s, a disciple of legendary CEO Lee Iacocca.

Formerly, he had implemented the $1.2 billion federal loan guarantee program that put Chrysler back on track after the company's near-collapse in the late 1970s. That government industry venture turned out to be profitable for all, Pappert said, as he explained how dealers fit into the picture and helped fuel Chrysler's dramatic turnaround. There were distinct parallels with the present-day crisis, he ventured.

At first, Pappert met with a special Congress committee, including Steny Hoyer, Chris Van Hollen, and Dan Maffei. He briefed them on Chrysler's comeback thirty years earlier as Detroit cheered the home team. He related the success of the government loan that rescued the automaker. Iacocca had struck the deal as Chrysler president in 1979 when he convinced Congress to gamble on Chrysler. The rest was history; Chrysler rebounded and thrived for some years. So did dealers.

The second meeting was with a few auto task force members. Ron Bloom abruptly stopped the session after about twelve minutes. Before that, Bloom had done most of the talking, asked almost no questions, and then dismissed the group, including Pappert. As if he was a busy man and they weren't. Most of that time Bloom spent knocking Pappert's credibility, Darvish heard later. As if he, Pappert, was on trial.

Bloom shot him down. According to Jack Fitzgerald, Bloom claimed he had his own "experts" on the subject and implied that Pappert was incorrect and outdated in his thinking. Later, Darvish learned Bloom's "expert sources" were those he had talked with three years earlier while advising the United Steelworker's union. That job was Bloom's claim to manufacturing expertise.

Pappert felt snubbed and left the room dismayed, wondering what had happened. It was clear that Bloom didn't care to listen to his advice on how Chrysler had handled a similar crisis, recalled insiders at the meeting. He had about three decades of experience in the car wars of the past, but that didn't matter to the new task-force chief. Not more, it seemed, than Chrysler's one-dollar sale price offer to the government. "They had their minds made up and had no interest in hearing about the past," said Rob Smith, who attended the Bloom and Pappert exchange. He called the Bloom dismissal "insulting" to Pappert.

In his third meeting, Pappert briefed a judiciary committee of Congress that would express their anger at the dealer situation. At least he was treated with more respect in that setting, Darvish observed. And Pappert's former boss, Lee Iacocca, had sent in a letter of support for dealers to the White House, after Darvish contacted him personally.

Darvish said, in the end, Pappert had been effective in influencing Congress members who were sitting on the sidelines. "He was good at convincing those members who were perplexed, or confused. After hearing Pappert; they had an 'ah-ha moment; now I get it,'" she said.

* * *

About mid-stream in August, some Congress members wavered on restoring dealers in whole. They began pushing for a non-legislative solution from the four dealer advocacy groups. Dealers and automakers needed to work it out, come up with a compromise solution. Compromise was the way of political life in DC, after all. And still GM and Chrysler had not come to the table.

Internally, Congress was still gathering facts, hearing more stories of devastation and ruin in their communities. They looked at the data on unemployment and economic impact if the closures stood. Assessing the damage, for the most part, they were appalled.

But other disappointments set in. One was that Representative John Conyers Jr. didn't step up earlier. "He kept promising we would have a hearing, and it didn't happen," Darvish said. Serving since 1965, the Michigan Democrat was the powerful chairman of the House Judiciary Committee and could have been influential earlier on, she thought. Later he at least voted for the measures before the House.

Michigan Senator Debbie Stabenow and Senator Carl Levin, also local institutions, remained on the quiet side, although Stabenow's staff told the A-team and local Michigan dealers the senator "wants to make dealers whole." The committee attributed the distancing to their strong union and corporate ties in the home of the Detroit Three. But their fight was about building the economy, contributing to a community, not tearing it down. And it wouldn't cost taxpayers anything to keep the dealers open, the committee kept stressing.

How could the dealer campaign be anti-union? This too was all about jobs in the midst of an economic meltdown when good jobs such as those at dealerships were hard to find, Darvish said. It was hard to fathom how unions, at least, could not evenly tacitly support their cause. Sure, they had their own battles for card-carrying members, just like NADA did. But this was about jobs and community welfare.

A Meeting of the Minds

On September 3, members of the key dealer advocacy groups met in Steny Hoyer's small meeting room in the Capitol Building. Unlike some visitors who climbed the steep steps up to the Capitol offices on the Hill, many of the attendees that day used a side entrance in order to clear security easier. Their names had been provided to guards earlier.

Home of the brave, land of the free. The twin US flags ripple above the Capitol's two front entrances. The national anthem theme perhaps plays in the minds of many visitors walking up those steep steps to the halls of Congress.

Leaders of CRDR, NADA, NAMAD, and ATAE were there to kick off a pivotal meeting—the first time all four groups were in the room together with representatives of Congress. The meeting included key staffers from the offices of Hoyer, Van Hollen, Maffei, Kratovil, Durbin, and Rockefeller.

At that time, Congress asked the four dealer groups to get on the same page. The instructions were simple. They needed to agree on a non-legislative solution that would garner support and show a united front to the automakers. The objective was to agree on a joint proposal Congress could present to automakers—and quickly.

By six that night, they still weren't close to an agreement they could all live with. What's more, the Capitol's doors were closing; they were getting kicked out.

Darvish proposed they continue in NADA's offices across the street and hammer out a proposal that night. There were a few supporters, namely her CRDR colleagues, Fitzgerald, Smith, and Spitzer. After some hemming and hawing, the meeting moved over to the NADA building.

In the NADA office, the sparring continued as they tried to craft a common language they could embrace. Going round after round, unity came hard. Each group had separate agendas, it seemed. Like everything else, this task had turned into a political football.

At around ten o'clock that night, they hit pay dirt. Somehow they managed to deliver a joint proposal to Congress leaders called Outline of Alternative Solutions, dated September 3, the same night. The proposal from the four dealer advocacy groups outlined their collective thinking on a non-legislative path to restoring dealers. It had been painfully arrived at, since nearly a month earlier when Darvish's struggle with NADA had been publicly laundered.

The next day the proposal was sent to Congress, who would use it as a tool, a wedge, with the automakers. Congress didn't have an actual approval role, Rob Smith said. "They were acting more in the role of an honest broker between dealers and the manufacturers at that point," he explained.

Smith called the joint proposal "a breakthrough" for all sides. He doubted that Congress could have made headway without the document in place. It showed Congress the dealer groups were trying to work with the automakers, even if the reverse wasn't true, he said.

Coming together was a big step for the dealer groups, and it seemed to tilt Congress in favor of the dealers even more since the automakers' lobbying attorneys, John Bozzella for Chrysler and Ken Cole and Joe Lyons for GM, had earlier called off negotiations with the dealers. The dealer groups were trying—what was wrong with the automakers?

The stalemate was like those unions and automakers encounter over especially divisive negotiating issues.

The September meeting of the four advocacy groups had shown the lawmakers they were serious about working things out. Darvish wrapped up their alternative proposal by saying, "We still believe we have tremendous political leverage with the bills in Congress but were asked to develop a non-legislative solution and in good faith we did so." They could still push to get legislation passed if GM and Chrysler did not agree on the latest terms set forth, she said. "It is the opinion of the committee that neither company has been negotiating with us in good faith."

Privately, Darvish hoped they might still have a shot at reinstating the dealers in whole with an act by Congress. She'd always believed that Congress was their best hope and was increasingly on their side. By then they had 272 votes in the House and forty cosponsors in the Senate.

They weren't done yet, but the four dealer groups had come a long way in finding some common ground. With a bill stalled in the Senate, they were united behind a proposal calling for arbitration and reasonable compensation for the cancelled dealers.

Ducks in a Row

By September 10, Darvish was sending memos out saying that the four key dealer advocacy groups were presenting a united front to Congress. There was strength in numbers, and the endless meetings with key members of Congress had moved the process along. The groups were heading for a showdown with GM, Chrysler, and the auto task force at this stage. They needed to get their ducks in a row, be on the same page, the advocacy leaders realized.

"It's unpredictable what will happen by the end of next week with the automakers and the White House task force," Darvish wrote to her groups. Should the key players—GM, Chrysler, and the task force—decide they won't cooperate with the proposal, "We will not be able to waste any time in getting refocused on the Hill."

Darvish continued: "We are treading on such uncharted waters that even the most experienced and expensive lobbyists in Washington were shocked by the accomplishments of all of our grassroots efforts. Based on my experience in the past three months there are no rules, steps, or procedures to walk anyone through this ridiculous travesty." At this point she could only hope they had laid the stepping stones to future success. "There is no attorney, lobbyist, or even therapist who can predict the outcome or results," she said.

That week, Darvish shared with her network some motivating words from President Obama. He had addressed the nation a few nights earlier and talked about the rewards of hard work and fair play. In effect, President Obama said, "A belief that in this country that hard work and responsibility should be rewarded by some measure of security and fair play. And an acknowledgment that sometimes government has to step in to help deliver on that promise."

Surely those words applied to Main-Street car dealers who had invested in hard work and fair play. Or those stranded on the lonesome highways of America. *If private businesspeople didn't stand for that, they stood for nothing*, Darvish, a patriotic woman, thought.

Damon Lester and his counterparts at NAMAD were also aligning themselves as advocates for their group. They were part of those seeking a consensus proposal and had been fighting the dealer cuts all along. Minority dealers were being wiped out at high rates. "Reducing the dealer body has absolutely nothing to do with the viability of the manufacturer," Lester said publicly.

Like the CRDR leaders, Lester continually pointed out that dealers run independently financed franchises. They were the middle group between the manufacturer and the consumer, acting as the voice of customers and a distribution channel for products. Like a Kmart or a McDonald's, they were not owned by product manufacturers.

The money issue and the automakers' response to it was becoming a broken record. Darvish and her A-team thought, *What part of that message doesn't the government or automakers get?*

As if there hadn't been enough meetings, Congress suddenly called for a September 17 powwow on the closed dealer situation with the automakers, the task force, and a few dealer representatives.

It was their world they were inhabiting, and they had to play by their rules, Darvish saw. "I didn't know about this until yesterday," she apologized to her groups by e-mail a few days earlier about the short notice. Dealers, she said, should attend only if they were interested in meeting with members of Congress.

There was tension in the air that day. The automakers were not offering a peace pipe, and there were no offers on the table. So far, the main lobbyists had refused to negotiate.

At the news conference at the Capitol, a bipartisan group of House members questioned GM and Chrysler on why they should close more than two thousand dealerships. The automakers gave their familiar litany: the cut dealers were a drain on their resources and budgets. They did not represent their profit-making dealerships; these were the failed dealers.

House Majority Leader Hoyer took the lead in questioning the automakers and auto task force. He still had a bone to pick with the task force, as did many other members of Congress. At the news conference, he again asked the task force members why these franchises should be closed and how that would save carmakers money.

The response, Hoyer said, was unbelievable: stone silence. "They could not tell me why shutting down any of those dealers would save money for the carmakers," the Maryland Democrat said, still amazed. The automakers had offered damaging testimony in bankruptcy court earlier in June, which the dealer groups came to dispute vigorously. That's when all the "evidence" about dealers as cost factors surfaced.

Unfortunately, the corporate spin took hold as the general public came to believe that dealers cost the company money and were poor performers. Public sentiment was not exactly on the dealers' side, judging from the auto task force. But the dealer advocacy groups knew otherwise, especially Darvish and her A-team.

The rest of September was a flurry of efforts to get Congress unglued on the dealer rights legislation.

Then, almost magically, in early October, GM and Chrysler began initial talks with dealers, knowing Congress's collective eye was on them. Like union negotiations with automakers, the talks bordered on confrontational and led to postponed decisions.

Chrysler maintained that they had used methodology in making the critical decisions as to whom they would cut. Most industry observers even agreed that the automakers had to slim down their swollen dealer count, which no longer met current market demands.

"The decision, though difficult, was based on a data-driven matrix that assessed a number of key metrics," Steven Landry, Chrysler's executive vice president for North American sales, had said earlier.

ATAE's Tim Doran again pressed the criteria hot button. He pointed out that dealers didn't believe logic or a systematic method was used to eliminate them. "The decisions were not made on merit. We assumed dealers were at the bottom end, but they're not. We need the guidelines used to evaluate dealers," he told the automakers.

"It was done dealer by dealer. Do you want a profile?" asked Pete Grady icily. He was the highest ranking Chrysler officer attending, along with John Bozzella, Chrysler's chief lobbyist. Grady stressed that everything Chrysler did was "along the lines of Genesis because of our product plans going forward."

Bozzella, the lobbyist in DC, reinforced Chrysler's position, which had not changed much from the start. They had a strategy and stuck to it. But a written document on Chrysler's position on dealer concerns had not surfaced yet.

Darvish found Bozzella to be "everything you'd expect a lobbyist to be, a hired gun, and on the slippery side." He was hot and cold, unpredictable. You never knew which Bozzella would show up.

But in the talks, Bozzella opened the window a crack, admitting Chrysler may have "made some mistakes" in their decisions. "We can't go back and undo what's been done," he said, adding, "we can't sustain independently branded dealers." This meant stand-alone one- or two-brand Chrysler dealers were out of the picture.

GM, however, *would* go back and review some questionable decisions. Earlier, GM offered every dealer a wind-down period and an opportunity for a review. The most weight on the metrics used was sales effectiveness, GM negotiators said.

Ken Cole, the chief GM lobbyist in DC, defended GM's stance that they used standards in deciding on which dealers would go. "We didn't reject dealers in bankruptcy like Chrysler did. We used a standard," he said.

By October 27, four months into their efforts, Darvish had grown more comfortable with her get-out-the-vote style. She still clung to a reed of hope that their original proposals to restore dealers unilaterally would see life. She continued to rally the troops, providing sample letters to write Congress that were customized for their use. She and her A-team tried to make it easy for them to blitz all their contacts and not worry about what to say, or how to say it. They could copy, paste, edit messages, and send via e-mail. She made sure dealers were well-scripted along the way.

Dealers under SIGTARP's Eye

Preparing dealers for SIGTARP questioning was another matter. It was somewhat like preparing for trial, and then appearing before a judge. It could be uncomfortable squirming under SIGTARP's investigative eye.

The SIGTARP office, located in downtown DC, was calling for dealer testimony on the cuts. Darvish met with their investigators for some hours. SIGTARP acts much like a federal prosecutor's office, doing discovery and obtaining evidence. Surprisingly, they had not received much "real data" in discussions with other sources. However, they had interviewed countless witnesses and spent time watching the dealers' personal videos that were sent. Her group also had provided each investigator with recent economic-impact packages that showed facts and figures related to closing the dealers.

"The SIGTARP focus is on facts and evidence," she reminded dealers who could be called upon by the investigators. She urged them to "back up your statements with facts and have numbers ready" on how much money they were charged for the various items manufacturers claimed they paid for—everything from product inventory, parts, signage, training, and advertising.

SIGTARP's office operates independently of Congress and the White House, and its members were committed to completing the investigation called for by Senator Rockefeller and Congress earlier, she wrote to dealers. Between Congress and SIGTARP, the ball was rolling on the issue of fair play in the dealer terminations. They weren't home yet, but they had momentum going.

November came. No vote yet, but the advocates spent more time hammering Congress to swing votes their way. They had to have a signed law in place before the end of the year, or it was no dice. Darvish and her A-team were wrangling over language in the bills that might survive the complicated political process and best help the dealers. It was a tougher go in the Senate.

In early December, more frustration set in. It was the late innings, and Chrysler threw the dealer groups a curve ball. The company wanted to change their position on how to resolve dealer concerns, throwing the advocacy groups off guard.

Chrysler issued a "Proposal to Resolve Dealer Concerns," dated December 3, 2009. In carefully crafted legal language, Chrysler said they were aiming for "transparency" on the rejected dealer process. They gave guidelines on binding arbitration terms, sensing that was the direction Congress was going in, and looking at dealer-compensation issues. In that document, they also called for a "face-to-face review process" with dealers. Dealer lawyers later said they didn't see that happen, at least not with most dealers.

Darvish and the committee leaders were livid. Why were they getting this formal document with such complicated language now? GM also pulled some last-minute maneuverings on their end, like the two legal teams were consulting on strategy to still fight the dealers. GM broke off talks to avoid legislation and the announced plans to give rejected dealers access to third-party arbitration, CRDR members believed.

The committee tried to fight the actions but knew the automakers were running out the clock, stonewalling at this late date. Or simply trying to win points with Congress, as if appearing to negotiate with dealers.

David Weaver and John Hughes, the key congressional staffers, told the dealer groups that Congress had to proceed with the legislation at hand. There was no time to keep working on the automakers with their stalling tactics. When push comes to shove, you go with what you have, they advised. It was now or never.

Darvish could see this was turning into an old-fashioned shoot-out movie. In her saner moments, she thought, *It feels like a movie unreeling before my eyes, but you can't make this stuff up.*

In the late hours, Darvish took stock again. She planned her next moves. On the advice of Dan Renberg, CRDR's attorney, Darvish called for her team to keep pushing on the critical votes, forget the setbacks with the automakers. Keep your eye on the prize; the Congress votes were what mattered now, Renberg reminded her and others on the committee.

Almost a week before the final countdown in the Senate, the heat was cranked up to get it done, for better or worse.

Chapter 11—Hometown Heroes

Did you ever know that you're my hero? You're everything I'd like to be …
—"The Wind Beneath My Wings," Bette Midler

America loves heroes. Hollywood fosters a multibillion-dollar industry that feeds off creating and promoting action heroes. Sports, rock, and other celebrity-creating machines also are based on the same premise: larger-than-life heroes. So far they're mostly men, but women are increasingly joining the ranks.

In times of major stress or upheaval the need is even greater to come in contact with them, to live vicariously off their energy, drive, and heroic accomplishments. The fact that it's mostly smoke and mirrors doesn't bother people. Americans spent more than $10 billion last year on movies, despite the deep recession of the past few years, according to a Yahoo online survey.

In the fight to save the dealers, everyday Americans were responding in a crisis like Hollywood heroes would. They *were* heroic in their actions those who observed them closely thought.

Many of the dealers depicted here could be called "hometown heroes." They are unsung heroes, not household names to the world at large. The average Joe and Josephine wouldn't recognize them on the street. But as activists in the campaign to save all dealers, they became the voice for the fallen dealers, or those who could not speak out. Most were not fallen in the sense of death or debilitating illness. But they did fall—often from great heights, as their lifework was abruptly taken away, their businesses stolen, their reputations smeared. The dealers who remained quiet sometimes were too wounded morally to speak out for the cause, or afraid of further repercussions. Many were not able to even tell family members of their loss.

To Tammy Darvish, the activist dealers she worked with emerged as heroes in their own right. After joining forces with CRDR, they kept fighting even in the face of insurmountable odds. They gave selflessly to help others when hope seemed gone. Some continued to help other dealers even after they lost their own businesses, hoping to spotlight the wrongs done by their former manufacturing partners with the blessing of government and the courts. Others continued the fight after winning the chance to get their own businesses back. They knew what it was like to think you'd lost it all.

They told their stories to Congress, government officials, judges, and lawyers. They got them out to media and other key influencers. Later, their collective voices shook the halls of Congress as a vote on dealer rights legislation was forced.

But in the portraits that emerge here, these heroes are not one-dimensional movie types. They hurt. They suffer and are able to admit their human failings. That's hard for most people to do. In the process, some described the painful loss of their livelihoods as a robbery, a mugging, a murder of the human spirit. Almost all of them called it an outrage, a betrayal. There were no polite terms or euphemisms like "lessons learned" or "shared sacrifice" in their language.

One of the unknown facets of the core group of CRDR members is that they formed a common bond that lived on far beyond the dealer rights campaign itself. Many support one another to this day. Like veterans of wars, combat buddies, they were shaped by the most horrific—and meaningful—experience of their lives. And they never gave up the fight to restore the rights of the whole group to regain their businesses. In many cases, like the CRDR leaders themselves, they put their own jobs on the line. They were eyewitnesses and participants in history—unwittingly changing it.

Most were ready to go to the mat to stay open—and keep others open. Like the three committee leaders, they wanted to make a difference for dealers now and for future generations, so the egregious acts they had lived through would not happen again to anyone else.

The dealer rights battle began raging in May 2009 as news of the terminations spread. Supporters came along who understood what dealers meant when they said a violation of constitutional rights and personal freedom had occurred. Media reports helped fan the flames. The wrongs done to thousands of dealers, their employees, and their families must be righted, the committee said. Their supporters grew to include Congress, city and state officials, legal teams, and dealership staff and customers.

Tammy Darvish maintained an e-mail base of thousands of contacts, including journalists and Congress members she kept in touch with regularly. It constituted a personal Facebook-style friends list. She kept them updated on legislative actions, dealers in the news, trouble spots, and the latest events.

Looking back, Darvish pondered the questions she often got: How do you keep going? Who helped you keep up the momentum day after day? Why, it was these very same people she communicated with and often cried with every day. They became her personal heroes. She created a mental and physical list that still sustains her.

Darvish didn't know what order to put them in so she put them in alphabetical order. Many became her A-team of go-to people, a few dozen hardy, driven souls. In her book, they're all batting a thousand. They each deserve their own book. Some of the leaders are profiled here.

* * *

Mark Calisi runs Eagle Auto Mall in Riverhead, part of New York's Long Island. His group sells a handful of brands—Chevrolet, Mazda, Volvo, Kia, and Chrysler GEM cars. He wanted to add Chrysler back into the lineup but needed to resolve the legal issues between them. Calisi will never forget the day he got his termination letter and later the "see-ya-in-court" papers from Chrysler. A high-performing Chrysler-Jeep dealer, he faced not only rejection but felt personally maligned in the process.

Only in Calisi's case, the turn of the screw put Chrysler in the spotlight for getting rid of him, even though his performance scores and profit record proved exceptional. "We were in the top 1 percent in working capital in the country. It was never a performance issue," Calisi said. Calisi is a high-energy straight-shooter, transparent, much like Darvish. His rapid-fire speech is peppered with slang and comes out exactly like he thinks it. It would be easy to understand why corporate types might not relate to the take-no-prisoners style of a Mark Calisi. With Calisi, you know which side of the fence you're on, no doublespeak.

As friends describe him, he's like a gentle bull in the china shop, but he doesn't destroy anything. He builds on the rubble, erecting a new foundation. "He's absolutely fearless, not afraid of anyone," Darvish said. She grew to admire Calisi immensely as he rushed to help the group intent on restoring dealer rights. She had often drawn on his strength when the chips were down.

"Mark thought nothing of calling up Jim Press or Pete Grady, the Chrysler VP in charge of sales and dealer relations, or NADA execs directly to let them know his thoughts. He was a great media instigator to get them to chase rumors or other lies put out there," Tammy recalls. "He could stand up to anyone."

With his Bronx-style New York accent, Calisi is almost a perfect caricature of a hard-charging New Yorker. Picture an older, solidly built Fonz from the 1970s–80s TV series *Happy Days*. Only talking with Calisi about his dealership experience isn't a feel-good comedy. Or think the hardboiled but emotional Detective Andy Sipowicz on TV's cop drama *NYPD Blue*. Under the sometimes tough exterior, Calisi has a soft spot for children and the disadvantaged, the underdog. He's a big supporter of charities and community fund-raising drives. He's big-headed yet big-hearted.

Yet Calisi has a sophisticated analytical side that understands the world of high finance and numbers. It's Calisi who explains the numbers to reporters who ask questions such as why GM would be better off with its own captive finance company. He loves marketing and dealing with customers too much to give it up. He's also an excellent pitch man to media and legal types. Always quotable, he was a dealer source in headline stories in major national newspapers, including *The New York Times, Wall Street Journal, Automotive News,* and *Ward's Dealer Business.*

This is no dealer slouch. A classic entrepreneur, Calisi had the first Chevrolet store in the nation to get hydrogen fuel stations for cars and is designated a priority dealer for Chrysler's GEM EV golf-cart style cars and the 2011 Chevrolet Volt, a combined electric-gas engine small car, which debuted from GM in 2010 in select market regions.

With the terminations, Calisi got ensnared in the politics of big business. As he explains it, e-mails surfaced among Chrysler execs who admitted his rejection had nothing to do with performance. His was superior. Chrysler staffers in the field offices called him "combative," "litigious," and other choice terms.

Field office staffers manage day-to-day sales affairs for the automakers. Those e-mail records were sealed and then finally subpoenaed and released by US bankruptcy Judge Arthur Gonzalez when Leonard Bellavia, acting as the dealers' lawyer in two cases, requested them in the legal discovery process.

He grew incensed when Judge Gonzalez disregarded facts that later came to light showing the dealer cuts were unnecessary. He and others saw Gonzalez as a pro-corporate federal judge after he found for Chrysler in their bankruptcy hearings. Nearly ninety dealers had agreed to serve as witnesses against Chrysler. To many, it seemed the veteran judge had made up his mind ahead of time in support of Chrysler's position.

Other dealers were puzzled that supposedly reputable judges and government officials didn't reverse their decisions, or make public comments on them as new facts surfaced.

Tammy Darvish and Calisi became good friends as a result of fighting on the same side of the dealer battlefield. "We are opposites in many ways, but we got to be pretty good friends. He was a great source of motivation, for us in CRDR, always," she said.

* * *

Mike Comiskey, a Chrysler dealer in the New Orleans eastern ward area, saw his Orleans Dodge Chrysler Jeep store decimated in the aftermath of Hurricane Katrina in 2005. Even though his insurance company (Chrysler Insurance) still owed him more than a million dollars for flooded vehicles, he rebuilt his dealership from the ground up after the hurricane.

After refurbishing his property, Comiskey got shipshape and sales picked up. But some months later, another catastrophe hit. This one was called "Operation Chrysler." In May, when he got the Chrysler rejection letter, he was stunned and emotionally devastated. "It all seemed too much," he said. He was given three weeks to shut down on June 9. Now he had truly lost everything. Only this time he couldn't rebuild. He was one of sixteen Chrysler stores to close across Louisiana; none remained in New Orleans.

He turned his shop, set on a three-acre lot, into a used car and parts operation. He cut staff in half, from a high of sixty-eight. After a good try, he had to shut down operations and find a job to support his family.

Sometimes life just dumps too much on you, Comiskey couldn't help thinking. "Things are pretty rough for me and mine right now, but we keep on fighting," he wrote to Darvish in the thick of things. Still, Comiskey rolled up his sleeves and said, "What can I do?" to help the dealer cause nationally and keep the momentum going, Darvish recalled.

He e-mailed the team constantly with updates and kept up pressure on legislators to investigate the dealer problem. What's more, Comiskey understood the pain other dealership owners and their people were going through. He served a community wiped out by disaster and knew the struggles of the working class. He closed shop but vowed to return.

He launched an e-mail campaign and phone attack on a grand scale, involving employees, friends, and family. "I called and met with any official that would take my call. This made the July fly-in event easy for me." He was geared up, his own campaign in place, and able to throw his support behind CRDR, despite his own misfortunes.

To keep going and support his family, who live in the New Orleans area, Comiskey took a temporary manager's job with nearby Premier Automotive. The prominent auto group, owned by Troy Duhon, operates multi-line import franchises near Comiskey's former store on Route 101, the area's dealer row that borders the New Orleans freeway system.

In November, eighteen months after his closure by Chrysler, he was planning his comeback. He wanted to open another dealership on his former site which he still held a lease on. That project is underway and he hopes to re-open shop in 2011. "Why another dealership? Aren't you fed up?" he is asked. "It's what I know how to do best," he says.

In a way, it's also his answer to the struggle he and others have endured. "What they've taken from us can't be replaced. In my eyes, bankruptcy is a vulgar term," he said.

* * *

Jeff Duvall, a northern Georgia dealer, is an unusual hero to add to the list. He continued to bring practical advice and resources to the dealer committee even after his own franchise was restored before the arbitration period. He had his private reasons for staying involved, but when pressed sometimes, he said in his good humored way, "Maybe I was suffering from survivor's shock."

Survivor's shock? It was a psychological term used to describe the mental anguish and guilt survivors of tragedies feel when they learned they survived, sometimes at the expense of others. It can be a tough mental trip. Duvall also wasn't afraid to tell it like it is, even after he was back in business, and he stood to lose again. That was a time when many dealers wouldn't speak out, worried they would lose more, or the automakers wouldn't like them.

During the ordeal of 2009, and even after, Duvall came out in support of the dealer campaign, putting funds into the committee coffers and working on Congress. He was a key example of Darvish's notion that those who can help should. He financially supported CRDR through the summer and until the arbitration hearings were completed in 2010.

But there was more to it for Jeff Duvall. He saw the crisis in the country and DC as "the darkest period in franchised automobile dealer history." He didn't think NADA's leadership was responding in kind, despite some of their public statements decrying the dealer cuts.

When differences arose between CRDR and NADA over the direction that legislative efforts should take on restoring dealers, he called John McEleney, the NADA leader at the time. McEleney called back from Santiago, Chile, Duvall said. At a critical juncture, McEleney had left a meeting with CRDR and congressmen the day before saying he had to catch a plane, Duvall recalled. It turned out McEleney flew to Santiago for Chile's version of a NADA dealer convention. That might be all right in different circumstances. But to Duvall, it didn't sit right. It was like "Nero fiddling while Rome burns," he thought. Dealers were on fire and getting burned to a crisp, while some with power stayed away.

Duvall considered himself one of the lucky ones. He won his dealerships back after negotiating terms that allowed him to "dual" his existing stores. He didn't know any dealers who could "make the onerous LOI work without getting some waivers," he said. Other factors played out in his favor during the closure period. "Since we are a rural dealer we were not burdened with a huge parts inventory, which I kept rather than almost giving away like many dealers had to do."

"With all the good luck I've had comes plenty of survivor's guilt," Duvall said. In fact, before he signed the agreement, he called the committee leaders to ask if his settlement would in any way harm other dealers' chances in arbitration. Darvish encouraged him to "accept the letter if it worked for me." *Imagine,* she thought, *giving up your own chance at the prize for the sake of others.*

Duvall also saw how generous the three CRDR leaders had been. "I shudder to think about how much of their own money they invested in dealers, not to mention their time, while possibly hundreds of GM [and Chrysler] dealers got their franchises back and never sent them a dime." His heart also went out to the dealers who supported CRDR and lost everything. He was sick at heart for them, wondering what he would do if he was in their shoes. But Darvish and the committee thought Jeff Duvall, of all people, gave more than they ever expected.

* * *

Jack Fitzgerald, one of the original leaders of CRDR, gained folk-hero status to his dealer followers and other industry observers. After five decades in the auto business, he was not afraid to speak candidly to higher-ups at the automakers. The risk-averse automakers generally preferred order takers. Fitzgerald was not one of those. It's perhaps those qualities that got him in trouble with the rainmakers who reward yes-men and women in corporate military-industrial-style hierarchies.

Fitzgerald is a down-to-earth, no-nonsense man, but a tactician and fact man. He was usually five steps ahead of anyone in the room with him. Politicians could take lessons on his style. But be careful: he tells it like it is. His thoughtful but fiery manner might belong to a top politician. His speeches and comments to Congress, major media, the auto task force, and dealership groups came across as campaign speeches of a man running for high public office. Would he ever run for public office? "I'm too honest for politics," he said when asked, laughing at the idea.

He and Alan Spitzer kick-started CRDR's "save the dealers" campaign in May, shortly after the announced closures. As a veteran of the leadership group, Fitzgerald had been in car sales and service since the mid-fifties. Before that, he sold safety systems door-to-door. It could be said of Fitzgerald that he suffers no fools and can be blunt with those who continually whitewash the truth. Like other ambitious dealers, he seems fearless in the face of adversity and won't kowtow to power. Fitzgerald often pointed out that Chrysler and GM were not making cars that *Consumer Reports* would recommend, accounting for their sales problems.

Fitzgerald is known as an innovator. His dealerships were among the first to develop green-power programs, and he has built a reputation as being pro-consumer, even at the expense of manufacturer relations. "Most dealers are afraid of retribution from the manufacturers. Jack, he's not," Ivette E. Rivera, a NADA lobbyist, told the *Washington Post,* following the cuts. "He helps put a face on it. When he speaks out, he has a lot of credibility."

In a *Fox TV* news broadcast in late October 2010, Fitzgerald upbraided the task force, which pushed Chrysler to thin its ranks and enter bankruptcy status. Chrysler then was able to remove dealers with an "Alpha" dealer consolidation project on the boards for years, refreshed as Project Genesis, a new-age name for a new-age Chrysler. By fall, Steve Rattner had long departed, so Fitzgerald and crew took on Ron Bloom, who indirectly replaced Rattner. Bloom had a new title of manufacturing czar, advising the administration on broad industry issues.

"I talked to Ron Bloom, and he was the most arrogant person I've ever met," Fitzgerald said after taking his measure. "Or maybe second, after Steve Rattner," he corrected himself. He recalled a meeting with Bloom and others during the legislative process. "Now I've been dressed down by drill sergeants before—I served my time [in the air force]—but he was something else," Fitzgerald said about a late July meeting between the Bloom-headed task force and dealers. (Rattner had departed by then.)

At that meeting, Fitzgerald said, Bloom dismissed them in twelve minutes after doing most of the talking. He also insulted former Chrysler VP Tom Pappert, who had worked for decades at Chrysler, helping to restore the company to prosperity after a government rescue loan. Bloom clearly wasn't interested in hearing about that period, the effect the cuts would have on employment, and the economy, Fitzgerald saw.

* * *

Yale King is the Colorado dealer who lost his Chrysler and Jeep stores in Longmont; his GM Buick-GMC store was later restored, but he was no longer the dealer. King was always ready with an instant motivational pep talk for Darvish and the A-team. She came to think of him as the "wisdom and conscience" of the group. He was often the one she turned to in times of personal distress, just to get her head straight.

King became actively involved at the very beginning of the dealer rights struggle, in May 2009. He made thousands of calls, and sent an equal number of e-mails to the dealer network and every lawyer and politician he could think of to help the dealer cause. In the height of the battle to win congressional votes, he was always on the front lines. Like others, he saw this as a domestic war, except it was the little guy against the big corporate interests and government.

Craig Allely, his lawyer in Denver, said of King, "At that time, only a handful of dealers understood the magnitude of what was happening, and even fewer stood up at the beginning. Yale was among those, along with Tammy, Jack, Alan, and a very few others." The two, dealer and lawyer, were in New York for the Chrysler bankruptcy hearings at the beginning of June. "Yale was among the very few dealers who early on objected to the Chrysler rejection motion and submitted briefs in opposition," Allely said.

"He is second to none in hard work and enthusiasm. He is thoughtful and honest, and a simple patriot," said Allely, who has known King for a long time.

King is a rah-rah America guy. He loves his country; he loves the car industry. The joy of his life is talking about his two sons, who serve in the military and fought in two recent Gulf wars. But he's said more than once, if he can send his sons to war to fight for his country, then he personally had to take a stand on fighting for the rights of citizens on their home soil. To him, the dealer rights issue was as big as that. And these were his peers.

Speaking in his soft Midwestern drawl (he's originally from Iowa), Yale King may have missed his opportunity to be a great orator in the tradition of Martin Luther King, or a politician. A deeply spiritual man, he drew on his faith to get him through the hard times. It's not a topic he's shy about.

Darvish worked closely with King and communicated with him from the very beginning through the final steps of the journey to restore dealer rights." Yale was the spiritual leader for the team, especially me," she said. "Whenever I would have a really bad day or hit a hard wall in our efforts, Yale could always find the good or some inspirational message to get me back in the saddle and running at a fast gallop."

In keep-up-the-spirit notes to Darvish, he would often draw on personal experiences he had witnessed or heard about among fighters in combat troops. He likened the dealer battle to combat situations. It was about survival, this dealer fight.

Here's one example. On a Friday night in late August of 2009, the weather was oppressive and the CRDR troops were weary. Suddenly Darvish received an e-mail from King. It was almost prescient. He spoke of a special US combat force, the 160th Special Operations Aviation Regiment out of Fort Campbell, Kentucky, four of whose members had died not long before during high-altitude training on Mt. Massive in Colorado, causing despair in the unit. But the elite military unit known as the Night Stalkers had a saying: NSDQ (Night Stalkers don't quit).

It was the "don't-quit" message that Darvish and others took to heart in the dark days, when the group felt the wolf howling at the door and defeat lying like an unwanted package on the doorstep. Dare you open it and look inside? Dare you raise your voice to power again?

She thought about King's "don't quit" message. To soldiers of old it might have been, "Remember the Alamo"; to athletes, football or otherwise, it might be, "Win one for the Gipper!"

According to King, the "don't-quit" theme was inspired by a book by General Jerry Boykin called *Never Surrender*. Boykin, a friend of King's, was a founder of the Delta Force. As a commander of that elite unit, Boykin was a subject in the movie *Black Hawk Down*.

Like an officer who wants to inspire his troops, King passed that "don't-quit" message on to Darvish and team. To the three CRDR leaders, he said personally, "I have been humbled and honored by the commitment of you three. I thank you all, and ask for prayers for this nation, our military, and those that will go and have come and I know that you three don't quit," King wrote. "I beg you to have strength."

Throughout his personal ordeal, King called his wife, Shauna, his "rock." Shauna King worked tirelessly at night and on the weekends, sending e-mails in the wee hours that would land in the morning as people arrived at work. She held a high-level position in a human service agency she had founded, but supported him emotionally as the strain grew, King said.

Yale King remained one of Darvish's ardent supporters over the long haul. He always ended his e-mails, perhaps to everyone on planet Earth, with "Positively, Yale." After the automaker debacles had cooled nationally and he knew he wasn't getting his Chrysler franchise back—an arbitrator found against him—King thought he would meditate and figure out his path. Then on September 7, 2010, his home was ravaged by wildfires that swept the Colorado canyon valley he lived in. He moved his family into a Boulder-area hotel after staying with relatives in cramped quarters. Even when he thought he had lost everything, King kept the others around him propped up with hope and support. It was his way.

* * *

Steve LaBelle, a GM dealer, ran a profitable Chevrolet operation in Bridgewater, Massachusetts. An assertive, disciplined man, he wouldn't take no for an answer. He kept on pushing—boulders, barricades, people, whatever stood in the way—to get his dealership back and help others. To his credit, he had the numbers and scorecard to back up his words. In the contest with GM, his dealership was reinstated. As fate would have it, GM then placed another dealer in his market area near Boston, wanting him to move to a smaller, less desirable market. He challenged that decision.

But it was LaBelle's connection to US Representative Barney Frank, the Massachusetts Democrat, that greased the skids for much of the political action that followed. Darvish was able to contact Barney Frank, and that led Frank to lobby fiercely for the disenfranchised dealers. Through Frank, LaBelle also enlisted the support of Senator Ted Kennedy, who was fondly called the "lion of the Senate." On his hospital deathbed, Kennedy made appeals to GM CEO Fritz Henderson and sales executive Mark LaNeve to change GM's approach on dealer terminations, LaBelle relates. Kennedy brought up LaBelle's case specifically. The Henderson letter may have been one of Senator Kennedy's final political stands, after lobbying for health care, before his death on August 25, 2009.

LaBelle said he reached Senator Kennedy through mutual friends. "Kennedy was very much for small business because it was the foundation this country was built on and what was happening was not what he wanted to see happen. I think that had he been healthy we would have seen his influence with the president in action to right this wrong much sooner," LaBelle said. Kennedy contacted GM, but LaBelle thought he may have passed away before they responded to his letter.

"I had received an e-mail from Mark LaNeve stating that Senator Kennedy had called him and he was looking at my case, but I think the senator was simply too sick to press on with the issue," LaBelle said.

But with clout such as Barney Frank, Chris Van Hollen, Steny Hoyer, Steve LaTourette, Dan Maffei, Roscoe Bartlett, Jay Rockefeller, and others lending weight to the dealer cause, the dealer movement gained importance among Democrats and Republicans in Congress. Although the administration's auto task force never "got it" when it came to the dealer issues, Congress did get it and eventually their support may have helped the president speed the legislation along, CRDR leaders thought.

Of LaBelle Darvish said, "Steve's good connection to Barney Frank was important to our ability to move forward and fuel the success of our legislation. We spent many hours together strategizing and Steve also was a big sounding board for Jim Tarbox." Tarbox was the East Coast dealer who stood out in the fight to convince Congress and other leaders of the automakers' hurtful actions.

"Steve was a generous and tireless contributor to CRDR efforts up through legislation and preparation for arbitration. His case was very unique so arbitration was not the major issue for him at the time, but he still remained involved as an advocate for everyone," Darvish said before LaBelle's own dealership doors finally closed. He was also able to uncover some mistakes the automakers made in selecting dealers for termination, a story on its own.

* * *

Richard Mealey stood out as a Chrysler dealer, deemed a Five-Star, the highest rating a Chrysler dealer can get. He had received most Chrysler awards and was even nominated for Time Dealer of the Year, a prestigious national recognition very few can claim. He was a former president of the Detroit Automobile Dealers Association, proving that old ties often don't survive in the new economy.

A high-profile dealer, Mealey chaired the North American International Auto Show, the world's third-largest auto show with a multi-million dollar charity fund-raising purpose, and was the second-largest Moparts dealer in Michigan.

He and his wife, Jackie, hail from the upscale town of Bloomfield Hills, Michigan. But the upscale didn't mean anything when Chrysler yanked the business they had poured their life savings into. A well-prepared Richard Mealey testified in Chrysler bankruptcy court hearings in late May 2009. Generally soft-spoken, Mealey was even more so in court. It was hard for him to verbalize the words he'd carefully prepared. At one point he could not continue, and the sentiment in the court was with him, Darvish recalled. Even a Chrysler lawyer sitting near her whispered Mealey should not have been on a list, or maybe was the last person on it. Mealey, who soon lost his dealership and countless investments, continued his fight for dealer rights, although he couldn't go up against Chrysler and all their resources. After four decades of service to one automaker, it was a betrayal. It all came out in bankruptcy court that morning in May.

"He was very emotional on the stand and I felt so sorry for him and other dealers testifying. Not only was he a great performing dealer in sales and service, he was among the top in the country in parts sales. His story was so sad, it made me cry while I was sitting in the courtroom," Darvish said.

Attending as a representative of the Unsecured Creditors Committee, it opened her eyes to what was going on in the modern-day version of car wars: dealers waging battle against the corporations, their lawyers, and big government. Between dealers such as Mealey, Mark Calisi, and Jim Tarbox, who also testified in bankruptcy court, Darvish began to understand how deep the terminations had cut into the finances—and hearts—of dealers. "I couldn't believe that the bankruptcy judge, Gonzalez, did nothing to help these dealers even though he had the power to do so," Darvish said.

She was sitting next to a Chrysler lawyer, in the courtroom when Mealey testified. "I looked at him so sadly and he looked pretty sad himself. He told me that out of 789 dealers Mealey was probably 788 on the list of 789, or even 789. Their own lawyer felt bad for Richard Mealey." That meant Mealey should never have been on the list, like so many others, she thought. He had the luck of the draw against him. Chrysler never explained satisfactorily to him why he was let go.

* * *

Jackie Mealey is Richard Mealey's wife of forty-five years, and together they have two grown children—girls formerly in the automotive business—and four grandchildren. She can be described as one who keeps things running behind the scenes. She's the organized type who sends birthday and holiday gifts early and remembers all the details: who likes what and why.

Young-looking and vibrant (some have described her as a Sally Field double), she likes to bake—chocolate chip cookies, brownies, and cupcakes are specialties. When hard times sidelined the Mealeys, she was a force behind Richard Mealey, supporting him as a good wife is inclined to do.

When he wanted to fly home early from bankruptcy court in Manhattan because it was taking five days instead of two in late May, she said, "No, no, you have to stay and finish this, Richard."

Her empathy for the rejected dealers ran as a strong electric undercurrent in her thinking. "[The dealers] I know are among the most ethical and righteous people I've ever known. All of the disenfranchised dealers are panicked about their futures," she said, her eyes wet. She described the dejection she and her husband felt as an "emotional paralysis," a time where they were treated as outsiders by Chrysler. The baffling part? This was the company they had supported their entire youth and now in late middle-age—the company that heaped upon Mealey one award after another. That was before the termination notice arrived, of course.

"The mental anguish has been indescribable. There is never any peace of mind. Every day is a huge worry and at one point I thought the only good part of my day is when I can see Richard finally sleeping because that is the only time he isn't worrying," she said twenty months after their ordeal.

At one point during their shut-down crisis when one of her grandchildren came up and climbed into her lap and said, "Lammie,"—their nickname for her—"why are you so sad?" she had to force a smile. "Kids can do that to you," she said. But that was much later when she could face things more bravely.

Jackie Mealey became highly active on the political front with CRDR and on her own, trying to fix what she called "a horrible injustice." She kept pushing the group and public figures to respond, try to do more. Darvish said of her, "She never would accept that much of what we did fell on deaf ears and blind eyes with the automakers, and the task force. She was more than relentless. My parents knew her and Richard for many years. They had won so many of the same awards at Chrysler and went on so many Chrysler reward trips together."

These ran from the Five-Star exceptional dealer to various sales-achievement recognitions, up through 2009, when they were axed. "If there was a CRDR award for most dedicated wife, Jackie would win that award hands down," Darvish said.

The Mealeys never ended up going to arbitration; costs were too prohibitive. Just what Chrysler wanted, they knew. Darvish tried to work out a deal for them through her contacts at Kia Motors America for a franchise, but getting financing was a problem for many dealers. It was the height of the credit crunch and even once-successful businesses couldn't secure the loans. They ended up settling with Chrysler shortly before their arbitration date, but it was a minimal amount.

In the meantime, Jackie Mealey and other dealer supporters worked behind the scenes to effect change. She sent personal appeal letters to every power figure she could think of—Chrysler executives, members of Congress, all the way up to President Obama and Rahm Emanuel, Obama's recent chief of staff. She outlined the scope of the dealer problem and the atrocities committed against dealers. Mealey would work on these memos with her dealer colleagues until she thought they were perfect. Most were thoughtful and well-crafted. One letter she and other dealers wrote and sent to President Obama (Emanuel too) in January 2010 appears in the back section of this book. (See appendix D.)

Jackie Mealey got no reply but wasn't altogether surprised. Emanuel resigned his post in October 2010 to run for mayor of Chicago. She hoped he was sick to hear about the dealer situation but doubted he even remembered their plight.

* * *

Patrick Painter represents an entire family of Painters in southern Utah who owned businesses—two Chrysler dealerships in Nephi and St. George, Utah—that were eliminated as part of the automaker's restructuring. Patrick Painter ran Painter Motors Chrysler Dodge Jeep truck and Chevrolet Buick Pontiac dealerships in Nephi; while his brother Phil ran the Chrysler-Jeep-Dodge dealership in St. George.

In all, ten family members were involved in running the businesses in the Utah towns, around for sixty-five years. Darvish said Patrick Painter, especially, became highly active in the charged political and organizing process that fueled the CRDR dealer campaign. He and his brother, Phil, lobbied valiantly on behalf of dealers and stayed in constant touch with CRDR throughout the legislative process.

Painter is a state representative in Utah, so he understood how politics work. In the beginning, it wasn't enough to save him and his family stores. Their Chrysler-Jeep-Dodge dealership in St. George was closed in the May roundup and soon gifted to a nearby dealer, who operated a chain of primarily import stores. Other dealers thought the gifting deal smacked of cronyism and deals struck behind closed doors, many of the culled dealers said. "I really got emotionally tied to the Painter family because they reminded me so much of our family-run business at DARCARS," Darvish said. "Patrick's father, James, was so sad that his own father's legacy was being stolen from his family, and all I could think of was how sad that would make my father to have such a long legacy and tradition with an automaker destroyed."

The tension between Darvish and NADA members intensified when she tried to defend the Painters and others who had been uprooted then watched their dealerships given away, gratis. She kept their stories alive to the media and talked about them openly to Congress, hoping to reverse the unfair growing practice of gifting closed dealerships to competitors. If there was any issue that enraged dealers more than losing their own franchises, it was that one.

Patrick Painter later was able to negotiate with GM to restore his Buick and Chevrolet franchises in Nephi, but the emotional and financial damage could not be erased.

* * *

Gina Russo is a dealer's daughter who helped run the family dealership, Lochmoor Chrysler-Jeep in Detroit. Their single-point dealership was on the cusp of a more prosperous area called Grosse Pointe, situated on an old-style boulevard called Mack Avenue. Her father, Gus Russo, who founded the dealership, continually performed at the top in Chrysler sales. He also was a friend and colleague of John Darvish. The two had known each other for more than thirty years. Once the dealer rights struggle united them, Gina Russo and Tammy Darvish discovered they had more in common than being successful dealers' daughters. And once the ax fell on car dealers, they got behind a fighting cause that changed their lives.

Russo, an energized and practical woman, jumped on board the CRDR train and made her presence known. Her letters and e-mails always stressed she was ready to help when needed, Darvish recalled. "She worked so hard and fought so hard to help save her father's business. She came to Washington whenever we needed her and she was great at keeping in constant contact."

According to several accounts, the new owner, who had been given the Russos' Chrysler-Jeep franchise to merge with his Dodge store, didn't waste any time luring the Russos' customers or announcing his dealership presence. At one point, his staffers parked a minivan in front of the Russos' closed building with a brightly colored sign showing an arrow pointing to his own dealership location a few blocks away. They hoped, of course, to capture any of the Russos' old customers who might drive by or go there. The Russos were still doing part-time sales and service business at the time.

After facing her battles in Detroit's car wars, Gina Russo became an advocate for dealer rights. She encouraged other activists to write letters, pressure Congress, and even the auto task force to listen to reason. She and her father appealed to Chryslers' top brass but got no resolution. The answers, if any, came from Chrysler lawyers who asked them to "cease and desist," or go away in "not nice" legal terms.

Gina Russo believed that what happened to car dealers could happen to any business owner. Dealers were not some unusual class of business, or people who did anything wrong. They were just minding the store, serving their customers, and often jumping to the factory's tune.

The big story behind the dealership cuts is not just about auto dealers losing their businesses, although the numbers were huge.

"What happened to us could happen to anyone in America. It was so wrong; that's why this story is so important to everyone in the country. This is about the survival of America's small businesses," Gina Russo said.

* * *

In some ways, Gus Russo is more reticent than his daughter, but even more enraged. He got involved and vocal on the dealer rights issues, but also grew skeptical that the automakers would change their positions. He appealed to the top at Chrysler, with Sergio Marchionne, but got little satisfaction there.

He believed Chrysler honchos in the field and at the top took a certain joy in being able finally to get rid of dealers they didn't want in the mix, those who might stand up to them. They couldn't wait to get rid of some of us dealers," he said of Chrysler leaders such as Steve Landry, Brian Schnurr, and even Jim Press. If bankruptcy hadn't happened, the automakers would have lost the poor performers anyway, or seen a lot of buy-sell deals going on, he said. Dealers sell their franchises for many reasons, but it often suggests financial duress, or a change in life circumstances, such as retirement. That didn't happen in great numbers at the time to indicate a trend.

After Russo lost his Chrysler-Jeep franchise, he didn't pursue arbitration to the end point, knowing their store—highly successful on all national scores—had also been gifted to another owner who had never sold Chrysler and Jeep models. But more than anything, Gus Russo had lost enough money—and sleep—to Chrysler power makers. He'd had it.

The Russos got a minimal settlement from the automakers for their losses. To this day, they are not in the dealership business after more than thirty years of serving customers. Many customers wrote letters of support and complained to Chrysler. They might as well have been shouting into the wind.

* * *

Mark Sims, a Lyndhurst, Ohio, dealer lost his Chevrolet store, his only dealership, with the cuts. Sims challenged Chevrolet later in arbitration but lost the case. In the process, he got involved with SIGTARP and had regular conversations with them to keep them informed.

Sims fought hard in the battle to restore dealers, even though his own Chevrolet store was lost. He made dealers aware that constitutional questions were being raised by experts and dealers on the unjust closings.

He pointed out that cities were caving in and allowing previous new-car-only zoning laws to be grandfathered in because they needed the revenue.

On November 17, there still was no firm vote in Congress. Sims suggested that CRDR step up the pace even more, aware that time was critical if the legislation was to pass before the end of the year.

"I had just spent twenty days on the Hill working for fairness and trying to light some fires. GM's Mr. Whitacre had committed to meet with dealers one-on-one but had not. It was all very frustrating for dealers, including Mark Sims," Darvish recalled.

Sims believed that GM's arbitrary and nonsystematic cutting of dealers should not be forgotten, and their practice of gifting dealerships or reassigning them to others, needed wide exposure. "This is the smoking gun that would force them to reactivate the rest of us," he told Darvish and CRDR.

Sims also worked the media and political angles hard, focusing attention on the national and local problems the dealers were having as a result of the terminations. "This guy should be in PR!" Darvish exclaimed.

It was Mark Sims who alerted Darvish and other dealers in late September about an ad that ran in a suburban Washington newspaper placed by a Chevrolet-Honda dealer who advertised for customers of a rejected dealer whose family dealership had served Chrysler for sixty-three years. The new Chevy-Honda dealer had been awarded the business although he had never sold a Chrysler product and didn't have a Chrysler-compliant facility that Sims knew of.

Darvish used the points Sims made in an e-mail to Congress alerting them to the situation and why this was just another violation of dealers' rights and a violation of the Fifth Amendment.

After the battle seemed to be over and the omnibus act was passed, with dealer legislation tucked inside and signed by President Obama, Sims stayed involved. He kept up the political pressure and helped orchestrate meetings with Congress and dealers. After the federal SIGTARP report came out in July 2010, he had a role in putting together a late press event, armed with new evidence.

Northeast Ohio dealers Sims, Alan Spitzer, and Halleen Chevrolet in North Olmsted were trying to get their closure decisions reversed, as if seeking last-minute clemency from the automakers.

Connected to that effort, Ohio Congressmen Steve LaTourette and John Boehner hosted a meeting at Sims' store near Cleveland that drew much press attention on the closed dealers in late October, right before the 2010 national midterm elections. It was staged to coincide with the GM final closure date of October 31. Dealers hoped to gain a reprieve for some of the remaining five hundred dealers who had not yet shut their doors.

After that time, perhaps unconnected, Representative Boehner was elected and would go on to serve as Speaker of the House as the Republicans gained majority seats in the House. LaTourette continued as a US representative and dealer advocate. The call of frustrated dealers was still echoing in the heartland.

* * *

Rob Smith served as Jack Fitzgerald's right hand throughout the campaign to restore dealer rights. Their stores in Maryland, Pennsylvania, and Virginia rate high in customer satisfaction. Ask someone in the area about where you might find the Fitzgerald folks, and they will point you to the main store in Kensington, Maryland, on Rockville Pike Road, a well-known, meandering highway. It winds for nearly thirty-seven miles from Wisconsin Avenue in DC and then twists from Bethesda to Kensington and further northwest.

Smith acted as Darvish's double in many instances. He had Darvish's back and knew her thinking and position on nearly every issue. He cautioned her when she was misfiring in a memo, or a critical issue, and his dry wit helped keep the mood a little lighter when the internal politics heated up with NADA, the automakers or other groups. He also did not seek credit for anything, letting her take center stage, where he thought she belonged. He was willing to work in the background, keeping the tone civil.

Darvish often called on his advice when drafting memos or letters on important issues. His reply notes were often cryptic affairs. But he was efficiently directing traffic, the course of action, often polishing her prose. "Take out [Dan] Inouye and soften it," he wrote as Darvish sent him an urgent e-mail about to go to the Senate from the committee. He thought her tone was too harsh.

Smith was a constant in the save-the-dealers campaign. Like the three committee leaders, he was a strategist and implementer. Darvish was glad to have people like Smith in the mix, and on her side. "We spent hours, days, weeks, months together and became very close friends," Darvish said of Smith. "He was a great fact checker and resource. Anytime I needed facts, figures, numbers, etc., he could produce them almost instantly. He attended every single meeting we had and took excellent notes. I even took him to my debriefing meeting with SIGTARP in July in case I was asked a question that I could not answer." Rob Smith always had the answer or could get to it by punching the keyboard on his laptop or hitting his BlackBerry keys.

Darvish called him "the best cheerleader anyone could have." Smith might be another Darvish clone, born with a heart of gold. Darvish often praised his skills. "Rob was a very valuable and important part of our team. All the while, he is a single dad raising three kids on his own and runs a teenage church group in his community." In his private life, Smith worked with church-affiliated youth groups and did other community fund-raising.

For his part, Smith said Tammy Darvish was often the first person he spoke to each morning and the last person he spoke to at night. He was an advisor, confidante and, in his levelheaded manner, steered Darvish and others on a straight course. Smith, who is process-driven, had worked for Jack Fitzgerald since the late 1980s and had seen his share of car wars and skirmishes with the big guys at General Motors, Ford, Chrysler, and other franchises that Fitzgerald had acquired over the years.

Both Smith and his boss, Fitzgerald, believe in backing up every assertion and claim they made with facts and statistics. Like Darvish, they had rooms full of records and notebooks on how the dealer termination saga unfolded and their own roles in it.

* * *

Alan Spitzer masterminded the creation of the CRDR group, while running the Spitzer Management Group out of Elyria, Ohio. In fact, in May 2009, he pulled in Jack Fitzgerald, a longtime colleague, and they began their own save-the-dealers campaign. As Spitzer tells it, the two had been friends since the late 1960s when they served on dealer councils and industry "dealer twenty" leadership groups together. Both became fervently committed to relentlessly pushing the dealer rights cause. "No" was not a word in his vocabulary when it came to closed dealers.

After they added Tammy Darvish to the team as their chief organizer and coleader, they became the "Big Three" in CRDR. As a group, they bristled at the bankruptcy methods of Chrysler and GM, who got a federal "kangaroo court" to buy their stories, Spitzer said. It wasn't bankruptcy but the process that angered them.

Spitzer was another listening post for Darvish and the fledgling committee. He teamed up Darvish with Alison, his daughter, thinking they would click. At the time, Alison was working in the dealerships in Elyria, near Cleveland. He also asked her to help coordinate events and the dealer campaign, once it grew legs and paperwork demands were increasing. And Alison was a natural for handling them.

Darvish recalled how Alan Spitzer regarded the sometimes last-minute requests she sent his way. "I would dump silly, problematic, very lengthy, and philosophical e-mails from people across the country on him and he would methodically and very factually deal with all of them."

Like Jack Fitzgerald, Spitzer had a world of patience with Darvish, just as he did with his daughter, whom he usually addressed as "honey." He enjoyed writing long e-mails explaining a position CRDR might take on an issue plaguing the group. "He would send us his own op-ed pieces now and then, and they were often quite instructional," Darvish said. Perhaps he was a frustrated newspaper editor, she thought, although he had a sharp eye for accounting.

Spitzer, a multi-line dealer in three states, handled press conferences and meeting call-ins for the group. He was also the financial guru, intent on raising money and a budget for the splinter group which the three leaders were financing solo for some time. Like Fitzgerald, he lost a high number of dealerships in the Chrysler and GM terminations. In fact, he referred to his dealer group as among the "most adversely affected" of the cancelled dealers, losing ten dealerships between Chrysler and GM. Only two were restored by Chrysler but were not yet operational at last contact.

* * *

Alison Spitzer, Alan's daughter, was involved from the beginning of the dealer campaign, even as Chrysler went to bankruptcy court in New York City. Growing up in the family business, she understood the issues the dealers were facing. When the group started up, she was pregnant and somewhat limited in her involvement, but after her baby girl was born, she went into high gear.

A techie, Alison Spitzer proved to be the supreme organizer. She kept the computers humming and schedules of meetings and events flying. She developed the group's highly secure website and also helped maintain it. A major role was coordinating the many events and meetings that were being added almost daily, including the big dealer rally that took place in mid-July on Capitol Hill, and coalesced Congress behind them.

She recalled the sweltering, humid day that drenched everyone in sweat. But there was work to be done, she said, and it helped for dealers and Congress people to come together for the greater good, she thought. "Any time you can talk about what you do as a group it's good. It's a very misunderstood industry," she said about the dealer role in the automotive industry. It was certainly a role the majority of Congress members and the public did not understand, she said.

As part of CRDR, she attended almost all the organized events, except when she took time out to give birth to her child. Spitzer would also be the point person at her father's dealer group. She took the role of coordinating the dealer network very seriously and gave it her all, Darvish said. The two worked fluidly as a team from the start.

* * *

Jim Tarbox, a rejected Chrysler-Jeep dealer, lost both his stores in North Kingston, Rhode Island, and Attleboro, Massachusetts. Tarbox, a poster child for the dealer fight, was determined to get wide-lens exposure on termination issues. He often acted as a source for TV and print stories as the issue grew legs.

A third-generation dealer and father of three young girls, Tarbox made news because his own story of loss was so poignant. He argued passionately about the dealer losses, especially his own, as a proven performer in his small-town markets.

In one vivid exchange with Congress in late July, he said in a bitterly passionate voice, "Let Steve Rattner give up everything he has, all his wealth, his home, his rights, and his job. Let him give it all up for the greater good. This letter shows how ridiculous and pompous a man can be!" This plea came after Rattner had sent a letter to Tarbox's Rhode Island Senator Jack Reed, suggesting that the cuts only affected one dealer in the state and that "sacrifices have to be made for the greater good."

"How in this country can this happen?" Tarbox asked Congress. It was the same question posed by dealers around the country who had lost so much.

Almost a one-man show, Tarbox's passion often carried the day. Later, some saw him as a broken man, desperate to get gross injustices righted.

"I met him when he testified in Chrysler's bankruptcy hearing. He was probably the most emotional of the dealers I met, and I got attached to him and his wife, Kim," Darvish said after the court proceedings. What she saw was a resolute Tarbox in court, embodying the depth of pain dealers felt about their losses.

Tarbox's many e-mails to dealers like Tammy Darvish could border on being harsh. "But I knew he had lost everything and was desperate to right some wrongs," she said. Tarbox, a dedicated one-brand dealer, was an example of the many dealers who were destroyed because of failed "brand loyalty."

Along with Mark Calisi and lawyers, he discovered e-mails from Chrysler execs saying they were cutting dealers for factors not related to performance but for personal reasons. "He and his wife made several trips to DC and were very active in putting heat on Congress when we needed it most," Darvish said.

On a happier note, it was Tarbox and his wife, Kim, who led to Darvish becoming enamored of dogs. In fact, Darvish had disliked dogs and never had a pet. Her friend and colleague, Rose Bayat, was a confirmed dog lover. Every time Darvish encountered Abby, Rose's dog, she recoiled from her slurpy manners. "Put her away somewhere," she told Rose when she visited. "Until I leave, please?"

"Okay," Rose said, complying, although she never quite understood how anyone could not love an innocent dog.

Then one night Darvish was having dinner with the Tarbox couple during the Chrysler bankruptcy proceedings in New York. Kim showed her a picture of their small dog, a Bichon Havanese. Darvish started thinking maybe it was time to give a dog a try. This one was pretty cute, and it might be nice for the kids to have a pet.

Next she found herself driving for four hours to see a similar Bichon at a breeder's farm. She went home without the dog. But a pet, specifically that kind of dog, stayed on her mind. When she called to buy it, the dog was sold. Now she really had pets on her mind. Looking around, she saw a Morkie puppy, related to the Yorkie breed, and decided this was the one. She finally said yes to a dog.

Willis arrived September 9, 2009. Accompanied by her brother, a dog expert, she picked the puppy up at Reagan National Airport. It was true puppy love. Willis became the new joy of her life. Her friends approved, saying she was expanding her horizons beyond cars and dealerships and politics. She was now a transformed pet lover.

The Lobbyists

Mary Jo Dowd, a partner and attorney with the Arent Fox law firm, first represented Jack Fitzgerald in Chrysler bankruptcy court in May and June and then was retained by CRDR to help with their legislative and lobbying efforts. Her strengths were analytical and often behind the scenes, working alongside legal partner Dan Renberg in their DC office.

Dowd was also well-versed in the constitutional issues that arose after automakers coldly terminated several thousand dealers, using what dealer advocate groups saw as questionable criteria. She worked endlessly to help Darvish deal with animosity and lingering tension coming from opponents. When problems arose with the NADA lobbying group, the well-oiled Washington DC–based dealer group, Darvish turned to Dowd for practical advice. NADA, founded in 1917, boasts about eighteen thousand paying members compared to CRDR's underfunded but passionate group of several hundred members, who worked together in a cohesive grassroots campaign style.

In her practical and efficient manner, Mary Jo Dowd helped keep Darvish and the A-team anchored and focused on the priority issues. In that way, she was able to hold the emotional damage at bay. She helped them answer the legal and lobbying challenges at each step of the way. She also acted as a morale booster, pointing out the CRDR group's—and Darvish's—many achievements even when they might doubt themselves. She often said that without CRDR the dealers would never have made it to arbitration, or gotten reprieves at GM, which restored hundreds without the expensive legal fees of arbitration.

Dowd had her own views on the need to wage the campaign for dealers. "Today it's Chrysler and GM; but tomorrow it could be Ford, Toyota, and others. If the dealer community did not step up this time it could continue to happen to anyone," she said.

Without Dowd and the legal team, the lobbying effort with Congress and the automakers' huge team of lawyers would have been a slower, more painful process, Darvish believed when assessing the legal group's impact.

* * *

Dan Renberg is the other Arent Fox attorney who worked closely with Mary Jo Dowd and CRDR in lobbying legislators and the other politically connected groups. Renberg was highly knowledgeable when it came to the legislative process and protocol. He knew who to reach, what buttons to push, and when to turn the heat up. He was invaluable in guiding Darvish and her A-team in "Politics 101," the legal side.

Renberg also spoon-fed CRDR leaders the language to use for the key cosponsors in Congress who were working with them to get the dealer bills passed in legislation. He understood the need for compromise and working things out among themselves and the automakers, as Congress cautioned the dealer advocacy groups. His ideas and language often served to underpin the congressional cosponsors' positions with the automakers and other legislative leaders as needed.

Hired initially by Fitzgerald's auto team, he helped make CRDR aware of the political nuances of their actions in dealing with Congress, elected officials, and with the other dealer advocacy groups, such as NADA, NAMAD, and ATAE.

In one instance in an upcoming press briefing during the July dealer rally on Capitol Hill, Renberg suggested it would not be wise to have Steve LaTourette, a Republican, sharing the podium with Democrats Van Hollen and Steny Hoyer, the House majority leader, especially if LaTourette might be critical of the Obama agenda. Even though LaTourette introduced the original and amended bills and was instrumental in their passage, Van Hollen and Hoyer were their best bets to get a bill passed in the House, and, after all, President Obama was their leader. They couldn't appear to be going against their president.

These issues were the kinds that needed to get ironed out well in advance, he advised his clients. Preparation was all.

Darvish viewed Renberg as the master drill sergeant and respected his professional guidance. "He gave us a lot of the marching orders and I would take his instructions on many occasions and then translate them into layman's terms," she said. Renberg's politically savvy ideas became the genesis and foundation of the hundreds of strategy-type e-mails that were sent out to CRDR members and auto industry leaders in the group's database—and to members of Congress.

His clear thinking also helped underscore the legislative proposals that CRDR leaders such as Fitzgerald, Spitzer, and Darvish crafted.

Most memos and resolutions had to pass muster with Renberg and cocounsel Dowd before being released. Luckily he acted quickly and didn't hold up progress, the CRDR leaders said.

Renberg also served as a key reporter after major events, such as the July 14 fly-in to Washington DC, the rally for dealers and Congress members, and key negotiating sessions with the automakers and Congress. It was that fly-in event that drew much national attention on the dealer closings and brought undecided members of Congress to the table, on the dealers' side, CRDR leaders believed.

The Congressional Staffers

On the Congress side, Darvish worked closely with a number of chiefs of staff and aides to the key members of Congress supporting the dealers. Some were more active with CRDR than others, but several stood out. They are, in alphabetical order:

Ben Abrams was deputy chief of staff for Congressman Democrat Frank Kratovil in Maryland. Abrams stayed abreast of all the dealer issues, often getting the CRDR team to the negotiating table with automakers and on Kratovil's calendar.

"Ben worked with CRDR on behalf of Representative Kratovil in our fight to get to the negotiating table and through all our negotiating meetings with Chrysler and GM trying to find a non-legislative solution," Darvish said.

With Abrams greasing the wheels, Kratovil became a strong supporter of the dealer legislation and helped the various dealer advocacy groups work together to find a compromise solution. He helped sway them toward a middle path that might pass muster in Congress in the long run and get the dealers the support they wanted. Later, Kratovil lost in his own personal bid to be reelected in the November 2, 2010 midterms, losing against Republican Andy Harris by almost 13 percentage points. The midterm wave of heavy Republican votes was felt in blue states like Maryland and Michigan, politicos said.

* * *

John Hughes served as the senior policy advisor for House Leader Steny Hoyer, second to Nancy Pelosi, at the time of the dealer legislation. Hoyer would be reelected in the midterm elections held in November, but no longer be second in command after the Democrats lost majority control in the midterms. The new order, now under Republican control, became effective in the new year, 2011.

"Hughes worked with CRDR on behalf of Hoyer in our fight to get to the negotiating table and through the negotiating meetings with Chrysler and GM. By this time, we were asked to try to find a non-legislative solution and craft a joint proposal with the other three main dealer advocacy groups," NADA, NAMAD, and ATAE, she said.

"Along with David Weaver, Chris Van Hollen's chief of staff, John Hughes was probably the staff member that I became closest to and really appreciated how he helped us prepare Congress for the vote, even though he was one of the toughest of the congressional aides," Darvish said. "He was very tough but always fair. Never emotional—it was always about business and getting the facts right at all times."

That rock-steady temperament and direct style would help Darvish through many long days and battles with everyone from the folks in NADA, the auto task force, and the skittish Congress members who sometimes wouldn't put their votes on the line until the end.

Eventually it all came to a head, a vote, and Hughes was a major player in making it happen by capably preparing Steny Hoyer on the issues, she said. It was Hoyer, after all, who took on Steve Rattner and the task force by continually challenging them on the dealer issues. He kept them wondering why the second-most-powerful person in the House was so agitated about "a few dealers," as Rattner referred to them.

"Why did he—Hoyer—do this?" Darvish was often asked questions like that. "Steny Hoyer got it, that's why," she answered. This was about jobs, thousands of people, and the loss of human rights. It was also about businesspeople and their rights being carelessly swept away.

* * *

David Weaver worked as executive chief of staff to Maryland Democrat Congressman Chris Van Hollen before moving to NASA in 2010. He became Tammy Darvish's close advocate and advisor on Capitol Hill. He also was a mentor and a teacher, tutoring her in the intricate workings of Washington DC, Capitol Hill, and getting around many political barriers that could appear like a land mine that needed clearing.

At first, Darvish was amazed that busy people like Weaver and the chiefs of staff welcomed her visits. Many of them, she came to realize, enjoyed meeting their constituents. Initially she had been afraid to approach them, but her confidence grew as she got to know them. Later, she tried to not be a pest, except when she had a reason to seek information, or in emergencies, to garner their support. Anyone who thinks the wheels of justice and lawmaking grind slowly has not spent a week in a busy congressman's office, she came to learn.

"David had a strong PR background, so he really understood the importance of feeding the media to keep the story alive and out there," she said. Darvish, who was used to priming the pump in her marketing role at her family-owned DARCARS, took the lessons to heart. And Weaver's influence and preparation made a huge difference, she knew, in getting Chris Van Hollen on board as a key driver of the bus in Congress, right up there with Hoyer.

"David always made sure that I had access to Representative Van Hollen whenever I needed it and became a real friend. He never dodged me and was always very responsive and helpful," Darvish said.

Although Van Hollen was reelected for a fifth term in Maryland in the 2010 November midterm elections, Weaver moved on. He accepted a promotion in a new position as assistant director of communications for NASA in November, but he still kept up on the dealer issues.

Darvish thought he would be missed on the political front but was happy he made a positive career move. *Who knew where he would end up next*? she wondered. Somewhere big, for sure.

The midterm elections of 2010 changed things in a big way for the country. Still, the passion to restore the rights of dealers lived on and would be seen in new ways and political methods with most of the all-star team still in place.

Chapter 12—Pride and Politics

Hubris: Wanton insolence or arrogance resulting from excessive pride or from passion.

—Webster's Dictionary

In another life, Steve LaBelle might have made an excellent private eye or probing investigative journalist. On October 7, five months after the announced cuts, the enterprising Massachusetts dealer uncovered a serious error that could have proven embarrassing, if not outright damaging, to GM's upper brass. Add to this "who-could-be-embarrassed" list their majority owner, the US government. Since Treasury had a 61 percent ownership stake in GM, the media dubbed them "Government Motors," once the *Wall Street Journal* proclaimed them as such.

It was a label the country's number-one automaker was trying to shed by paying off their loans early and gradually decreasing Treasury's majority ownership. If there's anything GM hates, it's playing second fiddle. It was a matter of pride, if not politics.

In May and June, as GM announced its two waves of dealer closures, the company would not release lists of dealers being cancelled, unlike Chrysler, citing dealer confidentiality.

LaBelle spent part of June at his keyboard in his office, aided by his staff, and at home trying to compile his own list. Using search terms like "GM dealers open" and "GM dealers closed," he clicked away until he found what he was looking for. Names of inactive dealers. He cobbled together the list of closed GM dealers after painstakingly scouring online lists of who remained and ferreting out who was gone.

He spent several days researching and calling dealers to verify information. Bingo. Finally he had a list. GM never released the names, but LaBelle shared his findings with the CRDR network of closed dealers. It turned out to be highly accurate.

More weirdness. The big "oops" LaBelle discovered happened on Fritz Henderson's watch. Henderson, the golden boy of the moment and the latest CEO at GM had been handpicked by the DC-based task force and the GM board to replace Rick Wagoner in April 2009.

LaBelle uncovered a problem that defied logic. He learned that a Chevrolet dealership in Wareham, Massachusetts, had filed bankruptcy on December 8, 2008, and was insolvent. But after this, the Wareham store received a "go-forward" congratulations letter from GM, welcoming them as a current and active GM dealer. They never made the list of dealers to be cut.

The dealership had been closed for months but received the June letter from GM stating they had been identified as one of the key dealers of the Chevrolet brand and would happily be continuing with GM.

Very strange indeed, he thought. The Wareham store had shut down on its own. He decided to bring these facts to the attention of Henderson, who soon responded that he had copied Mark LaNeve, GM's sales and marketing chief, and Ken Cole, a chief lobbyist at the time for GM in DC.

LaBelle himself was on the wind-down list of Chevrolet dealers, so he politely asked Henderson, "Was GM aware when they made these decisions that my direct competitor [a dealer fifteen miles away] was out of his lease, and another Chevy dealer twelve miles north has been facing financial challenges and was losing their floor plan?" A "floor plan" in dealership lingo is a financing procedure in which dealers finance excess inventory through the financial arm of a manufacturer or a local bank.

"What's more, the already closed 'point' [franchise] in Wareham was chosen to go forward? Perhaps these findings warrant another look at my appeal," he suggested.

The next thing LaBelle knew, he was in a meeting in DC with Ken Cole, GM's chief lobbyist, and Clarence Oliver of GM government relations. The meeting actually happened because Tammy Darvish had pushed for Chevrolet to review his case, he later found out. The word there was, he shouldn't have been cut based on his performance scores alone. GM honchos had said they were using sales, and customer satisfaction and profitability criteria, but here were three cases, plus his own, where the facts and decisions they made proved otherwise. "They found my appeal to be valid and my story compelling," LaBelle said.

It was clear to LaBelle that GM didn't know its own dealer base. Why did it take a discontinued dealer to tell them what was going on under their own noses? And if it happened here, what was going on elsewhere in the country? "This told me that GM or some of the decision makers didn't have a clue as to who should stay and who should go," he said. Those closure decisions involved more disturbing questions that didn't get answered.

LaBelle, of course, asked his GM contacts why he was let go in the first place. It was more than curiosity driving him. His livelihood was at stake. Beginning in early July, he asked GM officials, including Dan Adamcheck, a regional sales manager in the field, "How am I deficient? Tell me."

In September, he was again probing for specific termination criteria from field reps. "I got the same vague answers other dealers did—it had to do with my DPS [Dealer Performance Scores]." GM had said his scores were below the required levels. LaBelle argued that wasn't so. He was able to prove it by providing his scores, all well above those GM said they required.

What lie are we on now? he wondered.

At least the top GM execs were aware of his situation, he thought. Perhaps unrelated to these inquiries, LaBelle was brought back into the GM fold after making many more appeals. He was called a reinstated dealer. He figured the Ted Kennedy letter on his behalf to Henderson, the top guy, didn't hurt him either. His Mark Reuss appeals he wasn't so sure about.

But then another punch sidelined him. Like other returning dealers, he found himself "starved of products," meaning he couldn't get the vehicles he needed to sell and would be forced to shut down in the coming year. "How do you show good sales scores when you can't get the product?" LaBelle, like other dealers, wondered.

What hurt him as much as anything was the reaction of his employees when he told them in the fall of 2010 that he would be closing up shop after trying to make a go of it. He couldn't afford to stay in business selling used cars, and the new-car pipeline was shutting down. "They were mad. Somehow, they thought it was my fault," he said. That was almost as hard to take as GM's rejection.

* * *

Mistakes were made all around in picking the dealers, and even closing them, dealers and legal experts would argue. It took GM nearly six months following the closure announcements to publicly admit that maybe, just maybe, it had goofed here and there in selecting which dealers to be let go.

On November 11, 2009, the *New York Times* reported that Ed Whitacre, GM's chief executive, said publicly that the company "might have" made mistakes in some of its dealer-termination decisions. "We're not geniuses," Whitacre said. "We might have made a mistake or two, probably did somewhere along the way. We'd be happy to look at any situation and reevaluate it and maybe the answer comes differently," wrote *New York Times* reporter Nick Bunkley, quoting Whitacre.

Whitacre seemed to make these comments off-the-cuff to reporters at a press gathering while discussing the critical role GM and other manufacturers play in the US economy. These are the moments reporters love. Sometimes the best quotes come at unguarded times when the executives are not scripted, reporters will say. It can be fun watching them search for safe answers, without their "flaks" (PR staff) interceding, one reporter said.

At that time, GM was trying to earn some PR points with the public. Whitacre said GM would pay back $6.7 billion in cash that it owed Treasury, excluding the nearly $1 billion loaned to "old GM" that remained in bankruptcy. Another portion of the $50 billion loan would go to Treasury in the form of public stock offerings, by 2011, Whitacre said to the media. In all, GM alone got around $50 billion in federal aid, or public dollars. This didn't include loans to its finance arm, GMAC, which it later spun off, and it became Ally Bank.

A government report released earlier that November said taxpayers were unlikely to receive full payment of the $81.8 billion used to rescue automotive in the eleventh hour in that fatal time period between 2008 and 2009.

At least Whitacre's statements signaled that GM was willing to reconsider its position on dealers. It was as if the hostages, some at least, could be released.

The sick ones could possibly be brought back to life. In fact, GM later invited 661 dealers to return to their network, and more later. The offer came with strings attached. To come back, they had to meet rigid requirements imposed by the automaker.

And then the news of product-starved dealers began to roll out to media. It was the story of the day. But the new Chrysler Group LLC played a tougher game called "we won't back down" from an original position of the need to cut dealers to get competitive. They were consistent, if nothing else.

Chrysler spokespeople, the ones who interact with media and government, issued standard statements that appeared in press accounts, such as: "Chrysler Group LLC has complied fully with the letter and intent of the federal dealer arbitration statute by issuing a customary and usual Letter of Intent (LOI) to dealers that prevailed in arbitration and is engaged in constructive discussions with many prevailing dealers seeking to meet the financial and operation requirements of the LOI."

Toyota's Dealer Strategy

Earlier in a special congressional hearing in late July, GM and Chrysler lawyers, of course, defended the dealer closures as necessary for the financial health of the companies and remaining dealers. The lauded Toyota model played in their minds like a violin swan song in the desert night.

But what they perhaps didn't know about Toyota was how the automaker viewed dealers as part of their corporate and sales strategy. "At Toyota, we put the customer first, the dealer second, and Toyota third," Don Esmond, Toyota's North American vice president of sales, told reporters at an Automotive Press Association meeting in Detroit in October 2010.

It was a view of dealers that seemed diametrically opposed to that of domestics, especially of Chrysler and GM. During the sales debacle of 2008 and 2009, the automakers' solution was to slash dealers, especially in urban, small town, and rural areas, where their strengths in truck sales lie.

That view was diametrically opposed to what CRDR leaders believed. "You need more dealer coverage and presence in these areas, not less," said Jack Fitzgerald for CRDR. A CRDR report in October of 2009 noted that the domestic dealer count had fallen drastically since the 1990s. Chrysler, for example, already had lost 25 percent of its dealers between 2001 and 2008 through natural market forces. In that period, its sales volume went down 45 percent.

Even during the product recall crisis in early 2010, Toyota dealers stepped up to the plate, Esmond told reporters, and took exceptional care of customers. The recalls could have been even worse of a nosebleed for Toyota, but dealers cleaned up the bases, he indicated.

In a press huddle at the Detroit APA meeting, Esmond was asked if Toyota had plans to restructure its dealers given the cutbacks at the domestics, and due to slowdowns since the product recalls. He looked puzzled for a moment, as if thinking, *Why would we?* Then he said, "No, no. It works. Our dealers have the highest sales per outlet [in the industry]." Why fool with success? That was Toyota's view.

Esmond also told dealers at a national dealer meeting in Las Vegas in October after the Toyota product recalls hit, "The only way we're going to get out of this is to sell our way out." At that meeting, he thanked dealers for stepping up to take care of customers during the recalls. He praised the dealers for going above and beyond expectations in handling service customers.

"They did a fantastic job. We asked them to take care of the customer, and that's exactly what they did," he told journalists. By the end of 2010, Toyota had come back fairly strong, despite the product setbacks, industry watchers said.

Later, a government report from the National Highway Transportation Safety Administration (NHTSA) said the unintended acceleration problems in Toyota vehicles that led to a slew of recalls were not due to electronic control flaws, a big plus for the company. There were three known causes of unintended acceleration: improperly installed floor mats, sticky pedals, and driver error, according to a *CNN Money* report.

NHTSA enlisted the help of National Aeronautics and Space Administration (NASA) scientists and engineers to conduct the ten-month investigation. Toyota remained "bullish on the long-term progress of the economy" and was predicting a 15-million SAAR (seasonally adjusted annual rate) season in auto sales by mid-decade, Esmond said. He also predicted 2010 would result in about 11.5 million total SAAR units, depending on consumer spending. It was a higher forecast than many forecasted, but 2010 industry sales records showed he was spot on.

Esmond said Toyota expected to come back with a new North American product arsenal in 2011 and even more resources for its US dealers. Toyota also seemed to understand another key message dealers consistently gave automakers: "It's the product, stupid." And when you have slippage, quickly correct the course you're on.

* * *

At a July 2009 hearing with Congress, A GM lawyer who testified said the automaker would try to help the dealers by giving them cash settlements for their losses. At least they were willing to make some financial amends to many dealers, if not all.

And no, it didn't take a genius to see that the country was reeling and rocking with economic pain in 2009. Unemployment rates were at their highest level since the Great Depression in the 1930s, running 10 percent nationally. In hard-hit states, primarily in the Midwest and Alaska, the rates rose to 16 percent, or higher for some bigger cities. California, too, seemed to be shaking from factors other than earthquakes. Americans exuded a sense of anxiety expressed in opinion polls that showed 60 percent believed the country was in decline. This sense of fear and loathing seeped into the end of 2010, affecting the November midterm elections, which favored Republicans.

"There is a sense of rage out there with people," said Yale King in Colorado, who became politically entrenched after losing his dealerships. And there was a disconnect between government and what people wanted, he said. Politicians had yet to get their arms around the problem. Throwing multi-billions of dollars at the major players—from banks to Wall Street—hadn't solved the crisis.

Fact Box: Dealer Economics 101

Before the 2009–2010 crash, new-car dealers were vital to the economy:

- Total annual payroll for all dealers: $53.2 billion
- Total sales of all US dealers (new vehicles): $576 billion
- US dealer employment (new vehicles): 1.06 million people
- Total dealer advertising expenditures: $6.8 billion
- Total investment in parts inventory: $6.6 billion

Source: *NADA 2009 data*

With a full-blown economic crisis in swing, the free-enterprise system simply wasn't able to do its job of course correcting. The downhill landslide became global. Under normal circumstances, the economy would recover quicker if the market were healthier, if consumer and business spending were stronger, said students of free enterprise 101. But it wasn't happening—largely because jobs weren't there *now*, not in some future high-tech landscape workers weren't prepared for. And dealers who offered among the highest-paying jobs and economic base in a community were being forced out.

Like many of her colleagues, Tammy Darvish believed that free enterprise would take care of the poor performers automakers talked about. The market naturally takes out the underperformers, she said.

"If Ford, GM, and Chrysler are losing market share, you're going to have some bad dealers, but if they're losing market share, a lot of it has to do with the product, marketing, and everything else. If some dealers have to go, that's for the market to decide. It's not for someone to sit back and play God," she said. "The reality is, the dealer count had gone down in the twelve-to-thirty-six months before the terminations. That decline occurred through natural attrition. And in a free market, that's how businesses should go down."

* * *

After four long months of lobbying Congress, by September the pressure was mounting on the dealer advocates. Most of them had other businesses to run while the battles in Washington and Detroit heated up. At CRDR, their volunteer staff and skimpy marketing budgets were stretched thin. In some cases, dealers knew their import franchises were shoring up other parts of the business, including domestics.

Tammy Darvish had spent more than three months chasing lawmakers—and trying to run the complicated affairs of her family dealership chain. She tried to put her priorities in order. But restoring the dealers was still number one, as far as energy and time went. As far as her commitment went.

With the help of attorneys at Arent Fox and her own lawyer, Mike Charapp, she was preparing the key messages Congress members needed to sell the save-the-dealers campaign broadly. A heavy-duty month was ahead as Congress weighed legislation that could force GM and Chrysler to reverse their decisions despite arguing they needed to shrink their dealer base for competitive reasons.

In early September, Darvish and her group had managed to reach a compromise agreement with NADA and other key players among the dealer advocacy groups, ATAE and NAMAD. But the NADA relationship still was tricky, one that needed careful tending.

Walking the Tightrope

A few close insiders knew of Darvish's personal struggle with NADA. Here, she was on the board, representing the DC-area dealers, and she felt like an outsider. It appeared this was not a group that welcomed outsiders, or differing viewpoints. It seemed at times the officers were willing to hear positions that were consistent with their philosophy, but not opposing views.

"I feel like I'm walking the tightrope here—and that I'm being ignored at NADA board meetings," she told Utah dealer Patrick Painter. She knew him to be a good sounding board on the pain and politics issues after his own family business was yanked and then given to a nearby competitor and NADA officer. Painter was consoling as usual, but she still felt uneasy. Darvish felt it was her duty to speak out for the rejected dealers. She thought that was part of her job as a dealer representative to the NADA board. She knew pride and politics were enmeshed in most conflicts, but she didn't know how else to act. It was more than a matter of pride to her. She needed to be heard, to act on the dealer issues that consumed her life. For her part, Darvish knew that NADA was not in a position to fully throw their weight behind the affected dealers. She also was the one who sat through all the dealer testimony in bankruptcy court and later in arbitrations. Getting those close-up views, she was far more emotionally impacted by the dealers' plight than the NADA leadership.

Still, the NADA higher-ups were miffed when she suggested they leave negotiating on the closed-dealer issues to CRDR, who were better suited to represent rejected dealers since that was their single focus. She knew they had other priorities, but CRDR did not. Rejected dealers had no real voice through NADA; and CRDR was the logical group to press their case with Congress and the automakers, CRDR argued at the time. The advocacy groups were supposed to present a united front to Congress and the automakers, but they were internally fractured. In those days, Darvish often wondered how one mends a rift that had grown from political, as one faces on a job, to personal, like one also faces on a job. That's what it seemed like with NADA, although they weren't her employers.

In fact, the relationship with NADA became tense once Darvish became a front person for CRDR. She was fueled by the tragic dealer losses she witnessed and heard about. She was a woman who was not afraid to speak out. She couldn't call something she saw as wrong to be right.

She thought back to early August. She had pushed the hot button then, one that CRDR was continually playing. The automakers in a number of cases were reassigning dealers to take over the closed stores, often in their own neighborhoods. How could they say there were too many dealers, and then put in new ones?

As an example, she assailed practices such as Chrysler literally giving away dealer businesses that were often built on the work of multi-generations in families. She took on the Painter cause as only one example, asking Stephen Wade to step down from his leader role on the industry relations stabilization task force after he accepted the Painter deal. That NADA subgroup influenced dealer issues greatly, including negotiating payment concessions for closed franchises with the government and the Detroit automakers. He later stepped down from that position.

State legislators and national media such as the *Salt Lake Tribune* and *Automotive News* reported on the Wade and Painter deal. Stories appeared in the *New York Times* and elsewhere on the Painter family's ordeal. Wade himself granted media interviews on the subject.

Two powerful NADA leaders, John McEleney, former NADA chairman, and Ed Tonkin, NADA chairman with active dealerships in St. George, Utah, quickly scolded Darvish in writing regarding her memos to them. It was Ed Tonkin's words that stung hardest. In the coming weeks, however, John McEleney and others made public statements of their ongoing support and actions to help the closed dealers, perhaps spurred on by CRDR's actions to do so, some dealers speculated.

Peter Kitzmiller, a former NADA lawyer who heads up the Maryland state dealers association, said that when the advocating for shuttered dealers began, "NADA was slow on the draw. CRDR helped pull them along," even at a time when everyone was saying the bills didn't have a chance.

Kitzmiller added that "Jack Fitzgerald, especially, was a force of nature, not to be stopped. Like Darvish and Spitzer, he saw that what was happening was wrong" and set the wheels in motion as a change agent. Darvish's dealership allies also quickly backed her up, speaking out on issues such as the gifting of dealerships.

The closings were corporate cronyism run amok," said Jackie Mealey. She reflected other dealers' views as Chrysler especially closed a dealership, and then reopened another in the closed dealers' backyards, such as the Painter's in Utah, and their own in Michigan.

Jackie Mealey had become a good sounding board on what was bothering dealers most, Darvish found. Jackie, with Gina Russo (of Lochmoor Chrysler-Jeep in Detroit), had put together an economic-impact report of dealerships, something the auto task force didn't do, as far as they knew. They circulated the report to Washington and CRDR members.

"Clearly it showed that their [automakers'] knee-jerk reductions would have a staggering effect on dealers, employees, and their communities," Mealey said. She and Russo sent letters to senators, members of Congress, and even President Obama. They traveled to DC with other rejected dealers to lobby their cause. At times, it fell on deaf ears, Mealey and Russo would learn.

After the case of Richard Mealey came up in New York bankruptcy court, he was featured in major national papers as an example of the many rejected successful dealers. But that point was still lost on the task force deciders. There were many Richard Mealeys in the lineup of closed franchise owners, if they had only looked about, asked questions of dealers, and done due diligence.

In Richard Mealey's case, his closed Chrysler-Jeep dealership in Michigan had performed exceptionally in the Chrysler categories. His dealership performance records included 136 percent in MSR (minimum sales requirement, based on a top score of 100) in 2008, and 150 percent in 2009, before being shut down. His scores were far above what Chrysler required. The scores were also achieved at the most devastating time for auto sales in near history, especially in Michigan. Mealey also had continually upgraded his facilities, reflecting $9.3 million in investments. Mealey testified to all this in New York bankruptcy court earlier in May. Some who knew him said it was like taking an Olympic-caliber performer and calling him an amateur.

When it came to slashing the dealers, CRDR members thought the task force and Treasury had their minds made up, not analyzing the impact of what culling dealers meant, just as the bankruptcy court judges had their minds made up and sided with GM and Chrysler—perhaps the stakes were higher there than with dealers, as some have suggested. On the other side of the coin, the financial benefits for cutting dealers were mostly smoke and mirrors. GM and Chrysler both submitted estimated cost savings of shutting down dealerships, but dealers poked many holes in their theories.

* * *

With NADA, Darvish suspected the good-old-boys' network was in play. At the time, as a vice chairman, Stephen Wade was slated to become the top dog in 2011, the NADA chairman. Darvish commented on the conflict publicly and drafted a proposal to NADA requesting they recognize CRDR as the only suitable negotiating arm for the cut dealers. For this she had legal counsel from Arent Fox, CRDR attorneys and her own attorney, Charapp. Speaking for CRDR, she said NADA was "conflicted" on the closed-dealer issues otherwise, since their interests tended to lie with their entire network of dealers, unlike the focused CRDR group. At that point, the politics grew thick and steamy.

In her private moments, even when angry, she worried. She talked to Jack Fitzgerald, to her father, to her close dealership friends. They cautioned her to not get shot down in the line of fire. Fitzgerald especially kept telling her to stay focused, not veer off course. She was so passionate about restoring the closed dealers, it was easy to get emotionally embroiled. She knew that as much as anyone.

On August 7, she had written Phil Brady, who headed NADA then, citing the conflict CRDR saw. That memo had started the ball rolling. She was fairly new on the board, so she copied the board members, thinking she was following protocol. She was also representing the thinking of the CRDR group.

At the time, CRDR also pointed out that the NADA vice chairman was in a position of influence over other dealers and should step down from his leadership role on the industry stabilization task force, which affected dealers nationwide. Darvish said so, possibly a little too directly for some tastes. That officer and others "have purported to represent these very same dealers before the federal government and the auto task force," she wrote to Phil Brady.

That memo drew the NADA chiefs' ire even more. They were getting pretty upset with the woman from Maryland. She had broken the golden political rule. From their perspective, she had attacked one, or more, of their own. What was missing here was that NADA execs could not understand Darvish's overriding mission. In order to save all the rejected dealers, nothing was going to stand in her way.

"It was never our intention to attack anyone. The bottom line was we wanted to make sure the rejected dealers were represented," and had a chance to get their businesses back, Darvish would explain later as the gifting practice came into the spotlight.

She also pointed out what CRDR thought to be true. As the key dealer lobbying group, NADA was too focused on the manufacturers' criteria for terminating dealers, which were flawed. "NADA should abandon its quest to apply the manufacturers' factors … [the] firm insistence on the use of manufacturers' criteria calls into question its motivation and agenda," she wrote. It was a point the CRDR committee leaders made time and again.

But an angry Ed Tonkin, then chairman of NADA, responded to the points in her memo. On August 8, he penned a scathing reprimand. His three-page letter told Tammy Darvish exactly what he thought of her actions. In no way did he imply she had the courage of her convictions. Tonkin had heard and seen enough. To him, she had hung the dirty laundry in public. She had attacked *them.*

Tonkin said, in part, "I take great offense and umbrage with the many insinuations you make in your letter [to Brady, NADA president]; particularly those about Stephen Wade. I'm not sure what kind of picture you're trying to paint here, but it smacks of ugliness. Your questioning of Phil's and others' integrity and commitment to NADA's goals and objectives in representing all dealers is misguided."

He reamed her even more in writing, when he indicated he took the accusations personally. He was one of the "other" she referred to in her letter. Then he copied the entire board with his e-mail to Darvish, feeling justified because she had copied them with her earlier missive.

But the NADA tussle didn't end there.

On August 21, NADA chairman John McEleney assailed Jack Fitzgerald's recent e-mail asking NADA directors to reconsider NADA's ideas on the alternative solution to legislation. McEleney said that Fitzgerald's explaining of events was "not accurate," adding that CRDR presented a joint proposal on August 14 without NADA's or ATAE's "approval or knowledge." He said NADA had moved forward because "delay is not an option" and the group would continue their engagement on behalf of dealers. He again reaffirmed the group's efforts to "vigorously advocate on behalf of Chrysler and GM franchises who lost their dealerships," by seeking an alternative to legislation.

By August 24, an article appeared in *Automotive News* in which Darvish was quoted: "NADA is conflicted and should bow out of the campaign to get dealerships back." Speaking for the CRDR group again, she said NADA was seeking a non-legislative solution that would result in very few if any dealers being restored. She knew they needed Congress and the power of the law behind them to win this fight. She also knew that the votes, which would move the legislation along, were not yet in the Senate.

At the time, Congress had asked the dealer groups to work toward a "non-legislative solution"—the current catchphrase—and it was on the table. But the so-called solution was in direct opposition to CRDR's plea for restoring dealers unilaterally, Darvish and the committee said. It caused another split in the groups.

Automotive News had been covering the closed-dealer issue intensely all year. Another story came out four days later: "Rejected dealer talks: a rift over what's fair."

Some critics thought Darvish or other CRDR leaders were leaking sensitive information to media. Darvish explained that she and the leaders didn't contact the press or leak the so-called "rift" between the groups. When reporters called her, Darvish said she didn't sugarcoat what she thought was true: NADA should step aside. That position was well documented in CRDR's and her own communications to the group.

Clearly, Tammy Darvish was not winning friends and influencing people at the NADA lobbying group. By August 31, in the deep summer of the cuts, the political climate grew hotter, as the NADA-CRDR tussle spilled over. The dealer groups still hadn't agreed on a final alternative solution to present to Congress to show they were on the same page on the rejected-dealer issues.

It was then that Jack Fitzgerald again stepped up as the de facto leader of the CRDR group. In essence, he backed up Darvish's assertions which were made after all as a CRDR leader. He outlined the key differences on why CRDR should represent terminated dealers in the effort to negotiate a resolution of the two bills in Congress, HR2743 (House) and S1304 (Senate).

It was the committee's thinking that rejected dealers weren't being fully represented by NADA because they weren't members. Fitzgerald knew the NADA bylaws. They specifically limited membership to entities that are "engaged in the business of new motor vehicle retailing." That rule by itself excluded the dealers rejected by GM and Chrysler, since they were no longer eligible to receive new products.

"How can NADA purport to represent dealers who are no longer members?" Fitzgerald queried the group. But unknown to him, NADA had hastily given itself wiggle room on closed dealers. The dealer lobbying group did not want to lose more members in a fragile economy; the auto industry was in precarious shape too. In response, NADA had devised an amendment that allowed terminated dealers to stay or join as "sustaining members." But they would have no voting rights and could not serve as board members, the ones who call the shots. In effect, they paid their dues but surrendered their power, CRDR leaders thought.

"About 90 percent of NADA members did not lose franchises," Fitzgerald pointed out, since their members included all US dealers, international and domestics. So their base was not the disaffected dealers CRDR was solely representing. He further called NADA's action of creating a loophole—the sustaining member category—"duplicitous."

Fitzgerald also brought up the Stephen Wade matter. He quoted a recent article in Utah's daily paper, the *Salt Lake City Tribune*, in which Wade, said, "They're not going to give those franchises back to any of those Chrysler dealers. Not one of them in the country." Wade apparently used this as a rationale for why he assumed the franchise, not wanting to see it go to Las Vegas speculators or other outsiders who didn't really have the interest of the community in mind. They would build it up some, sell it, make their money, and get out, he feared.

Then CRDR crafted a statement that said, "As we have stated repeatedly during this process, our Committee to Restore Dealer Rights is the only organization to advocate solely on behalf of the disenfranchised dealers, their employees, and families without duplicity."

Maryland dealers association president Peter Kitzmiller added that the massive dealer cuts represented a unique period in automotive history, that was almost hard to fathom. "Looking back, it's impossible to find some other instance in history where this happened—I think it's the first time it has ever happened," he said.

Many dealers in the field backed up the CRDR views that NADA wasn't focused on the rejected dealers enough. Many didn't like the fact that NADA was backing the automakers' original criteria. "[NADA officials] have never faced anything like this—the dealer crisis—before," said Georgia dealer Jeff Duvall. At the time, Duvall was working on his own reinstatement battles, so staying on the front lines opposing the automakers was risky for him, he knew. But he would have his say.

Better leadership might have helped "bring NADA through the darkest period in franchised auto dealer history," he added.

Jeff Duvall's dealerships were eventually reopened, but he continued to support the group financially in their lobbying efforts. On July 8, 2009, in the thick of the battle, he was worried that more dealers weren't contributing to help the CRDR lobbying group defray expenses. "Are any of the state associations or NADA contributing financially?" he asked Alan Spitzer, the group's financial guru.

"Every dealer in the country should be concerned," Duvall said. "They could be next."

It had happened now and it could happen again. Precedents were what the auto industry and its cordon of lawyers were all about.

Spitzer replied that NADA, the largest entity, was not contributing financially to the group, although they had pledged to provide assistance for the July dealer rally and the evening dealer reception at which they spoke. That pledge eventually fell through, CRDR learned. They never found out the reason.

Early on, Spitzer, acting as the group's administrator, had sent out pleas for contributions, noting as CRDR usually did, they were voluntary but gratefully accepted. "As many of you know, your co-chairs—Jack, Tammy, and I—have pretty much been full-time politicians for the last few weeks." As leaders, the three were bankrolling the group as much as they could. His pitch for money did not fall on deaf ears. Dealers often stepped up to the plate.

In the year of the cuts, on August 27, Yale King in Colorado got pretty stirred up with NADA leadership too. He had talked with Phil Brady, the NADA president, about where the dialogue on restoring dealer rights with CRDR and other groups was going. King grew more politically active as the months passed and a firm vote was yet to be cast by Congress on dealer legislation.

"We discussed the conflict-of-interest issue. I did not get an answer from Brady, but he shared with me that NADA membership had varying thoughts on it," King later said.

Perhaps innocently, given it was Yale King asking, he wondered if NADA had done any kind of survey to see how many dealers wanted to or had the financial capability to come back in "under the NADA proposal aiming at a compromise of sorts with the automakers?" According to King, Brady replied, "No, can you imagine if that got out to the press." Apparently, King surmised, he was more concerned about media and image than the dealers' interests.

In his earnest, forthright manner, King said he didn't think there was "anything wrong with the truth and maybe it could help with the resolution process." He'd always taken the middle ground on many political issues but was pretty sure he knew what side the dealers would come out on.

The legitimate query on profitability of dealers was tossed asunder as if it were either too hot to handle, or someone didn't want to answer it. Likely the latter, King thought. At the end of his talk with Brady, Yale King walked away, saying only, "We agreed to disagree." Another stalemate, or another standoff.

It seemed that no one, at least as far as most dealers knew, had done a study of dealer profitability on either the terminated dealers, or the remaining "go-forward" dealers.

Who was profitable and who was not? There was much anecdotal evidence, but as a whole, no one seemed to know what everyone wanted to know.

Unknown to some dealers, an internal Chrysler document that supposedly came from the Chrysler dealer planning group surreptitiously surfaced. Most dealers did not have access to it. Apparently, the automaker knew full well who among its remaining dealers was profitable and who was not. There was even data comparing the terminated dealers to the remaining ones.

So far, a verifiable, objective profitability study of the terminated dealers was missing. Anecdotally, many dealers showed high profits, sales, and the ability to satisfy their customers, legal experts said. Leonard Bellavia, attorney for about forty dealers in the arbitration hearings against the two automakers, said most of the dealers he represented had been profitable and healthy before being cut.

But the Chrysler data—including multiple charts of numbers and statistics—was not readily shared with dealers who were arguing for their livelihoods, and this was startling. The internal report showed that of the retained Chrysler dealers—those 2,386 who stayed—51.5 percent were profitable in 2008, compared to 59.1 percent in 2006, an economically healthier year. Of the cut dealers, 43.2 percent showed profits in 2008, versus 59.1 in 2006, a similar drop to the retained group. That was less than an 8 percent difference between the two groups. The closed dealers could argue, as many did, that they were not supplied products in the latter stages of 2008, accounting for their lower numbers.

Many dealers, even returning ones (meaning they were invited back after signing required agreements), would continue to see product shortages. Some were seeing them even earlier, in 2008, one of the evaluation years. Making money and showing a good bottom line of returns are always topmost in any business setting.

* * *

At the Chrysler campus in Auburn Hills, Michigan, another game of cards was being played out. The game was called Stop the Dealers at All Costs.

On November 4, 2009, Peter Grady told the media that Chrysler was shrinking its dealer network to fit current market conditions. He'd also made these points in bankruptcy court in June when he stated a strong case for eliminating dealers as part of the company's plan to carry out Project Genesis, its dealer consolidation effort.

The plan to reduce dealers to get the optimum dealer network size was in line with Genesis, Grady said, in order for existing dealers to get a return on investment. At that point, there was no mention of government intervention or of emulating a foreign model. To Chrysler, cutting dealers to get their house in order and allow maximum dealer profitability seemed a natural course of affairs.

As Grady explained it, Chrysler's efforts to consolidate dated back to 1991 when they combined Chrysler and Jeep. "Then in 2001, with the Alpha project, we wanted Chrysler, Jeep, and Dodge under one roof to increase throughput," he said in customary corporate speak. "That became Project Genesis, which gives us the optimal number of dealers."

He added that in June 2009, after the bankruptcy, the company rationalized what they called a "sustainable and competitive" dealer network. "Rejection was difficult and necessary, but we had fair and equitable criteria. We looked at the number of dealers in a market, financial capability, customer satisfaction index, and competitive brands in the same locations."

But by then, the auto task force was pushing the import-transplant dealer models on the Detroit Two. Transplants referred to the import makers who built and invested in US plants and facilities. Grady and Chrysler execs claimed the rejected dealers had low throughput, or sales volume. "Fewer than 60 percent sold Chrysler-Jeep-Dodge. And only 38 percent in metro markets sold CJD. Today, 80 percent have all three [brands]. And 63 percent are in metro markets. By 2011, 100 percent of our dealers will have all three brands," he projected grandly. By then the rejected dealers would be gone.

Grady claimed customer convenience would be "enhanced by having all three brands in one location." He argued that existing dealers would be more profitable and sell more vehicles. Network profitability remained a challenge, Grady admitted. He spoke of a pilot program in San Francisco where the regional dealer had one main store, additional services, parts centers, and a sales boutique. There are exclusives sales managers and sales consultants at that store.

What's so unique about this? Toyota, Honda, Nissan, GM, and other upper-tier makers had been promoting boutique-style facilities for years. They referred to them as "image stores" for the brands.

Grady also shared what he considered glowing Chrysler news. With Marchionne ensconced in the leader's seat, a Fiat-500 plan was under way. They would bring the micro-car from Italy to Detroit. It was an attempt to appease Washington and the environmentalists strong on the West and East coasts that the company cared about the environment and in cutting "America's addiction to gasoline," as President Bush's speechwriters had put it. Many dealers were skeptical it would sell in big numbers in the States.

Chrysler was on a growth spurt, Grady said. It seemed that cutting dealers had enabled them to make all kinds of progress and fine-tune their dealer network. "Since June 10, dealers have committed to building twenty new buildings and two hundred major renovations. They have an archway design to separate us in the marketplace." He said the dealer network was expected to be fully consolidated by 2011.

With Chrysler's network tinkering, Grady projected that dealer throughput would increase from 340 units to 750 in 2014. That was apparently a big jump from the death days of 2008 when dealers saw much lower average throughputs per store. Throughput refers to the total annual sales of vehicles per dealership. It's just one measure of how dealers do.

But as Colleen McDonald, a rejected Michigan dealer put it, high throughput does not always mean a successful dealer. "Chrysler talked about how throughput was a great way to measure a dealers success. Which is not always the case. Many dealers who sell a lot of cars fall short in the customer-satisfaction area," she said.

And David Ruggles, a former dealership manager and current auto columnist, called throughput "a flawed concept" that had little to do with automaker or dealer profits.

Grady also failed to mention that many of the terminated dealers would have upgraded their stores earlier while in business and often had done so before being cut out of the action. And many did sink multimillions into upgrading their facilities at Chrysler's request. They were among the scrapped dealers.

Would cutting dealers be the solution to Chrysler's problems? A wise dealer would have said, "It's the product, stupid," as many of them did. And Chrysler's sales figures, if excluding fleet sales, suggested cutting dealers hadn't helped them in overall customer retail sales.

Even Internet bloggers and posters questioned the fuzzy logic of cutting more dealers to get more sales. Bloggers were asking, "How the heck do you suddenly sell more cars by removing the dealers?" It didn't add up.

More Warning Shots

By that winter, the NADA fight should have been long over. Tammy Darvish was tired of playing defense. The dealer advocacy groups had compromised and sent a September agreement on alternative solutions to Congress that was shared with the automakers. Congress had finally acted and passed a law that addressed dealer rights.

But it didn't end there. This time it was Stephen Wade himself who fired the next salvos. He wasn't done dissecting the issue between the committee to restore dealers and NADA. He picked his moment. Darvish heard from him directly on December 17, coincidentally right after Obama had signed the historic funding act, including the dealer economic rights portion.

Wade protested Darvish's criticism of his actions in accepting the offer from Chrysler to run the terminated dealership across the street. Wade had been a dealer since 1973. He owned a number of stores, including nine domestic and foreign brands on twenty-five acres in St. George.

"It would make [Wade's] dealership the only Chrysler-Jeep-Dodge franchise between Provo, Utah, and Las Vegas, Nevada, since the automaker severed ties with eleven Utah dealers in May," the *Salt Lake Tribune* reported in late August of 2009.

Wade seemed to have missed her point, Darvish thought after she got his letter. Her concern was about the conflict-of-interest issue, and the gifting of dealerships at large which were going on nationally.

Wade also knew that Obama had signed the bill into law and that the Painters wanted their store back, so fearing "the bad guys" from Vegas moving in was a moot point, Darvish thought. "Why not at least allow the Painters the respect of getting through arbitration because you know that Chrysler is going to say they can't have two dealerships operating across the street from each other," she reasoned.

She felt strongly that Wade should have waited until after the arbitration hearings concluded to step in. It would have leveled the playing field just a little.

Perhaps the precedent of gifting dealerships and businesses had been set at the top of Chrysler.

On June 1, shortly after the Chrysler hit list was announced, Fiat SpA CEO Sergio Marchionne was named chief executive at Chrysler LLC, its former name. The new company name didn't change much. It became Chrysler Group LLC after emerging from bankruptcy.

In Sergio style, he boldly refused to pay a dime for the sinking automaker that was burning through billions in cash loans from the US government. Marchionne, of course, got his way. Even the fiscally aggressive task force under Steve Rattner couldn't tame the resolute leader.

It seemed a perfect storm of pride and politics converging together, much like the CRDR group had witnessed all along. Those who were opposed dug in their heels and wanted to stay that way. Looking back on the chain of events that transpired, Darvish and her allies tried to see things on balance. They had won some, they had lost some.

After months of playing tug-of-war, at least a compromise solution and proposal had been crafted by the four dealer advocacy groups, including CRDR and NADA. At least in public they looked unified, as if they had reached common ground.

But in the end, at Chrysler and somewhat at GM, the dealer cuts came down to hubris, or too much pride to back down, many closed dealers believed. Their reasons were cloaked in catchwords like "competitive factors," "cutting non-performers," and "cost-reduction measures." But their rationale on dealers was based on false premises, CRDR said in many statements at many times.

In the analyst community, consultants who complained publicly about the automakers' accelerated cuts were few in number. David Cole at CAR, and J. D. Power analysts were among them. Cole, especially, pointed out that culling rural and small-town dealers ignored the oversaturation of some metro markets and hurt GM and Chrysler's strength in smaller markets, where imports were not yet a presence.

J. D. Power analysts argued that, especially in the case of Chrysler, the cuts would "create a wave of chaos amid a serious economic crisis that was already full blown."

Many in the analyst community seemingly thought the dealer cuts were necessary due to new market forces and a downsized economy. Most, after all, were advocates for the automakers' interests. And the surviving dealers were actively selling stores and carried the weight in achieving sales results in fiercely competitive times, like it or not, they reasoned.

James Bell, executive market analyst at Kelley Blue Book (kbb.com), said, "The wave of dealer closings that were part of the reorganizations at auto manufacturers has been very painful but economically obvious, as many were remnants from a long-gone US market that saw Ford, GM, and Chrysler enjoy a much larger overall share that these manufacturers themselves are predicting will not return."

He added, reflecting the manufacturers' spin, "The dealers that have been retained now have an opportunity to sell a greater volume of new and used cars with higher profitability, as all three manufacturers are working to raise average new-car transaction prices while also closely monitoring supply and demand in order to support both short- and long-term residual values."

The king of fair pricing for consumers, Jack Fitzgerald, had an answer to this: "What they did was raise the price of vehicles for consumers by cutting back on the retail network. More competition is good for customers, not less," he said. Costs again were being passed on to the customer, who also footed the bill for the industry overhaul, courtesy of the auto task force.

In the late innings, dealers such as Patrick Painter became more vocal on the need for Chrysler and GM to change course. Painter, at least, thought it was encouraging to see top GM CEO Ed Whitacre take responsibility for the damage done to dealers, especially before the vote in Congress came due.

"It was somewhat heartening to see Whitacre come clean on this. I think he is doing damage control for GM," Painter told dealers. He suggested having their supporters in Congress, such as Chris Van Hollen or Steny Hoyer, hold a press conference to say now that GM had come forward, Chrysler should stop "making an enemy of every customer, dealer, state legislator, and Congress and give up being in the legal business and make peace with everyone. They need to get back to the business of building great cars."

It was more than a suggestion. He firmly believed it. "How much in wasted resources, time, and heartache has been lost with this stupid attitude of suing the hell out of everyone? Mr. Whitacre appears to be ready to call a truce. Why not Sergio?" he asked pointedly.

New York dealer Mark Calisi said, "We need to stop this negativity and get back to selling great cars and trucks. The retail sales numbers would be up if the rejected dealers came back. They took out the wrong dealers." Calisi later said that at least GM reconsidered its moves against dealers and brought some back. "They should be commended; they did a great job in backtracking on the issue," he said.

After arbitrations ensued, Chrysler stood its ground and kept the legal machinery humming. Florida dealer attorney Mark Ornstein at one point estimated that Chrysler was spending at least $1 million monthly in legal fees alone defending against the dealers.

Patrick Painter also put it bluntly by saying to his confidantes, "I want to know why [these] crappy dealers with their lousy facilities were kept and others were rejected. I want to be reinstated on the same basis that was used for them. Obviously, they must be feeling some pressure from Senator Rockefeller's letter" to SIGTARP.

Senator Jay Rockefeller in West Virginia strongly endorsed legislation to reverse the decisions to close the dealers. Rockefeller had clearly stated his position a number of times. "It's a national tragedy," he said about the dealer cuts in early June, when he presided over a special commerce committee hearing. Rockefeller pushed for a special investigation into the dealer closures which led to SIGTARP.

Another sticky wicket was surfacing for the two automakers. So far, the termination criteria that dealers had been asking for were not clear yet in the rejected dealers' minds. They had not received objective criteria on who went and who stayed. That alone made it easier to think it was a vendetta or popularity contest at work.

Ohio's Tim Doran, who headed the auto executives' trade group, had continually pressed the automakers and Congress to provide transparent and measurable closure criteria. At times, he knew he was pushing a thorn into the side of the automakers. But he knew this was only fair, and dealers deserved to know why they had been shut down.

Some dealers received criteria later when the issue surfaced in the cold light of court as the lawyers came to town. Then, in the summer of 2010, a report published by SIGTARP'S office said it could find no basis in fact to close the dealers, especially in the hurried approach of the automakers, including not finding cost savings to automakers. "The acceleration of dealership closings was not done with any explicit cost savings to the manufacturers in mind," concluded Neil Barofsky, who headed the investigation.

The SIGTARP report also said that GM estimated its cost savings of $1.1 million per terminated dealership, while Chrysler said it was going to save $45,500 per closed dealership. As the audit investigators came to see it, "The difference in these estimates alone casts doubt on their credibility." The auditors seemed to believe the variant numbers warranted investigation.

Further, the audit found inconsistencies in how GM went about closing dealerships, adding that 364 dealers were kept open that qualified for termination, according to the criteria they saw. "There was little or no documentation of the decision-making process to terminate or retain dealerships with similar profiles," the SIGTARP audit said.

Dealers, analysts, lobbying groups, many members in Congress, and now SIGTARP, were calling foul, as it turned out. Their cries would echo throughout the US legal system. But that also came too late to save the majority of dealers whose lives had been hollowed, and in many cases, destroyed.

More fireworks would soon follow.

Chapter 13—Showtime in Congress

I do not think there is any other quality so essential to success of any kind as the quality of perseverance. It overcomes almost everything, even nature.
—John D. Rockefeller

The countdown was beginning.

It was showtime in the halls of Congress. The feature film was *Save the Dealers*, as if they were an endangered species, but one unknown to most preservationists.

Keep the dealers closed or give them a lifeline? The votes would decide. And they were imminent.

Even in the final days, CRDR appealed to NADA and its board to keep pushing the legislation with Congress members. Darvish urged NADA to keep the fires lit under the Senate, especially with Senator Durbin, the Democratic leader and chairman, the power point. Urge the Senate to accept the House version with an arbitration process alternative, she said. It was their best shot.

"Like many of you, I feel this position comes with certain responsibilities that are moral and ethical, as opposed to political. So while I feel no obligation to do so, I will apologize right now for offending anyone with my rhetoric. We are in a unique position to be able to help. Remember, there is a fine line between those who can help and those who need help," Darvish wrote.

Chevrolet dealer Steve LaBelle grew even more active. So did Mark Calisi, Mark Sims, Jeff Duvall, Yale King, and others on the A-team. On voting days, the team stuck to legislators like flies on sticky paper. They built a virtual cordon around the lawmakers. In some cases, LaBelle said, "We walked them up to their seats on the floor so they wouldn't or couldn't *not* go in and vote."

For her part, Darvish fired off more e-mails to push buttons and pull in Senate support, even as the House was casting their votes. She reminded them of a December 7 resolution floating in the House that addressed arbitration for the rejected dealers. "There's no backing down now," she said.

She wrote to dealers in a late e-mail: "The flawed GM and Chrysler proposals are not sufficient and we need help from Congress. As of that night, December 7, the House Appropriations Committee had put forth a fair and transparent arbitration process intended to benefit all rejected, terminated, and wind-down dealers, using the manufacturers' language."

A joint appropriations group indeed had passed an arbitration resolution that favored the rejected dealers a few days earlier. But that was not final.

To close, she offered excerpts of a letter from a dealer's wife, who described the effect of their closed Chrysler and Chevrolet dealerships in wrenching terms. To protect the owners' privacy, she omitted names and personal information. "It could have been any of us writing this," Darvish said simply about the anguished note, detailing a dealership with its back to the wall.

As the political machine kicked in harder, Darvish did her best to explain what was happening and why to her base. She knew that bills had been flying through both houses of Congress since early summer to resolve the festering disputes. It was confusing even to her, and she'd been in the thick of it all along.

"I know this all sounds very complicated, but I can tell you that this train was long gone back in June when we started the fight. But with the tenacity, dedication, and around-the-clock efforts of all dealers across the country not only are we in a better place, but we all made a huge statement in Washington of how important and vital dealers are in America," she said to the dealer groups in another e-mail.

Giving her shortcut version of events in Congress, Darvish's ongoing updates served as an anatomy of the bills moving first sluggishly and then quickly through the lawmakers' chambers. "Our congressional champions insisted that we negotiate in good faith with the companies, and we did so for three months knowing that the exercise was simply of little or no benefit to those that have suffered so greatly," she reminded her peers. The LaTourette Amendment that survived "was our best shot at getting the affected dealers back in business," Darvish wrote.

Her friendly advisors in Congress had counseled her on this very issue. Compromise was best. It was the way Congress and politicians did business. She herself had learned the art of compromise when she stumbled on trip wire trying to push a joint proposal through with NADA and the other advocacy groups.

She credited the House supporters who had gotten the bills this far, especially Ohio's Steve LaTourette, whose alternate text remained in the appropriations bill that survived the flurry of revised bills, each with separate, confusing numbers attached. And without Steny Hoyer and Chris Van Hollen's leadership in the House, and their staff, there would be no legislation, she knew. There had been many other heroes, too many to mention here.

The cosponsor support was clear at least. In the House, there were 286 cosponsors who favored supporting the legislation (HR2743). Of these, 169 Democrats voted yes and 117 Republicans did so. In the Senate, forty-eight Senators, or twenty-nine Democrats and nineteen Republicans agreed to sponsor the final bill (S1304). Cosponsors however might differ from actual votes cast.

For one thing, they have to show up for the vote. A lawmaker could sign on as a sponsor and then not vote on a measure, or its reverse. It happens with busy schedules and if commitments are not altogether firm. In this showing, it appeared the vast majority of both House and Senate members could cast "yea" votes, if they showed up. In government parlance, that meant a resounding yes.

The House reacted quickly at the end, working nights and a weekend to get fair, transparent arbitration language woven into the final bill that went to the Senate. If it stalled there, they would be shot down.

Darvish and CRDR also worried about the erosion of state franchise laws designed to protect dealers at the state level. She made a last-ditch appeal to remind legislators to "make sure language is adopted for the protection of state automotive franchise laws to be included in the agreement being crafted by the Senate now."

Then in her best salesperson's style, she inserted the closer. "Now is the time we can really make a difference for the thousands of dealers who are counting on us. Act now; it's never been more important to stand with dealers," she urged.

The House and Senate took almost four days to wrestle over the bills. An agonizing four days. It was then in the hands of the Senate. The finalized bill would go to the president of the United States, Barack Obama.

On December 10, it happened. The House of Representatives voted. They unanimously approved substitute legislation called the Omnibus Appropriations Act (HR 3288), which included parts of the resolution to restore the economic rights of closed dealers by including binding arbitration. Binding meant what it said. Final. *Fait accompli.*

In fact, much of LaTourette's original language was intact in the flurry of changes. The Ohio representative from an economically battered state had carried the day.

* * *

After the bill passed in the House, Darvish felt something that was in short supply for too long: a sense of relief. She could breathe a little easier. The people, the decision makers—at least in the House—understood the dealers' plight. The dealers were still looking for their shot of redemption. It was now in the Senate's hands.

How long did they have to wait to get answers to the questions that had tormented them for seven months?

Three days.

It was Sunday, December 13, when, in an emergency weekend session, the US Senate gave dealers their holiday wish early. The Senate ended the raging 210-day debate by voting for the new Omnibus Appropriations Act (HR 3288), a bill similar to the House's version. The vote was 57 to 35, better than expected.

It was December 13, but it felt like New Year's Eve to the Darvish A-team and all of CRDR. Surely a time to celebrate. Kick up one's heels.

But the next step was to send the appropriations act to President Obama for signature before it could become law. The president could hold it up, veto it, or move it forward with his signature. He had the power of the pen, and the office.

On December 16, a Wednesday, President Obama signed the legislation that would give the rejected dealers a chance to plead their cases in a neutral arbitration setting. The dealer portion, earlier called the Dealer Economic Rights Act, was tucked into the larger legislative package.

It would take a miracle to pull off a victory in Congress, the naysayers said along the way. Considering where they—a fledgling CRDR group—had started, they had let their vision and passion guide them.

At last. Darvish and her team and dealers across the country exuded a real sigh of relief. They didn't pop champagne corks in victory, though. Most went home and slept.

The legislation that Obama signed was a $446 billion spending bill called the Omnibus Appropriations Act. The unwieldy act looked like a book and contained the dealer arbitration provisions that had flown through Congress in one form or another, finally spearheaded by Democrat Steny Hoyer, the House majority leader, and Democrat Dick Durbin of Illinois, the Assistant Senate majority leader. It was now fait accompli.

Magically, Dick Durbin from Illinois had come around in the Senate to push it through. In an about-face, he backed the principles the dealers had been advocating—transparency in Chrysler's dealer termination decisions, an opportunity for a third-party review for reinstatement, and reasonable reimbursement of expenses for dealers.

The president's official signature kicked off another seven-month process as cases were scheduled to be heard with the American Arbitration Association, considered a neutral third-party arm. The Triple A was not tied to the government or the automakers. Their teams were supposedly independents comprised of retired judges, retired attorneys or attorneys with law firms, or other specialty arbitrators.

At that point, the Dealer Rights Act was the law of the land. That meant GM and Chrysler had thirty days to send letters to the owners of the several thousand rejected dealerships informing them of their rights under the new law and spelling out the reasons that their franchise agreements had been terminated.

Then the affected dealerships had forty days to give notice whether or not they intended to seek arbitration. Arbitration must be completed within six months, and dealerships that won cases were slated to receive a Letter of Intent from the automakers within another fourteen business days.

It all seemed dry and procedural, but underneath was a dealer victory. In actuality, it was just the beginning of another lengthy process that would throw dealers, lawyers, and courts into a strange and expensive brew of hearings, appeals, and more legal wrangling.

Unsung Heroes

The unsung heroes in Congress, who took great care to shepherd the dealer bills through Congress and keep them alive were:

Rep. Steny Hoyer—D-Maryland

Rep. Chris Van Hollen—D-Maryland

Rep. Steve LaTourette—R-Ohio

Rep. Roscoe Bartlett—R-Maryland

Rep. Betty Sutton—D-Ohio

Rep. Dan Maffei—D-New York

Rep. Frank Kratovil—D-Maryland

Sen. Chuck Grassley—R-Iowa

Sen. John (Jay) Rockefeller—D-W. Virginia

In the end, it would pit dealer against dealer as corporate lawyers and the automakers found loopholes to award closed franchises to more favored parties. The modern age phenomena called "gifting" was born. Another challenge, another fight, was brewing.

How the Dealer Drama Unfolded

Milestones in the seven-month journey, from the announcement of dealership closures to arbitration approvals:

- **May 14:** Chrysler announces 789 dealership terminations.
- **May 15:** GM announces first round of planned dealer cuts; about 1,350 eventually targeted for closure.

- **June 3:** Maryland dealer Jack Fitzgerald and Arent Fox law firm draft legislation to reverse closures.
- **June 8:** Rep. Dan Maffei, D-NY, introduces bill to restore dealership franchises.
- **June 18:** Sen. Charles Grassley, R-Iowa, introduces similar bill.
- **July 13–14:** Hundreds of dealers mobilized by Committee to Restore Dealer Rights fly to Washington to lobby lawmakers.
- **July 16:** House passes legislation to reverse dealer closures by a 219–208 vote.
- **Sept. 3:** With legislation stalled in Senate, dealer groups unite behind proposal for rejected-dealer arbitration and compensation.
- **Sept. 30:** GM, Chrysler begin settlement talks with dealer groups.
- **Dec. 3:** GM, Chrysler break off talks; announce arbitration with original termination criteria.
- **Dec. 9:** Conference committee of House and Senate leaders passes arbitration bill with criteria more favorable to dealers.
- **Dec. 10:** House passes similar legislation, 221–202.
- **Dec. 14:** Senate passes same bill, 57–35, sending it to President Barack Obama.
- **Dec. 16:** Obama signs bill into law as part of omnibus act.

Source: *Automotive News, December 21, 2009*

Chapter 14—Who's Phoenix?

"It makes a difference to this one," the woman said,
throwing the lone starfish back into the ocean.
—Loren Eiseley, "The Star Thrower"

"Call me Mark," said the president of GM North America when Tammy Darvish arrived at his office half an hour before their appointed time on March 24.

Darvish apologized for the time and said she could wait in the lobby until nine. She found herself a little nervous in his presence. He was, after all, the president of the world's second-largest automaker, General Motors. Her father had been a GM dealer for years, but it wasn't often you got a personal meeting with the man at the top.

Actually, Darvish had arrived nearly an hour early at GM's global headquarters in Detroit. She'd taken a late-night flight from Washington DC's Reagan Airport to Detroit Metropolitan Airport. That airport is called Detroit Metro, but really is in the semi-rural area of Romulus in Western Wayne County, about a forty-minute drive from downtown Detroit if one obeys the speed limit. Add another five or ten minutes to your trip to ask for directions if you get lost inside the maze-like GM Renaissance Center—RenCen, as most locals refer to it. The seventy-two-floor building, known for its confusing tower layout, was indeed a labyrinth of structures housing offices, businesses, shops, and restaurants.

That morning, Darvish window-shopped a little and then found the sets of elevators going to the thirty-eighth executive floor in tower five where GM's upper brass are located. She was still early. At one point she thought about stopping for a cup of tea, but changed her mind. *No snafus this morning, please God,* she thought. She believed in being early, especially to important meetings. And this one could be a game-changer.

What's interesting is how Darvish first "met" Mark Reuss. It had been through an Internet connection on an *Automotive News* Web chat website allowing users to ask questions on dealer issues, including reinstatements.

Darvish had replied to Web chats to the GM writer whose code name was "Phoenix." This Phoenix was encouraging and wrote back promptly, obviously enjoying the secrecy. At this point, the writer could be anybody in GM, Darvish thought. Except this poster had some power over dealers, it was clear. Phoenix responded to a Darvish post on March 9, finding her comments illuminating. The Web posts appear here unedited.

"I do read the comments here and I do listen. Every day. Most nights, and all weekends. I am trying to make things right here. I am trying to put the face on GM again. With dignity, with honesty, with care. To rebuild the company and its dealers back to greatness. I talk to dealers—lots—every day," Phoenix wrote, after posting one note that promised dealers would be called about their GM status.

"We are doing this with care of others' privacy and feelings too. Each case is different. Each dealer's wants and desires are different. Not getting a call does not automatically mean you are 'out.' In many cases it means we want to actually talk to you and come to a mutual agreement of your wants and the business we are in together. This takes more time. Please just understand what we are doing here—making the company fit for battle again in the market. No agendas, no sneaky tricks. There is history to overcome, and we cannot snap our fingers and say 'it's ok.' But just know I want trust and success again—with honesty and integrity. Just like you all do. I expect the nasty comments, but we will only fix this by actions not words—over time."

Many dealers did not get the promised call, Darvish wrote in a post, more of a reminder meant to grab attention than anything. The Darvish dealerships, of course, were among those, not getting notices.

In her direct Darvish style, she sent a response to "Dear Phoenix" on March 9, at 10:21 p.m. She didn't want to engage in cloak-and-dagger antics, so she baited the GMer probably more than she should have:

"Very ironic to hear words like 'trust, honesty, integrity' etc. from someone who hides behind an a.k.a. as they post a comment. Come on … 'with dignity, with honesty, with care.' Help us out here. Enough with the games as two thousand-plus dealers have been through more than enough this past year. Many dealers that did not get the 'call' (including myself) called the 800# as directed in the PR stunt last week only to be told 'you need to prepare for arbitration.' Further, when pressed about the meeting that was said would happen in the PR stunt the response was 'only after you sign a discussion agreement (confidentiality agreement) and it won't change anything.' You can be sure that we have ALL of these cases accounted & documented. The only [thing] missing with this picture (besides who you really are) is exactly what you profess to be—truth, honesty, integrity. Put up or shut up!"

What she wanted to say but didn't, was, "Who are you, Phoenix? 'Fess up, will you?"

The next morning, at 9:06, Phoenix replied in abbreviated posting style, as if reading her mind: "Not trying to hide behind anything. Phoenix = me, Mark Reuss. Friday not a PR stunt, and while I am an engineer I am trying to do what is right. Was not here through all this so I apologize but I do care deeply and do listen. Would never attempt to imply everything is ok but trying to treat all correctly. I am far from perfect, but I am, with our team, doing our best. Thank you."

Double wow! she thought. Not only had Phoenix come out of cyberspace hiding, he turned out to be the president of GM. This was a big fish she had on the line, if it was true. She wanted to believe it was. Who could impersonate being Mark Reuss? Who would dare?

Now that she knew who Phoenix was, Darvish worried a little about her own boldness earlier. But she gathered up her courage and pressed on. Firing off another quick post, she invited Reuss to meet her for coffee, anywhere in the country; she'd be there. She wanted to talk about the rejected dealers. So far her Chevrolet dealership had not been reinstated. But she had no intention of pleading her own, or her father's, dealership case.

Mark Reuss did one better. He invited her to meet at his office in Detroit on March 24.

* * *

Flying to Detroit, Darvish had one mission in mind. She was going to talk about the terminated dealers, some of whom were being reinstated or negotiating a compensation deal. Some were going through the arbitration process approved only this past December by federal law.

Maybe at that time Mark Reuss wanted to be called one of the GM good guys. Maybe small miracles do happen in this disaster story that began unraveling nearly a year ago, Darvish thought. Could there be a happy ending here? She could only hope on a wing and a prayer.

Appointed by Ed Whitacre in December 2009, Reuss at least had gasoline in his veins. A car guy, he was the son of Lloyd Reuss, a GM president in the early 1990s. Lloyd Reuss served under Robert Stempel in the engineering era of GM. Mark Reuss had returned stateside fresh from GM stints in Australia and New Zealand and then briefly headed global engineering. If he played his cards right, he could be fast-tracked to the top CEO spot, a rising star, the thinking went.

Now she'd come full circle and was face-to-face with Reuss in Detroit. Their conversation was pleasant, even informal. Reuss offered coffee; she drinks tea. She sipped the coffee politely, feeling a little intimidated.

Still, Reuss was cordial, even casual in his demeanor, she saw. Friendly and approachable just like his reputation was said to be. He smiled a lot, which put her at ease. She had asked that there be no advisors, lawyers, or PR staff present. This was not a photo op. She wanted to talk openly. He honored the request. She had paid for the trip, of course. There was no discussion about that earlier.

She immediately brought up the rejected dealers. That was why she was here, after all. She clarified again that she wasn't there to talk about the DARCARS' dealerships. Reuss said he understood her point, and the purpose of her visit, but said he would do whatever he could for them; he had a lot of respect for the Darvish name and reputation on the East Coast.

They talked beyond their appointed time of a half hour. Even when she reminded him about the time, he waved it off. He seemed starved for direct dealer feedback, she thought. Well, maybe it was because he was still new at this job and, of course, not many dealers walked directly into his office. What she didn't understand was there was no learning curve for Mark Reuss, no dress rehearsal. He had to get it right, even the dealer problem.

They parted like old friends.

Darvish caught her flight back to DC that day, feeling encouraged. She actually inhaled and exhaled, not holding the tension in so tightly. Maybe GM had a chance with Mark Reuss at the helm. Maybe dealers had a fighting chance too. Arbitration was still in its early stages, beginning in February.

To many, Reuss signaled a new day at GM, open to hearing dealers out, willing to rock the boat a little. So unlike the old GM and the members on the government auto task force. His boss, Ed Whitacre, already said they might have made some mistakes in the terminations, so the top exec left a window open for revisiting the dealer closures. There was talk about bringing back large numbers of GM dealers before and after the arbitrations ended.

In one media report, Reuss had said, "Dealers are a big priority for GM." And this: GM's large dealer network "used to be one of our main, massive strengths," Reuss said during a media test drive of the new Chevrolet Cruze in 2010. "I still think that's true. It can be true with the right dealers."

That was good news, coming from a top GM leader, Darvish thought. So far, it was looking hopeful with Mark Reuss, and she noted that Reuss had the touchy-feely thing down pat. He seemed to be a people person, as she had heard.

After their Detroit meeting, Reuss quickly sent an e-mail to Darvish, thanking her for the visit that day. He said, in part, "The effort and conversation was something I will never forget. Your information validates our actions, and we will not let America and its dealers down. You are a true American success story, and I am honored to know you. I also have the answer to your question, 'why am I here.' The answer I believe may lie in a higher power than we understand. Thanks from America, GM, and all the dealers. Your friend, Mark."

And Reuss's stand on dealers seemed to represent a desire by the new GM leadership team to avoid the expense of litigating and closing dealerships, now signaling that that move was not critical to restore the company to profitability. She believed he was delivering on his promise. GM also saw the effect on retail sales for Chrysler and themselves.

Later, she wrote about the Reuss visit to her dealer contacts. "The truth is I never expected he would take me up on my offer … Mark listened, took notes, asked many questions, and was the first person from GM throughout this entire process who never made any excuses or justifications for anything that happened in the past. He genuinely was there to learn, and I felt he appreciated the value of all the research prepared by the CRDR team."

But Darvish also remembered the dealers, the many who had gone through hell; many had not survived. Many were not coming back into the fold. She wasn't sure about her father yet.

Dealers on the Ropes

Steve LaBelle, a Chevrolet dealer in Bridgewater, Massachusetts, grew to have a different view of Mark Reuss. He had felt encouraged by his contacts with the amiable new GM leader at first. When LaBelle approached him early in his tenure at GM, where he'd been recruited by Ed Whitacre, Reuss had seemed personable enough.

Like a few other dealers, LaBelle was on the ropes after he was reinstated as a Chevrolet dealer. His franchise was reinstated after he appealed the opening of a new dealer in his market area, which he claimed would do him irreparable harm and hurt his sales. But LaBelle's case was tricky. In late January, he had filed for arbitration to be reinstated under the new law. In February, GM sent him a letter to notify him that a new dealership had been approved in his market area. LaBelle filed an injunction to prevent that from happening until his arbitration was completed in late June. Then GM turned around to reinstate him with an LOI, which virtually rendered his arbitration moot. He was in a tough spot, reinstated but receiving almost no new products.

Before all that happened, he had contacted Mark Reuss in January after reading a story in *Automotive News* about Reuss taking his son to Flint, Michigan, to the site of Buick City and the former Buick headquarters. Flint, one of the most devastated industrial spots in the country, was almost wiped out after GM shut down plants, including Buick City.

About seventy miles north of Detroit, Flint gained minor notoriety as the site for filmmaker Michael Moore's satiric debut *Roger and Me,* which came out in December 1989. In the "mockumentary," Moore chases GM's Roger Smith around the country, camera in hand. He wanted to ask Smith about the harm he was doing to Flint with GM's massive downsizings. For the sake of the plot, of course, Moore never meets up with CEO Smith. And one story has it that GM professional staffers were not allowed to see the controversial film at the time.

Fast forward about twenty years. Another story in which Mark Reuss talked about taking his son to see the former Buick City in Flint appeared in *Fortune* magazine in February 2010. The sprawling manufacturing complex, once Flint's pride, was off Saginaw Road, a main highway running through the city's heart. It connected former factory towns, such as Pontiac, Saginaw, and Bay City, Michigan. The facility was designed as GM's answer to the Toyota City plant in the same-named Japanese city.

At one time, before the I-75 freeway to the west of Flint was built in the 1960s, Saginaw Road was the major north-south connector to the downtowns of large and small cities that grew up around it. The massive Buick City complex closed when GM deemed it noncompetitive due to an influx of cheap Japanese cars. Its demise left a gaping hole in the heart of Flint and area workers who had enjoyed among the highest-paying union jobs in the country, in the world.

In Buick City, "The massive manufacturing complex, which once employed twenty-eight thousand workers, represented an unsuccessful attempt to compete with the integrated production of Japanese manufacturers. As GM's volumes declined, it became obsolete; it was closed in 1999 and was demolished in 2002," the *Fortune* story said.

According to Reuss, his thirteen-year-old son looked around at the utter devastation of downtown Flint. Except for a few pawnshops, thrift stores, and fast-food restaurants, it looked deserted. Incredulous, the young boy asked his father what had happened here. Pondering his options, Mark Reuss decided to tell the truth. "We could not compete," he said simply.

For Reuss, the admission was even more poignant because he had worked there as a young engineer—and for another reason. Buick City had been created by his father, Lloyd Reuss, when he held the top jobs at the Buick complex for about a decade, beginning in the mid-1970s.

Buick's headquarters was adjacent to the plant and employed thousands of white-collar managers who ran Buick's expanding global division. Many GM executives in training got their starts in Flint, including Bob Coletta, who headed the Buick group after attending GMI (General Motors Institute), the company's engineering school. Lloyd Reuss and his young son, Mark, did stints there. But the Buick facility was scaled back after GM gradually relocated its professional staff to the RenCen after 1996.

In fairness, though, well-paid auto workers were themselves abandoning bigger industrial cities like Detroit, Flint, Cleveland, and Kokomo, Indiana, for cleaner suburbs with better schools, like their white-collar counterparts. That point is well made in a 2010 book by two *Indianapolis Star* newspaper reporters called *At the Crossroads: Middle America and the Battle to Save the Car Industry.*

The book examines the collapse of the US auto industry from a Midwest perspective. Indiana, they maintained, is the country's second-largest automotive manufacturing state after Michigan. They further dissected the fall of Flint, once the hub of the GM auto industry.

Flint, of course, was the birthplace of GM in 1908; and it signaled the growth of the UAW after 1935 under labor leader Walter Reuther. It's the town where workers won the right to organize as a result of the forty-four-day UAW sit-down strike of 1936–37 that was to fuel labor unrest in other big industrial cities.

Why did big industrial cities like Detroit fail? Some blamed it on the advent of major shopping malls in the suburbs where developers, businesses, and residents soon followed. When J. L. Hudson's (later named Marshall Fields and Macy's) department store, a major Detroit landmark, pulled out of downtown Detroit in 1983, critics said it was like a death knell had sounded in the city, once the fifth-largest in the country.

But the reasons for manufacturing failing, especially in Detroit, are a complex stew of work loss, urban flight, and new macroeconomic trends. Detroit's decline had more to do with the loss of manufacturing jobs than anything, auto observers said. Many industrial jobs went to the suburbs, then south, and then further overseas to developing countries. A good number were outsourced and automated out of existence as robots replaced line workers. The BRIC nations (Brazil, Russia, India, and China) with their ready supply of cheaper labor stood to benefit.

* * *

Steve LaBelle, touched by the story about Reuss and son in Flint, wrote to Reuss in January of 2010 to tell him so. At that time, he carefully brought up his own dealership situation in Massachusetts, saying he had just requested that the placement of another dealer, McGee Chevrolet, in his market area not be approved at that time.

His appeal to Reuss was almost father-to-father. He mentioned that after receiving the wind-down notice, he had gone home to break the news to his wife and son. It had been painful. "The American Dream we had accomplished, of owning a successful Chevrolet business, had been destroyed in the blink of an eye," he said. He related that his son, like Reuss's, had asked why it had happened. He had not yet been able to answer that question, LaBelle told Reuss. He wrote to Reuss again on March 1. He further explained that another Chevrolet dealer was moving into his area of responsibility and it was the exact location LaBelle had asked for, saying that it limited his chances for a fair arbitration hearing, which was pending. He asked that the move be stopped, pending the outcome of arbitration.

Mark Reuss later called LaBelle, apparently in response to his March letter. The congenial Reuss said he would try to do something. After that, LaBelle was reinstated, but it was through a legal sleight of hand. He couldn't get enough products to sell. Over about a six-month period, he'd received twenty-five to thirty new cars to sell. Despite his reinstatement, he believed he was being product-starved like other dealers who had been terminated.

The Reuss father-and-son trip through Flint was a grim reminder of what had transpired in the US auto industry and on Main-Street America. The reasons were complex, of course, and you couldn't blame one culprit alone. But it was still a crying shame, LaBelle thought.

Flint and Detroit, as symbols of industrial America, seemed to fail. Maybe kids today don't understand the lessons of what happened in America's manufacturing sector. A "don't-know-don't-care" catch-all teen slogan permeated young minds.

Maybe they didn't care, but these were the high-tech and management workers of the future, Tammy Darvish thought. Movies like *Roger and Me,* and books such as *The Machine That Changed the World* and *The Reckoning* weren't on their radar screens. Their nods to history, or the future, were in far-off fictional realms like *Star Wars, The Lord of the Rings,* the Harry Potter series, and more recently vampire books/flicks such as *Twilight.*

But the present drama was not about cyber-wars with imaginary villains and heroes shooting laser weapons and extracting fake blood. This was about car wars between real people being waged on a political and global level. And the victims were real people too, who hurt and suffered; their blood was real. People like their parents, relatives, and neighbors who would lose jobs through no fault of their own as technology, outsourcing, and cutbacks permeated the car culture.

Circa 2009, GM was talking about leaving Detroit, the once-industrial city they propped up, for the suburbs. That would spell ruin for a once-flourishing industrial magnet now hammered with nearly the worst unemployment rate in the country, high crime statistics, and failing companies. Like other cities dependent on one industry, it was in decay. "A few cars, bars, and weirdos" was a bumper sticker slogan often seen at the time.

Later, LaBelle thought about Reuss, his Flint story, and the demise of the Main-Street dealers. In the Flint area, perhaps a dozen dealers had shut down. He saw the parallels. "They destroyed the American dream for us," he said.

For LaBelle, it was personal too. Reuss and other GM execs had failed to deliver on the promise to help his dealership survive. He was still feeling the product squeeze.

LaBelle was forced to close his dealership in October 2010, letting his employees go. He was left to ponder his options. Of Mark Reuss, he concluded, "He's just another salesman, telling you what you want to hear."

* * *

"I am a fellow Italian businessman at Lochmoor Chrysler Jeep in Detroit. I want to express how my feelings have been betrayed by those who you are looking to for accurate information regarding the inner workings of your customers, the dealers." Agostino, or "Gus" Russo, began his letter to Sergio Marchionne this way on a night in June. He didn't know the independent-minded Marchionne, raised in Canada and trained as an accountant, was not one to be swayed by the "fellow-Italian" line.

As the CEO of Fiat in Italy he'd brought that stalled company, not well regarded for its product line, back from the brink. Some viewed him as one of the better auto executives in the world, right behind Carlos Goshn of Renault-Nissan, who was hailed as the top global automotive executive.

There was hope that Marchionne could restore the new Chrysler to prosperity. Russo wasn't so sure about that. He wasn't naming names in his letter, but privately he was furious that his dealership had been gifted to another nearby dealer, who had never sold the Chrysler and Jeep brands, only Dodge.

Russo continued in his letter: "Lochmoor Chrysler Jeep was your only Chrysler and Jeep dealer in the city of Detroit. We were with Chrysler for thirty years, one of the top fifty [performers] in the country, and year after year we were one of your most profitable dealers. In the 1990s Lochmoor was one of the Alfa Romeo dealers for many years; we were one of the top performers for Fiat in sales and service. In May, decisions were made to close hundreds of dealerships. I know you feel this is not your problem; you have said 'my conscience is clear.' Well, that may be true, but I feel you should hear the truth about what truly transpired during the times that you also have called fair and equitable.

"If you take a few minutes to review the numbers between Lochmoor and the dealer that was chosen to remain, you will be wondering what in the world happened here! My sales and service numbers far exceed anything [the gifted dealer] did in the years we did business."

Indeed, Russo was a top Chrysler sales dealer nationwide for years. What he got for his efforts, or deep concern, was a curt cease-and-desist order from Chrysler's hard-line attorney shortly after writing. He'd served for more than thirty years, and a newcomer (Nardelli and then Marchionne) walked in and it's all over. Thinking about it, he could only shake his head. He moved around nervously as he surveyed his dealership, anything to keep the rage at bay.

The cease-and-desist response was a classic lawyer's scare tactic. It was the same kind of reply Tammy Darvish had received when she approached Marchionne and his dealer chief Pete Grady that year. Clearly they did not want to communicate directly with the terminated dealers. All the action was being orchestrated by Chrysler lawyers with dealers at this point.

Gus Russo couldn't believe how the company had changed since he started with it. There was no human contact or personal voices in this company anymore, especially for those deemed outsiders, the Russos saw. The information was all controlled by lawyers and public-relations people laundering the messages of higher-ups.

For more than a year, Russo's daughter Gina contacted everyone she could think of to intervene in their case and that of other dealers. In that time, she formed a close bond with Jackie Mealey in Troy, and the two sent personal letters, e-mails, and called everyone they could think of in a power position—from Chrysler, all the way up to the auto task force and President Obama. They heard nothing.

"It all fell on deaf ears," Gina Russo said.

Like other dealers, the Russos tried to sell used cars and parts to customers until late October of 2009. They became active in Tammy Darvish's save-the-dealers campaign nationwide. That fall, they decided to shut down and were forced to let their employees go.

At times, Gus Russo halfheartedly watched TV, some sports or other programs that caught his eye. He would suddenly spring out of his chair and scream, "Those bastards! They took away everything from me!" Gina Russo could hear her father, and she would bite back the tears, as did her mother, if she was in earshot.

* * *

Loyalty to people, to one another on jobs, and even in many relationships had gone out the door. The American dream had soured, according to some accounts. The media was documenting it.

Arianna Huffington's 2010 book *Third World America: How Our Politicians are Abandoning the Middle Class and Betraying the American Dream* paints a grim picture of what's wrong with the country. Huffington, a Greek immigrant, is editor-in-chief of Huffington Post Media Group.

"Every day, Americans, faced with layoffs and tough economic times, are forced to use their credit cards to pay for essentials such as food, housing, and medical care—the costs of which continue to escalate. But, as their debt rises, they find it harder to keep up with their payments. When they don't, banks, trying to offset losses in other areas, turn around, hike interest rates, and impose all manner of fees and penalties," Huffington wrote.

President Barack Obama, ten days after taking office in 2009, also recognized the problem. "It's like the American Dream in reverse," he said. That's how he described the plight of Americans hit by the shattered economy. His description fell short of a real fix, despite more multibillions of dollars poured onto the problem. The dream had turned into a nightmare for millions of people. And the debt was being passed on to future generations.

If anything, Obama had too much on his plate as president, some dealers thought. As a supreme delegator, he obviously listened to the people he put in place, including the auto task force who reported to Treasury's Geithner and chief economic counsel Larry Summers. They in turn listened to the task force. But everyone wanted to please the president and their superiors. No one said Stepford Wives didn't exist in government too.

Even Jack Fitzgerald, the outspoken leader of the CRDR group in Maryland, thought President Obama meant well in saving GM and Chrysler, but he got bad advice from the task force—all the president's men—on the dealer issues. While the talk was of "shared sacrifice," they didn't bother to look at how it would affect the real American people, the ones losing jobs and all they had worked for.

"I think President Obama wanted to do right. But [the task force] made a mess of Detroit. And they put more people out of work in the country than they saved jobs in Detroit," Fitzgerald said on national television. The dealer closures only compounded the problem of job loss, not job creation, he said.

It was clear that the leaders in Washington could often diagnose the problem but didn't know how to fix it.

* * *

As they looked at how far they had come, the Darvish camp and her A-team often didn't give themselves credit. Like people who suffer from compassion sickness, they often felt they had not done enough for other dealers, not themselves.

Sometimes Tammy Darvish beat herself up. Unknowingly, she had become an activist, but it was still hard to take—when the results are not those you wanted. "Those who can help should help; it's what I did," she would remind herself. It was the way she got by sometimes, speaking her own slogans.

She would not take a victim's posture. But she couldn't help but wonder what they had won. Of course they got the right to arbitrate with supposedly neutral arbitrators who barely understood how the dealership process worked. She couldn't blame them; not many people understood before the dealers themselves tried to tell their stories, to Congress, to media, to America.

Still, the corporate spin machine dominated public perception: too many domestic dealers existed to sustain the current marketplace. Automakers and the task force argued that they could not be competitive in today's market with the old dealer structure, designed for times when the US makers faced less foreign competition and sales were higher.

What the automakers failed to tell the public was there was also a time when they designed and produced more products in the United States, when their factories were humming and their dealers were selling cars because the companies were committed to US jobs. That landscape had changed. The producers of America had often gone overseas. The economic meltdown was global. China, in fact, became GM's biggest market. And the BRIC countries (Brazil, Russia, India, and China) were prospering.

For some, the dream was over. They had not won the skirmishes or the war. This was not a stalemate. *It is what it is,* Darvish thought. She could only point to the results of that long harsh winter as 2009 turned the page to 2010. The year, the cataclysmic events were about to become history. With one stroke of the pen, on December 16, President Obama signed into law the fate of dealers across the country, giving them the right to arbitrate in a neutral third-party setting before a panel, including an arbitrator assigned by the American Arbitration Association.

The dealer advocates had won resounding bipartisan support for restoring dealers across the country. That bipartisanship vote was almost unheard of in the realm of modern-day politics. Fewer than 1 percent of all bills brought before Congress do this well, the CRDR leaders said.

Those were facts.

The media reported that, in their way, Jack Fitzgerald, Tammy Darvish, and Alan Spitzer had made history. Theirs was a classic heroic tale of defeat and survival, their admirers said. As a united dealer group, they had helped lift the death sentences of many Chrysler and GM dealerships.

But by 2010, middle-class America was still feeling betrayed by forces bigger than themselves. If you're out of work or facing the prospect of diminished resources, it can make you feel that way. Ask Joe and Josephine America. Dealers, for the most part, understood the plight of average Americans. Many dealer personnel in closed dealerships were worried. The dealer terminations had brought a change in their own lifestyles—and for their families and the communities they did business in.

On balance, many considered Darvish and her A-team victorious. At the outset, the oddsmakers told them to hang it up. No one would bet on them in this horserace. "If you think they're going to win against the power structure, I've got some beachfront land in Florida to sell you for forty bucks an acre," the grim reapers joked. If you don't mind swampland, that is.

Maryland Rep. Chris Van Hollen called their efforts a huge "victory of David over Goliath." When it started out, he was among the unknowing at the congressional end. But Van Hollen, Hoyer, Rockefeller, Kratovil, and LaTourette were among the roll call of unsung heroes for the A-team, Darvish said.

Attorney Mary Jo Dowd with Arent Fox, the DC legal lobbying experts, worked closely with Darvish and CRDR in the long months leading up to Congress's votes and the president's signature. Several times, Darvish contacted Dowd for advice when she was struggling with thorny issues, ranging from internal problems with NADA to ways to approach Congress.

"So how should I say this?" she might ask Dowd.

Dowd would send back a quick reply. In her calm, straightforward manner, Dowd tried to bolster Darvish's confidence as much as provide legal counsel. Anyone who fought the battles that Darvish was fighting could suffer from feelings of self-doubt at times, Dowd knew. And Darvish, as an introspective woman, was willing to share her fears.

Later, after the arbitration decisions came down in July, Dowd said, "Darvish and her team need to take credit for the wins and for the 661 non-arbitration negotiations that happened at GM and the others who could get back into their businesses. It's not just the final arbitration numbers that count, but those dealerships that were kept by the companies, count too," she said. "These cases were settled out of court and dealers were able to save money and legal fees. Those were huge wins. [Tammy and her team] should not sell themselves short."

America's Debate: Losing the Dream

Are we losing the American Dream?

An opinion poll conducted by *ABC News* and Yahoo in 2010 showed that nearly 45 percent of those surveyed thought that "the American Dream" was a thing of the past. It "once held true" but no longer does, respondents said. Only half the country believed the dream "still exists." The poll was conducted against a background of dismal statistics on growing unemployment, poverty, inequality, and Americans without health insurance. An even higher number of Americans—more than 60 percent—thought the country was heading in the wrong direction.

Are we losing the American Dream?

Darvish asked herself that question many times along the journey. She had hoped for real change with Mark Reuss in place at GM. He, at least, seemed to care and signaled a new attitude toward dealers and the way GM did business with them; a new leadership team at GM could make a difference. But listening to dealers' stories following arbitration, where they indicated they weren't getting what they needed in products and support, she had to wonder. The future would brighten and then cloud up again, just like the weather. No predictability any more.

If anyone, even Mark Reuss, asked her what their dealer group had accomplished in 2009, Darvish might say, "We didn't save all the starfishes, but we saved a few. The classic poem, "The Star Thrower," portrays a woman consoling herself after rescuing at least one starfish of millions by throwing it back into the sea. Darvish and the A-team did far better, of course. But they too had to remind themselves that every person, every case is uniquely important. The "few" in the dealer world, according to Mary Jo Dowd, numbered in the thousands who at least had a fighting chance to win back their businesses or negotiate settlements on their closed dealerships.

Chapter 15—Exile from Main Street

The world breaks everyone and afterward many are stronger at the broken places.
—Ernest Hemingway

Just because you're paranoid doesn't mean they aren't out to get you.
—Author unknown

It's like this. You're invited to the home of a friend or close business associate. You bring food or a bottle of nice wine, or a dessert. You've always been the giving kind.

You walk in the door. It's a fancy place, a friendly place, you recall. You've been here before. Holidays, celebrations, dinners, or parties of one kind or another. Camaraderie, warmth, acceptance set the tone at these festive gatherings.

But the mood in the air is somehow different on this night. No one talks to you; no one looks your way. Eyes are averted. No cordial greetings or slaps on the back. No, "How's business, buddy? How's the family, the golf game going?" Not even, "What have you got for me, any news?" The nonverbal cues say "Go away."

Suddenly, you're a stranger at the party. It's not like they don't care. They just don't want you here. You are shunned, an outcast from the tribe. And you don't know why.

That's what thousands of businesspeople felt like when their car dealerships, their lifework, vanished. Everything they'd built was suddenly yanked out from under their feet.

You leave your wine, your offering, or whatever you brought. But you take your crushed spirit and go home, alone and forlorn. If you have someone close you can talk to later, you tell them about it. Most likely you bottle it up inside. You stew. The problem festers. Questions mount. What happened back there? Why me? If it goes on long enough, this pressure, you will likely develop medical problems—high blood pressure, high cholesterol, heart attacks, and stroke are all linked to high stress levels.

Change the festive locale. Make it a business function. Perhaps it's an anniversary or milestone birthday celebration as a business owner—a car dealer, or anyone. The feelings are the same. A sense of rejection and betrayal follow you home.

From Insiders to Outsiders

When they think back to what happened in 2009 as the automakers announced they were shutting down several thousand stores, dealers describe their experience—and the revelation—as surreal. Paranoia was growing among those targeted for closure, but being entrepreneurs, they wondered how they might change things, make them work. But they couldn't turn back the clock.

Now they were strangers in their own world, outsiders looking in.

Suddenly, you're a pariah, someone rejected by others. That's how Richard Mealey described it. "It's clear they don't want you on the team anymore. And you don't know why," he said. Mealey ran a successful Chrysler and Jeep store for forty-three years in the Troy Motor Mall among twenty-seven other franchise owners in Troy, Michigan. He was located on a major boulevard called Maple Road, the area's prime commercial strip. Chains such as Whole Foods, Walmart, Target, Kohl's, Home Depot, Starbucks, and various restaurants, banks, and strip malls had opened nearby in the last few decades.

* * *

When people are asked what keeps them up at night, the response is usually a deeply personal or financial problem, or workspace issues. But George McGuire described the memory of being cast out of GM as his personal nightmare. Almost eighteen months later, it was still surreal, a horrific dream. Like other dealers, he was living out his worst nightmare in his waking hours.

McGuire was a Chevrolet dealer in Shakopee, Minnesota. He said the experience of being cast off will never leave him. It's as if all the rejected dealers were suddenly marked with a sign. "It's like everyone had gotten their teeth bashed in," McGuire said. "But the problems weren't with the dealer network. It was a bloated [automaker] management system and that of course was getting saved by the government."

The culled dealers were asking the government only for free enterprise to be allowed to take hold, he said, no taxpayer money. Being kicked to the curb was enraging to dealers like McGuire, who only wanted to continue running their businesses. "We were not asking for a bailout like the automakers did. But nobody should choose that you fail," he said. "It's like wanting to go to a party, but you're not invited. The corporate insiders pick and choose who comes. When you were a terminated dealer they looked at you differently."

You were suddenly damaged goods, thrown on the reject pile. *It's like they'd like us to go away. Just disappear. Like we did something wrong, but we didn't know what.* That was the feeling many dealers described.

Local dealer marketing meetings are often hooplas where colleagues meet-and-greet one another. McGuire recalled a recent meeting in his Minnesota region where everyone was invited—except the rejected dealers. *Screw them,* he thought. He crashed the party. Big mistake? In some ways it was. "It was like being made to wear the scarlet letter. I was the bad guy here, but I didn't do anything wrong," he recalled.

At that meeting, he felt isolated, alone. *If they would only speak to me, or even look at me,* he thought. "It was like I was somehow subhuman, invisible," said McGuire. He suddenly knew how some minority people must feel when they're the only ones at an event or gathering. You could be among a million people and still be alone. It was a lonely, desolate feeling.

* * *

Gina Russo helped run her father's Lochmoor Chrysler-Jeep store in Detroit until the day it shut down. After helping lock up the store and saying farewell to lifelong customers, she observed, "Our government conspired to ruin America's most successful businesses. I never imagined this would happen to us. How could the task force allow Chrysler to manipulate the law?" Russo asked, still in disbelief many months later. Gus Russo, her father, had started the business more than thirty years ago. Lochmoor had placed at the top or near the top in Chrysler sales nationally for years. It was hard to fathom. Why would Chrysler let high-performing dealers go? she asked. The competition had never been more fierce or the stakes higher as auto sales plunged nationally.

Gina Russo remembered a phone conversation Jim Press had with all the dealers nationwide before he left Chrysler late in 2009. Press insisted that Russo (and other dealers) buy cars then and there to help save the struggling automaker. Press said he "had a long memory" and he would "remember who you are," if they didn't order, Russo recalled. The veiled threat was loud and clear. Dealers such as Russo did buy cars, even though they didn't need them. They had always been team players and supported the factory. "Inventory clearance sales" had become popular marketing jargons for such reasons. The Russos had 338 vehicles in inventory when they were shut down. That meant they had bought those vehicles outright—with only twenty-eight days to sell them and all the parts inventory on hand. They had insider knowledge that the gifted dealer down the street had bought no new cars at the time. "If we hadn't ordered them, we wouldn't have lost all that money," she said. It wasn't as if playing ball with Chrysler had earned them any points.

In the end, Chrysler did not buy back a single car or part from them, as the automaker had told Congress they would do with the cancelled dealers. Gus Russo still laments what Chrysler, GM, and the government did to ruin businesses like his. "I was raised to believe if you work hard, you will be rewarded. With blatant disregard to our rights, and all the years of hard work and investment in our business, with a swoop of the pen at Chrysler, or a chain letter, it was all over," he said.

Russo remembered the promise that Jim Press represented to the company and dealers when he joined Chrysler in 2007. He and other dealers would be keenly disappointed. "At Chrysler, he was just another empty suit," Gus Russo said.

* * *

When she thinks back to what happened in 2009, Tammy Darvish was often perplexed, even almost two years after the closures. As the automakers suddenly announced they were shutting down several thousand stores, dealers were in a state of shock. Many didn't know where to turn or who to ask for help.

When the CRDR group formed with Alan Spitzer pulling in his old friend, Jack Fitzgerald, and then Darvish, it was a beacon of hope. Many thought the auto task force meant well in trying to save the automakers and even the UAW. But when it came to the dealers, and to an extent the parts suppliers, they were out of their league, dealers believe. Inexperience and naiveté of a highly complex industry took their toll on the task force, and ultimately dealers and other stakeholders, they observed. Their advice to President Obama to cut the dealers would backfire. They just didn't know it at the time.

In his book *Overhaul*, Steve Rattner paid the dealers scant attention. In a chapter called "Dealer Nation," he devotes only a few pages to dealers. And then it is to proclaim that he is confused as to why questions about the closed dealerships deluged his office. Most of that chapter, like the book, primarily deals with the GM and Chrysler restructurings.

If anyone is looking for explanations or an understanding of what led to the dealer debacle, go elsewhere, dealers who have read the book say.

David Ruggles, a former dealer-manager and a columnist for *Ward's Dealer Business* magazine, says in reviewing *Overhaul*, "The book did nothing toward mitigating my anger over the dealer terminations. But it did reinforce the importance to the nation of the Troubled Asset Relief Program, an idea proposed by Bush's Treasury Secretary Hank Paulson and passed by Congress after the Lehman Brothers collapse in the fall of 2008, without which it is unlikely that the auto industry bailout would have been possible."

But it was the righteousness and arrogance of the decision makers that ultimately got to dealers. Tammy Darvish took note of how they could hide behind masks and power, as if they could will the dealer problem to go away, or just ignore it. After all, they controlled the fates of many people, unions, and voting blocks. They could slash thousands of employees from their rolls, from production plants, from supplier companies—why not these few thousand dealers?

No matter what else happened, Darvish felt one true thing emerging. The implications of lying under oath were astounding. "If you have power you don't have to tell the truth." That was the message being sent to young and old, she thought. And it was wrong, just like the whole dealer-termination business was wrong. Neither pride nor politics should be allowed to get in the way of the truth, dealers such as Darvish thought.

"We can't let this go away. Too many lives have been destroyed with no accountability. Where is the justice?" Darvish said to her e-mail groups. "Is it because you're in a position of power you don't have to tell the truth? What are we telling our children?" Darvish asked colleagues in those days when the dealer debacle threatened to destroy them in greater numbers. "Is it okay to lie if you have the power?" It was, after all, a numbers game, one in which bean counters excelled. In courts, arguing in financial terms, they placed the dealers under their toxic-assets label, an inconvenient drain on their resources. GM, which once hailed dealers and suppliers as family under programs such as "targets for excellence," now made them targets for closure. Chrysler, which suffered from perennially lower marks in dealer satisfaction than other automakers, took a hard line and cut without mercy and perhaps consideration of the effect on dealers and communities.

In Maryland, Jack Fitzgerald said that the inexperience of the auto task force was a chief culprit in the dealership closing debacle. "No one on the task force ever made a car or sold one. And they did not listen if anyone tried to talk to them," he said in a *Fox News* interview in late 2010.

"The task force spent more than eighty billion dollars in taxpayer money on the auto loans without getting the advice of dealers," Fitzgerald said. "They're elitists. And elitists think they can do whatever they want because they know best." That's why Rattner was called the "car czar," he said. "A czar can do a perfect job innately, with no one questioning him."

More Rumblings in Motown

The auto industry has always represented dynamic change. But never more so than in the last decade. Dealers have always managed to ride out the rough waves. The weak do not survive; they're eaten by market forces. That's what many entrepreneurial business leaders believed.

Chrysler dealers especially had it rough. Going back to the Daimler-Benz alliance, the German Daimler managers did not want the dealers so strongly in the mix, dealers recalled. Daimler bought Chrysler in 1998, hailing a "merger of equals" opportunity. They often pressured dealers to take products they didn't want or need. When Cerberus's Nardelli came along, he gave the field staffers more autonomy, empowering them even more. That's why Chrysler dealers were happy when Jim Press arrived; here was someone who had the dealers' interests in mind. At least that's what they thought, judging from his record at Toyota.

And Press had grown out of the dealer distribution system; he was one of them. But that was then, this was now. The times were truly changing.

The corporate rumblings in Detroit would continue. The whooshing sound was not of cars speeding by, but of executives departing.

The continuing churn of leadership and shuffling of field operations in Detroit meant that long-term relationships were discarded and there were always bigger fires to put out. Leaders came in who were inexperienced in the industry and didn't understand what the dealer system meant to their company or profits. No wonder loyalty—to dealers, to employees—went out the window, some auto insiders said.

Companies like GM and Chrysler were being hollowed out, and loyalty was a thing of the past. That's perhaps another reason Detroit could not copy a Toyota model that still had a corporate mind-set that rewarded employee loyalty and dealer relationships.

But bankruptcy is another animal. The deep restructurings brought cataclysmic changes that only compounded the erroneous thinking at the corporate level. At the tops of government and other mega companies, everyone was looking for the leader on a white steed to ride in and save the day. They wanted another Jack Welch at General Electric, Steve Jobs at Apple, Bill Gates at Microsoft, and Warren Buffet in the finance world, and now they had Alan Mulally at Ford Motor.

There was great hope—and pressure—put on the shoulders of Ed Whitacre at GM. Whitacre got a good look at the expectations and gracefully bowed out before his expected departure date. With his accumulated wealth and accomplishments he didn't need the challenge, or the aggravation.

On August 12, 2010, Whitacre suddenly announced at an analyst and media phone-in session in Detroit he was resigning from the top GM CEO job, effective September 1. He would continue in a chairman role, often from afar. The news bomb came barely a week after Whitacre delivered a speech at the Management Briefings Seminar (MBS), an annual gathering of top auto executives and suppliers in Traverse City, Michigan.

Neither Whitacre nor other top GMers breathed a word of his plans, at least not to the press, at the MBS, a largely informal gathering where much free time is spent on the fabled Jack Nicklaus golf course, sailing Grand Traverse Bay, and in social get-togethers. But his sudden departure would leave GM and its government majority owners scrambling to fill the top spot again. They had trouble finding a leader with the right skills and temperament when Whitacre reluctantly took the job, pressed by the task force and GM board. And, like its Chrysler rival nearly thirty miles to the north of Detroit, GM had been rotating their top leaders since the upheaval in late 2008.

"My goal in coming to General Motors was to help restore profitability, build a strong market position, and position this iconic company for success," Whitacre said in resigning. "We are clearly on that path. A strong foundation is in place and I am comfortable with the timing of my decision."

Whitacre lasted a little more than eight months on the job, far short of what was expected when he signed on. The tall Texan was well-liked for his informal manner and famous drawl—and decisive thinking. With his departure, GM was cycling through four CEOs since the government loans rescued them in late 2008 and early 2009.

Whitacre's successor was Dan Akerson, a fresh GM board recruit in July of 2009. Even then he meant new blood to a tired organization in the eyes of the auto task force, which had helped draft him. Nearly a year later, he was left with the daunting job of sorting out the mess left at GM since Rick Wagoner's departure. One of the first tasks of the car czar and his junior czars was firing Wagoner, followed by Fritz Henderson, both GM lifers. Out with the old, in with the new, the auto task force thinking went—and better yet if they had no GM and auto blood in them.

Once sacred cows such as internal promotions on the corporate ladder were cast asunder.

Now, Akerson would flip the switch and go from board director to running the slimmed down shiny new GM the task force created. Wonderful buzz words that the power brokers came to believe themselves.

Ousting Fritz Henderson in December of 2009, followed by Whitacre's quick departure the next September, suggested that the glitter of the shiny new GM was not as brilliant as some wanted it to seem. His beating a hasty retreat back to Austin, Texas, surprised many auto insiders, even at GM.

According to GM, Akerson was slated to assume dual roles of chairman and CEO by January (2011). Like other recent board recruits, he lacked automotive experience. But these days that was considered an asset, not a handicap, by the shapers of the new GM in Washington DC

A former managing director of the Carlyle Group, the largest private investment firm in the world, located in Washington DC, Akerson also had served as a top exec in the telecommunications field. Deemed a practical, decisive thinker in the Whitacre mold, Akerson was a naval graduate from the Annapolis Naval Academy in Maryland. He was known as a tough, practical man admired for his street cred in both technology and finance arenas. Above all, he was a money man, another sign that GM was shifting leadership gears from engineering and product wisdom to finance and investments.

Two other candidates were considered by the board for the top perch as chief executive. The board looked at two more of their own, Steve Girsky and Patricia Russo (no relation to Gina or Gus Russo in Detroit). Girsky, considered razor sharp and a former auto analyst, had been groomed to serve on the board by Ron Gettelfinger, the fiery leader of the UAW. That might have become Girsky's liability since Gettelfinger wanted him focused on UAW issues and boosting languid GM stock prices quickly, according to Steve Rattner's *Overhaul* book. Another issue: he lacked the desired solid executive management experience. Russo also came up short on the executive managerial skills side.

That left Akerson, who didn't much like the idea of living in Detroit but finally accepted when pressed by GM's board and the former auto task force. That group, later headed by Ron Bloom, was acting as manufacturing counsel to the Obama administration.

Whitacre resurfaced in San Antonio in mid-October saying that an initial public offering (IPO) from GM was imminent. Now a board member, he seemed to be finishing the job he was hired to do: run the new GM and make it attractive enough for public investors. Prime the pump to sell stock, so to speak.

On October 13, Whitacre said that stock shares were likely to be priced between twenty and twenty-five dollars in the IPO by the automaker in November. "It's a little too early to tell, but somewhere in there," he said, responding to questions from *Reuters News* on the IPO timeframe at a business event honoring him near his home in San Antonio. That's not what happened as the business press tells it.

"I can't say how much we'll sell, but I can say we'll have a successful IPO sometime in November," he said. That at least proved prescient. Whitacre's comments represented the first time that a GM official spoke about the public offerings. Whitacre said he could not say how large the GM IPO would be but predicted it would be successful in reducing the US government's 61 percent stake in the automaker.

Since then, the game of musical chairs among lleaders has played on. Akerson was the fourth CEO at GM in about eighteen months. For a company known to move slowly in making decisions, this was lightning speed. Akerson also had not been a big fan of Fritz Henderson, who the task force thought was not effecting change quickly enough, according to the first task force.

From the start, GM's goal was to get out from under the government's yoke. That was beginning to happen the following November, when the government's stake went down to about 33 percent and IPO prices rose higher than even Whitacre predicted. Chrysler, meanwhile, had churned six CEOs in about ten years, and upper managers who survived were dizzy with the speed of change at the once slower-paced number-three US automaker. The rapid-fire changes suggested that fear motivation indeed could be a powerful motivator.

There were many theories as to who created the dealer hit lists. There's some agreement among legal experts and dealers that it was a combination of Detroit execs and field staff closer to the dealers.

But the churning of upper-level execs continued. They too were no longer wanted, were cast out.

It seems that many of the people who compiled or sanctioned the lists—at many levels—were gone by 2010. Jim Press, Steve Landry, Brian Schnurr, and other field reps at Chrysler resigned. Pete Grady was a main driver of the dealer changes, and he remained under Marchionne at last scrutiny, one of the few upper execs to survive. At GM it was a little different, but after Mark LaNeve, Rick Wagoner, and Fritz Henderson left, it was not exactly easier for the culled dealers. They were still fighting for their rights.

Now, many of those former high-powered, highly paid execs were on the loose. The consultancy positions usually open to movers and shakers looked less appealing. If you're a classic hard-charging type A personality as these leaders tend to be, a future on the ranch or fishing in lakes near the cabin can be a less cheerful proposition than when it was a seasonal getaway from the pressure-cooker job.

Rick Wagoner landed an advisory position on the *Washington Post* board of directors. Fritz Henderson reportedly had taken a cushy three-thousand-dollar per hour consulting position, though part time, with GM, which apparently recognized it was short on institutional knowledge. And Bob Nardelli landed high up in a paper firm called New Page Corp., a Cerberus company. In recent years, he bounced around three other industries, including automotive. Jim Press for a short time advised the Nissan-Renault alliance.

* * *

On October 26, 2010, Rattner was slated to speak at the Detroit Economic Club, to recount the good work his task force did in saving GM and Chrysler. What better setting to do this in than in Motown itself? The shiny new GM he raved about was only a few blocks from where he would speak.

Presumably, he would plug his new book, *Overhaul*, which was selling briskly at the time.

In a reversal of fortune, Steve Rattner, the former head of the task force and advisor to the president, was suddenly among the invited and then the uninvited. A week before his scheduled appearance, the Detroit Economic Club (DEC) sent out a media alert. The Rattner talk was canceled. DEC President Beth Chappell said she decided to cancel the talk following reports of an ongoing investigation of Rattner's involvement in an alleged influence-peddling scheme. The Securities and Exchange Commission (SEC) had been investigating whether Rattner and his private-equity firm Quadrangle Group in New York paid kickbacks to get access to business from the state's $125 billion public pension fund. Quadrangle had served as an indirect money manager of the pension fund. News reports at the time said Rattner needed $6 million to fight the charges against him.

Chappell told news media that she decided against his visit due to the ongoing SEC investigation, saying it "doesn't seem appropriate to have him speak."

To be fair, the Rattner investigation was made known to the White House when he was named to the top task-force job in February 2009, before everything began unraveling. Rattner also reportedly paid $400,000 of his own money to be vetted for the short-lived federal post. White House Press Secretary Robert Gibbs confirmed the Rattner disclosure facts about the investigation at the time.

* * *

The political pressure had not ended with the passage of the dealer rights law in mid-December of 2009.

The Special Inspector General for the Troubled Asset Relief Program (SIGTARP) report came out in July 2010. Federal watchdog Neil Barofsky and his team of investigators indicated that dealers had not received fair treatment during the economic upheaval. The report concerned itself with the Wall Street bailouts, dealer closures, and how the huge pot of TARP money was spent.

"It is not at all clear that the greatly accelerated pace of the dealership closings during one of the most severe economic downturns in our nation's history was either necessary for the sake of the companies' economic survival or prudent for the sake of the nation's economic recovery," the SIGTARP report said.

The claims that the dealer cuts were needed to reduce their costs also were not adequately assessed or explained, the SIGTARP report claimed. After SIGTARP surfaced, Tammy Darvish fired off a letter asking a House panel to look further into the issue of the GM and Chrysler dealership terminations. She and her coleaders asked for nothing short of a full investigation of who was responsible for the harsh and hasty cutbacks.

"We ask that there be some sort of accountability for the gross error in judgment on behalf of the auto task force in addition to those that we believe committed perjury in federal bankruptcy court and in congressional hearings," Darvish wrote for CRDR.

Darvish's letter did not name names or who she thought might have committed perjury, a criminal activity. But the facts were out there—in the public domain. She sent the memo to members of the House Oversight and Government Reform Committee, the main investigative group, headed by Rep. Ed Towns, D-New York.

That letter came two days after the government watchdog's findings that the US Treasury Department's auto task force ordered an acceleration of GM and Chrysler dealer cuts without adequately considering their effect on the Detroit Two's viability, local markets, or jobs.

For its part, NADA also took a strong stand on SIGTARP. Chairman Ed Tonkin released a statement in July agreeing with the SIGTARP findings. He quoted Sen. Jay Rockefeller, the West Virginia Democrat and chairman of the US Senate Committee on Commerce, Science, and Transportation. Rockefeller issued a statement, saying, "This report shows that Congress did the right thing when it gave all dealers the right to appeal terminations before a neutral arbiter. It is my hope that this report will send a clear message that unfairness in the termination process will not be tolerated."

Analyst David Cole, who headed an automotive research center in Michigan, spoke with auditors of SIGTARP in October of 2009. Automakers are cutting into their own strengths which are "in rural and modest markets rather than in large metro areas in which imports do better," Cole cautioned.

What GM and Chrysler did under pressure to get quick federal dollars needed to survive was cut into the very markets they were succeeding in—cutting into bone, analysts like Cole have said.

Cole, a forty-year auto expert who advised executives at the car companies, was appalled at the dealer decisions. On his own initiative, he also spoke to Ron Bloom at the auto task force, pointing out that the dealer cuts would harm the economy and the auto industry even more. "These cuts did not make sense to me," Cole said to media and government officials. But the decisions were cast in minds of stone in DC and Detroit, it seemed.

Rattner, dealing with his own legal problems, criticized the original SIGTARP report as "silly" and vindictive. Again, he didn't see what all the fuss was about with dealers. He would repeat this claim throughout 2010.

To the administration's chagrin, the dealer question wasn't going away. In October of 2010, the pressure was renewed to look at dealer closures even further at the automaker and government levels.

The special investigators from SIGTARP were back too. Perhaps the special investigators, like Congress, were incensed that Treasury and the task force weren't listening to them. This time, the investigators seemed to be focusing more closely on the dealer cuts.

Interestingly, Tim Geithner's Treasury group disputed the earlier July SIGTARP findings, asserting that Treasury hid losses associated with bailing out the AIG investment group. The *New York Times* wrote on October 27: "The United States Treasury concealed forty billion dollars in likely taxpayer losses on the bailout of the American International Group earlier this month, when it abandoned its usual method for valuing investments, according to a report by the Special Inspector General for the Troubled Asset Relief Program."

On Sunday, October 17, ten days before the *New York Times* story on Treasury, *Automotive News* published an article under the headline "Dealer-closure audit may signal focus of US probe." SIGTARP investigators appeared to be probing deeper into misconduct in the dealer cuts "but won't say who or what they are looking at," the paper reported.

"What clues might a July audit offer into the federal investigation of possibly illegal actions during the General Motors and Chrysler dealership terminations last year?" the reporter asked, referring to SIGTARP. "However, investigators have been given the files of auditors in the same office that compiled a July report critical of the handling of dealer cuts by the Obama administration, GM, and Chrysler. A review of that report suggests concerns of auditors that might also highlight areas under scrutiny in what the office's spokeswoman has described as a 'follow-up' investigation," *Automotive News* reported.

"Many disparities arose during the ongoing investigation—such as the companies' cost-savings estimates, lack of documentation for termination criteria for dealers cut and those kept with similar profiles," the story said.

The *Automotive News* report concluded, "Still, if nothing else, the auditors flagged unanswered questions that they felt have not been adequately addressed by the main actors."

The trade paper had long been reporting on the dealer-closure issues since that story broke in May of 2009. The news story on SIGTARP returning, however, seemed to raise more questions than it answered. Media follow-up on the SIGTARP probe and the audit itself appeared to go dark, like winter itself falling on the country.

Still, Jack Fitzgerald said the SIGTARP findings represented a significant step for closed dealers. "It confirmed what we as dealers have been saying all along," he said. "The dealers should never have been closed."

"Pay for the Loss"

One dealer, who didn't want to be named, compared it to taking out any profitable business in the country—from grocery stores to restaurants. "Suppose you live in a city and someone, like the government, comes in and says it wants to cut out half the pizza places in town, and the few remaining franchises are then given the businesses of the closed ones, free. That would be horribly wrong. You can't take someone's business and give it to someone else. It's so un-American," he said. But that's what happened in his case—and many other dealers who were cut.

"Someone's got to pay for the pain, the loss," he said. That did not happen, in many cases.

The free-enterprise system should decide which dealer stays open and which closes, many dealers believed. Free enterprise should work within itself and not be government controlled as long as you play by the rules and do the job, dealers told Tammy Darvish and CRDR.

It was, as President Bush had said at the end of his term, a sad day for the free-enterprise side. And if you play by the rules, do what's right, you should be protected, his successor, President Obama said. In the dealers' cases, some said it seemed like a major crime against society had been committed and no one was made to pay. They were not protected.

Colleen McDonald, the former Chrysler and Chevrolet dealer in the Detroit area, also said someone's got to pay for the losses dealers sustained. Even those not terminated outright saw major financial drains in their businesses; and those who agreed to return also faced astronomical expenses and loss of customers not experienced by the untouched dealers.

"I know it's wrong; it's illegal and unconstitutional," said McDonald, who was seeking legal redress. "It's a very sad time in our country when this can happen to independent businesspeople."

McDonald was one of many who said someone had to pay for the fact that too many dealers on Main Street had been forced from their businesses. That was the consensus coming loud and clear from the rejected dealers in the heartland of America.

* * *

On October 20, with the midterm elections nearly two weeks away, John Sackrison thought the time was right to propose another bold idea. Sackrison, president of the Orange County Automobile Dealers Association in California, called on Darvish for help. He drew her attention to an important upcoming date for GM. October 31 had been set as the final wind-down day for GM dealerships forced to close.

Sackrison suggested putting the problem squarely in the Obama administration's lap. Since they claimed to want to save jobs and, of course, owned 61 percent of GM at the time, they might be open-minded and issue an eleventh-hour edict. This one would cost taxpayers nothing. It would be free. "Perhaps they would want to take the opportunity to save jobs by not closing these dealerships. I know it's a long shot, but I wanted to get your thoughts—and see if CRDR is interested in pursuing this," he proposed.

Sackrison related the story of dealer Tim Mullahey in his district, who would lose his fifty-employee store with the GM shutdown deadline of October 31. Mullahey had employed about one hundred people between his Chevrolet and Ford operations but let go of half of them.

In Fullerton, California, the Chevrolet store had been doing solid business there for eighty-one years. They were ready to close permanently, unless an eleventh-hour rescue happened. Sackrison was doing whatever he could to help dealers like Tim Mullahey and their employees. So far, they had been propped up by their Kia and Ford businesses, after losing Chevrolet.

"Mullahey Chevrolet is still a profitable business with an active floor plan source, good banking relationships, and annual taxable sales around thirty million dollars," Sackrison pointed out. "Tim also owns three successful Ford dealerships and is a great poster child for this effort. This store has been in Fullerton since 1929 and has survived the Great Depression, WW II, oil embargos, GM factory strikes, declining sales, and is surviving in the current economic crisis," he said.

What could CRDR do to help dealers such as Mullahey at this juncture? Sackrison asked. As much as Darvish wanted to act on dealer requests such as Tim Mullahey's, GM had beaten her to the punch. There was no rescue plan for dealers like Mullahey.

Unfortunately, Tim Mullahey did not survive the legacy of the auto task force, or GM's late power play. At the end of October 2010, GM officially terminated the five hundred dealers.

Mullahey closed down his Chevrolet store at the end of October as scheduled. He had no choice, he said. Still a Ford dealer, Mullahey thought that even if the government had not bailed out GM, Chevrolet as a brand would have survived. "Chevrolet represented 130 percent of the value of GM. Someone would have been acquiring Chevrolet," he said right before the closing.

What dealers did now was up to the lawyers, and any help the committee and their dealer groups could provide. Everyone was studying SIGTARP and its possible ramifications for dealers. The legal process was kicking in.

Experienced trial lawyer, attorney Richard Faulkner in Dallas thought there was a high probability that the dealer closures will come before the US Supreme Court. Too many people had been harmed; too much was at stake. Investigators at SIGTARP continued to add fuel to the fire. Dealers could only hope they were serious and would again exercise due diligence, forcing the government and courts to act responsibly.

Chapter 16—Legal Eagles Take Aim

Freedom is never given; it is won.
—A. Philip Randolph, US Civil Rights Leader

The lawsuits were flying. The rights of terminated dealers blew in with the spring winds in 2010 and kept on raging. The issue was not going away.

Public perception grew that the battle was almost over after Congress passed the dealer rights law packaged as part of a huge omnibus act to keep the government running another year. In a politically motivated environment President Obama signed the act on Wednesday, December 16, 2009. With his signature, a sense of renewed hope arose, for the first time in seven months, that dealers might win back their businesses.

The new law did not provide for automatic reinstatement of franchises. Congress passed legislation that gave dealers the right to an appeal through a review of independent arbitrators. These cases are not conducted as court trials but instead are heard by a neutral legal review panel. Dealers and automakers could also be represented by their lawyers. Owners of former Saturn, Hummer, Pontiac, or Saab franchises at GM were not eligible to file appeals, even though the brands were being discontinued as part of the restructuring.

Although CRDR fought for dealers to be reinstated as a group to their pre-bankruptcy status, they took the next best thing—the chance to win businesses back through arbitration.

"While CRDR had hoped for legislation that would automatically restore all dealer agreements, our champions in Congress made clear that it was not possible to get that relief at this time," Tammy Darvish told her supporters after the law passed.

The American Arbitration Association (AAA), the assigned review group, began hearings in late February, almost ten months after the original dealership terminations. India Johnson, senior vice president of the AAA, said that regional panels vetted the cases and were bound to a completion timetable defined in the new law. As it turned out, Ohio, Illinois, Pennsylvania, and Michigan were the most heavily represented states in arbitrations, which made sense since they suffered the greatest number of dealer cuts.

Between GM and Chrysler, 1,575 cases came up for appeal through AAA. The cases needed to be concluded by the end of June but dragged through July before all was said and done. Dealers could represent themselves, or bring their lawyers. The majority of dealers, of course, opted for legal representation, not understanding the complexities of law. Some had weeks, others months to prepare.

But questions soon were swirling about the effectiveness of arbitration and arbitrators themselves, who came from a pool of lawyers, retired judges, accountants, and others certified by the AAA. Like the US jury system, arbitration may be an imperfect process, but it's the best there is, some attorneys said.

Experienced and retired trial judges often make the best arbitrators, said Mike Charapp, the DC-area dealer attorney. "The arbitration panels have many attorneys who are willing to sit as arbitrators, but there are not an overwhelming number of retired judges. Retired judges still make the best arbitrators. They have judicial demeanor and a history of decision making. Lawyers who have never been judges, generally are not as experienced in this area," he explained.

After the hearings were over and complaints arose, Charapp still defended the process. "The arbitration process for dealers was invaluable. Dealers would have had no opportunity to get their stores back or to get more realistic compensation without the arbitration process," he said.

By July 26, the automakers and dealers had their decisions. The results hardly contained big surprises. The automakers won the majority of cases. Of the appeals heard by arbitrators, Chrysler said it "prevailed" in 70 percent of cases, lower than they wanted. GM's success rate was 63 percent. Michael

Palese, a Chrysler spokesperson in Detroit, said of the 418 former dealers who filed for arbitration against Chrysler, 150 settled privately and 130 cases were withdrawn or dismissed. And thirty-two Chrysler dealers won in arbitration hearings out of 108 total cases heard by arbitrators.

That meant Chrysler won 76 cases, according to company internal reports. Chrysler Group reiterated that fact that it had prevailed in 76 of 108 arbitration decisions with rejected dealerships after erroneous media reports put the number at Chrysler 73 wins of 105 decisions. In GM's final tally, arbitrators decided in favor of GM in 39 cases and in dealers' favor in 23 cases. There were 62 total arbitrations, according to GM spokeswoman Ryndee Carney.

GM's overall dealer numbers were lower because GM offered settlements and Letters of Intent (LOIs) to dealers to rejoin the business before and after arbitrations, according to Carney. Of the 725 rejected GM dealers who received agreements, all had signed them, Carney said. To return to the fold, dealers had to meet specific GM criteria.

Chrysler and GM kept their settlement amounts confidential, but attorney Richard Faulkner, a former law professor who specializes in arbitration, pegged the Chrysler settlements as averaging about $100,000 per dealer in cases, if they were offered. GM, meanwhile, came in with higher offers. Once a settlement was reached, GM and Chrysler imposed confidentiality restrictions on dealers to not disclose the amounts.

In Orlando, Florida, attorney Mark Ornstein, who handled numerous arbitration cases and at the time matters were being arbitrated, estimated the Chrysler payments were in the seventy-five-thousand-dollar to one-hundred-thousand-dollar range. "At the time, Chrysler in many cases was legally obstructive and did the minimum good they could do for dealers," he said. Ornstein's firm, Killgore, Pearlman, Stamp, Ornstein and Squires, represents nearly one hundred dealers nationwide.

Ornstein also estimated that Chrysler, at least, spent about $15 million in arbitration legal fees alone against dealers. Other arbitration attorneys agreed that was a reasonable estimate.

Following the arbitration hearings that ended in July, dealers wondered why the recently bankrupt automakers would spend so much taxpayer-funded money to keep dealerships closed.

Former Detroit metro dealer Richard Mealey posed a different possible solution that might have changed the tide for Chrysler and dealers. If Chrysler had given the affected dealers about $500 million collectively after it shut them down, their (Chrysler's) problems might have gone away, Mealey suggested. Each dealer could have received a settlement amount equivalent "to each vehicle sold the previous two or three years," he said. That would average about $600,000 per dealer, Mealey figured. The amount could be apportioned by sales volume, so high-volume sellers would get about $2 million, medium-volume dealers about $1 million, and smaller-volume stores $500,000, he suggested.

The actual settlements were much lower than Mealey's estimations and didn't cover all dealers. Instead, the automaker chose to fight the appealing dealers in courts and privately at far more cost and great psychological damage. Even if they won in arbitration or signed agreements to return to the fold, most dealers didn't come out ahead, some lawyers argued.

Either way, "It's a hollow victory; it didn't ring true," New York attorney Leonard Bellavia said of the dealer arbitration wins. He represented nearly forty dealers in the cases. Why hollow? Dealers who won were being asked to agree to harsh requirements and improve their facilities at a cost of millions, or spend even more money in litigation, he noted. Most Chrysler dealers did not sign the agreements that bound them to fulfill "onerous conditions" if they returned, he said.

A big question was why dealers would fight to resume ties with a company that publicly tossed them aside. Chrysler's retail sales, excluding fleets, were down more than 25 percent after they filed bankruptcy. In later months, they would report better overall numbers, but those were beefed up because of strong fleet sales, dealers said. GM sales were slowly inching upward and their products were even performing better in *Consumer Reports* reviews, the golden scorecard.

Chrysler retail sales were down 26 percent in June of 2010, the first year after the bankruptcy period. The company then saw a 25 percent drop from the dismal 2009 retail sales reported after that, experiencing its worst months ever, said Jack Fitzgerald, a major seller of Chrysler products in his market. There's a correlation between those numbers and a 25 percent drop in dealers, he noted.

The dealer cullings were supposed to result in higher profits for the remaining dealers, those "go forwards" the automakers talked about. Indications are that was not yet a reality in May, 2011, about two years after the closings.

Analyst Tom Libby at R. L. Polk Company in Woodcliff Lake, New Jersey, said that event would take longer to happen, and depended on the two automakers relying less on fleet sales in reporting their aggregate sales. Both Chrysler and GM include a significant number of fleet sales when reporting their sales successes, he noted. "We will have to wait longer to see if they get away from that practice," he said in May.

Secret E-mails and Arbitrations

Another important development occurred on the legal path. Former Chrysler dealers Jim Tarbox in Rhode Island and Mark Calisi in New York were able to obtain secret e-mails exchanged between Chrysler managers released by US Bankruptcy Judge Arthur Gonzalez in April in time for their arbitration hearings. The previously sealed e-mails proved that the company shut them down for reasons not related to performance, the dealers said.

In an early April appeal to the bankruptcy court, Bellavia, their attorney, asked that the rejected dealers be allowed to use the e-mails in their upcoming arbitrations. In their suit, the dealers asked Judge Gonzalez in New York to allow them to use the e-mails as evidence. The e-mails had previously surfaced in the public domain but had remained sealed, along with thousands of pages of Chrysler documents, by Gonzalez, who presided over the bankruptcy cases, so they couldn't be used in other legal proceedings.

Chrysler lawyers immediately countered and objected to the dealers' request, citing the sanctity of the bankruptcy court's seal order the former year. At that time, the bankruptcy court had "determined that sufficient legal and factual bases existed to establish just cause for confirming the confidentiality of the documents," Chrysler lawyers said in fighting the unsealing.

But Bellavia got the court's permission and proceeded with the appeal. In court, Bellavia, who represented thirty-one rejected Chrysler dealerships in bankruptcy proceedings, quoted from the previously secret internal e-mails while questioning a Chrysler director in court the year before.

Like Tarbox, Calisi was crying foul ball. Calisi related these events to media and others long after the court proceedings.

In Calisi's case, a May e-mail in question was written by Bill Doucette, Chrysler's Northeast regional manager in New York, and sent to Phil

Scroggin, the regional business center director who supervises field managers. That e-mail related a conversation Doucette had concerning Calisi with Peter Grady, the Chrysler VP in Detroit. According to the testimony, Doucette said in his e-mail to Scroggin, "Just talked with Pete, he simply said that the dealer (Calisi) has to go, too litigious, etc.; it's not a performance issue," though.

Grady expressed concern that the cases could be hard to prove because performance was not the problem. Chrysler had built their arguments on cutting out underperformers. When Bellavia questioned Scroggin in court, the Chrysler exec replied: "All I can tell you is that the e-mail—the words are the words, and there is quite a bit of discussion that went on afterward as it did with all dealers."

"There was no performance issue," Calisi told reporters later and repeated many times. "We were well capitalized and profitable." The e-mails proved it, especially when Pete Grady indicated in the e-mail exchange the company might have a tough time in their cases because the dealer performance scores were so good, he said.

Since Calisi's livelihood was at stake, in June of 2009, he wrote to Jim Press, the big boss at Chrysler, to recount the events of his termination. He said that he had listened to Pete Grady's entire May 29 testimony concerning Eagle Auto Mall, his dealership group. In the testimony, Grady read the e-mail from William Doucette to Scroggin, his boss, Calisi related.

Calisi also wrote: "One of the reasons Chrysler gave for terminating dealers was so remaining dealers would have an opportunity to earn additional capital to invest into their franchises, but this dealer chosen in my market wasn't willing to do that in the last forty years, while I have built an eleven-million-dollar facility at Chrysler's request. This dealer was kept because of a personal relationship and to punish Eagle Auto for not giving in to the unfair and unjust practices of the Northeast business center at Chrysler."

He didn't hear from Press after that letter, but he did go to arbitration and won his case. The secret e-mails and discussions between the execs were big factors, Bellavia said. "These Chrysler e-mails were extremely helpful in winning Calisi's case and settling Tarbox's case against Chrysler," Bellavia said. He thought the suppressed e-mails were prime examples of what was wrong in the dealer rejection cases.

It showed that the termination process "was nothing more than a backslapping brotherhood of Chrysler executives enjoying two weeks of bankruptcy code power to play God with the livelihoods of dealers," Bellavia told *Automotive News.*

In Calisi's case, Chrysler also said he was let go because, as a multi-line dealer, he shared Chrysler-Jeep space with the Kia, Mazda, and Volvo brands he sold. In the Jim Tarbox case, he had legally protested the location of a competing dealer in his market area, causing him trouble later, Bellavia said.

Calisi and Tarbox were among the small group of dealers who would win in arbitration rulings against the automaker later that spring. Tarbox later settled with Chrysler for a confidential undisclosed amount; Calisi won arbitration but refused to sign a prohibitive agreement to return to Chrysler. He had bigger fish to fry.

But a seemingly minor incident went to the heart of the judicial matter for some dealers. Judge Arthur Gonzalez was officiating at Calisi's hearing in bankruptcy court when he began to scold Bellavia for a minor transgression in an exchange on the internal e-mails. At one point, Gonzalez reprimanded Bellavia, saying he was out of line after the attorney corrected Calisi, his client, who had mispronounced Peter Grady's name as "O'Grady." Bellavia, perhaps injecting humor into the tense moments, said, "Let's not make Mr. Grady more Irish than he is," prompting the judge's stern warning.

After the hearings concluded, some dealers thought Judge Gonzalez took a pro-corporate stance and was hardly receptive to the dealers and their attorneys. Questions speculated in the dealer ranks about the judge's neutrality. Some legal experts, however, wondered if it was the size of the case or whether the huge national importance of the Chrysler group case affecting hundreds of thousands of jobs nationwide may have influenced the judge's decision somewhat.

Calisi remained perplexed some twenty months later. He wondered why Grady could present conflicting testimony on the dealer closures and face no repercussions. Yet Gonzalez chose to pounce on Bellavia for a relatively trivial matter of a mispronounced name. "It made me realize how one-sided this whole thing was and convinced me the judge was in Chrysler's corner all along," Calisi said.

Before legislation was passed by Congress granting dealers the right to arbitrate, key executives said the dealers did not need to be terminated and did not cost the automakers money. Dealers wondered why at that point a reputable judge would not use the proper legal or public forum to set the record straight. Was this a matter of pride, or prejudice? Was there no precedent for such admissions? Those were the kinds of questions dealers later asked each other and their lawyers.

There were new facts coming out continuously, and old ones being tossed out, that the dealer cuts were unnecessary. Even Mike Manzo, Chrysler's chief financial expert had testified to that effect in late May of 2009—that Fiat did not require the dealer terminations to swing the takeover deal. Jim Press later told dealers and a Congress subcommittee he believed the cuts were not warranted, refuting earlier statements.

Lawyers too dissected the original bankruptcy decision in 2009 of Judge Gonzalez, who sided with Chrysler on the grounds that the dealer restructurings were necessary to move ahead with the Fiat deal. "The simple truth is that Fiat did not see dealer restructuring as a material issue to the sale closing. They didn't insist upon it. Therefore, Old Chrysler had no reason to reject the dealers," wrote one CRDR legal scholar.

After the arbitration hearings concluded, dealers like Calisi and Tarbox still did not feel vindicated. Like their peers, they wondered why the corporate players behaved so arrogantly, as if they knew they were untouchable and fully protected by the federal bankruptcy court decisions.

In Orlando, Mark Ornstein defended a case where Deland Dodge, based in central Florida, went up against Chrysler early on. Gilbert Dannehower, Deland's owner, became the first US dealer to win in arbitration against Chrysler in May 2010. Despite his win, Dannehower had to sue in Florida state court to get Chrysler to comply with the arbitrator's award. That case was kept hanging around long afterward, as Chrysler countersued and used federal law to trump state laws.

Like the Calisi and Tarbox cases, Dannehower was a proven performer, the number-one auto retailer in Deland at the time he was cut. "He was an acknowledged stellar performer and his arbitrator, retired Judge Amy Dean, went out of her way to acknowledge it in her arbitration award," Ornstein said.

"These terminations were decisions made in the heat of bankruptcy, from a twenty-thousand-foot view," Ornstein told *Ward's Auto*. "And Congress, when giving the dealers the right to arbitrate, allowed them to tell their individual stories," he said.

Ornstein was one of many lawyers who noted that the July SIGTARP report coming from federal watchdog Neil Barofsky's office confirmed what dealers and their attorneys were saying all along. The decision to close dealers was unnecessary, and the task force may have acted hastily with no basis for ordering the dealership closures.

Like many other dealers, Dannehower refused to sign the Chrysler agreement after winning arbitration. He couldn't live with the language it contained about dealers nearby being able to object to Deland's being a Dodge dealer and the steep investment returning dealers must make to remodel their facilities.

Under Florida law, Ornstein said manufacturers cannot require dealers to upgrade their facilities. There's a lot of language in the state law that doesn't allow manufacturers to run roughshod over dealers, who are private businesses. The demands on dealers are even more unreasonable because the auto business has been decimated over the past few years, and many dealers have already shut down or are financially troubled, Ornstein said.

Tammy Darvish, who attended the Deland arbitration hearing, was shocked to see dealers testifying against dealers like Deland, who were struggling for their livelihoods. This pattern would emerge in other arbitration hearings too. Again, a fallout of the terminations was to pit dealers against dealers, their peers.

How all the disputes will play out is still a matter for the courts, lawyers, and legislators. But the power of state franchise laws protecting dealers and businesses had been substantially weakened through the federal courts, some dealers and legal experts said.

Others defended the state franchise laws as working on behalf of dealers, despite the power of federal bankruptcy law.

Mike Charapp said, "There is no question that federal bankruptcy law trumps state franchise law. Through use of the rejection process, a bankrupt franchisor [i.e., automaker] has the opportunity to reject the ongoing agreements with its dealers." His firm handled thirty-three arbitrations and won or settled favorably twenty-eight of those. He represented Darvish's dealerships among others. But he still defended the state law's role in protecting private businesses. Well after arbitrations concluded, Charapp advised dealers to keep in mind: "The only way that federal law trumps state law is through the bankruptcy process. It is important for dealers and others to understand that. Their state law rights are intact and they have the ability to exercise them." It was a point he stressed with many of his clients.

The idea of entitlement or privilege among government players also surfaced among the lawyers and dealers. In Yale King's fight for his Colorado franchises, he was instrumental in getting the state of Colorado to pass several laws that were enacted by the governor to add extra protection to franchise rights.

One was the "right of first refusal," so that if a manufacturer brought a franchise back into the same market, the terminated dealer would have the right of first refusal or be given adequate compensation for the loss. Another law came after Chrysler sued the Colorado Attorney General, the Colorado Department of Revenue, and the Colorado State Department of Motor Vehicles. It essentially said that every day a franchisor did not honor the franchisee's rights, a substantial financial penalty would be levied against the franchisor, in this case the automaker, on a daily basis, according to King's lawyers.

Nationwide, former Chrysler dealers found the legal fees of fighting the manufacturers prohibitively expensive. Some were defeated by costs alone. Many dealers were not producing incomes at former levels. Yale King was among them. He and his partners got hit by both manufacturers. "We were fighting both GM and Chrysler at state and federal levels nationally. It tapped us out," King said.

King saw that Chrysler's legal machinery was always in motion, and so was the calculator. In light of legal wrangling with Chrysler and the State of Colorado, King's attorneys warned him the litigation could drag on for years and cost hundreds of thousands of dollars more in fees. After a year, his partnership had already spent around a half-million dollars and had little to show for it, King said.

By that point, GM and Chrysler had received billions in federal aid to keep operating. Federal money, as in taxpayer money, King and other dealers would often remind others. But dealers were on their own dime.

Craig Allely, the Denver attorney who represented King and his group, said, "The auto task force and executive branch of government thought in their arrogance that what they were doing was so important—and that their plan was the only one that could work. Assisted by the courts, they felt entitled to trample on the procedural and substantive rights of private citizens."

Another chief culprit for dealers was the US bankruptcy court experience, Allely added. "The bankruptcy courts permitted the automakers and the task force to accomplish their goals—no matter what laws were stretched to the breaking point for the executive branch. The idea that courts should uphold the law even in times of crisis was ignored," Allely said. It came as a stern observation from a lawyer on the firing lines of Western America.

The arbitration hearings concluded and results were reported by early August. By then, more legal action, primarily against Chrysler, was building. Dealers were still enraged at how they were treated.

"It's been a slow death, very stressful for dealers," said Colleen McDonald in Farmington Hills, Michigan. She and her husband, David, ran Chrysler and GM franchises in three local towns before being shut down. She also had a long-term business partner at the Dodge store in Taylor. The mostly family-based operation had existed for about thirty years until that fatal year of 2009. The closings did grave damage to dealers and families. The terminations led to suicide, illness, and depression in some cases, but dealers wouldn't give names. Much of the damage remained anecdotal and undocumented. Dealers were still paying the price emotionally and financially of termination several years later.

As part of its legal maneuverings, Chrysler had begun consolidating dealer legal cases in specific venues, such as Michigan, their home turf, dealer attorneys said. The McDonalds had pursued legal remedies against Chrysler in a Michigan case filed in Detroit federal court following arbitrations. Chrysler, meanwhile, was suing dealers back and forth, and attempting to move the legal action to federal court in Michigan and venues that were closer to their corporate offices in Auburn Hills.

In the end, dealers like the McDonalds felt they had little control. Even their court cases against Chrysler were being remanded to states Chrysler requested. "State franchise laws were supposed to protect us," Colleen McDonald said. "But automakers found a big loophole," via federal court protection, she thought.

Two years later, McDonald was still in a legal holding pattern waiting for her case to be resolved against Chrysler a year after arbitrations concluded. She and her business partner from Century Dodge (and her husband) opened a Sears Auto Center in February of 2011 while selling used cars and running a body shop in their original Taylor location. Weathering the tough economic climate, especially in Michigan, was proving to be another major hurdle.

Overall, dealer reaction to winning the right to appeal in arbitration was mixed. Some got fired up and wanted their franchises back, no matter what. In the early stages that was particularly true. In a dealer survey in 2009, Tammy Darvish said all the dealers CRDR talked with wanted their stores back.

And later, as bitterness and legal costs mounted, some dealers backed down. Other dealers were so angry at their treatment by the automakers, they had little interest in returning to the fold. When asked if he would return to Chrysler if something could be worked out, Richard Mealey said, "Never in a million years." The hurt ran too deep. He also got burned in settlement negotiations and needed to start rebuilding another business.

Those Not-So-Innocent LOIs

During and after arbitration hearings, the automakers lobbed dealers yet another fast ball. A seemingly innocent Letter of Intent (LOI) was delivered to the dealers who won in arbitration. The devil was in the details of the agreement letters from both Chrysler and GM. Upon careful reading, dealers and their lawyers found that the LOI language was stacked against them. They objected, saying the terms were prohibitive and financially unfeasible.

Chrysler and GM were asking cancelled dealers to sign the terms of the LOI, or cookie-cutter agreements, before they could resume business operations and sell new vehicles again. However, dealer lawyers complained that the LOI was "unduly onerous" and prohibitively expensive. The terms made it almost impossible for dealers to get back in business and show profits in due time. All the while, they were being measured on profitability.

Chrysler, for its part, called the LOIs "usual and customary" for their dealer network. But dealers argued that the agreement they received was not usual or customary. The continuing dealers, those "go forwards," using company lingo, did not have to comply with rigid LOI agreements and did not, in many cases, have to spend their own money to upgrade their facilities, the rejected dealers said. Dealers getting LOIs said they would prevent them from getting back into business mainly because of the steep investments required. Many said they were tapped out financially and had had no new products, or very few, to sell. A good number were becoming used-car dealers against their will.

The hitch was that dealers could get their franchises back if they could meet requirements, such as access to financing, adequate cash reserves, an approved location, and build new facilities as needed at a time when loans and credit approvals for consumers and dealers were drying up.

"In the worst automotive market ever, the automakers were still telling dealers to invest in facilities," Mark Ornstein observed. In some cases, dealers had already done so, but the upgrades weren't sufficient. Those with cash would do better. But many dealers didn't have the means to compete and get back to business.

In Chrysler's case, twenty-nine dealers signed the documents, which included the negotiating dealers, Chrysler said. GM had better luck—and for a reason. Of the 725 rejected GM dealerships that received LOIs, all had signed them in the required time period, the company's spokesperson said. Why the disparity between the two automakers?

In general, GM seemed to escape some of the dealers' wrath. Lawyers made a convincing case for why that was so. According to Ornstein, the GM experience tended to be more positive because the company got the message that "dealers are an expense-neutral cost item" and then proceeded to bring more dealers back. That switch-up speeded up with Ed Whitacre's new stance and Mark Reuss entering the executive team. Earlier, GM, like Chrysler, claimed a key reason to shut down dealers was because of the cost expense. But CRDR, major media, and SIGTARP disputed the cost factor, perhaps changing minds quicker.

The GM incentives were also greater than those from Chrysler—understandable perhaps because GM was a larger volume automaker. And unlike Chrysler, GM softened their position on bringing back dealers, inviting them to rejoin while avoiding expensive court battles and fees.

"GM provided more information and actually made an effort, though limited, to comply with the federal statute. The company was also smart enough to undo some of the auto task force's poor decisions and reinstate dealers," said Richard Faulkner, one of the sharpest legal automaker critics.

Another glitch arose for Chrysler dealers. The letters Chrysler gave dealers offered little information to work with, Faulkner said. In his view, Chrysler did not want the dealers back, no matter what. "Chrysler took a very hard, scorched-earth, screw-the-dealer approach. It consistently did the absolute minimum plausibly defensible to help dealers," he said.

Based on documents his firm later obtained, the automaker was working with the AAA "to eviscerate even the minimal remedy of the arbitration awards," Faulkner said.

Even as the results poured in, lawyers were of two minds on the benefits of arbitration overall for dealers. One theory, called the "repeat player effect," said the corporate win rate was preordained. According to a study from Cornell University professor Alex Colvin, arbitrators naturally tended to favor bigger employers and corporations, thinking that might lead to feathering their nests up the road, Faulkner explained. In his study, Colvin had dissected thousands of arbitration cases and found the results pretty much matched the Chrysler outcomes in terms of wins for the less powerful plaintiffs, whether employees or dealers.

Mike Charapp thought the arbitration process was a win for dealers who would never have had a chance otherwise. "Without the arbitrations, dealers would have had no opportunity to get their stores back or to get more realistic compensation."

He also thought dealers would fare better if a retired judge sat on their arbitration panel. "But when you get a bad arbitrator, there is little you can do about it, and there really is no method of collaterally attacking or appealing an arbitration decision," he conceded. The results, according to the new law, were final. No appeals. And the "retired-judge factor" was true in fewer than 10 percent of cases, lawyers estimated. Getting the judge in a case seemed to be a matter of luck, and the odds were against it numerically.

Despite dealer protests, legal and otherwise, Chrysler repeatedly said it was in compliance with the federal dealer arbitration law in its treatment of dealers. "Chrysler Group LLC has complied fully with the letter and intent of the federal dealer arbitration statute by issuing a customary and usual Letter of Intent to dealers that prevailed in arbitration and is engaged in constructive discussions with many prevailing dealers seeking to meet the financial and operation requirements of the LOI," Mike Palese, a Chrysler spokesperson, said.

The company also said that trimming its dealer count was part of its overall consolidation plan and would improve profits for the remaining dealers.

Further, Chrysler PR staffers punted media inquiries on dealer terminations, often using carefully prepared statements. Their responses usually consisted of comments such as, it was "inappropriate to discuss matters now in litigation." One oft-repeated claim was that "the decisions to select dealers for the company's optimized dealer network were carefully considered as part of Chrysler's Project Genesis plan." And, they said, "Placing all four brands under one roof in modern facilities has already resulted in enhanced profitability for the Genesis dealerships, and it is well documented that, due to Chrysler's optimized network, existing dealers are already enjoying increased profitability and are making significant investments in their dealerships on track with the $500 million investment objective outlined in Chrysler's business plan on November 4, 2009," Chrysler staffers stated.

The pity was that not many rejected Chrysler and GM dealers were up and running after winning in arbitration, selling the products they loved and once vigorously promoted.

"I do not know of one dealer who won arbitration or was offered reinstatement who is back to selling new vehicles with Chrysler," co-owner of Crossroads Superstore Jack Haigh told *Ward's Dealer Business* magazine, three months following arbitrations. But Haigh said he knew "plenty of dealers that Chrysler gave franchises to who have new Chryslers on the ground and are selling and servicing cars without the LOI mess that we got." He owned GM and Chrysler stores in rural Atoka, Oklahoma.

Jay Cimino at Phil Long Automotive in Colorado Springs, Colorado, said the same thing as Jack Haigh. He didn't see Chrysler dealers getting back into business, including his own. He lost a Chrysler-Jeep franchise and was still in limbo in December 2010, waiting for legal proceedings to wrap up. He thought nothing would happen for Chrysler dealers until the spring, if that.

"This thing has already cost us a pretty penny," he said. "What happened to rejected dealers in this country is corrupt and criminal."

More Legal Chess Moves

While some dealers waited and worried, lawsuits against Chrysler were occupying lawyers' calendars. The legal tidal waves continued as dealers' lawyers battled against postponements and delays.

There were new developments in legal action against Chrysler in late 2010. In a federal suit on behalf of Quality Jeep Chrysler Inc., a rejected dealership in New Mexico, a federal judge found on November 18 that Chrysler won in about 92 percent of arbitrations completed by AAA, Faulkner related. That is well above the 70 percent rate Chrysler claimed after the cases concluded in August 2010.

The Quality Chrysler case was filed in US district court in New Mexico. Federal judge Paul Kelly claimed, citing document references, that about 418 dealers pursued arbitration or initiated action against Chrysler and only 32 prevailed. It appeared the judge used the total number of cases initiated number, while Chrysler based the 70 percent on total arbitrations concluded.

What's more, by 2011, Chrysler issued a new franchise agreement for all dealers requiring that future disputes with the automaker undergo arbitration. Chrysler also stipulated that AAA serve as the arbitrator in such cases, a handy arrangement, according to Faulkner.

"The new Chrysler requirements are a chapter-and-verse way of sticking it to the dealers again," Faulkner said.

Automakers had "lawyered up" to take on the dealers who were often financially broken. In arbitration, Chrysler and GM lawyers far overpowered the dealer attorneys and resources.

"Five to six Chrysler lawyers charging stratospheric rates would oppose one or two lawyers in our cases," said Richard Faulkner, who advised on and handled multiple dealer arbitrations.

Attorney Bellavia cited similar numbers, saying dealer resources could not match those of the automakers, and they were better off joining in group suits. Unity again was power.

And Jack Haigh, the Oklahoma dealer, summed it up for other dealers by saying, "Chrysler spared no expense in hiring attorneys. They have deep pockets and will fight forever. I do not have the resources in Oklahoma to fight them. That is why we joined with other dealers and hired [one of] the best attorneys in the automotive field [Len Bellavia] to take them on." Haigh's group had joined in the New York–based group lawsuit against Chrysler in 2010.

In late December, there were more legal chess moves on Chrysler's part. The company submitted a federal court document requesting discretion in placing reinstated dealers who won in arbitration. This latitude applied to reinstating more than twenty dealerships in Michigan, Ohio, and four other states, according to *Automotive News*. Accustomed to controlling the action, Chrysler wanted to give franchises to reinstated dealers in locations they chose, but, "The dealers contend they should have their old stores back in their original locations," the paper noted. That fight will take time to resolve.

Dealers were still concerned about the culpability of the corporate players who may have lied to get them ousted. Would those who testified in courts and to Congress be held accountable? Wasn't that the law? they wondered. The questions could only be raised, although answers were not readily available.

Attorney Faulkner advised that any lie under oath is actionable by the Department of Justice if charges are brought against the offending parties. Any lies told under oath, whether in court, before Congress or even in arbitration testimony can result in perjury charges, Faulkner said. "Lying under oath is always an extremely poor decision, even if that is what a witness sincerely believes is best for the administration or what the executive branch of the government suggests it wants." Or even if a high-up boss or executive says it's expected, or demanded.

Constitutional Rights Battle

But the tide was to turn again in the contentious legal battles between automakers, the government, and dealers. For many, closing down dealerships impinged on dealers' constitutional rights, as legal experts and dealers believe.

Tammy Darvish, along with dealers such as Frank Blankenbeckler, Mark Sims and Jack Fitzgerald, had long argued that dealers' Fifth Amendment rights were being violated with the unlawful seizure or taking of property by the automakers—and by association, the government.

Numerous legal firms, including Bellavia's, had filed suits against Chrysler Group on behalf of petitioning dealers. Some of these were denied. Still, Leonard Bellavia stood his ground, saying, "It's an unauthorized taking of private property that violates the Fifth Amendment."

For most of late 2010, Bellavia's firm was in the middle of the Chrysler discovery process and facing a great deal of "stonewalling and postponements," he said. But Bellavia said his firm was able to overcome venue request changes by Chrysler, keeping a major case affecting six dealers he was representing in a New York court, rather than shifting it to Chrysler's backyard.

And the government, as in the auto task force, was increasingly in dealers' sights. Many more dealers were pressing onward with legal suits against Chrysler and the federal government. In a landmark case coming out of Texas, dealers banded together to take on government representatives. They filed a class-action suit in late September that claimed the federal government required Chrysler and GM to scale back the franchises of thousands of dealers and set up the termination play. The government intervention was based on a flawed dealer model used by the imports and not applicable to US franchises, dealer attorneys—and dealers—said.

"Dealers are seeking to be fully paid for their property damages," said Faulkner, who filed the class action suit, along with several other attorneys. "Without need and, on a theory, the federal government demanded that GM and Chrysler immediately terminate a huge number of car dealers or be denied obtaining billions of dollars of TARP (Troubled Asset Relief Program) money," Faulkner told media.

Acting as cocounsel, attorneys Harry Zanville of San Diego, California, and Kevin Buchanan of Dallas, Texas, joined up as the class-action leaders of the legal team. That suit asserted that both GM and Chrysler submitted to the government's requirements and speeded up the dealer terminations, as well as increasing them substantially because they had no choice under the bankruptcy requirements. The lawyers added dealers to the class-action suit throughout the year.

Colonial Motors, a former GM dealer in Branchburg, Mississippi, and Finnin Motors, a former Chrysler-Jeep dealer in Dubuque, Iowa, initiated a suit on behalf of more than a thousand dealers, saying unnecessary government economic regulation caused the dealer franchise terminations.

In late October, dealer Mark Sims in Ohio told the *Cleveland Plain Dealer* that a group of dealers there may appeal to the US Supreme Court. They were discussing options with their lawyers.

Then in early 2011, Leonard Bellavia, representing about eighty mostly Chrysler dealers nationwide, with more likely to join, filed a lawsuit against the federal government in the US Court of Federal Claims in DC, designated for cases brought under the takings clause. Eligible GM dealers could join the suit too, Bellavia said, but most of the early interest came from the spurned Chrysler dealers.

Bellavia said he anticipated "a fifteen-round fight ahead with the government, and appeals that will possibly go to the Supreme Court." As part of discovery, his firm asked to see everything the auto task force did in their work connected to dealer terminations while employed at the White House in 2009.

He also joined forces with Roger and Nancie Marzulla, a DC firm he called "the foremost experts in government takings"—or seizure of private property. Roger Marzulla was a former legal appointee in President Reagan's administration in the 1980s before starting up his own East Coast law firm.

Bellavia thought the class-action suit against the government could take more than a year to settle, but the lawyers were seeking "an expedited trial" based on the emergency nature of the underlying bill signed by President Obama (Section 747) into law in December of 2009.

* * *

Another ripple in the legal waves appeared in fall of 2010. The federal investigation of wrongdoing in terminating the dealers, SIGTARP, was back. The investigators had issued a report damaging to the administration, task force, and automakers in mid-July of 2010. That earlier probe included the possible abuse of TARP bailout funds that went to key players, including GM and Chrysler, *Automotive News* reported in mid-October.

The federal inspectors investigated the government, GM, and Chrysler in their handling of about twenty-three hundred projected US dealership closures. Under Neil Barofsky, the SIGTARP office appeared to again be looking into "possible legal misconduct" on the dealer closures and use of TARP funds, according to *Automotive News*. The SIGTARP office would not disclose the targets of the investigation or the latest actions being probed, *Automotive*

News said. But auditor files used in preparing the earlier July audit on dealer terminations during the automakers' bankruptcies had been turned over to the investigators, the SIGTARP office told the trade paper.

The July report from SIGTARP indicated that the widespread dealership closings were not vital to the two automakers' survival and unnecessarily resulted in thousands of nationwide job losses in the depth of the recession.

Dealers continued to contact the SIGTARP office in DC, making inquiries. According to media reports, there seemed to be little official action coming from the investigative team. And the SIGTARP office did not respond to requests for information after those news reports, reporters said. At CRDR, the dealer advocates had other questions. Had evasive responses to the federal auditors' questions delayed release of the critical report issued July 18? That report of the audit came out a few days after dealer arbitration hearings concluded. That meant dealers had no recourse to the audit findings in their arbitration cases against automakers. CRDR leaders thought that report, if released earlier, could have made a difference in their chances.

* * *

Richard Sox is a lawyer with the firm of Bass Sox Mercer and is based in Tallahassee, Florida, specializing in representing auto dealers. Sox said in August that his firm handled arbitration filings for seventy-four GM and Chrysler dealers who hoped to get their franchises back. Almost half those dealers were reinstated very early in the process, primarily by GM, he said. "There are lessons to be learned for all dealers, not just those holding GM and Chrysler franchises, through this incredibly unique process which included many hours of settlement discussions with GM and Chrysler representatives, document review, and hearing testimony," Sox said.

Earlier, Sox had called the Chrysler termination criteria, based on MSR factors, "fraught with the potential for error."

For dealers in the Chrysler and GM camps, the legislation itself that led to arbitration hearings by supposedly neutral arbitrators was a victory—at least it was a moral victory.

Elaine Vorberg, the Chicago attorney who represented her father, Nicholas D'Andrea (Buick-Pontiac-GMC), in arbitration proceedings against GM, described the feelings of powerlessness that dealers like her father felt at the time. "There was no good-faith effort coming from GM earlier. We did not know who to go to, or what to do. At times we waited for direction (from GM field people). But normally we just had to slog through the muck the best we could," she said. She often was not taken seriously by the corporate entities and their lawyers when she asked them questions. "We had no power and so weren't taken seriously when questions about the process or the proposed wind-down were raised. Sign the agreement, or else," was the message, she said.

Dealer advocates, such as CRDR, finally made the most difference in outcomes, she thought. Yet Vorberg believed many lessons were learned from the experience, for all dealers involved. "The issues here are really compelling. It's amazing how it all came together—the dealer battles, legislation, legal challenges—in the face of an über-popular president.

"It took the dealers banding together through CRDR and the advocacy groups to make it happen," Vorberg said. And now they're coming together through the legal process, filing joint suits, and consulting one another as well as lawyers, she noted.

Looking back at the ordeal dealers faced, attorney Elaine Vorberg looked at the struggle, especially with GM, a little differently. "In the aftermath, I get the sense that GM has more respect for its dealers than it once did. For years, Detroit underestimated its sales and distribution partners that went about selling the cars that 'nobody wanted to buy' (an Obama comment), not just on their business acumen, but on their integrity and their heart. Perhaps it's the humbling experience of having to be bailed-out by the

Other Arbitration Highlights:

Polls showed that Ohio, Illinois, Michigan, Florida, and Pennsylvania were most heavily represented by dealers seeking arbitration in 2010, according to India Johnson, the AAA group's senior vice president.

A *CNN Money* story in 2010 reported that the highest number of arbitration appeals came from Ohio, Illinois, Pennsylvania, Michigan, and California.

The top numbers of appeals were from Ohio (116), Illinois (106), and Pennsylvania (97).

Those states were followed by Michigan, 82; California, 71; Texas, 67; New York, 60; North Carolina, 52; Wisconsin, 51; Florida, 49; Missouri, 48, Minnesota, 38; Kansas,37; Georgia, 31; and Virginia, 31, according to *CNN Money*.

government and still going bankrupt that realigned some sensibilities," Vorberg said.

Attorney Faulkner in Dallas said the battle likely won't end with the joint suits against the automakers and government. "These cases are likely to interest the US Supreme Court because of the constitutional issues involved," he said. His firm and others had filed suit in October against the federal government, and many smaller suits were in play, primarily against Chrysler.

"The federal government has never in the history of the country taken business properties like this, so the Supreme Court is going to want to be able to delineate a precise limitation of the federal government's power to seize private property. The operative mechanism to get there is the takings clause of the US Constitution.

"Proponents of limited government see this as the temporary nationalization of the automotive sector by especially incompetent government bureaucrats who destroyed a huge percentage of small businesses who historically made it (automotive) work," Faulkner said, still seeking to get justice for damaged dealers at the end.

The special investigators under SIGTARP could still push the legal action into federal courts on a compelling national issue affecting the rights of private citizens and entrepreneurs in America, dealer lawyers said.

"We can only stay tuned," said Tammy Darvish. "I'll stay involved."

The Final Tallies

Chrysler Group
Arbitrations concluded: 108
Decisions for company: 76
Decision for dealers: 32
Decisions pending: 0
LOIs sent to CG dealers: 82
LOIs signed by dealers: 29
Total number of matters initiated: 418
Withdrawn, dismissed, or abandoned matters: 130
Arbitrations settled: 151
Total remaining active issues: **0**
Source: *Chrysler Group LLC, August 2010*

General Motors
GM dealers filed 1,176 appeals for reinstatement
Arbitration cases completed with decisions rendered: 62
Decisions for dealers: 23
Decisions for company: 39
Letters of Intent sent to dealers: 702
Individual resolutions with other dealers: 408
Cases dismissed: Four
About 4,500 dealers will comprise the new GM dealer network
Source: *General Motors, August 2010*

Epilogue: Fixing Humpty Dumpty

Betrayal is the only truth that sticks.
—Arthur Miller, US playwright and essayist

Can the trust between car dealers and the manufacturers who terminated them ever be restored? Can dealers put the hurt and distrust aside and go on from there? Can you forgive your executioner, the one who betrayed you? These are deep, troubling questions. Some legal experts and dealers say they don't know the answers.

But here's a clue: GM managed to bring back a good percentage of dealers and not alienate others by offering restitution to them, even if it was under extreme pressure and not always full restitution. GM backtracked on some targeted dealers and gave a big number, more than 650, a chance to return. Chrysler never offered that option to a sizeable number.

To the end, there were opposing views and debates on who ordered the cuts, provided the names of those to be cut, and who exactly made the decisions. Were decisions made in corporate offices, private meetings, e-mails, or in more social settings? No one knows where all the bodies are buried, or they're not talking if they do. Jim Press probably could, where Chrysler is concerned, if only he would.

Using Minnesota Chevrolet dealer George McGuire's analogy, the cohorts were still playing "Pinkie Swear" and were sticking to their stories and scripts.

In Tammy Darvish's view, the corporate yes-people and shills were paid to be silent. Big salaries and bonuses can be persuasive motivational tools, even for the reluctant. So can signed confidentiality agreements that companies require for those who depart or accept golden parachutes on the way out. Telling corporate secrets or insider dope is understandably a big no-no. But standing up for right versus wrong is another matter. Darvish and CRDR members staked their careers on it.

Dallas attorney Richard Faulkner observed that after winning in bankruptcy court, Chrysler and GM thought they were home free. "People at GM and Chrysler clicked their heels and said 'yessir' to Mr. Rattner, Mr. Bloom, and crew. They thought they would never be held personally accountable and sloughed off the costs on the poor taxpayers," he said summarily.

Long after the arbitrations were settled, attorneys were still weighing the options. The best remedy now may be in lawsuits and courts—perhaps even in the US Supreme Court, as Faulkner has suggested.

Faulkner gave his assessment of the damage done. "Sadly, neither the bankruptcy judges nor the auto task force understood that the dealers are the only real customers of the manufacturers. Only a federal bureaucrat could think it was a good idea to use bankruptcy to kill off your customers."

Another fallout could hit Chrysler, who took the harder line against dealers, Faulkner said. The lack of dealerships in certain areas of the country could drive customers away, and not to the closest GM or Chrysler store. "They may have a hell of a time selling vehicles in large parts of America. I would be amazed if Chrysler survives," Faulkner said in November of 2010.

And in Orlando, Mark Ornstein, who also handles properties for clients, thought investment in Chrysler properties could be risky business. "I would not invest in a Chrysler-Jeep-Dodge franchise now," Ornstein advises his clients. That may prove a problem for Chrysler if desirable dealer buyers from other brands won't invest in a Chrysler-Fiat franchise. Even with Fiat, the new Italian small car being marketed like a new designer label by Chrysler, it's still risky. The small sporty car reentered the US market in 2010 after a twenty-seven-year absence. It's priced, starting around $15,500, to compete with entry-level models of chief competitors—GM, Ford, Toyota, Honda, and Nissan.

But those risks Ornstein mentions are all speculation. The marketplace will be the key decider as dealer advocates long have maintained.

Obsessed Dealers

In the beginning, not many auto insiders thought that CRDR, a fledgling, underfunded advocacy group, could get Congress on their side, let alone force the legislative issue. They would never get a law passed that was supported by the majority of members of Congress, on both sides of the aisle, many said. That just didn't happen in American politics. But neither did the plan to annihilate more than several thousand dealers. It was unprecedented in American automotive history.

There weren't enough of them to fight the power brokers, CRDR leaders heard repeatedly. Their membership numbered fewer than five hundred, compared to more than sixteen thousand members of NADA.

But the small group earned their stripes. *Automotive News* wrote about CRDR on December 21, after the legislation passed that granted arbitration rights to dealers: "Their story is marked with dedication, dealer connections and a lot of their own money. … These dealers became obsessed with getting their stores back. It led to several political battles, including a significant fight with the National Automobile Dealers Association and other groups—without a guarantee of success."

Fewer than twelve people in all of Washington were betting on them when they started their precarious journey in early June until the final vote days in Congress. Darvish learned of that wager through a high-ranking member of Congress right after the House and Senate votes were counted. But members of Congress in both chambers overwhelmingly put their faith in the rejected dealers.

Their anthem—no guts, no glory—was alive. Passion and determination finally won out. It was a little like the Bad News Bears team defeating the New York Yankees in the World Series. A miracle victory.

They weren't exactly popping corks from champagne bottles after the votes, but there was a palpable sense of relief in the CRDR camp. After the surprising upset in Congress, Darvish wrote CRDR members and her dealer base, "There are a lot of highly paid expert lobbyists in Washington scratching their heads right now. What all of you pulled off as a team now is going to be documented in history."

Months after the group took their fight to Congress, Jack Fitzgerald revisited the path taken. "Originally they told us we did not have any chance of success. They told us the train had left the station and it wasn't possible to get legislation approved. The Capitol Hill staff said 'work it out,' at first, asking for a non-legislative solution. And then we learned the auto task force was our enemy," he said.

"Later, we had some of the most conscientious members of Congress on both sides of the aisle on our side." The dealer issue aroused bipartisan support because they "saw dealers in their states getting ripped off," he said in his usual candid manner. And the recrafted LaTourette plan laid the groundwork for widespread sympathy for dealers among lawmakers in both parties of Congress.

The dealer movement indeed got big names in Congress behind it. Fitzgerald ticked off a number of sponsors. "We had Ted Kennedy, John Kerry, Steve LaTourette, Steny Hoyer, Chris Van Hollen, Chuck Grassley, and many others in support." Even Senator Dick Durbin, initially neutral, came around near the end. (See appendix E for sponsor lists.)

The auto task force, under Steve Rattner, never understood the real impact car dealers had on the economy and on retail sales. Even in a mid-November (2010) meeting with Automotive Press Association journalists in Detroit, Rattner insisted that Fitzgerald was severely underperforming, having only sold three new Chryslers in 2008. This was the same argument Rattner gave House Leader Steny Hoyer who questioned him on certain rejected dealers in 2009, such as Fitzgerald and Darvish. Hearing his ludicrous claims, Fitzgerald blasted Rattner for his statements. He had no idea where Rattner got his information. When told about the low number of sales Rattner cited for his group, Fitzgerald replied, "Untrue. [Rattner] makes up the facts as he goes along. We sold more than a thousand Chrysler brand vehicles retail in 2008 and eleven hundred with fleets, the largest Chrysler dealer in our county."

Assessing the damage done to dealers, Fitzgerald posed another perplexing question: "How did it benefit GM to close Oldsmobile [in 2000] and Chrysler to close Plymouth and Eagle, both good brands?" Even with brand eliminations and dealer cuts, "They still ended up going bankrupt," and were in trouble for decades, he said. "They had some lousy products—that's been their problem all along."

Those *Consumer Reports* guides that survey millions of owners at a time don't lie, Fitzgerald said. Of the Detroit Three, Chrysler usually fared the worst on the CR surveys—even after the cuts. GM, too, struggled to get a good showing on the quality reports from consumers.

As for Steve Rattner, he had to pay the piper in late 2010 for his role in an alleged kickback scheme involving his New York investment company, Quadrangle. Rattner agreed to pay $10 million to settle the lawsuits brought by New York's attorney general Andrew Cuomo. The influence-peddling allegations against Rattner involved the state's pension fund and went back to 2004. As part of his fine, Rattner also was banned from appearing in any capacity before any public pension fund in New York for five years, according to a December 30, 2010 *Reuters* story.

Rattner had previously agreed to pay $6.2 million to settle an SEC lawsuit over his conduct. That deal included a two-year ban from the securities industry. "It's a good way to stay out of jail," an auto analyst opined when he heard about his agreed SEC-related payments. Cuomo, then the state attorney general, brought his office's two lawsuits against Rattner in 2009. Cuomo became New York's governor on January 1.

The Rattner drama is not over, many dealers believe.

Like other dealers, Jack Fitzgerald believes there's more to be uncovered about Steve Rattner. "You don't get to be in your fifties and suddenly become clever," he said, referring to Rattner's settlement on the SEC and New York state lawsuit charges. Fitzgerald says he's not alone in this belief. Many dealers talk to him in dealer meetings, voicing similar views, he said.

His partners at Quadrangle distanced themselves from Rattner, according to media reports, including *Dow Jones Financial News* and *CNN Money* in 2010. That's a serious matter in his (Fitzgerald's) eyes. "Partnership is a sacred relationship, a trust. You can go through a lot of spouses, but not business partners," he quipped.

Was it all worth it for the automakers? The cost, the alienation of customers and dealers? What price or value do you place on constitutional and human rights? The CRDR leaders grappled with those kinds of issues long afterward. They always concluded what happened to car dealers was wrong and unnecessary—and unconscionable.

GM would report profits early in 2011, but not because they had cut the dealers, media reported. An *Automotive News* opinion piece indicated that profitability of the remaining dealers might still be wishful thinking.

In May of 2011, *Automotive News* said in an opinion piece that "wildly profitable" remaining dealers were not being seen.

"When General Motors and Chrysler shed nearly 2,800 dealerships, one major supposition was that the remaining dealerships could be wildly profitable and better represent their brands in individual markets across the country. That hasn't happened yet, and it may be some time before it does," *Automotive News* wrote.

"Surviving dealerships have bounced back. Data from the National Automobile Dealers Association show that last year the average dealership had a net pretax profit margin of 2.1 percent of sales, the strongest margin since 1986. But the improved results were due more to actions taken by domestic and import dealerships to reduce costs during the downturn—plus record low interest rates on floor-plan loans—rather than increased throughput at GM and Chrysler stores," the story continued.

Who's to Blame?

The debate continued to rage over who was to blame for throwing the dealers under the bus. Almost two years later, dealers thought the "who-to-cut" decisions were in the automakers' hands, while the auto task force gave the marching orders to seriously trim the dealer networks.

DC-area attorney Mike Charapp still believed that in many cases, staff managers in the field at Chrysler and GM gave feedback on which dealers would go, with Detroit and Auburn Hills, Michigan, corporate offices rubberstamping the decisions. That certainly proved true in the Jim Tarbox and Mark Calisi cases with Chrysler.

Jack Fitzgerald thought the level of cuts was government ordered. "The 25 percent cuts were task-force determined. I'm certain of it. Everything we told Congress was later verified by the SIGTARP people," he said. "The task force put a gun to the head of the automakers. Jim Press later confided it to Tammy and others. There was no data to substantiate the cuts," he said.

Dealers such as the Carlsons in Anoka, Minnesota, blamed the automakers first. The decision on who to cut was "decidedly in their hands," after receiving marching orders from the task force, with the financial strings attached, said Karen Carlson.

Some dealers wondered at the turn of the screw on the automakers' part. Why did they expend such huge resources to take out the dealers? Was it all a matter of pride and inability to back down, the reasons why some wars are fought?

"Did Chrysler dislike the thirty-two dealers who won in arbitration so much that they had to fight with every resource they had?" Jack Haigh in Oklahoma asked. The bitter legal battles gave the answer. "But the total decision was made in Detroit and the regions as to who stays and who goes," Haigh believed. "The new Chrysler Group accepted all the go-forward or continuing dealers of the old Chrysler, with no letters of intent." They had a strategy and stuck to it, he said.

Haigh summed up what many other dealers were saying. "What were we asking for? We were just asking to be put back in our businesses—where we were before these bad things happened. It's not all that complicated, and it would not have cost the automakers or taxpayers a thing."

Haigh also lamented the hardships brought to communities and families with the dealer cuts. The data on what dealers contribute to communities and employment rolls began surfacing as a result of the dealer debate. "It's sad for a lot of communities and people who rely on dealer goodwill. All that's been eroded," Haigh said. "The task force and automakers should have said, 'Let's keep the car dealers in business, and those terminated should be invited back.' The message should have been, 'Let's go sell some cars. Together,'" he said.

Many legal experts, dealers, and consultants believe as Mark Ornstein does: the cuts were designed to take out the dealers that automakers didn't want on the new team. Ornstein, for one, said, "The automakers used [bankruptcy] as an opportunity to get rid of dealers they don't want."

Some dealers are proving to be exceptions to the lament of "no one's back in business yet." The numbers may be small but are no less important.

Lee and Karen Carlson reopened their Cadillac and Chevrolet franchises in Minnesota, and are hoping for the best. The Carlsons' ordeal finally ended last May. Their GM franchise, Main Motors, was in the family for ninety-one years when it closed. They were reinstated after GM officials visited their dealership and perhaps saw the negative spin from publicity on their closing.

Karen Carlson didn't care how it happened, just that it did. "We're over the moon, we're so excited. A lot of people, especially CRDR, worked very hard to make this happen," she said, crediting the group's lobbying efforts with Congress. The couple became high profile when news stories and an appeal on national TV spotlighted their cause. Their daughter, Gretchen Carlson, a *Fox News* host, appeared on the Glenn Beck show and appealed to GM publicly about her parents' plight. That seemed to carry some weight.

Karen Carlson also commended Mark Reuss for "bringing sanity to the dealer process at GM." Another positive outcome for them was in working with new GM managers with new attitudes in Chicago and Minneapolis who were helping them reenter the business, she related. "I'm happy as a lark we're back because we have the best two field managers for Cadillac and Chevrolet we've ever had," she said. The Mocks in Wentzville, Missouri, were back in the Dodge-Chrysler-Jeep business on March 1, 2011, after prolonged legal battles with the automaker in the courts. Without CRDR, the dealers thought, they would not be in the position they were to reopen.

There were others, mostly in the GM camp, who were not able to talk about their agreements to continue. Chrysler maintained in media accounts that more than twenty stores were back in business. Dealers were hard-pressed to name one or two. But moving on is a position the returning dealers say they can live with.

* * *

More than a year after the dealer rights legislation was passed, Tammy Darvish was able to look at the big picture. It didn't change her mind. It seemed so simple: the concept of fighting for what you believe in is so right, yet so hard to do.

She was being hailed as the dealer advocate who stirred up a movement but still wore her analyst hat on the closings. It didn't take a rocket scientist to understand the fundamentals. Reopen the dealers and watch sales go up. It would have helped sagging employment statistics too. And it didn't have to cost billions of dollars to defend on all sides, draining dealers, the companies, taxpayers, and the government.

The notice to reopen could have been via a phone call or a letter. Just like it started. Or it could have been in a national dealer meeting. It would have given the automakers a positive PR boost. She could see the headline now: "GM and Chrysler Reopen Closed Dealerships, Revive the Economy."

Instead, they signed off on a national tragedy that spelled gloom and disaster. "The truth is none of this had to happen. Taking away someone's hard-earned business and livelihood is so unethical, so wrong," Darvish told her dealer groups. "I'll believe that to my dying day."

She thought about her father, toiling in the auto industry for more than forty years, building a small family business, watching it grow bigger and employing many relatives and people—almost two thousand—in communities in three states. That was nothing to scoff at.

Her other pet project often arose when she spoke of the dealer struggle: "To restore dealers to their pre-bankruptcy levels would have restored jobs and given back to communities that have been so devastated." It would have been a positive sign of faith in America, in the American people. She believed that in her heart.

The reinventing of the auto industry by the task force had a surreal, mysterious quality to some dealer observers, especially the decimated ones. You had to fight to get information and facts, they said. The process was hardly transparent and open. It was like a sinister force was orchestrating the events.

Darvish thought that, in the end, it seemed real victory was illusive, even after billions of dollars were spent by automakers, the government, and dealers. Most of the dealers were not restored wholly. Her father's Chevrolet dealership was reinstated, but not the closed Chrysler stores.

Attorneys might be among those who benefit, but some still didn't like what they saw happening. "They're spending taxpayers' money on attorney fees and other legal matters," Mark Ornstein said, knowing he was one of the attorneys. "If all thirty-two dealers who won arbitration were to be reinstated right now, it would be a shot in the arm for Chrysler," he said after the arbitrations. It would be a PR win for the auto companies, he and others believed, and good for the economy.

Except for not selling cars and chasing away dealers confirmed as decent and hardworking, the closures did very little for America, Ornstein said. "Right now, dealers are still failing because of a lack of financing. Banks still treat dealers as diseased entities and they're still terminating dealers," Ornstein said. He also worried that the public and media focus was no longer on the car dealers, and dealer groups may need to become activists again.

Indeed, CNN's Anderson Cooper and NBC's Brian Williams had other hot stories to chase. And Keith Olbermann and Oprah Winfrey left their respective networks. Popular *NBC* talk-show host and satirist Jay Leno, a certified car nut, also seemed to turn away from the dealer debate. He could have made a difference, some dealers thought, even if in comic jest. To be fair, *Fox News* covered the dealer crisis to a greater extent than other media in the early stages, some dealers said. As did top editors and reporters at *Automotive News,* all backed by Keith Crain, founder of Crain Communications.

Dealers need to sharpen their focus to survive in the future, attorney Mike Charapp said. "I am advising dealers now that they need to operate their businesses as wise business people using all of the knowledge they have acquired over the years. The franchisors are strong-arming dealers more than they ever have, but the state laws have never been better and state laws do control, absent another bankruptcy," he said.

Whiz Kids in DC

The whiz kids from Wall Street, as one lawyer called them, guided the restructuring of an industry responsible for almost 20 percent of US retail sales. Ironically, that guidance came after the fall of many Wall Street firms and banks.

It's well documented that Rattner's "team auto," who advised Treasury and President Obama on the auto restructuring lacked fundamental knowledge about the auto industry. The task force members spent perhaps a day in Detroit before making their decisions and most of that time was spent visiting GM's Technical Center in Warren, nearly twenty miles east of Detroit and an older-line Chrysler assembly plant also in the suburbs. Giving a nod to labor, they took a brief walk through the UAW Solidarity House in Detroit before rushing back to catch their flight to DC, reportedly anxious to leave town.

A *New Yorker* article published on November 1, 2010, called Steve Rattner to task for misunderstanding Rick Wagoner's accomplishments at GM, anxious to paint him as the culprit. "But, especially given the mess that Wagoner inherited when he took over, in 2000—and the inherent difficulty of running a company that had to pay pension and medical benefits to half a million retirees—[Wagoner] accomplished a tremendous amount during his eight-year tenure [as CEO]. He cut the workforce from 390,000 to 217,000. He built a hugely profitable business in China almost from scratch: a GM joint venture is the leading automaker in what is now the world's largest automobile market. In 1995 it took forty-six man-hours to build the typical GM car, versus twenty-nine hours for the typical Toyota. Under Wagoner's watch, the productivity gap closed almost entirely," the reporter wrote.

So it's little wonder that the task force didn't understand how US dealers fit into the industry picture.

Bob Dilmore, the former GM VP who now consults with dealers, was among the biggest critics of how the dealer debacle was allowed to happen. He believed it was time to hold up the mirror to the new GM and Chrysler so they could see the old great companies and their leaders, compared to what had emerged. Not even a government-hatched "shiny new GM" could compare with the past. He recalled when "GM was a truly great company—one of the largest corporations in the world and held in high regard by everyone." To own a GM car once was considered a status sign among the domestics, having arrived.

He added, "Having served in an executive position in the central office of Buick Motor Division in Flint, I came to know the real leaders, the movers and shakers at GM, as well as at Buick. These were intelligent people, moral people; whose leadership was very apparent. They recognized their dealer body as GM's greatest asset. Harlowe Curtice, chairman and CEO of GM [1952–1958] initiated the Quality Dealer Program. We all lived by the standards established. We respected dealers as business partners," he said.

That was then and this is now, he admits. "To see the depths to which this once great company (GM) has fallen is frankly heartbreaking. The actions of the current management against dealers at both GM and Chrysler are not only unjust and immoral; they will prove to be self-destructive," he said. "Under the guise of the necessity of their restructuring plans, GM and Chrysler attempted to convince 'all the president's men' that getting rid of 25 to 40 percent of their dealer body will save them into prosperity."

Dilmore summarized what many believed about the dealers who were rejected. The real reason for terminating dealers "under the umbrella of a Chapter 11 bankruptcy, was to eliminate dealers who stood up to them. They saw these dealers as refusing to be team players on a team that was very obviously losing the game. Less than a year ago, GM was literally forcing their Hummer dealers to build an idiotic Quonset hut building that never moved the sales needle, and then they announced to the world that they were selling Hummer. Actions such as these have destroyed GM's credibility," he said.

He also worried that the dealer-trashing may have eliminated many of the country's risk takers, the bold entrepreneurs who helped shape the industry. The kind who built the American Dream.

Mark Calisi added, "Car dealers were part of the American fabric that fought in wars, gave up their lives, or started up businesses on a dime." It was because of such efforts that future generations could aspire to be president, run for public office, own a business, and build their dreams, he believed. "Now many of those businesses have been destroyed."

Other respected industry leaders were critical of what transpired between Detroit and DC in 2009 once the Wall Street rejects jumped in.

Former Chrysler CEO Lee Iacocca, in mid-December 2010, told the *Detroit News*, "The [Obama auto task force] called me for my advice, but they didn't follow it too well." He had spoken with top federal officials in the spring of 2009. "Keep your hands off of [the auto companies]," Iacocca had said to task force cochairman Larry Summers, President Obama's top economic adviser, according to the *News* story. "You can't run a business out of Washington, DC." He added, "There is no fairness in bankruptcy."

Michelle Malkin, in her "Dealergate" articles on Creative Syndicate was appalled by the way the task force treated dealers. "Rattner's auto-czar successor, Ron Bloom, is a far-left union lawyer … who opined that 'the blather about free trade, free-markets and the joys of competition is nothing but pabulum for the suckers,'" she wrote.

Malkin also uncovered a truth in SIGTARP's pages. "In search of the rationale for Team Obama's bizarre, job-killing exercise of power over thousands of small-car dealerships, the TARP inspector general may have stumbled onto the truth from Bloom. On page 33 of its report, Barofsky writes that 'no one from Treasury, the manufacturers, or from anywhere else indicated that implementing a smaller or more gradual dealership termination plan would have resulted in the cataclysmic scenario spelled out in Treasury's response; indeed, when asked explicitly whether the Auto Team could have left the dealerships out of the restructurings, Mr. Bloom, the current head of the Auto Team, confirmed that [they] 'could have left any one component [of the restructuring plan] alone,' but that doing so would have been inconsistent with the president's mandate for shared sacrifice," she wrote.

GM North America President Mark Reuss talked about transparency and wanting to do well by the cancelled dealers. But by March 2010, after he took the top helm, much harm had been done. Reinstated dealers were still going out of business and not getting products to sell. And at the time of the final GM deadline for closing the last five hundred wind-down dealers on October 31, there were few reversals of those decisions. The executions stood.

Almost a year later, Reuss confirmed that GM would likely add dealerships in key markets on the East and West coasts. That meant challenging the imports on their own turf. The company was looking at new points in primarily the Los Angeles and San Francisco markets where GM was not performing well. There was no talk of offering those points to closed dealers.

According to the *Detroit News* in early February 2011, Reuss said, "We know that our footprints on the coasts have been destroyed" through GM's 2009 bankruptcy, the 2008–09 financial crisis, and what he called "twenty years of bad product." This in itself was a candid admission on more company mistakes from a top-level auto executive who had seen it all.

And GM's initial public offering stock sold for thirty-three dollars per share in mid-November, exceeding former CEO Ed Whitacre's prediction of up to twenty-five dollars per share. Shareholders were not getting rich yet, but GM looked to be rounding the bend. There was talk of IPO stock going even higher. And GM was looking to reduce the government's ownership stake from 61 percent originally to 33 percent, *Reuters* said in November 2010. With its positive stock and sales performance and ability to pay off loans far quicker than scheduled by the end of the year, GM's future looked bright.

Meanwhile, as late as December, Chrysler was gobbling up pricey land deals in California to open new dealerships in import-dominated markets such as Los Angeles. It was also recruiting new dealers there. A downtown Los Angeles store would be a showcase for selling its coming lineup of Fiat-based small-car products, according to media reports.

Not to be outdone by GM, the Chrysler group said it would repay all its government loans nearly six years early, by summer, 2011, or sooner. The company's goal was to raise Fiat's stake in Chrysler to 51 percent, from 19 percent, as soon as possible and to prepare the company for public stock offerings, as GM did. By spring, Fiat had a 46 percent controlling share of Chrysler and repaid its government loans, reportedly by credit card.

Where SIGTARP Is Heading

Where is the dealer campaign heading now? By 2011, dealers around the country wanted to get the closure issue back on the radar of investigators and journalists. Legal action was still ongoing, with the action shifting to the cases against the federal government.

In Maryland, Tammy Darvish saw something else that was worrisome. Neil Barofsky was the key to continuing investigating the dealer terminations. He made conclusions that looked positive for rejected dealers, but was suddenly quiet, she said. Now what? It was a question many dealers, affected or not, were asking.

As of this writing, SIGTARP seemed to be in a holding pattern on further investigations on the dealer closures after its initial audit was released. The SIGTARP office in DC could not confirm in March 2011 that Christy Romero, the acting inspector general, would reopen the investigation into dealer closures or TARP funds' usage.

But dealers still believe much lies in the hands of the SIGTARP investigators, capably led by investigator Barofsky, through March, at least. Dealers flooded the SIGTARP office with calls and letters in 2010. Barofsky, who had a reputation of being an independent thinker who did not bow to political pressure, was held in high regard by most dealers.

"The only honest person in the whole game is Neil Barofsky and his group of investigators. A lot of people are counting on him," Mark Calisi said in late December.

Two months later, the picture changed drastically at SIGTARP, and so had Calisi's message. On February 14, 2011, Barofsky tendered his resignation to President Obama and Timothy Geithner at Treasury. "It's a very sad day for America when such a hardworking, honest person like Mr. Barofsky is no longer looking out for the interests of the American people," said Calisi.

Barofsky, a former federal prosecutor who headed SIGTARP, said his work was largely done and it was time for him to move on from government service. That at least was the official word at the time. His resignation was effective March 30. Kristine Belisle, SIGTARP communications director, said in March no replacement had been named for Barofsky yet. That position is presidential and Congress-approved. "It is up to the White House to decide who will replace him," and when, Belisle said.

Barofsky was pursuing an academic career at New York University's law school, she said. Meanwhile, Christy Romero moved into the acting inspector general for SIGTARP slot, from deputy inspector general.

Tammy Darvish observed that Barofsky had spent at least a year investigating the dealer closures and TARP use, now dealers could only wonder what would come of it. Yale King in Colorado only hoped that Barofsky's successor also proved to be tough and independent-minded like Barofsky and "not some pushover."

The SIGTARP chapter may yet be revisited or rewritten, many auto observers believe.

On January 5, Democrat Sheila Jackson-Lee in Texas introduced a House bill that aimed to help terminated dealers who are not reinstated. Jackson-Lee's bill, Automobile Dealers Fair Competition Act of 2011 (HR75), will prohibit "certain restraints of competition adversely affecting automobile dealers," if passed, said the bill overview. An early read suggests the bill could affect manufacturers who filed a 363 bankruptcy clause and violated franchise agreements, Darvish said. It was one of the few bills in Congress that picked up the threads of the 2009 legislative fight.

Personal Sacrifices

Initially, the CRDR team did not relish the task of taking on the automakers or the auto task force empowered to fix the Detroit Two and shrink the dealer body. But two years later all of them would do it again, with the wisdom that hindsight often brings.

The personal sacrifices made by CRDR were different than those "shared sacrifices" that government leaders called for as Obama launched his young presidency. The dealer sacrifices came from hard times too. But they came from the heart and pure determination. The three leaders also provided plenty of elbow grease and money into the campaign. Their anthem of "no guts, no glory" carried the day.

"So was the personal sacrifice worth it?" Jack Fitzgerald was asked in December 2010, long after the dealer battles subsided. He considered the question before answering, as if recalling the highs and lows along the way. "There are a lot of people in business who would not be in it now," he said.

Hundreds of GM dealers lived to see another day, a stay from execution. Of Chrysler dealers, thirty-two won in arbitration. Yes, that's thirty-two out of nearly eight hundred. But that's still better than a worst-case scenario. And many more were negotiating their returns, or pursuing legal action. At GM, arbitrators found for dealers in twenty-nine cases, but hundreds more were settled or negotiated to return.

In Fitzgerald's case, "We saved six out of ten of our franchises slated to be cut," he said. Sixty percent isn't bad when you look at the alternative, he thought.

In Ohio, Alan Spitzer, who enlisted Fitzgerald and Darvish to help breathe life into CRDR, was still in business selling other vehicle brands and fighting for dealer rights. Spitzer had lost ten stores, got two back, and negotiated on several others for settlements.

Spitzer also said he had several private chats with President Obama in Ohio and with Congress members in late October. Along with several closed Ohio dealers, he helped orchestrate meetings with Congress members in his home state to try to delay or reverse the remaining GM closures before the November midterm elections.

US House Representatives Steve LaTourette and John Boehner, who became House speaker after the midterm elections, hosted public meetings at the urging of Spitzer, Mark Sims, brothers Eric and Mark Halleen, and Ron Marhofer, all Ohio dealers who had lost businesses.

It was important to keep shining a light on the issues, the dealers thought. Or the veil of darkness on information flow could fall again.

And Darvish's DARCARS' group? With three cancelled dealerships, they negotiated settlements on two Chrysler franchises and signed a continuation agreement with the Chevrolet store after drawn-out talks.

In the fight to save the dealers, was the personal sacrifice worth it? For Darvish, it's like asking if you would still have the baby, knowing in advance everything you would go through. But Tammy Darvish says unhesitatingly, "Absolutely, yes."

Looking at the big picture, many of the disenfranchised dealers were given a fighting chance. In some cases, GM and Chrysler negotiated settlements. Some dealers turned the page and ventured into new careers or businesses that could lead to better days ahead. For many dealers the legislation that passed both houses of Congress was not a clear-cut win. But it led to the arbitration process ordered by Congress that gave them a chance to tell their stories in a forum that for some made a difference. The fight is not over for others.

Leonard Bellavia spoke with dealers who wanted nothing more to do with Chrysler and were only seeking reimbursement for losing their franchises. "Many Chrysler dealers were filing for arbitration simply out of the need for some personal vindication. Some dealers are indifferent whether they win. They don't want to go back to a company that doesn't want them. They just want their stories told."

Other dealers, like Gus Russo in Detroit, had had enough. "Chrysler approached us about discussing a settlement, and everyone knew Lochmoor Chrysler-Jeep would win in arbitration, but the reality was, you couldn't put Humpty Dumpty back together again," Russo said. There was too much toxic water under the dam. Too much hurt and despair to go back. He needed to move on.

Denver attorney Craig Allely said, "One hundred years from now, people will not care whose rights were trampled on, but they *should* care that people's rights were trampled on, all supposedly in the name of the greater good, as determined by the executive branch. That the checks and balances of the three branches of government were ignored for a time should be a matter of historical and personal interest to all."

Still, the fight to save American businesses and surface the thorny economic issues of dealers would not have been possible without the efforts of the three CRDR leaders, informed sources said. "This was in many ways a victory of David over Goliath," said Maryland Democrat Chris Van Hollen, who helped escalate the dealer campaign to highly visible levels. "There were lots of groups involved in the effort, but this trio played an especially effective role."

Restoring Their Honor

Jim Estle, a dealer in Defiance, Ohio, contacted Tammy Darvish In late September. "I am one of the fifty terminated Chrysler dealers that had their franchise given back before arbitration. I want to tell you how grateful I am for all you have done for not only myself but for all of the fellow dealers you have assisted over the past year. I have finally settled with Chrysler this week and ordered cars yesterday. What an ordeal!"

Estle's was more than a typical thank-you note. Estle wanted information. He asked for help on dealer-restoration issues, even at that late stage. This was nearly sixteen months after their battle began. Darvish was still the dealer go-to person on the business side.

Darvish was still earning other supporters. One comment came to her through a third party from Karen Carlson, the restored dealer in Minnesota. This one spoke volumes to her. "I can't thank that woman [Darvish] enough. What she did for dealers is remarkable."

Carlson's words got Darvish to remember the note that arrived in June 2010, a Father's Day weekend, after many arbitration cases had been heard. This one also got her going. She shared it with her coleaders. "Tammy: On behalf of my family and our employees, I cannot begin to express how grateful and fortunate we are to know you. We received word yesterday that the arbitrator assigned to our case ruled in our favor. Few understand the lengths you have gone to or price you have paid for me to sit here today writing you this e-mail.

"Whether it was Jack's leadership, Alan's supporting evidence supplied through the CRDR forum, or Tammy's single-spaced multi-page e-mails providing us with the latest information and inspiration, the work you have undertaken has impacted many more families like mine than you realize. In four days, we will be celebrating Father's Day, and I cannot thank you enough for providing my dad with the present of getting his good name back and taking a step closer to regaining a business he started on his own in 1972." The note was signed by Bill Hahn Jr., the dealer at Village Chrysler-Jeep in Royal Oak, Michigan.

And in Wentzville, Missouri, Century Dodge-Chrysler-Jeep reopened March 1, 2011 after being shut down for almost two years. Operated by brothers Frank and John Mock, the dealership owners had filed a landmark lawsuit against the Chrysler group in 2010 and won.

"To the best of our knowledge, we are the only contested Chrysler dealer in the country to open our doors since the massive terminations in May 2009," they wrote to the three CRDR leaders in late March. "Without the courageous and tenacious efforts of the CRDR spearheaded by you (three), we could not have succeeded," they wrote. Their letter was signed personally by the four family members who run the franchise—John, Frank, Brian, and Kevin Mock. For Tammy Darvish, those words, like the others, were the thanks of a lifetime. It was all she needed. In a way, she had accomplished her personal mission. She had, in part, helped restore the honor of many dealers, including her father's. They were telling her so.

Postscript from San Francisco: Special Delivery

Darvish was attending the 2011 NADA convention in early February in San Francisco. After an evening dinner sponsored by research group J. D. Power and Associates at the Palace Hotel, she stopped at a drugstore to buy a Diet Coke before walking back to her hotel.

At the Four Seasons hotel the man getting on the elevator with her looked familiar. She thought it was Steve Rattner, but didn't say anything. He looked at her quizzically too. She knew Rattner was speaking the following morning at an AFSA meeting.

The could-be Rattner guy got off on the tenth floor; hers was the fourteenth. Before returning to her floor, Darvish walked down and caught his room number. She formed a plan.

In her room, a basket of wine, cheese, and crackers had been sent earlier courtesy of the Washington Area New Automobile Dealers Association.

Feeling like a sleuth, she still had to confirm who the mystery guest was. She called the hotel from her cell phone, saying, "Can you connect me with Room 1007?" The operator asked her to verify the guest's name. "Steven Rattner," she replied. The clerk thanked her and connected the call. After hearing it ring, she hung up.

She sat down immediately and wrote a quick note on hotel stationery and then attached her business card. "Dear Mr. Rattner: Welcome to San Francisco. We read about the sacrifices you made having to forfeit lunches at the Four Seasons in Manhattan for tuna fish sandwiches on cheap red leather government couches in government offices, so maybe this will make up for it. By the way, pour a glass of wine, sit back, and think of the 789 Chrysler and two thousand-plus GM private businessmen and businesswomen whose lives you destroyed for *no* reason other than greed and ignorance. Just think, more than 170,000 direct lives were rocked because of *you*. SIGTARP vindicated these people but most still lost everything. Simple math and common sense must not have been part of Harvard's curriculum. Anyway—break a leg tomorrow at the conference. The Q&A will be great. Karma sucks."

She signed it, "Sincerely, Tamara Darvish."

Then a final step: she took the letter and gift basket to the front desk and asked them to deliver it immediately to Room 1007. To make sure it reached the right person, she rode with the hotel clerk in the elevator and watched him deliver it.

In her room, she thought about fate and karma again. The stop for the Diet Coke had done it. Timing was everything—and fate had delayed her for the few minutes it had taken to encounter Rattner.

She was able to sleep well that night in San Francisco. She wasn't so sure about Steve Rattner.

Acknowledgments

We would like to sincerely thank those who gave guidance and good advice and kept the faith in the more-than-year-long journey to defend dealer rights, and thus served as the stimulus in creating this book. We especially thank dealers for their many insights and candid stories. It was most unfortunate that these tragic events brought so many hard working Americans together, but as a team we were the *David* that beat *Goliath*.

There were so many dealers and their families who shared their time, resources, and heartfelt encouragement that we certainly can not name them all individually. The diligent veracity of these many dealers was pivotal at a time when they were abandoned by those that greatly lacked the courage to do what was right. Having no where else to turn, these dealers also put their faith and support into CRDR. Together, we proved that citizen activism is a force to be reckoned with regardless of economic, demographic, or political cachet.

Without a doubt, none of it would have been possible without the true determination and fortitude of my CRDR founders and coleaders, Alan Spitzer and Jack Fitzgerald. Supported by their individual A-Teams including Alison Spitzer and Rob Smith, they envisioned the dream and started the engine. They were committed to bringing the *train back to the station*, and then righting a wrong that unnecessarily created so much loss and suffering for thousands of Americans. God bless them both.

External to CRDR, special thanks for all ATAEs of state dealers associations including Don Hall of the Virginia Auto Dealers Association, Peter Kitzmiller of the Maryland Auto Dealers Association, Gerry Murphy of the Washington DC Auto Dealers Association, and Damon Lester, President of the National

Minority Auto Dealers Association. They had a strong presence and supported our efforts from day one, and most importantly, they stayed true and loyal to their reason for being.

We also want to acknowledge Tim Doran, who headed the Automotive Trade Association Executives group (ATAE) and is president of the Ohio Automobile Dealers Association. His effort was a major catalyst in encouraging other dealers associations to do the right thing and stand behind the affected dealers.

A very special thanks goes to Crain Communications and their outstanding team at Automotive News for never letting this story get swept away. Reporter Neil Roland was a great educator in ethics, fact finding, and telling the story to readers.

A very special commendation and appreciation goes to our fearless members of Congress and their most invaluable staff members who kept the hope alive, the legal teams and media engaged and the unscrupulous "lobbyists" under control. Their active support was evident that all Americans do have a voice and all Americans do matter. Thank you to Leader Steny Hoyer and the entire Md team led by Chris Van Hollen, Donna Edwards, Roscoe Bartlett, Frank Kratovil, Elijah Cummings, John Sarbanes, Dutch Ruppersberger, and Senators Barbara Mikulski and Benjamin Cardin for coming together in a bipartisan way to be the first State to have all members of Congress in support of HR2743/S1304. We appreciate all 336 House and Senate members for working together to support all of our efforts. Thank you Congressman Steven LaTourette for the "Hail Mary" – it was brilliant.

Thank you Dr. Timothy G. Nash and my other professors and mentors at Northwood University, my alma mater, who believed in me at a time in my life when not many did. Dr. Nash was my very first professor and still continues to be a truly valued and personal friend and mentor. His coaching and lessons related to the values of an entrepreneurial and free-enterprise society provided a great source of ethical values that have guided my life and career for decades. Individual freedom and individual responsibility encouraging function from a foundation of ethics and integrity were some of my life's greatest lessons. For that, I thank him from the bottom of my heart.

Thank you to my Executive Assistant, Courtney Wallin-Seufert for not only making this dream of a project a reality, but for your relentless efforts in all that you do. You are a great source of encouragement for myself and my children, and we love you very much. And to Rose Bayat, who has saved my life more than once since we met in the dorm M13 of Northwood University. You are the loving friend that everyone needs in their life. LU2. And, last but not least, to my husband and children who continue to support me as I pursue my passions. My children will forever be my greatest inspiration for all that I do.

And lastly, a heartfelt tribute to John Darvish, my father, for providing endless opportunities not only to me and my family but to hundreds in our industry. He is a true hero.

Appendix A

EDWARD M. KENNEDY
MASSACHUSETTS

United States Senate
WASHINGTON, DC 20510-2101

July 22, 2009

Fritz Henderson
Chief Executive Office
General Motors Co.
P.O. Box 33170
Detroit, Michigan 48232

Dear Mr. Henderson:

I'm writing to request GM to reconsider the closure of the LaBelle Chevrolet dealership of Bridgewater, Massachusetts. The dealership has received a wind-down agreement, but its sales and customer service record suggest that a review of this decision is needed.

According to Steve LaBelle, the owner of LaBelle Chevrolet, his dealership earned a dealer performance score of 76 in 2008—above the target level GM set for a dealership to receive a wind-down agreement. Mr. LaBelle also tells me that LaBelle Chevrolet ranks in the top 30 percent in capitalization for GM dealerships, and was in the top 10 percent for profitability in 2007, 2006 and 2005. His dealership sold nearly 1000 new Chevrolets between 2005 and 2008.

I also understand that LaBelle Chevrolet has never received a written warning from GM on policy, that the dealership has met all sales requirements, that it has consistently met or exceeded standards in Customer Satisfaction Information scores, and that it exceeds Dealer Standard Working Capital by 200 percent.

Despite inquiries to GM from Mr. LaBelle, he has not received a specific explanation as to why his dealership was given a wind-down agreement. The closure is obviously a serious issue for the dealership, but it is also a serious issue for the surrounding community, and I urge you to reconsider the decision.

With respect and appreciation, and I thank you for considering this request.

Sincerely,

Ted Kennedy

Edward M. Kennedy

Appendix B

LEE IACOCCA & ASSOCIATES

August 11, 2009

To Whom It May Concern:

During all these months of the economic downturn and in particular the crisis within the American Automotive Industry I've remained uncharacteristically quiet. The daughter and friend of a family of east coast dealerships have kept me abreast of the situation concerning dealership closings. In her most recent communication, she stated she'd be going before congress one more time to plead the case of dealer closings. She seems to believe words from me could alter what is already very much in motion.

During my 50+ years in Detroit I supported dealers and was proud to be considered a friend. I've been advised a broad brush was used when deciding which dealerships were no longer viable. And, since I am not privy to the criteria used, it's nearly impossible to comment or chastise those that made the cuts.

However, from my experience dealers are very much the backbone to communities across the country. They employ people, sell cars, participate in their local service organizations and, are involved in a host of intangible activities that enhance all citizens. When it came time to raise money to renovate The Statue of Liberty and Ellis Island, dealerships did more than their share. Just recently diabetes research was greatly assisted by the family of Chrysler dealers. As a group they continually step up to the plate when asked. So, I am unaware of the dealers costing manufacturers money.

It is my hope that Congress and anyone else currently in charge will look very closely prior to altering for good what is the fabric of America.

Respectfully,

Lee Iacocca

LI/ns

190 NORTH CANON DRIVE, SUITE 306
BEVERLY HILLS, CALIFORNIA 90210
PHONE: (310) 247-1352 FAX: (310) 247-8206
LAI@IACOCCAASSOCIATES.COM

Appendix C

Facts the Auto Task Force Probably Didn't Consider

Source: NADA DATA from Auto Exec - May 2008, Chrysler Dealer Closure List, GM Dealer Closing - Wash Post

* Includes Estimated 2000 Domestic/Import Duals Dealers (U.S.) - Source: Paul Taylor NADA

STATE	TOTAL New Car Dealerships	Exclusive Import Dealerships	Exclusive Domestic and Domestic Import Duals *	Chrysler Closures	GM Announced Closures	GM Proposed Closures	TOTAL Closures	Remaining Exclusive Domestic and Domestic Import Duals *	Percent Reduction D3	TOTAL Dealership Employment	Estimated Job Loss From Chrysler and GM Dealer Closures
Arkansas	267	74	193	8	17	16	41	152	21.5%	8,811	1,366
Indiana	521	132	389	25	48	46	119	270	30.7%	21,882	5,012
Iowa	369	77	292	22	46	44	112	180	38.5%	12,177	3,709
Kansas	258	69	189	17	29	28	74	115	39.1%	10,062	2,886
Michigan	759	158	601	39	58	56	153	448	25.5%	36,432	7,343
Minnesota	438	101	337	18	39	38	95	242	28.1%	19,710	4,259
Missouri	494	123	371	27	14	14	55	316	14.7%	21,736	2,399
Montana	132	40	92	4	16	15	35	57	38.5%	4,224	1,134
Nebraska	213	45	168	8	21	20	49	119	29.3%	6,603	1,527
North Dakota	96	18	78	8	6	6	20	58	25.4%	3,168	653
Ohio	958	296	662	47	79	76	202	460	30.6%	41,194	8,697
Oklahoma	299	78	221	12	17	16	45	176	20.5%	20,033	3,042
South Dakota	117	19	98	7	16	15	38	60	39.2%	3,510	1,153
West Virginia	169	50	119	17	25	24	66	53	55.6%	6,253	2,447
Wisconsin	597	129	468	18	50	48	116	352	24.8%	21,492	4,185
Wyoming	70	21	49	5	6	6	17	32	34.3%	2,450	588
73.7 - 86.1 % D3 UIO	**5,757**	**1,430**	**4,327**	**282**	**487**	**470**	**1,239**	**3,088**	**28.6%**	**239,737**	**50,401**
Alabama	345	128	217	12	33	32	77	140	35.4%	16,560	3,689
Alaska	38	16	22		0	0	0	22	0.0%	2,280	0
Idaho	123	44	79	3	8	8	19	60	23.7%	5,781	880
Illinois	934	302	632	44	66	64	174	458	27.5%	42,964	7,990
Kentucky	298	109	189	9	23	22	54	135	28.7%	13,112	2,385
Louisiana	337	118	219	16	10	10	36	183	16.3%	18,198	1,925
Maine	144	55	89	4	14	14	32	57	35.4%	5,328	1,166
Mississippi	242	92	150	6	38	37	81	69	53.8%	9,438	3,146
New Mexico	140	57	83	3	10	10	23	60	27.3%	7,420	1,201
Pennsylvania	1,161	404	757	54	90	87	231	526	30.5%	51,084	10,158
South Carolina	326	136	190	11	24	23	58	132	30.6%	14,996	2,676
Tennessee	420	162	258	14	30	29	73	185	28.3%	22,260	3,867
Texas	1,346	490	856	51	55	53	159	697	18.6%	87,490	10,341
64.6 - 73.7% D3 UIO	**5,854**	**2,113**	**3,741**	**227**	**401**	**387**	**1,015**	**2,726**	**27.1%**	**296,911**	**49,424**
Arizona	256	153	103	5	11	11	27	76	25.8%	29,184	3,034
Colorado	284	131	153	13	15	14	42	111	27.8%	17,040	2,549
Delaware	65	32	33	3	2	2	7	26	21.0%	4,030	430
Florida	948	484	464	33	35	34	102	362	21.9%	76,788	8,244
Georgia	603	242	361	13	24	23	60	301	16.7%	33,768	3,369
Nevada	118	59	59	5	3	3	11	48	18.5%	10,974	1,013
New Hampshire	169	78	91	6	6	6	18	73	19.6%	7,098	747
New York	1,112	464	648	28	60	58	146	502	22.5%	48,928	6,420
North Carolina	692	272	420	14	36	35	85	335	20.2%	32,524	3,983
Oregon	274	129	145	9	21	20	50	95	34.7%	13,974	2,564
Utah	153	60	93	10	6	6	22	71	23.4%	9,333	1,329
Vermont	97	36	61	2	8	8	18	43	29.1%	2,813	514
Virginia	551	234	317	25	26	25	76	241	24.0%	33,060	4,566
55.1 - 64.5% D3 UIO	**5,322**	**2,374**	**2,948**	**166**	**253**	**244**	**663**	**2,285**	**22.5%**	**319,514**	**38,763**
California	1,594	877	717	32	65	63	160	557	22.3%	133,896	13,418
Connecticut	320	169	151	7	11	11	29	122	19.0%	14,400	1,288
DC	2	2	0	0	0	0	0	0		64	0
Hawaii	66	36	30	1	2	2	5	25	16.4%	5,082	380
Maryland	358	190	168	17	21	20	58	110	34.7%	23,986	3,904
Massachusetts	478	216	262	12	29	28	69	193	26.3%	23,422	3,381
New Jersey	574	296	278	29	33	32	94	184	33.8%	32,144	5,256
Rhode Island	63	41	22	1	3	3	7	15	31.3%	3,339	365
Washington	383	191	192	15	18	17	50	142	26.2%	23,363	3,073
40.2 - 55.1% D3 UIO	**3,838**	**2,018**	**1,820**	**114**	**182**	**176**	**472**	**1,348**	**25.9%**	**259,696**	**31,064**
Total	**20,771**	**7,935**	**12,836**	**789**	**1,323**	**1,277**	**3,389**	**9,447**	**26.4%**	**1,115,858**	**169,652**

*** There are 2,000 import franchises dualed with domestic brands so the total import count is actually 9,935**

Appendix D

January 25, 2010

Subject: Letter to President Obama

Dear President Obama,

We are writing this letter to address an American tragedy that we are pleading with you to read and help with.

You commented last week that you felt you were out of touch with the American people. We applaud your realization and hope you can understand what truthfully happened to real businesses in America by reading our letter.

We are the profitable car dealers that were disenfranchised when the car czar was misinformed that the dealers cost Chrysler money. It has been stated and proven since by Jim Press and others that the dealers pay for everything and do not cost the corporations anything... We are their ONLY customers! This is why Chrysler sales have dropped dramatically in the past six months.

President Obama, please do not abandon us! No one has considered the lives of these families, their employees, customers and the trickle down to their communities. When these dealerships were closed, the mortgages, taxes, contracts on equipment, utilities, LIFO, storage, all still haave to be paid and without any income, most of these dealers will go bankrupt. It costs hundreds of thousands of dollars to close these buildings down and they are zoned for dealerships, so most of the properties cannot be sold.

Because of a three-week bankruptcy, these hard working Americans' lives are ruined. We have been successful business owners for decades and now we have nothing! Our futures are gone, and we are still trying to figure out how to survive.

We appreciate the bill you signed providing an arbitration process to get our franchises back, but most of them have been GIVEN to the dealer down the street. Obviously, in those cases, the arbitration process will be a moot subject. Some of the dealers that have received these dealerships are now trying to sell them to make a profit on our losses.

Plus, it will cost thousands of dollars to litigate this, and the lawyers will all benefit, but we are all very strapped. We are not the underachievers that we were portrayed to be during the bankruptcy, but we don't want this to be just a moral victory.

We are appealing to you to provide fair compensation to these innocent, hard working citizens. Billions of dollars were given to these corporations to stay in business, yet everything was taken from the dealers. Before the bankruptcy, there was a franchise law, so that something like this could never happen. To take personal property from a private citizen and give it to someone else is immoral and also breaks the Fifth Amendment.

We are hoping we can get this letter to you, so you can personally help our desperate situation. We were never offered buyouts, bail-outs and we have no pensions. We have all proudly invested our savings into these businesses, only to lose it all by these catastrophic decisions made without any due diligence. These decisions are the cause of the double digit unemployment, many bankruptcies and several suicides.

We all admire and respect the help you are trying to distribute throughout the world and only hope you will realize the depth of this crisis as well to your beloved American citizens.

We hope to hear from you soon before all is lost.

Respectfully,

Disenfranchised Detroit auto dealers

Appendix E

Cosponsors of Senate Bill S1304

Sen Grassley, Chuck [IA] (introduced 6/18/2009)
Sen Baucus, Max [MT] - 7/21/2009
Sen Begich, Mark [AK] - 7/7/2009
Sen Bennett, Robert F. [UT] - 7/7/2009
Sen Bond, Christopher S. [MO] - 12/4/2009
Sen Brown, Sherrod [OH] - 9/8/2009
Sen Brownback, Sam [KS] - 6/23/2009
Sen Bunning, Jim [KY] - 10/26/2009
Sen Burr, Richard [NC] - 7/9/2009
Sen Byrd, Robert C. [WV] - 12/8/2009
Sen Cardin, Benjamin L. [MD] - 6/24/2009
Sen Casey, Robert P., Jr. [PA] - 7/21/2009
Sen Chambliss, Saxby [GA] - 7/6/2009
Sen Cochran, Thad [MS] - 9/25/2009
Sen Collins, Susan M. [ME] - 7/31/2009
Sen Crapo, Mike [ID] - 7/14/2009
Sen Dodd, Christopher J. [CT] - 8/6/2009
Sen Dorgan, Byron L. [ND] - 7/31/2009
Sen Feingold, Russell D. [WI] - 7/9/2009
Sen Franken, Al [MN] - 9/30/2009
Sen Harkin, Tom [IA] - 7/6/2009
Sen Hatch, Orrin G. [UT] - 7/27/2009
Sen Inhofe, James M. [OK] - 7/15/2009
Sen Isakson, Johnny [GA] - 6/25/2009
Sen Johanns, Mike [NE] - 7/20/2009
Sen Johnson, Tim [SD] - 9/17/2009
Sen Kennedy, Edward M. [MA] - 6/24/2009
Sen Kerry, John F. [MA] - 6/23/2009
Sen Kirk, Paul Grattan, Jr. [MA] - 10/15/2009
Sen Klobuchar, Amy [MN] - 7/6/2009
Sen Kohl, Herb [WI] - 7/13/2009
Sen Landrieu, Mary L. [LA] - 7/13/2009
Sen Lincoln, Blanche L. [AR] - 7/14/2009
Sen Martinez, Mel [FL] - 7/6/2009
Sen Mikulski, Barbara A. [MD] - 6/25/2009
Sen Nelson, Bill [FL] - 7/6/2009
Sen Nelson, E. Benjamin [NE] - 9/24/2009
Sen Reed, Jack [RI] - 9/10/2009
Sen Risch, James E. [ID] - 7/14/2009
Sen Roberts, Pat [KS] - 6/25/2009
Sen Rockefeller, John D., IV [WV] - 7/23/2009
Sen Snowe, Olympia J. [ME] - 7/14/2009
Sen Specter, Arlen [PA] - 7/10/2009
Sen Tester, Jon [MT] - 7/16/2009
Sen Udall, Mark [CO] - 7/9/2009
Sen Vitter, David [LA] - 12/2/2009
Sen Whitehouse, Sheldon [RI] - 9/10/2009
Sen Wicker, Roger F. [MS] - 10/29/2009
Sen Wyden, Ron [OR] - 9/17/2009

Cosponsors of House Bill H.R. 2743

Rep Maffei, Daniel B. [NY-25] (introduced 6/8/2009)
Rep Ackerman, Gary L. [NY-5] - 6/11/2009
Rep Aderholt, Robert B. [AL-4] - 6/26/2009
Rep Adler, John H. [NJ-3] - 6/16/2009
Rep Akin, W. Todd [MO-2] - 6/26/2009
Rep Alexander, Rodney [LA-5] - 6/15/2009
Rep Andrews, Robert E. [NJ-1] - 6/18/2009
Rep Arcuri, Michael A. [NY-24] - 6/23/2009
Rep Austria, Steve [OH-7] - 6/23/2009
Rep Baca, Joe [CA-43] - 6/23/2009
Rep Bachmann, Michele [MN-6] - 6/10/2009
Rep Baldwin, Tammy [WI-2] - 7/10/2009
Rep Barrow, John [GA-12] - 6/11/2009
Rep Bartlett, Roscoe G. [MD-6] - 6/8/2009
Rep Barton, Joe [TX-6] - 7/10/2009
Rep Berkley, Shelley [NV-1] - 9/23/2009
Rep Berry, Marion [AR-1] - 6/11/2009
Rep Bilirakis, Gus M. [FL-9] - 7/9/2009
Rep Bishop, Rob [UT-1] - 6/10/2009
Rep Bishop, Sanford D., Jr. [GA-2] - 6/10/2009
Rep Bishop, Timothy H. [NY-1] - 6/9/2009
Rep Blackburn, Marsha [TN-7] - 7/16/2009
Rep Blumenauer, Earl [OR-3] - 6/12/2009
Rep Boccieri, John A. [OH-16] - 6/16/2009
Rep Boehner, John A. [OH-8] - 7/22/2009
Rep Boozman, John [AR-3] - 6/15/2009
Rep Boren, Dan [OK-2] - 7/8/2009
Rep Boswell, Leonard L. [IA-3] - 6/9/2009
Rep Boucher, Rick [VA-9] - 7/16/2009
Rep Brady, Kevin [TX-8] - 9/29/2009
Rep Brady, Robert A. [PA-1] - 7/13/2009
Rep Braley, Bruce L. [IA-1] - 6/9/2009
Rep Broun, Paul C. [GA-10] - 6/12/2009
Rep Brown, Corrine [FL-3] - 6/9/2009
Rep Brown-Waite, Ginny [FL-5] - 7/8/2009
Rep Burton, Dan [IN-5] - 6/11/2009
Rep Butterfield, G. K. [NC-1] - 6/11/2009
Rep Buyer, Steve [IN-4] - 7/8/2009
Rep Calvert, Ken [CA-44] - 6/26/2009
Rep Camp, Dave [MI-4] - 9/16/2009
Rep Campbell, John [CA-48] - 6/10/2009
Rep Cao, Anh "Joseph" [LA-2] - 6/10/2009
Rep Capito, Shelley Moore [WV-2] - 6/12/2009
Rep Capuano, Michael E. [MA-8] - 9/29/2009
Rep Cardoza, Dennis A. [CA-18] - 7/16/2009
Rep Carney, Christopher P. [PA-10] - 6/11/2009
Rep Carson, Andre [IN-7] - 6/9/2009
Rep Carter, John R. [TX-31] - 7/16/2009
Rep Cassidy, Bill [LA-6] - 7/8/2009
Rep Chaffetz, Jason [UT-3] - 7/31/2009
Rep Chandler, Ben [KY-6] - 6/9/2009
Rep Clay, Wm. Lacy [MO-1] - 6/9/2009
Rep Coble, Howard [NC-6] - 6/19/2009
Rep Coffman, Mike [CO-6] - 6/23/2009
Rep Cohen, Steve [TN-9] - 7/16/2009
Rep Conaway, K. Michael [TX-11] - 6/26/2009
Rep Connolly, Gerald E. "Gerry" [VA-11] - 6/10/2009
Rep Conyers, John, Jr. [MI-14] - 10/14/2009
Rep Costa, Jim [CA-20] - 6/11/2009
Rep Costello, Jerry F. [IL-12] - 6/10/2009
Rep Courtney, Joe [CT-2] - 6/16/2009
Rep Crenshaw, Ander [FL-4] - 6/26/2009
Rep Cuellar, Henry [TX-28] - 6/10/2009
Rep Culberson, John Abney [TX-7] - 6/23/2009
Rep Cummings, Elijah E. [MD-7] - 7/16/2009
Rep Dahlkemper, Kathleen A. [PA-3] - 7/22/2009
Rep Davis, Artur [AL-7] - 6/8/2009
Rep Davis, Geoff [KY-4] - 6/10/2009
Rep Davis, Lincoln [TN-4] - 6/15/2009
Rep Deal, Nathan [GA-9] - 6/10/2009
Rep DeFazio, Peter A. [OR-4] - 6/8/2009
Rep DeGette, Diana [CO-1] - 7/16/2009
Rep Delahunt, Bill [MA-10] - 6/18/2009
Rep DeLauro, Rosa L. [CT-3] - 6/16/2009
Rep Dent, Charles W. [PA-15] - 7/22/2009
Rep Diaz-Balart, Lincoln [FL-21] - 6/9/2009
Rep Diaz-Balart, Mario [FL-25] - 6/15/2009
Rep Doyle, Michael F. [PA-14] - 6/9/2009
Rep Driehaus, Steve [OH-1] - 6/11/2009
Rep Edwards, Donna F. [MD-4] - 7/10/2009
Rep Ehlers, Vernon J. [MI-3] - 6/19/2009
Rep Ellison, Keith [MN-5] - 6/15/2009
Rep Etheridge, Bob [NC-2] - 6/23/2009
Rep Farr, Sam [CA-17] - 6/11/2009
Rep Forbes, J. Randy [VA-4] - 7/9/2009
Rep Fortenberry, Jeff [NE-1] - 6/16/2009
Rep Foster, Bill [IL-14] - 6/10/2009
Rep Frank, Barney [MA-4] - 6/9/2009
Rep Frelinghuysen, Rodney P. [NJ-11] - 6/10/2009
Rep Fudge, Marcia L. [OH-11] - 6/9/2009
Rep Garrett, Scott [NJ-5] - 7/9/2009
Rep Gerlach, Jim [PA-6] - 6/10/2009
Rep Giffords, Gabrielle [AZ-8] - 6/10/2009
Rep Gingrey, Phil [GA-11] - 6/19/2009
Rep Gohmert, Louie [TX-1] - 6/15/2009
Rep Goodlatte, Bob [VA-6] - 6/18/2009
Rep Gordon, Bart [TN-6] - 6/24/2009
Rep Grayson, Alan [FL-8] - 6/11/2009
Rep Green, Al [TX-9] - 7/8/2009
Rep Green, Gene [TX-29] - 6/9/2009
Rep Griffith, Parker [AL-5] - 6/23/2009
Rep Guthrie, Brett [KY-2] - 7/8/2009
Rep Hall, John J. [NY-19] - 6/8/2009
Rep Hall, Ralph M. [TX-4] - 7/22/2009
Rep Halvorson, Deborah L. [IL-11] - 6/12/2009
Rep Hare, Phil [IL-17] - 6/9/2009
Rep Harper, Gregg [MS-3] - 7/9/2009
Rep Hastings, Alcee L. [FL-23] - 6/15/2009
Rep Heinrich, Martin [NM-1] - 6/8/2009
Rep Herseth Sandlin, Stephanie [SD] - 6/23/2009
Rep Hill, Baron P. [IN-9] - 6/26/2009
Rep Hinchey, Maurice D. [NY-22] - 6/10/2009
Rep Hinojosa, Ruben [TX-15] - 6/11/2009
Rep Hodes, Paul W. [NH-2] - 6/10/2009
Rep Hoekstra, Peter [MI-2] - 6/16/2009
Rep Holden, Tim [PA-17] - 6/9/2009
Rep Holt, Rush D. [NJ-12] - 6/26/2009
Rep Honda, Michael M. [CA-15] - 6/11/2009
Rep Hoyer, Steny H. [MD-5] - 6/8/2009
Rep Hunter, Duncan D. [CA-52] - 6/15/2009
Rep Jackson, Jesse L., Jr. [IL-2] - 6/10/2009
Rep Jackson-Lee, Sheila [TX-18] - 6/11/2009
Rep Jenkins, Lynn [KS-2] - 6/10/2009
Rep Johnson, Henry C. "Hank," Jr. [GA-4] - 6/15/2009
Rep Johnson, Sam [TX-3] - 7/8/2009
Rep Johnson, Timothy V. [IL-15] - 7/31/2009
Rep Jones, Walter B., Jr. [NC-3] - 6/10/2009
Rep Jordan, Jim [OH-4] - 6/18/2009
Rep Kagen, Steve [WI-8] - 6/16/2009
Rep Kanjorski, Paul E. [PA-11] - 6/10/2009
Rep Kaptur, Marcy [OH-9] - 6/18/2009
Rep Kennedy, Patrick J. [RI-1] - 7/13/2009
Rep Kilpatrick, Carolyn C. [MI-13] - 9/21/2009
Rep Kilroy, Mary Jo [OH-15] - 6/10/2009
Rep Kind, Ron [WI-3] - 7/8/2009
Rep King, Steve [IA-5] - 6/11/2009
Rep Kingston, Jack [GA-1] - 6/16/2009
Rep Kirk, Mark Steven [IL-10] - 7/28/2009
Rep Kissell, Larry [NC-8] - 6/12/2009
Rep Klein, Ron [FL-22] - 7/9/2009
Rep Kline, John [MN-2] - 6/18/2009
Rep Kosmas, Suzanne M. [FL-24] - 6/9/2009
Rep Kratovil, Frank, Jr. [MD-1] - 6/8/2009
Rep Lamborn, Doug [CO-5] - 6/12/2009
Rep Lance, Leonard [NJ-7] - 7/10/2009
Rep Langevin, James R. [RI-2] - 6/16/2009
Rep Larsen, Rick [WA-2] - 6/10/2009
Rep Larson, John B. [CT-1] - 6/12/2009
Rep Latham, Tom [IA-4] - 6/11/2009
Rep Latta, Robert E. [OH-5] - 6/18/2009
Rep Lewis, Jerry [CA-41] - 10/22/2009
Rep Lewis, John [GA-5] - 7/8/2009
Rep Linder, John [GA-7] - 6/18/2009
Rep Lipinski, Daniel [IL-3] - 7/13/2009
Rep LoBiondo, Frank A. [NJ-2] - 7/8/2009
Rep Loebsack, David [IA-2] - 6/9/2009
Rep Lucas, Frank D. [OK-3] - 6/18/2009
Rep Luetkemeyer, Blaine [MO-9] - 7/8/2009
Rep Lujan, Ben Ray [NM-3] - 6/12/2009
Rep Lummis, Cynthia M. [WY] - 6/26/2009
Rep Maloney, Carolyn B. [NY-14] - 6/9/2009
Rep Manzullo, Donald A. [IL-16] - 6/8/2009
Rep Markey, Betsy [CO-4] - 7/13/2009
Rep Massa, Eric J. J. [NY-29] - 6/9/2009
Rep Matheson, Jim [UT-2] - 6/19/2009
Rep McCollum, Betty [MN-4] - 6/9/2009
Rep McCotter, Thaddeus G. [MI-11] - 6/9/2009
Rep McGovern, James P. [MA-3] - 6/18/2009

Rep McIntyre, Mike [NC-7] - 7/8/2009
Rep McMahon, Michael E. [NY-13] - 6/8/2009
Rep McMorris Rodgers, Cathy [WA-5] - 7/28/2009
Rep McNerney, Jerry [CA-11] - 10/14/2009
Rep Meek, Kendrick B. [FL-17] - 6/16/2009
Rep Melancon, Charlie [LA-3] - 6/26/2009
Rep Mica, John L. [FL-7] - 7/10/2009
Rep Michaud, Michael H. [ME-2] - 6/9/2009
Rep Miller, Brad [NC-13] - 7/28/2009
Rep Miller, Candice S. [MI-10] - 7/16/2009
Rep Miller, Gary G. [CA-42] - 6/26/2009
Rep Miller, Jeff [FL-1] - 6/23/2009
Rep Minnick, Walter [ID-1] - 10/14/2009
Rep Mollohan, Alan B. [WV-1] - 7/28/2009
Rep Moore, Gwen [WI-4] - 6/12/2009
Rep Moran, James P. [VA-8] - 7/16/2009
Rep Moran, Jerry [KS-1] - 6/10/2009
Rep Murphy, Christopher S. [CT-5] - 6/12/2009
Rep Murphy, Patrick J. [PA-8] - 6/9/2009
Rep Murphy, Tim [PA-18] - 6/23/2009
Rep Murtha, John P. [PA-12] - 6/19/2009
Rep Napolitano, Grace F. [CA-38] - 6/10/2009
Rep Neal, Richard E. [MA-2] - 12/8/2009
Rep Nye, Glenn C. [VA-2] - 7/8/2009
Rep Oberstar, James L. [MN-8] - 10/22/2009
Rep Olson, Pete [TX-22] - 6/19/2009
Rep Ortiz, Solomon P. [TX-27] - 6/10/2009
Rep Pallone, Frank, Jr. [NJ-6] - 6/15/2009
Rep Pascrell, Bill, Jr. [NJ-8] - 6/12/2009
Rep Pastor, Ed [AZ-4] - 7/8/2009
Rep Paul, Ron [TX-14] - 6/15/2009
Rep Paulsen, Erik [MN-3] - 6/8/2009
Rep Payne, Donald M. [NJ-10] - 7/9/2009
Rep Perlmutter, Ed [CO-7] - 6/23/2009
Rep Perriello, Thomas S.P. [VA-5] - 6/10/2009
Rep Peterson, Collin C. [MN-7] - 6/26/2009
Rep Petri, Thomas E. [WI-6] - 7/9/2009
Rep Pierluisi, Pedro R. [PR] - 6/26/2009
Rep Pingree, Chellie [ME-1] - 6/18/2009
Rep Pitts, Joseph R. [PA-16] - 7/22/2009
Rep Platts, Todd Russell [PA-19] - 6/24/2009
Rep Poe, Ted [TX-2] - 6/11/2009
Rep Polis, Jared [CO-2] - 7/16/2009
Rep Pomeroy, Earl [ND] - 6/15/2009
Rep Posey, Bill [FL-15] - 6/8/2009
Rep Price, David E. [NC-4] - 7/28/2009
Rep Putnam, Adam H. [FL-12] - 7/8/2009
Rep Radanovich, George [CA-19] - 7/9/2009
Rep Rahall, Nick J., II [WV-3] - 6/19/2009
Rep Rehberg, Denny [MT] - 6/11/2009
Rep Reichert, David G. [WA-8] - 12/8/2009
Rep Roe, David P. [TN-1] - 6/12/2009
Rep Rogers, Harold [KY-5] - 6/19/2009
Rep Rogers, Mike D. [AL-3] - 6/10/2009
Rep Rogers, Mike J. [MI-8] - 10/8/2009
Rep Rooney, Thomas J. [FL-16] - 7/8/2009
Rep Ros-Lehtinen, Ileana [FL-18] - 6/9/2009
Rep Roskam, Peter J. [IL-6] - 7/16/2009
Rep Ross, Mike [AR-4] - 6/15/2009
Rep Rothman, Steven R. [NJ-9] - 6/10/2009
Rep Royce, Edward R. [CA-40] - 6/15/2009
Rep Ruppersberger, C. A. Dutch [MD-2] - 6/18/2009
Rep Ryan, Tim [OH-17] - 6/12/2009
Rep Salazar, John T. [CO-3] - 7/28/2009
Rep Sanchez, Linda T. [CA-39] - 6/23/2009
Rep Sanchez, Loretta [CA-47] - 6/16/2009
Rep Sarbanes, John P. [MD-3] - 6/24/2009
Rep Schakowsky, Janice D. [IL-9] - 7/16/2009
Rep Schiff, Adam B. [CA-29] - 7/10/2009
Rep Schmidt, Jean [OH-2] - 6/15/2009
Rep Schock, Aaron [IL-18] - 6/12/2009
Rep Schrader, Kurt [OR-5] - 6/15/2009
Rep Schwartz, Allyson Y. [PA-13] - 7/10/2009
Rep Scott, David [GA-13] - 6/11/2009
Rep Scott, Robert C. "Bobby" [VA-3] - 6/9/2009
Rep Sestak, Joe [PA-7] - 6/12/2009
Rep Shadegg, John B. [AZ-3] - 7/8/2009
Rep Shea-Porter, Carol [NH-1] - 6/8/2009
Rep Shimkus, John [IL-19] - 6/11/2009
Rep Shuler, Heath [NC-11] - 6/11/2009
Rep Simpson, Michael K. [ID-2] - 6/23/2009
Rep Sires, Albio [NJ-13] - 6/15/2009
Rep Smith, Adam [WA-9] - 6/16/2009
Rep Smith, Adrian [NE-3] - 6/10/2009
Rep Smith, Christopher H. [NJ-4] - 6/23/2009
Rep Snyder, Vic [AR-2] - 7/16/2009
Rep Space, Zachary T. [OH-18] - 6/10/2009
Rep Speier, Jackie [CA-12] - 6/12/2009
Rep Spratt, John M., Jr. [SC-5] - 6/26/2009
Rep Stearns, Cliff [FL-6] - 6/24/2009
Rep Stupak, Bart [MI-1] - 10/22/2009
Rep Sutton, Betty [OH-13] - 6/8/2009
Rep Teague, Harry [NM-2] - 6/15/2009
Rep Terry, Lee [NE-2] - 6/18/2009
Rep Thompson, Bennie G. [MS-2] - 6/15/2009
Rep Thompson, Glenn [PA-5] - 7/10/2009
Rep Thompson, Mike [CA-1] - 7/16/2009
Rep Tiahrt, Todd [KS-4] - 6/16/2009
Rep Tiberi, Patrick J. [OH-12] - 6/11/2009
Rep Tierney, John F. [MA-6] - 7/16/2009
Rep Titus, Dina [NV-3] - 9/23/2009
Rep Tonko, Paul [NY-21] - 6/15/2009
Rep Turner, Michael R. [OH-3] - 6/18/2009
Rep Van Hollen, Chris [MD-8] - 6/8/2009
Rep Visclosky, Peter J. [IN-1] - 6/18/2009
Rep Walz, Timothy J. [MN-1] - 7/16/2009
Rep Wamp, Zach [TN-3] - 7/8/2009
Rep Wasserman Schultz, Debbie [FL-20] - 6/11/2009
Rep Waters, Maxine [CA-35] - 6/12/2009
Rep Weiner, Anthony D. [NY-9] - 6/10/2009
Rep Welch, Peter [VT] - 6/9/2009
Rep Westmoreland, Lynn A. [GA-3] - 6/16/2009
Rep Wilson, Charles A. [OH-6] - 6/9/2009
Rep Wilson, Joe [SC-2] - 6/23/2009
Rep Wittman, Robert J. [VA-1] - 6/10/2009
Rep Wolf, Frank R. [VA-10] - 7/8/2009
Rep Wu, David [OR-1] - 6/16/2009
Rep Young, C.W. Bill [FL-10] - 6/15/2009
Rep Young, Don [AK] - 7/9/2009

Glossary

The following is a guide to industry-specific terms and concepts used in this book. Please note the terms or acronyms might be used differently in another industry.

auto task force: The Obama administration–appointed group that formed in mid-February of 2009 to restructure the Detroit auto industry, specifically Chrysler and GM. The two automakers had applied for massive federal funds to keep operating during the President Bush and President Obama administrations.

blue sky: The term refers to the value over and above the hard assets that a dealer pays in order to purchase a business from another dealer, or investments made. Blue sky is also sometimes referred to as "goodwill." For example, if an individual works for twenty-five years to build up a business and then sells it, the buyer pays for all his or her previous hard work and investments. It's not unlike selling a totally renovated home.

CAR: The Center for Automotive Research is an automotive think tank in Ann Arbor, Michigan, that specializes in research, conferences, and a staff of auto-related analysts and experts.

CSI: Customer satisfaction index is an industry rating of the customer experience in a dealership in which he or she buys and services a vehicle. These scores are used by manufacturers as part of determining a successful dealership. Surveys are sent by the automaker and returned to them. CSI surveys are a way to measure satisfaction with the vehicle or manufacturer and the dealership. They may not actually reflect the customer experience at the dealership.

DART: An acronym for "dealer analysis and reporting tool." This is the General Motors dealer performance calculation, based on a scoring system GM uses that looks at several criteria: profitability, minimum sales responsibility achievement, working capital, and customer satisfaction.

Detroit Two: In the automotive world, the term commonly refers to Chrysler and GM.

Detroit Three: Chrysler, GM, and Ford Motor Company.

DPS: Dealer performance summary: A DPS score is calculated using a combination of sales performance, customer-satisfaction scoring, working capital standard, and dealership profitability. Dealers were able to access the DPS calculations through the dealer website.

five-star dealer: The classification refers to Chrysler's internal award to their best dealers. It measures a record of sales, service, and performance.

floor planning: A system of financing that permits dealers to borrow money to buy goods, which become the security for the loan that is repaid when the merchandise is sold.

Letter of Intent: Or LOI, an agreement letter that Chrysler and General Motors required cancelled dealers to sign in order to return to the dealership network, even if they won in arbitration hearings. Dealers and their lawyers believed the terms were often onerous and financially prohibitive.

MSR: Minimum sales responsibility is set at 100 across the board. Many factors go into calculating this score, including vehicle registrations and state averages, to assure the manufacturer is getting its fair share of the market.

SAAR: An acronym for "seasonally adjusted annual sales rate." Auto manufacturers report monthly, quarterly, and annual sales rates, showing the actual sales in a given period and comparisons to earlier applicable periods.

SIGTARP: The SIGTARP (Special Inspector General Troubled Asset Relief Program) office was created and supported by President George Bush and President Barack Obama to manage and keep a checkpoint on the appropriate use of TARP funds. Through TARP, American taxpayers funded hundreds of billions of dollars in programs to stabilize the financial system and promote US economic recovery. The SIGTARP office was responsible for assuring that those managing and using TARP funds acted appropriately, consistent with the law and in the best interests of the country.

After a yearlong study, the SIGTARP office issued a report in July 2010 that determined that the shutdown of auto dealers in 2009 was based on insufficient auto task force consideration and analysis of the cost of thousands of lost dealership jobs and the actual benefit to the companies' viability.

throughput: An automaker term that members of the auto task force and automakers attempted to assign to the retail experience of a customer to evaluate their sales performance. Throughput refers to the total annual sales of vehicles per dealership—one measure of how dealers do in overall performance.

Major Organizational Acronyms

AIADA: American International Automobile Dealers Association

ATAE: Automotive Trade Association Executives

CRDR: Committee to Restore Dealer Rights

GMMDA: General Motors Minority Dealers Association

NADA: National Automobile Dealers Association

NAMAD: National Association of Minority Automobile Dealers

NOTE: There are various state dealer trade associations identified with their proper names: CADA, or California Automobile Dealers Association; MADA, Maryland Automobile Dealers Association; etc. They operate independently of the national trade group, NADA.

About the Authors

Tamara Darvish helps operate her family's thirty-four US franchises as part of the mega-dealer DARCARS Automotive Group, the nation's sixteenth-largest auto group, according to auto journals. She has been active in the auto industry for twenty-seven years. She has earned numerous industry awards.

Lillie Guyer is a US journalist who has specialized in automotive, business, and technology reporting for more than twenty-five years. She has covered all the automotive giants.

Bibliography/Index

(including references to articles and publications cited)

Page numbers in **bold** indicate photos.

A

AAA (American Arbitration Association), 305, 321, 342, 354, 356
ABC News, 9, 10, 323
Aberdeen SD, 54–55
Abrams, Ben, 96, 98, 273
Adamcheck, Dan, 278
AFSA, 382
AIADA (American International Automobile Dealers Association), 45, 93, 396
AIFP (automotive industry financing program), 19
Akerson, Dan, 331–332, 333
Alfa Romeo, 318
Allely, Craig, 255, 351, 380
Ally Bank, 114, 279
Altavilla, Alfredo, 209
American Arbitration Association (AAA), 305, 321, 342, 354, 356
American Dream, 1–3, 6, 42, 111, 157, 163, 166, 176, 192, 316, 319–320, 323, 375
American International Automobile Dealers Association (AIADA), 45, 93, 396
American public
  automakers feeding myth to, 65
  and automakers' loans, 10
  automakers lying to, 197, 204
  and bailouts, 12, 38, 40
  on battle almost over after passage of dealer rights law, 341
  corporate spin machine and, 321
  and criteria for closures, 210
  GM trying to earn PR points with, 279
  and killing of the Main-Street car dealer, 5
  not seeing dealer issue on national television, 115
  paying scant attention to dealer problems, 135
  perception that dealers cost company money and were poor performers, 241
  perception that dealers must have done something horribly wrong, 92
  on understanding of auto industry, 269
Anderson Economic Group, 50
Ann Arbor MI, 136, 211, 394
Anoka MN, 3, 122, 369
anti-Chrysler sentiment, 53, 172, 185
anti-GM sentiment, 185
arbitration, 179, 306, 307, 341–343, 351, 352, 354, 356
Arent Fox, 95, 110, 271, 272, 283, 287, 307, 322
Aston Martin, 136
At the Crossroads: Middle America and the Battle to Save the Car Industry, 315

ATAE (Automobile Trade Association Executives), 57, 98, 208, 222, 238, 242, 283, 289, 396
"A-team," 65, 79, 89, 95, 100, 104, 107, 137, 204, 210, 227, 231, 235, 237, 240, 243-244, 248, 254, 271-272, 301, 320
Atoka OK, 109, 355
Attleboro MA, 56, 168, 269
Auburn Hills MI, 26, 75, 351, 369
auto company/industry restructuring, 16, 18- 20, 22, 29, 34, 137
auto dealers. *See also specific dealerships and dealers*
activist dealers, 247
appointments with Congress, 225, 266
arbitration opportunity for, 306
as automakers' customers, 65, 114, 186, 198, 317, 365, 390
automakers declaration of war on, 29
claims of being singled out for retribution, 170
closures as surreal, 325
closures not making sense, 52, 77, 140, 188, 198, 203, 211, 336
concern about culpability of corporate players who may have lied, 357
"continuing" dealers, 30, 91, 120, 132, 166, 178, 214, 215, 277, 352, 370
data on. *See* data
as David over Goliath, 322, 380
"dealer hit list," 44, 45, 58, 297, 333
economic-impact report of dealerships, 286
emotional stress of, related to closures, 187
emotions of, 184
employees, impact of closures on, 47, 164, 322
as entrepreneurs, 1, 13, 19, 139, 174, 197, 217, 249, 325, 375
feeling betrayed, 51–52, 55, 70, 131, 158, 163, 186, 195, 247, 259, 317
feeling outraged, 158, 160, 171, 195
as funders of community activities and charities, 182, 191
"go forwards," 30, 94, 277, 344, 352, 370
health risks of, related to closures, 112–113, 116, 174, 187, 351
as "hometown heroes," 121, 161, 166, 246–248, 251, 253, 321
identity theft of, 217
initial talks with GM and Chrysler, 242
lack of objective profitability study of terminated dealers, 293
lawsuits against automakers, 2, 218, 341, 356, 357, 358–359, 381
legal costs of, 64, 350, 352
letter to President Obama, 390
life-insurance policies of, 184
lobbyists for. *See* lobbyists
Main-Street dealers, demise of, 5, 113, 185, 197, 317, 338
minority auto dealers. *See* minority auto dealers
as missing voice on auto task force, 36
"move forwards," 30
myths about. *See* myths
number receiving notices from Chrysler, 49
overpowered by Chrysler in arbitration, 179
as part of solution, not problem, 109
percent cut, 29, 51, 52, 65, 69, 117, 131, 157, 159, 192, 193, 198, 269, 344, 369, 374
performance not the issue, 60–61, 125, 169, 202, 208, 248–249, 270, 278, 345, 346
performance of. *See* DPS (dealer performance summary)
pitted against other dealers, 163
as political campaign contributors, 223
powwow with automakers, task force, and Congress, 241

as product starved, 77, 180, 182, 278, 280, 316
projected job losses, 36
rally, 4, 75, 175, 194, 220, 226–227, 230–235, 269, 272–273, 291, 307
range of services at, 229
reactions to winning right to appeal in arbitration, 352
relationships with auto makers, 22–23
rights train, 66, 79, 121, 263, 302, 366, 384
seeing closure issue as train wreck, 93, 135, 197
seeing closures as vendettas, 5, 56, 167–168, 170, 299
settlements from automakers. *See* settlements with closed dealers
shrinking of US dealer base, 29
Steve LaBelle researches list of closed dealers, 276–277
survey of closed dealers, 204
survivor's shock, 252
as taxpayers and employers, 13, 35, 114, 177, 182–184, 198, 223
thinking closure notices a mistake, 58
victory for, 306
as vital to the economy, before 2009–2010 crash, 282
wanting to fight with legal action, 59, 62, 63, 64
YouTube videos of, 162
Auto Exec, 201
auto industry
downsizing, history of, 29
as major engine of economy, 11
reorganization of internal operations, history of, 30
restructuring of, 16, 18, 19, 20, 22, 34, 137
Auto Nation, 114
auto task force
and auto dealers, 18
on auto dealers' slimming down, 50
bad advice from, 320
consultants to, 39
and dealer cuts, 32
defined, 394
facts probably not considered by, 389
on fewer dealers equaling better performance, 34
Fitzgerald on, 64–65, 159
fixing the automotive industry as job of, 116
on GM's and Chrysler's dealer cuts, 51
initial work of, 16
lack of understanding of impact dealers had, 367
message to GM and Chrysler, 158
Obama announcement of, 11
overhaul job complete, 21
perceived agenda of, 99
splitting up ownership pie for GM and Chrysler, 26
taking credit for saving jobs, 117
time frame of, 17
and US Congress on restructuring decisions, 34
US Congress's bone to pick with, 99
watchdog's findings about, 336
automakers. *See also* Chrysler Group LLC; GM (General Motors); *specific automotive brands*
arbitration with closed dealers. *See* arbitration
assigning dealer placements to third parties, 5, 163, 178, 180, 186
claims of dealer costs to, 128, 241, 353
claims of significant savings with closures, 36, 126, 127, 128, 129, 137, 170, 287, 300, 337
on criteria for closures, 208–210, 242, 278, 299–300
familiar litany of, 241
hubris of, 297
lawsuits against, 2, 218, 341, 356–359, 381
legal costs of, 52, 299
Letter of Intent (LOI), 218, 280, 306, 313, 343, 352–355, 395
and negotiations with dealers, 239

and number of arbitration cases, 342
private jet PR disaster, 9, 10, 24, 93
reassigning dealers to take over closed stores, 285
as risk-taking leaders, 200
secret e-mails among executives, 345–346, 347
seeking non-legislative solution to dealer-closure problem, 135
stalling tactics of, 244
"Stop the Dealers at All Costs," 293
talk about buying out dealers, 54
views about dealer closures, 40
Automobile Dealers Fair Competition Act of 2011 (HR75), 378
Automobile Trade Association Executives (ATAE), 57, 98, 208, 222, 238, 242, 283, 289, 396
automotive bonds and bondholders, 27
automotive brands. *See specific brands*
Automotive Industry Financing Program (AIFP), 19, 37
Automotive News, 45, 68, 99, 109, 125, 126, 135, 214, 217, 218, 225, 249, 285, 289, 307, 309, 313, 337, 347, 357, 360–361, 366, 368, 369, 373
Automotive Press Association, 280, 367
AutoNation, 159

B

B. Bogdewic Chevrolet, 111
bailouts
and American public, 12, 38
of auto industry, 9–10, 16, 23, 25, 93, 109, 114, 193, 207–208, 211, 328
and dealers, 97, 326
specific to GM (General Motors), 23, 25
bankruptcy hearings, 50, 90, 91, 94, 184, 185, 250, 255, 270. *See also* Gonzalez, Arthur J.
bankruptcy law, 349
Barber, Chuck, 51
Barber, Fred, 51–54, 179–180
Barber, John, 51
Barber, Sam, 51
Barber Brothers Inc.'s Chrysler stores, 51
Barber's Chrysler, Dodge, and Jeep, 51
Barclays Capital, 39
Barlett, Roscoe, 119
Barofsky, Neil, 64, 203, 300, 335, 349, 360, 377–378
Bartlett, Roscoe, 31, 258, 306
Bass Sox Mercer, 360
Bayat, Rose, 67–68, 74, 117
Beale, Howard (fictional character), 202–203
Belisle, Kristine, 378
Bell, James, 298
Bellavia, Joe, Sr., 140
Bellavia, Leonard (Len), 33–34, 131, 140, 168, 188, 250, 293, 344, 345, 347, 356–359, 380
Bellavia Gentile & Associates, LLP, 33, 168
belt-tightening, 13
Belvidere IL, 201
Bentleyville PA, 111
Bethesda MD, 201
Biegler, Steve, 54–55
Big Three
of auto industry, 1, 15
of CRDR, 95
Bing, Dave, 189
bipartisan support, in US Congress for dealer issue, 31, 37, 98, 99, 103, 105–106, 107, 205, 232–233, 241, 258, 321, 367
Birmingham Chrysler Jeep (BCJ), 58, **148**, 183, 184, 186
Black Hawk Down (movie), 256
Blankenbeckler, Frank, 3, 99, 176–177, 178, 357
Bloom, Ronald (Ron), 16–17, 20, 100, 116, 134, 236, 254, 332, 336
Bloomfield Hills MI, 259
blue sky (goodwill), 57, 394
BMW, 34, 50, 201, 206

Boehner, John, 265, 266, 379
Boeing Company, 11
Bogdewic, Bruno, 111–112
Bogdewic, Bruno, Jr. (Chip), 112–113, 218
Boston Consulting Group, 39
Boykin, Jerry, 256
Bozzella, John, 239, 242
Brady, Phil, 216, 287, 288, 292
Branchburg, MS, 358
BRIC nations (Brazil, Russia, India, and China), 315, 321
Bridgewater MA, 129, 154, 180, 257, 313
Brunswick ME, 177
Buchanan, Kevin, 358
Buffet, Warren, 330
Buick, 50, 60, 122, 133, 140, 159, 161, 194, 206, 254, 261, 262, 313–315, 360, 374
Buick City, 313, 314
Bunkley, Nick, 279
Bunnell, Jim, 202
Bush, George H. W., 121
Bush, George W., 10, 11, 21, 294

C

CADA (California Automobile Dealers Association), 396
Cadillac, 50, 122, 133, 176, 177, 189, 191–192, 201, 206, 229, 370, 371
California
  and arbitration appeals, 361
  Chrysler buying land in, 376
  economic pain in, 282
  as high in dealership closures, 201
California Automobile Dealers Association (CADA), 396
Calisi, Mark, 3, 125–126, 128, **150**, 168, 169, 170–171, 248–250, 259, 270, 299, 301, 345, 347, 348, 369, 377
campaign to save the dealers, 19, 36, 79, 181, 253, 266, 267, 283, 319
Canadian government, 26, 27, 28
Cape Cod MA, 102
CAR (Center for Automotive Research), 136, 187, 211, 297, 394
"car czar," 16, 20, 31, 194, 329, 331, 390
Carlisle Chevrolet-Cadillac and Chrysler-Jeep, 176, 177
Carlson, Gretchen, 371
Carlson, Karen, 3, 122, 369, 370–371, 381
Carlson, Lee, 3, 122, 369, 370
Carlyle Group, 332
Carney, Ryndee, 343
Carter, Jimmy, 28
Cascade Auto Group, 101
Casper, Jim, 183
Cedar City UT, 55, 171
Center for Automotive Research (CAR), 136, 187, 211, 297, 394
Century Dodge Inc., 197, 352
Century Dodge-Chrysler-Jeep, 381
Century Motor Corp., 217–218
Cerberus Capital Management, 11, 15, 16, 21, 22, 25, 28, 44, 138, 139, 329, 334
Chappell, Beth, 334
Chapter 11 bankruptcy, 28, 158, 374–375
Charapp, Michael (Mike), 95, 124, 204, 283, 287, 342, 349–350, 354, 369
Charapp & Weiss LLC, 95
Chayefsky, Paddy, 202
Chevrolet, 48–50, 53, 57, 58, 71, 99, 102, 111–113, 121–122, 125, 129, 133, 140, 142, 144, 154, 161, 165–166, 167, 174–177, 180, 182, 188, 192–193, 196, 197–198, 202, 205–206, 210, 218, 229, 233, 248–249, 257, 261, 262, 264–265, 277, 301–302, 310, 313, 316, 326, 328, 339–340, 364, 370–372, 379
Chevrolet Cruze, 312
Chevrolet Malibu, 206
Chevrolet Volt, 10, 249
Chicago IL, 159

China
as one of BRIC nations, 315, 321
Rick Wagoner building business in, 374
strength of Buick in, 50, 133
Chrysler (brand), 13, 19–20, 32, 34, 38, 46, 48, 56, 58–59, 61, 70–71, 76, 78, 109, 126, 143, 151, 160, 168, 176, 179, 183, 190–191, 197, 201, 209, 228, 248, 254, 261–264, 269, 286, 296, 347, 351, 355, 358, 365, 371. *See also specific brands*
Chrysler Corporation, 44, 204
Chrysler Financial, 18, 133
Chrysler GEM, 125, 248
Chrysler Group LLC
Alpha dealer consolidation project, 254, 294
altering institutional memory, 190
announcement of dealership terminations, 306
arbitration with closed dealers. *See* arbitration
bailout of. *See* bailouts, of auto industry
bankruptcy filing, 158
bankruptcy hearings. *See* bankruptcy hearings
bankruptcy protection, 28, 38
breaking off talks, announcing arbitration, 307
on buying back cars and parts from closed dealers, 327
cease-and-desist response to Gus Russo, 190, 263, 318
challenging Colorado State laws, 64
change in position on how to resolve dealer concerns, 244
churning of upper-level execs, 333
claiming significant savings with closures. *See* automakers, claims of significant savings with closures
claims of dealer costs to, 128
compared to GM on dealer issue, 136
consolidating dealer legal cases, 351
on cutting quarter of dealer network, 51
data, 183, 292–293, 363
on decision to close Jim Tarbox dealership, 169
on decision to cut dealers, 51
decrease in retail outlets, 117
decrease in retail sales, 344
decrease in sales volume, 281
estimated cost savings per terminated dealership, 300
on excess dealers, 199
five-star dealer standing, 44, 60, 77, 92, 258, 395
history of reorganization, 44
"hit list," 44, 45, 58, 297, 333
initial news of closures, 45
initial talks with dealers, 242
Jim Press's calls to dealers on list, 46
legal costs of, 52, 299
management problems, 206
Marchionne as CEO of. *See* Marchionne, Sergio
as new name of Chrysler LLC, 25
new ownership of, 27
no reply to request from CRDR to negotiate, 100
notices to dealers, 29, 49, 187
number of arbitration cases from closed dealers, 342–343, 356
as one of Detroit Three or Big Three, 1, 15, 395
as one of Detroit Two, 1, 394
outcome with dealers, 364
placing competing businesses close together, 56
playing we-won't-back-down, 280
product problems, 206
products as lacking in appeal, 171
Project Genesis dealer consolidation plan, 33, 38
Proposal to Resolve Dealer Concerns, 244
questions about long-term viability of, 133

requesting discretion in placing reinstated dealers, 357
saying it would repay loans early, 377
secret e-mails among executives, 67, 169–170, 270
settlement talks with dealer groups, 307
settlements with closed dealers, 186, 264, 343, 344, 352, 379
throughput, 295
visit to Hill, 135
Chrysler LLC
announcement about shut downs, 4
approved loan to, 11, 18
bailout. *See* bailouts, of auto industry
CEO, 9
in need of partner, 16
new name, Chrysler Group LLC, 25
offered up for sale, 15, 26, 163, 236
as one of Detroit Two and Detroit Three, 1
restructuring of, 20, 22
termination letters from, 3
what to do about, 21, 23
Chrysler Unsecured Creditors Committee, 50, 70, 90, 91, 117, 222, 259
Chrysler-Fiat agreement, 26
Churchill, Winston, 157
Cimino, Jay, 355
class-action lawsuits, 2, 358, 359
Clayton GA, 66, 133, **155**, 174
Cleveland OH, 315
Cleveland Plain Dealer, 359
Clinton, Bill, 116
Clinton, Hillary Rodham, 17, 86
CNN Money, 281, 361, 368
Cole, David, 136, 187, 210–211, 297, 336
Cole, Ed, 211
Cole, Ken, 239, 243, 277
Coletta, Bob, 314
College Park MD, 48
Colonial Motors, 358
Colorado, state franchise laws, 60, 61, 63–64, 350
Colorado Attorney General, 61, 350
Colorado Department of Motor Vehicles, 61, 350
Colorado Department of Revenue, 61, 350
Colorado Springs CO, 355
Colvin, Alex, 354
Comiskey, Mike, 3, 172–174, 250–251
Committee to Restore Dealer Rights (CRDR). *See* CRDR (Committee to Restore Dealer Rights)
conditional loans, for GM and Chrysler, 12, 16, 22
conspiracy theorists, 140
constitutional rights, 1, 80, 98, 106, 176–178, 247, 357–358
Consumer Reports, 22, 208, 254, 344, 367
"continuing" dealers, 30, 91, 120, 132, 166, 178, 214, 215, 277, 352, 370
Conyers, John, 212
Conyers, John, Jr., 237
Cooper, Anderson, 373
"cover-your-ass" (CYA) tactics, 204
Crain, Keith, 373
Crain Communications, 373
CRDR (Committee to Restore Dealer Rights)
announcement about dealer rally, 233
on arbitration versus reinstatement of dealers, 341–342
author as member of, 2
as beacon of hope, 328
on behalf of all closed dealers, 209
on being only organization to advocate solely on behalf of disenfranchised dealers without duplicity, 290
benefits of, 361
building of "A-team," 65–66
clarifying misperceptions and innuendos, 137–141
as the "committee," 6

common bond among members of, 247
as David over Goliath, 322, 380
dealer rally. *See* auto dealers, rally
difference made in dealers' lives by, 122
doubters of, 124
federal legislation as goal of, 224
financing of, 108, 214, 291
formation of, 19, 93–95
growth of, 77
hitting the Hill, 222, 228–230, 235
and hurry-up-and-wait for Congress, 232
lack of financial support from NADA, 291
legal costs of, 108–109
letter asking for US House panel, 335
lobbying, costs of, 95, 108–109, 291
lobbyists for, 95, 228, 271–273, 322
march on Washington, 110
Mark Calisi's stepped-up role with, 170
meeting with four dealer groups and Congress, 238
needs of, 108
as obsessed dealers, 366
and Omnibus Appropriations Act HR3288, 304
and Outline of Alternative Solutions, 238
personal sacrifices made by, 378–380
planting the seeds for, 57
position of, 97
position on needing more dealer coverage not less, 280
reaction to Chrysler's Proposal to Resolve Dealer Concerns, 244
requesting support from NADA, 102
rumor about settlement talks, 100
on SIGTARP report, 360
success of, 305, 366
tension with NADA, 214, 215–217, 289
and united front with other dealer groups, 239
website, 69
Creative Syndicate, 375
CRM (customer relationship management), 23
Crossroads Superstore, 109, 176, 355
CSI (customer satisfaction index), 59, 62, 394
CSM Worldwide, 158
C-Span, 89
Cuomo, Andrew, 368
Curtice, Harlowe, 374
customer relationship management (CRM), 23
customer satisfaction index (CSI), 59, 62, 394
customers
  anti-Chrysler and -GM sentiment of, 185
  auto dealers as automakers' customers, 65, 114, 186, 198, 317, 365, 390
  complaints from, 198
  dealers as voice of , 240
  holding tight to money, 224
  "orphaned" customers, 54
  reaction from, on closings, 53–55, 133, 172, 206, 211, 264
Cuyahoga Falls OH, 101
CYA ("cover-your-ass") tactics, 204

D

Daimler, 132, 205, 329
Daimler-Benz, 28, 329
Dalgleish, Charles, Jr., 191
Dalgleish, Doug, Jr., 191
Dalgleish, Douglas, 191
Dalgleish, Keith, 191
Dalgleish Cadillac, 191–192
D'Andrea, Nicholas, 159–160, 194
D'Andrea Buick-Pontiac-GMC, 159, 194, 360
Dannehower, Gilbert, 348–349
DARCARS Automotive, 2, 13, 46, 48, 68, 71, 75–76, 88, 117, 262, 379

DART (dealer analysis and reporting tool), 201, 202, 209, 394
Darvish, Bonnie, 82
Darvish, Jamie, 48, 119
Darvish, John, 5, 13, 45–46, 48–49, 57, 71, 75, 82, 91, 139, **156**, 223, 262
Darvish, John, Jr., 48, 119
Darvish, Judy, 48
Darvish, Tamara (Tammy)
activities of, 69–70
at AIADA spring conference, 45–47
appreciations for, 121–123, 381–382
arranging meetings with Tom Pappert, 235
and art of compromise, 303
background, 82–85
call from Yale King, 62
"call-to-action" memos, 158
as coleader of CRDR, 6, 19, 32, 57, 67, 94, 267
counsel from colleagues, friends, and family to, 287
as CRDR at-large media person, 96
at dealer rally reception, 221–222, 226
on dealers' Fifth Amendment rights, 357
described, 80–82, 85–86
e-mails, 62, 69, 77, 96, 97, 100, 105, 108, 120, 123, 158, 226, 232, 241, 248, 256, 266, 268, 270, 288, 302, 312, 329, 381
executive vice president of DARCARS Automotive, 14
family, 71–74, 80–83, 162. *See also* Fallahi, Hamid; Nadia; Nima
feeling she had not done enough, 320
on free-enterprise system, 283
get-out-the-vote style of, 243
as hearing sounds of screaming souls, 119–120
as history maker, 321
hitting the Hill, 88–89, 96–97, 119, 222
humor, 195
on implications of automakers lying under oath, 328–329
Jack Fitzgerald as mentor and sounding board, 95
Jim Press's apology to, 212
and letter asking for US House panel, 335
as looking at the big picture, 371–372
at meeting informing Fairfax VA store members, 48
meeting with Mark Reuss, 309–313
as member of Unsecured Creditors Committee, 91–92
memo to Congress, 40, 42–43
memo to Phil Brady, 287, 288
motivation of, 119–120, 178, 233–234
note and gift to Steve Rattner, 382–383
on personal sacrifices made, 380
photo of, **146**, **156**
press conferences on dealer rights issue, 74
proposal to NADA to recognize CRDR as negotiating arm for cut dealers, 287
at rally press conference, 4, 231
reason for getting involved, 68–69
reason for organizing dealers, 87
rebuke from NADA, 215, 216
Rob Smith as double for, 266
with SIGTARP officials, 243
sitting in US bankruptcy court, 90
and struggle with NADA, 262, 283–285, 287–289, 296
Tammy-in-distress calls, 117–119
"A-team." *See* "A-team"
Yale King's "don't-quit" message, 256
Darvish, Terri, 82
data. *See also* statistics
from Auto Exec, 201, 389
from auto industry, 24
from Chrysler, 183, 292–293, 363
CRDR compilation of, 127, 201
from dealers, 183, 292–293

from J. D. Power and Associates, 138
from media sources, 27–28
from NADA, 35, 65, 98, 101, 138, 157, 201, 231, 269, 282, 389
from R. L. Polk, 117, 138, 227
dealer analysis and reporting tool (DART), 201, 202, 209, 394
"dealer economic rights" bills, 79
Dealer Economic Rights Restoration Act (HR2743), 98, 155, 305
dealer groups
breakthrough on Outline of Alternative Solutions, 238–239
compromise agreement among, 283, 296, 297
"dealer hit list," 44, 45, 58, 297, 333
Dealer magazine, 68
dealer performance summary (DPS), 181, 210, 278, 395
Dealer Rights Act, 306
"Dealergate," 139, 375
dealers associations
American International Automobile Dealers Association (AIADA), 45
California Automobile Dealers Association (CADA), 396
Detroit Automobile Dealers Association, 183, 191, 258
General Motors Minority Dealers Association (GMMDA), 192, 208, 396
Georgia Auto Dealers Association, 175, 226
Maryland Automobile Dealers Association (MADA), 285
National Automobile Dealers Association (NADA). *See* NADA (National Automobile Dealers Association)
Ohio State Dealers Association, 222
Orange County Automobile Dealers Association, 339
Washington Area Dealers Association, 222
Dean, Amy, 348
Dearborn MI, 136
Deese, Brian, 20
Defiance OH, 381
Deland Dodge, 348–349
DeLorean, John, 200
DeMint, Jim, 31
Democratic National Committee, 17
Democrats, 6, 21, 31, 37, 105, 139, 141, 272, 303
Dependable Dodge, 121, 132–133
Detroit Automobile Dealers Association, 183, 191, 258
Detroit Economic Club (DEC), 334
Detroit Free Press, 189, 191
Detroit MI, 3, 21, 24, 26, 153, 182, 189, 191, 286, 315, 316, 326, 330, 369
Detroit News, 375, 376
Detroit Three, 1, 15, 237, 367, 395
Detroit Two, 1, 194, 207, 215, 294, 394
Deutsche Bank, 39
DeWindt, Jonathan, 183
Diaz, Fred, 61
Dilmore, Bob, 119, 133, 196–197, 205– 208, 217–219, 374–375
Dodge, 38, 48–49, 51–52, 61, 76, 78, 115, 121, 125, 132–133, 143, 150, 152, 159–161, 165, 169–174, 186–187, 191, 197–198, 215, 250, 261–263, 294, 296, 318, 348–349, 351–352, 365, 371, 381
Don Yenko Chevrolet, 111
Doran, Tim, 209, 222, 242, 299, 385
Doucette, William (Bill), 204, 345, 346
Dow Jones Financial News, 368
Dowd, Mary Jo, 95, 271, 322, 323
DPS (dealer performance summary), 181, 210, 278, 395
"dualed," 61, 176, 205, 209, 252
dually owned dealerships, 61
Dubuque IA, 358
Duhon, Troy, 251
Durbin, Dick, 238, 301, 305, 367
Duvall, Jeff, 66, 133–134, **155**, 174–175, 225–226, 230, 251–253, 291, 301

Duvall, Louie, **155**, 174, 225, 226
Duvall Chrysler-Dodge-Jeep, 133
Dylan, Bob, vi

E

Eagle Auto Mall, 125, 248, 346
Eddy, Chuck, Jr., 214
Eiseley, Loren, 308
Elyria OH, 56, 267, 268
Emanuel, Rahm, 17, 116, 261
Engel, Peter, 164
Engel, Rich, 164
Engel, Rob, 164–165
Enterprise, 114
Esmond, Don, 280, 281–282
Estle, Jim, 381

F

Fallahi, Hamid, 73–74, 81
Farmington Hills MI, 197, 351
Farrell, Diana, 20
Faulkner, Richard, 340, 343, 354, 356, 357, 362, 365
federal bailouts. *See* bailouts
Feinberg, Steve, 15, 138
Feldman, Matt, 20, 28
Fiat, 23, 25–28, 131, 138, 209, 317, 348, 365, 376–377
Fiat SpA, 16, 38, 297
Fiat-500 plan, 294
fight song, 66
Finnin Motors, 358
first refusal rights, 61, 350
Fitzgerald, Jack
- answers to automakers' spin, 298
- appearance on *C-Span*, 89
- on auto task force, 19, 64–65, 159, 329
- background, 223–224
- as co-founder of CRDR, 6, 32, 93–95, 267
- on Congress's bipartisan agreement, 106
- on CRDR, 366–367
- on CRDR rate of success, 379
- at dealer rally reception, 221, 223, 225
- on dealers facing the market dilemma, 20
- on dealers' Fifth Amendment rights, 357
- drafting legislation to reverse closures, 110, 307
- as force of nature, 285
- on Fritz Henderson's claims, 127–128
- as history maker, 321
- hitting the Hill, 222
- as hometown hero, 253
- as innovator, 254
- as leading by example, 114
- on level of cuts being government ordered, 369
- as mentor and sounding board to Tammy Darvish, 95, 287
- message from GM re: negotiating with CRDR, 100
- on NADA conflict issue, 289–290
- as numbers man, 116
- as one closed dealer, 34–35, 46–47
- as one of Tammy Darvish's business associates, 74, 88, 117–119
- on personal sacrifices made, 379
- photo of, **142**, **146**, **147**
- on President Obama, 320
- Rob Smith as right-hand man to, 14, 101
- on SIGTARP findings, 338
- on Steve Rattner, 368
- on team of bill crafters, 98
- wanting to represent affected dealers, 56–57

Fitzgerald Auto Malls, 14, 20, 34, 56, 127, 155, 229
five-star dealer standing, 44, 60, 77, 92, 258, 395

Flint MI, 30, 313–314, 315, 316, 317
floor planning, 102, 126, 130, 179, 277, 339, 369, 395
Florida
  and arbitration appeals, 361
  law regarding facilities, 349
Ford, 16, 48, 51, 129, 174, 206, 233, 271, 283, 298, 339–340, 365
Ford, Bill, Jr., 136
Ford, Henry, 9
Ford Motor Company
  CEO, 9
  cracking code with midline sedans, 206
  eating GM's lunch, 224
  impact on, of letting Chrysler go, 23
  increase in sales and profits, 54, 208, 224
  as one of Detroit Three or Big Three, 1, 15, 395
  pre-Alan Mulally, 136
  and resist of federal bailout, 11, 93
  response to crisis-type problem, 135
  restructuring of, 16, 137
  winnowing of dealer ranks, 136
Ford Motor Credit Company, 133
Fortune, 18, 137, 213, 314
Fox News, 140, 254, 329, 371, 373
Frank, Barney, 105, 119, 130, 154, 205, 257, 258
Franklin, Aretha, 194
free-enterprise system, 12, 166, 190, 199, 205, 283, 326, 338, 385
Freres, Lazard, 17
Fullerton CA, 339

G

Galeana, Carl, 132
Gannon, Jack, 204
Gates, Bill, 330
Gaye, Marvin, 67
Geithner, Timothy (Tim), 11, 17, 18, 31, 38, 320, 337
General Motors Acceptance Corporation (GMAC), 18, 114, 133, 193, 279
General Motors Company, 25, 30, **153**
General Motors (GM). *See* GM (General Motors)
General Motors Holding Company, 25
General Motors Institute (GMI), 314
General Motors Minority Dealers Association (GMMDA), 192, 208, 396
Genesis. *See* Project Genesis dealer consolidation plan
Georgia Auto Dealers Association, 175, 226
Gerber, Robert, 39
Gettelfinger, Ron, 332
Gharib, Mina, 14, 68, 117
Gibbes, Robert, 335
Gibbs, Robert, 12, 140
Gibbs, Tommy, 132, 212–213
Giffords, Gabrielle, 107
"gifting" of dealerships, 162–163, 179, 183, 186, 262, 265, 286, 288, 296, 306
Girsky, Steve, 332
glossary, 394–396
GM (brand), 13, 19, 20, 34, 38, 46, 48, 52, 56, 58–62, 71, 109, 121, 122, 144, 151, 157–160, 162, 176, 179–180, 189, 194, 197, 201, 209, 228, 254, 257, 277, 308, 351, 355, 358, 365, 370. *See also specific brands*
GM (General Motors)
  admiting mistakes in picking and closing dealers, 279
  altering institutional memory, 190
  announcement about shut downs, 4
  announcement of first round of planned dealer cuts, 306
  approved loan to, 11, 18
  arbitration with closed dealers. *See* arbitration
  bailout of, 23, 25. *See also* bailouts, of auto industry
  bankruptcy decision, 39
  bankruptcy filing, 158

as bleeding badly, 16
boutique-style facilities, 294
breaking off talks, announcing arbitration, 307
challenging Colorado State laws, 64
churning of upper-level execs, 333
claiming significant savings with closures. *See* automakers, claims of significant savings with closures
compared to Chrysler on dealer issue, 136
DART (dealer analysis and reporting tool), 201, 202, 209, 394
decrease in retail outlets, 117
dismantling of, 20
estimated cost savings per terminated dealership, 300
on excess dealers, 199
federal aid amount, 279
as Generous Motors, 202
as Government Motors, 276
history of reorganization of, 44
"image stores," 294
initial news of closures, 45
initial public offering (IPO), 332–333, 376
initial talks with dealers, 242
looking to reduce government's ownership stake, 376
loss of market share in 1980s, 224
losses in 2008 and 2009, 25
mistakes on product side, 206
new name, General Motors Company, 25
new ownership of, 27
notice to DARCARS Automotive, 49
notices to dealers, 29
number of arbitration cases from closed dealers, 342–343
and offer of cash settlements, 282
and offer to review some questionable decisions, 243
as one of Detroit Three or Big Three, 1, 15, 395
as one of Detroit Two, 1, 394
outcome with dealers, 364
placing competing businesses close together, 180
profits of, in early 2011, 368
Quality Dealer Program, 374
refusal to negotiate with CRDR, 100
restructuring plans, 22
settlement talks with dealer groups, 307
settlements with closed dealers, 159, 167, 193, 208, 209, 264, 282, 343
"a shiny new GM," 21, 25, 374
statistics on dealer issue, 363
talks about leaving Detroit, 317
Technical Center, 373
termination of dealers, 340
willing to reconsider position on dealers, 279–280
"wind down," 3, 29, 47, 52, 57, 116, 180, 187–188, 191–192, 198, 202, 243, 316, 339, 361, 376
GM Dealer Appeal Group, 60
GM Minority Dealer Advisory Council, 193
GM Renaissance Center (RenCen), 21, **153**, 308, 315
GMAC (General Motors Acceptance Corporation), 18, 114, 133, 193, 279
GMC, 50, 60, 133, 159–161, 194, 201, 206, 229, 254, 360
GMI (General Motors Institute), 314
GMMDA (General Motors Minority Dealers Association), 192, 208, 396
"go forwards," 30, 94, 277, 344, 352, 370
Gonzalez, Arthur J., 38, 91, 168, 170, 183, 185, 250, 345, 347, 348
Goolsbee, Austan, 20
Goshn, Carlos, 16, 26, 317
Grady, Peter (Pete), 39, 128, 129, 131, 169, 242, 293–295, 318, 333, 345–346
Grassley, Chuck, 98, 110, 205, 306, 307, 367
Grosse Pointe MI, 189, 262
Group One, 114

H

Hahn, Bill, Jr., 381
Haigh, Jack, 109, 176, 355–357, 370
"haircut," 46, 139
Halleen, Eric, 379
Halleen, Mark, 379
Halleen Chevrolet, 265
Harris, Andy, 273
Harry Potter series, 316
Hastings, Reed, 137
Hawkinson, Doug, 157
Heath, Tom, 46–47
Hemingway, Ernest, 44, 324
Hemi-powered trucks, 52
Henderson, Fritz, 24, 29, 39, 50, 126, 130–131, 181, 204, 257, 277–278, 331, 333–334
Hertz, 114
"Highway 61 Revisited" (song), vi
Hitchcock, Alfred, 69
Holiday Automotive, 197
Holiday Chevrolet Inc., 197
Home Depot, 45
Honda, 34, 113, 129, 201, 294, 365
Honda Accord, 206, 265
Hoyer, Steny, 31, 34–35, 36–37, 96, 98, 105–106, 110, 119, **146**, 205, 227, 235, 237–238, 241, 258, 272, 274, 298, 303, 305–306, 322, 367
Huffington, Arianna, 319
Huffington Post Media Group, 319
Hughes, John, 96, 107, 119, 244, 274
Hummer, 29, 127, 158, 341, 375
Huntington Chevrolet, 193
Hutchison, Kay Bailey, 31
Hyundai, 129, 140, 201
Hyundai Motor America, 206

I

Iacocca, Lee, 44, 119, 139, 200, 204, 235–236, 375, 388
Illinois
    and arbitration appeals, 361
    decimated by auto crises, 104
    as heavily represented in arbitrations, 342
    as high in dealership closures, 201
imports (auto), 13, 33, 53, 117, 171, 201, 206, 227, 294
Indiana, as second-largest automotive manufacturing state, 315
Indianapolis Star, 315
initial public offering (IPO), 332–333, 376
ISH Automotive, 158
It Takes a Village (H. R. Clinton), 86

J

J. D. Power and Associates, 138, 297, 382
J. L. Hudson's, 315
J. P. Morgan Chase, 39
Jack Wolf Pontiac-Cadillac-GMC Inc., 201
Jackson-Lee, Sheila, 378
Jacksonville FL, 49
Jaguar, 136
J.D. Power and Associates, 22, 38
Jeep, 28, 32, 38, 46, 48, 51–52, 54–55, 56, 58–59, 61, 70, 76–78, 123, 125–126, 133, 143, 148, 159–161, 164, 168–170, 172–174, 176–177, 179, 183–185, 187–188, 190–191, 197, 248, 250, 254, 261–264, 269, 286, 294, 296, 317–318, 325–326, 347, 355–356, 358, 365, 371, 380–381
Jefferson, Thomas, 88
jobs, loss of, as result of dealer closures, 4–5, 36, 97, 98–99, 106, 107, 137–138, 157, 184, 203, 223, 231, 233, 237, 274, 320, 336, 347, 395
Jobs, Steve, 330
Johnson, India, 342, 361

K

Kelley Blue Book, 298
Kelly, Paul, 356
Kennedy, John Fitzgerald (Jack), 221
Kennedy, Ted, 130–131, 154, 181, 205, 257, 278, 367, 387
Kensington MD, 14, 266
Kerry, John, 367
Kersenbaum, Tim, 185–186
Kesey, Ken, 128
Kia, 125, 129, 201, 248, 339, 347
Kia Motors America, 261
Killgore, Pearlman, Stamp, Ornstein and Squires, 343
Kilpatrick, Kwame, 189
King, Martin Luther, Jr., 111
King, Remington, **151**
King, Rex, 58, 59, **151**
King, Sebastian, **151**
King, Shauna, 58, 256
King, Yale, 3, 58–64, 68, 121–122, **151**, 202, 209, 254–257, 282, 292, 301, 350, 378
King, Yale Blake, **151**
King Auto Group dealerships, 59–61
Kitzmiller, Peter, 65, 166, 285, 291
Kokomo IN, 315
Konkal, Paul, 183
Koronis Motors, 157
Kratovil, Frank, 32, 96, 98, 110, 238, 273, 306, 322

L

LaBelle, Steve, 121, 129–131, **154**, 180–182, 206, 210, 257–258, 276–279, 301–302, 313, 316–317
Land Rover, 136
Landry, Steven (Steve), 204, 242, 264, 333
LaNeve, Mark, 135, 181, 202, 257–258, 277, 333
Lanham MD, 49
LaRiche, Lou, 58
LaRiche, Scott, 58
Las Vegas NV, 152
LaSorda, Tom, 26, **145**, 212
LaTourette, Steve, 31, 98, 103–104, 105, 107, 110, 205, 227, 258, 265–266, 272, 303–304, 306, 322, 367, 379
LaTourette Amendment, 104, 232, 234, 303
lawsuits against automakers, 2, 218, 341, 356–359, 381
lawyers
  for auto dealers. *See* Allely, Craig; Arent Fox; Bellavia, Leonard (Len); Bellavia Gentile & Associates, LLP; Buchanan, Kevin; Charapp, Michael (Mike); Charapp & Weiss LLC; Dowd, Mary Jo; Faulkner, Richard; Ornstein, Mark; Vorberg, Elaine; Zanville, Harry
  for automakers. *See* Bozzella, John; Cole, Ken; Lyons, Joe
  for CRDR. *See* Dowd, Mary Jo; Renberg, Dan
Lazard, 18
Lee, Brian, 62–63
legal costs
  of auto dealers, 64, 350, 352
  of automakers, 52, 299
  of CRDR, 108–109
legislation and legislative efforts, 28, 32, 37, 77, 95, 103, 104, 105, 107, 110, 141, 208, 220, 224, 227, 228, 230, 232, 233, 234, 239, 241, 244, 258, 264, 265, 272, 273, 283, 288, 289, 292, 299, 301, 303, 304, 305, 307, 341, 347, 360, 361, 366–367, 371, 380. *See also* US Congress; US House; US Senate
Lehman Brothers, 18, 328
Leno, Jay, 373
Lester, Damon, 192, 240
Letter of Intent (LOI), 218, 280, 306, 313, 343, 352–355, 395

Levin, Carl, 237
Lexus, 50
Libby, Tom, 345
The Life of Reason or the Phases of Human Progress (Santayana), 196
"Like a Rock" (song), 53
Lincoln, Abraham, 125
Lincoln-Mercury, 16
Livonia Chrysler Jeep Inc., 197
Livonia MI, 197
lobbying
  costs of, by CRDR, 95, 108–109, 291
  groups, 98
lobbyists
  for auto dealers, 57, 98, 117, 254, 288, 289, 290
  for automakers, 68, 239, 241–243, 277
  for CRDR, 95, 228, 271–273, 322
  NADA as, 77
Lochmoor Chrysler-Jeep, **148**, 188, 262, 286, 317–318, 326–327, 380
LOI (Letter of Intent). *See* Letter of Intent (LOI)
Longmont CO, 3, 58, 59, 121, 254
The Lord of the Rings, 316
Los Angeles Times, 24
Lunt, Jim, 55, 171, 172, 178
Lunt, Mitch, 55–56, 171–172
Lunt Motor Co., 55
Lutz, Bob, 200, 206
Lyndhurst OH, 142, 264
Lyons, Joe, 239

M

The Machine That Changed the World, 316
Macy's, 315
MADA (Maryland Automobile Dealers Association), 65, 166, 291, 396
Maffei, Dan, 32, 98, 110, 235, 238, 258, 306, 307
Main Motors, 122, 370
Main Street
  compared to Wall Street, 40, 164
  as home of dealerships, 111, 113
  in trouble, 203
Main-Street dealers, demise of, 5, 113, 185, 197, 317, 338
Malkin, Michelle, 375
management briefings seminar (MBS), 330
The Man Who Knew Too Much (movie), 69
manufacturing in US, failing of, 18, 315, 316, 321
Manzo, Mike, 348
Marchionne, Sergio, 16, 25–26, 40–41, 115, 129, 137–138, **143**, 167, 189–190, 212, 294, 297, 317–318
Marhofer, Ron, 188, 379
Marhofer Chevrolet, 188
Marinos, Chris, 197
Mark Sims' Chevrolet, **142**
marketplace, as decider, 166, 365
Marshall, Jim, 226
Marshall Fields, 315
Maryland, dealer closures in, 228
Maryland Automobile Dealers Association (MADA), 65, 166, 291, 396
Marzulla, Nancie, 359
Marzulla, Roger, 359
Massarelli, Rocco, 77
Mazda, 16, 125, 229, 248, 347
MBS (management briefings seminar), 330
McAllen TX, 77
McClennan, Marni, 76–77
McDonald, Colleen, 197–198, 295, 338, 351–352
McDonald, David, 197–198, 351
McEleney, John, 32, 252, 285, 288–289
McElwee, Carrie, 51
McGee Chevrolet, 316
McGuire, George, 49, **144**, 165–167, 325–326, 364
Mealey, Jackie, 3, 80, 92, **149**, 160, 186, 259–261, 286, 319

Mealey, Richard, 3, 32, 58, 70, 92, **148**, 160, 183–186, 203, 217, 258–260, 286, 325, 344, 352
media. *See also specific media outlets*
on American Dream souring, 319
on brashness of CRDR, 124
coverage of dealer issue, 3, 5, 44, 64, 115–116, 216, 229, 247, 319, 373
dubbing of GM "Government Motors," 27, 276
dubbing of Steve Rattner "car czar," 16, 20
erroneous reports in, 343
on Jim Press's leaving Chrysler, 212–213
on *Overhaul* (Rattner), 116
portrayal of dealers, 110
response to automakers' claims of significant savings with closures, 126
on SIGTARP, 337, 360
on Steve Rattner and Quadrangle, 368
on Wade and Painter deal, 285
Mellencamp, John, 53
Mercedes-Benz, 50, 201, 205
Michigan
and arbitration appeals, 361
Chrysler consolidating dealer cases in, 351
as heavily represented in arbitrations, 342
as high in dealership closures, 201
reinstating dealerships in, 357
tough economic climate in, 352
middle-class America, 15, 321–322
Midland MI, 84
Midler, Bette, 246
Miller, Arthur, 364
minimum sales responsibility (MSR), 51, 209, 286, 360, 395
minority auto dealers, 192, 240. *See also* NAMAD (National Association of Minority Automobile Dealers)
misperceptions
about bad dealers, 223
about dealers and their role in automakers' decline, 134
about dealers as economic liability for automakers, 137–138
about dealers' position on auto industry bailout, 109
Mitsubishi, 53, 129, 179
Mock, Brian, 382
Mock, Frank, 218, 371, 381–382
Mock, John, 218, 371, 381–382
Mock, Kevin, 218, 382
Mock family, 218
Moore, Michael, 30, 313
Morgan Stanley, 18
Morgan UT, 51
Morie, Bill, 226
Motor Trend Car of the Year, 206
"move forward" dealers, 30. *See also* "go forwards"
MSR (minimum sales responsibility), 51, 209, 286, 360, 395
Mulally, Alan, 9, 11, 16, 93, 136, 137, **145**, 208, 330
Mullahey, Tim, 339–340
Mullahey Chevrolet, 339
Murphy, Gerry, 222
Murray, Jill, 98
myths
of auto dealers being part of automakers' business, 97, 114, 130
on automakers giving dealers cars on consignment, 130
of dealers as "rip-off artists," 113–114
of dealers draining automakers' bottom line, 65
of dealers paying advertising charge per car purchased, 128
of "too many dealerships," 89, 163

N

NADA (National Automobile Dealers Association)
clout of, 221

and conflict-of-interest issue, 216–217, 292, 296
CRDR as independent from, 94
CRDR problems with, 271, 290–292, 301
data from, 35, 36, 65, 98, 101, 138, 157, 201, 231, 269, 282, 369, 389
fighting for constituents, 208–209
and good-old-boys' network, 287
hitting the Hill, 110
Jeff Duval on NADA's leadership, 252
meeting with CRDR, NAMAD, and ATAE, 238
membership and dues, 36, 77, 108, 175, 271, 292, 366
Michelle Primm message to, 101
as one of dealer advocacy groups, 57, 272, 274, 297, 396
position on reductions, 32
and pre-rally reception, 222
relationship with CRDR, 283
stand on SIGTARP, 336
taking middle stance, 100
and Tammy Darvish appointment to creditors committee, 90
tension between NADA and Tammy Darvish, 262, 283–285, 287–289, 296
tension with CRDR, 214–217
Nadia, 71, 73, 74, 162
Nai Nan Ko, 123
NAMAD (National Association of Minority Automobile Dealers), 67, 98, 108, 192, 193, 208, 238, 240, 283, 396
Nardelli, Robert (Bob), 9, 15, 22, 25, 26, 45, 93, 131, 138, 213, 329, 334
NASA (National Aeronautics and Space Administration), 281
Nashville Chrysler dealership, **149**
Nasser, Jacques, 136
National Association of Minority Automobile Dealers. *See* NAMAD (National Association of Minority Automobile Dealers)
National Economic Council, 17
National Highway Transportation Safety Administration (NHTSA), 281
National Public Radio, 45
NBC News, 110
NBC-WDIV TV, 191
Nephi UT, 162, 261, 262
Network (movie), 202
Never Surrender (Boykin), 256
"new car co," 28, 29, 30
New Orleans LA, 3, 172
New Page Corp., 334
New York Times, 18, 20, 28, 279, 285, 337
New Yorker, 373
The New York Times, 249
NHTSA (National Highway Transportation Safety Administration), 281
Nightly Business News, 45
Nima, 71–72, 74, 80
Nissan, 201, 294, 365
Nissan-Renault, 16, 26, 334
North American International Auto Show, 258
North Kingston RI, 3, 56, 168, 269
North Olmsted OH, 265
Northville MI, 158
Northwood University, 84

O

Obama, Barack, 9, 11, 12, 17, 21, 22, 31, 116, 181, 240, 261, 296, 305, 319
Obey, David, 104, 105
Ohio
and arbitration appeals, 361
Chrysler reinstating dealerships in, 357
as heavily represented in arbitrations, 342
as high in dealership closures, 201
Ohio State Dealers Association, 222
Oklahoma OK, 176
Olbermann, Keith, 373
"old car co," 28, 29, 30, 212

Oldsmobile, 29, 367
Oliver, Clarence, 277
Omnibus Appropriations Act HR3288, 304, 307, 341
One Flew Over the Cuckoo's Nest (Kesey), 128
Orange County Automobile Dealers Association, 339
Orlando FL, 343, 348, 365
Orleans Dodge-Chrysler-Jeep, **150**, 172, 250
Ornstein, Mark, 299, 343, 348–349, 353, 365, 370, 372–373
"orphaned" customers, 54
Osias, Brian, 20
Outline of Alternative Solutions, 238
Overhaul: An Insider's Account of the Obama Administration's Rescue of the Auto Industry (Rattner), 21, 35, 37, 93, 116, 140, 194, 214, 328, 332, 334

P

Painter, James (Jim), 3, **152**, 160, 161–162, 175, 262
Painter, Patrick, 162, 216, 261–262, 283, 298, 299
Painter, Phil, 160–164, 216, 261–262
Painter family, **143**, 161, 163–164, 178, 285, 296
Painter Motors, 261
Palese, Michael (Mike), 342–343, 355
Pappert, E. Tom, 119, 235–236, 254
Paulson, Hank, 10, 21, 38, 328
Paynesville MN, 157
Pennsylvania
  and arbitration appeals, 361
  as heavily represented in arbitrations, 342
  as high in dealership closures, 201
Penske group, 114
Phil Long Automotive, 355
Pierce, Mitch, 59
"Pinkie Swear" game, 165, 168, 364
Plymouth MI, 58
Pontiac, 29, 60, 106, 122, 127, 158–160, 174, 194, 201, 206, 261, 314, 341, 360
Potomac MD, 81
Premier Automotive, 251
Press, Jim, 26, 33–34, 38–39, 46, 59, 77, 131–132, **145**, 170–171, 199, 204, 211–213, 264, 327, 329, 333–334, 346, 364, 369
Press, Linda, 213
Price, Tom, 226
Primm, Michelle, 101
Project Genesis dealer consolidation plan, 33, 38, 61, 169, 197, 205, 242, 254, 293, 355
property seizures, 74, 86, 98, 176, 178, 205, 357, 359

Q

Quadrangle Group, 16, 334, 368
Quality Jeep Chrysler Inc., 356

R

R. L. Polk, 117, 138, 227, 345
Ram, 38, 169
Randolph, A. Philip, 341
Rattner, Steven, 16–18, 20–23, 25–26, 28, 30–31, 34–37, 65, 93, 100, 116, 140, **144**, 168, 194, 214, 223, 228, 328, 332, 334–336, 367–368, 373, 382–383
Rayburn, Sam, 227
Rayburn House Office Building, 227
The Reckoning, 316
Redford, Robert, 161
Reed, Jack, 30–31, 269
Regan, David, 222
Reid, Harry, 104
Renault SA-Nissan Motor Co., 213
Renault-Nissan, 213, 317

Renberg, Dan, 95, 222, 245, 271, 272–273
Republicans, 6, 31, 105, 139, 272, 303
"R-E-S-P-E-C-T" (song), 194
"retired-judge factor," 305, 342, 348, 354
Reuss, Lloyd, 311, 314–315
Reuss, Mark, 206, 278, 309–317, 323, 353, 371, 376
Reuters, 9, 51, 332, 368, 376
Reuther, Walter, 315
Richard Auto Center, 76–77
Richmond Hills GA, 197
right of first refusal, 61, 350
Rivera, Ivette E., 254
Riverhead NY, 3, 125, 170, 248
Roberts, Desmond, 192
Robinet, Michael, 158
Rockefeller, John D., 301
Rockefeller, John (Jay), 31, 105, 110, 238, 244, 258, 299, 306, 322, 336
Rockville MD, 48, 68, 201, 223
Roger and Me (movie), 30, 313, 316
Romero, Christy, 377, 378
Ron Marhofer Auto Family, 188
Rothschild, Inc., 39
Royal Oak MI, 381
Ruggles, David, 295, 328
Rupert, Christine (née Van Burkleo), 77–78
Russert, Tim, 110
Russo, Agostino (Gus), 3, **148**, 188–191, 262–264, 317–318, 326, 380
Russo, Gina, 3, **148**, 188–189, 191, 262–263, 286, 319, 326
Russo, Patricia, 332

S

Saab, 29, 127, 130, 158, 341
SAAR (seasonally adjusted annual rate), 281, 395
Sackrison, John, 339
Salt Lake Tribune, 285, 290, 296
Sam Rayburn Building, 227
Santayana, George, 196
Saturn, 29, 127, 129, 158, 192, 341
Schnurr, Brian, 204, 264, 333
Scroggin, Phil, 169, 345, 346
seasonally adjusted annual rate (SAAR), 281, 395
SEC (Securities and Exchange Commission), 334
Section 363 bankruptcy ("363"), 20, 28, 54, 158, 378
Seger, Bob, 53
settlement talks, rumor about, 100
settlements with closed dealers
  with Alan Spitzer, 159, 379
  with DARCARS Automotive, 379
  in general, 167, 208, 343
  with Greg Williams, 193
  with Jeff Duvall, 253
  with Richard Mealey, 186, 344, 352
  with Russos, 264
Shakopee Chevrolet, **144**, 165–166
Shakopee MN, 49, 165, 167, 326
"shared sacrifice" theme, 12, 17, 31, 199, 218, 247, 320, 376, 378
Shroyer, Angela, 173
Shyon, 162
SIGTARP (Special Inspector General for the Troubled Asset Relief Program), 19, 40, 64, 105, 118, 170, 194, 203, 209, 243–244, 264–265, 299–300, 335–338, 340, 349, 360–362, 369, 377, 395
Silver Spring MD, 13, 48, 71, 215, 222
Sims, Mark, 121, 233, 264–266, 301, 357, 359, 379
Smith, Rob, 14–15, 74, 88, 95, 101, **155**, 162, 195, 221–222, 228–232, 238, 266–267
Smith, Roger, 22, 30
Sowles, Bill, 177–178
Sox, Richard, 360
Spanish Fork UT, 51, 179, 180
Special Inspector General for the Troubled Asset Relief Program (SIGTARP). *See* SIGTARP (Special Inspector General for the Troubled Asset Relief Program)

Spitzer, Alan, 6, 19, 32, 56–57, 80, 88, 93–94, 109, 127–128, **146**, 159, 222, 265, 267–268, 291, 321, 379
Spitzer, Alison, 95, 221, 226, 231, 268–269
Spitzer Management Group, 267
Sproule, Simon, 213
St. George UT, 3, 152, 160, 161, 196, 261, 262
Stabenow, Debbie, 237
Stagg, Marilyn, 102–103
Star Wars (movie), 316
"The Star Thrower" (Eiseley), 308, 323
state dealer trade associations, 396. *See also specific associations*
state franchise laws, 32, 54, 60–63, 169, 177, 207, 303–304, 349, 350, 351
Staten, Marjorie, 192
statistics. *See also* data
  to counter myth of "too many car dealers," 89
  final tally from automakers, 363
  on Metro Detroit impact from rejected dealers, 182–183
  on minority dealers cut, 193
  on profitability of Chrysler dealerships, 293
  on serving communities, paying taxes, and trickle-down effect on employment, 114
Stempel, Robert, 311
"Stepford Wives," 168, 199–200, 216, 320
Sterling Heights MI, 50
Stewart, Jimmy, 69
Stockwell, Michelle, 96
"Stop the Dealers at All Costs," 293
Stow OH, 188
Studebaker, 28
Sullins, Bob, 109, 176
Summers, Larry, 11, 17–18, 20–21, 23, 214, 320, 375
Sun Country Chrysler, Dodge, and Jeep, 160
Sundance Film Festival, 161
suppliers, 5, 11–13, 18, 22, 29, 31, 90, 114, 117, 135, 164, 184–185, 203, 231, 328–330
Sutton, Betty, 107, 119, 306
SUVs, 201
Sweeny, Brian, 202

T

Talley Motors, 140
Tarbox, Jim, 3, 56, 70, 168–169, 170, 184, 258–259, 269–270, 345, 347–348, 369
Tarbox, Kim, 270
TARP (Troubled Asset Relief Program), 9–10, 12, 18, 37, 38, 40, 114, 203, 328, 335, 358, 360
Taylor MI, 351, 352
Tea Party, 6, 97
Team Auto, 20
Tenafly NJ, 164
Texas
  and arbitration appeals, 361
  dealers' class-action suit coming out of, 358
  as high in dealership closures, 201
Third World America: How Our Politicians Are Abandoning the Middle Class and Betraying the American Dream (Huffington), 319
"This Is Our Country," 53
"363" (Section 363 bankruptcy), 20, 28, 54, 158, 378
throughput, 295, 396
Time Dealer of the Year, 258
Time magazine, 68
Toccoa GA, 174
Tonkin, Ed, 215, 222, 285, 288, 336
Towns, Ed, 335
Toyota, 13, 39, 48, 50, 113, 129, 132, 201–202, 206, 211–213, 224, 229, 271, 280–282, 294, 329, 365
Toyota Camry, 50, 206
Toyota City, Japan, 50

Toyota Corolla, 206
Toyota dealer/sales model, 33–34, 39, 50, 132, 158, 205, 280–282, 330, 374
Toyota Motor Corporation, 24
Toyota Motor Manufacturing, 12
Toyota USA, 131
transplant automakers, 13
Traverse City MI, 330
Treasure Island FL, 212
Tricsity Computer Solutions, 185
Troubled Asset Relief Program (TARP). *See* TARP (Troubled Asset Relief Program)
Troy Auto World, 217
Troy MI, 3, 58, 92, 183, 185, 214, 319, 325
Troy Motor Mall, 183, 185, 325
Twain, Mark, 125
Twilight, 316

U

UAW (United Auto Workers), 11, 20, 27, 90, 106, 199, 315, 328, 332
UAW Solidarity House, 373
UAW's Voluntary Employee Beneficiary Association (VEBA), 27, 28
UBS, 39
unfair performance scoring, 61
unions, lack of support for dealer campaign, 237
United Auto Workers (UAW). *See* UAW (United Auto Workers)
United Dodge, **152**
United Steelworkers of America, 16–17
Unsecured Creditors Committee, 50, 70, 90, 91, 117, 222, 259
US Capitol, **154**
US Congress
  appointments with auto dealers, 225, 226
  bipartisanship of, on dealer issue, 31, 37, 98–99, 103, 105–107, 205, 232–233, 241, 258, 321, 367
  call for powwow on closed dealer situation, 241
  and compromise as way of doing business, 303
  CRDR schmoozing of, 222
  engaging in process of restoring dealers, 4, 19, 135
  influence of Tom Pappert on, 236
  introduction of legislation in, 232
  Outline of Alternative Solutions proposed to, 238
  passage of arbitration bill, 307, 341
  passage of law on dealer rights, 296, 341
  as path to getting problem fixed, 94
  pitted against auto task force, 37
  push for non-legislative solution for dealer issue, 236, 238, 289
  significant events in, spring 2009, 110
  Spitzer, Fitzgerald, and Darvish sharing stories with, 102
  staffers to CRDR, 273–275
  Tammy Darvish memo to, 42–43
  votes, 230–232, 235, 244–245, 247, 255, 264, 292, 298
US Constitution
  as being trampled, 4
  Fifth Amendment, 8, 98, 178, 265, 357, 358
US Court of Federal Claims, 359
US House
  Appropriations Committee, 104, 302
  bill amendment, 103–104
  bill HR75, 378
  bill HR2743, 31–32, 43, 98–99, 107, 179, 220, 233–234, 290, 303, 392–393
  bill HR2750, 98
  bill HR3288 (Omnibus Appropriations Act), 304
  bill sponsors, 107, 179, 233, 303, 367
  Energy and Commerce Subcommittee, 176

Judiciary Committee, 134, 168, 192–193, 237
Oversight and Government Reform Committee, 335
panel initial vote requiring GM and Chrysler to restore dealer franchise agreements, 103
votes, 103, 104, 194, 237, 239, 274, 302–304, 307
US Senate
bill S1304, 43, 98, 99, 103–105, 179, 220, 290, 303, 391
bill sponsors, 99, 104–105, 179, 239, 303, 367
Committee on Commerce, Science, and Transportation, 31, 105, 336
votes, 289, 303, 304
US Supreme Court, 340, 359, 362, 365
US taxpayers, impact of auto industry problems on, 21, 25, 38, 203, 279
US Treasury. *See also* Geithner, Timothy (Tim)
GM payment back to, 279
investment in automakers, 37, 38
as majority owner of GM, 27, 276
New York Times' story on, 337
as taxpayers' overseer, 18

V

Van Burkleo, Bill, 77
Van Hollen, Chris, 31, 36–37, 96, 98, 106, 119, 135, **156**, 223, 235, 238, 258, 272, 275, 298, 303, 306, 322, 367, 380
Vero Beach FL, 121, 132
Village Chrysler-Jeep, 381
Volvo, 16, 48, 118, 125, 136, 248, 347
Vorberg, Elaine, 122, 157, 159, 190, 194, 360–362

W

Wade, Stephen, 285, 287, 288, 290, 296
Wagoner, Richard (Rick), 9–10, 16, 23–25, 58–59, 93, 126, **145**, 193, 331, 333–334, 373–374
Wall Street
compared to Main Street, 40
and restructuring of Chrysler and GM, 18
Wall Street Journal, 27, 55, 249, 276
Wall Street refugees, 21, 64
Wall Street rejects, 375
Wall Street whiz kids, 373
Wallace, Bill, 178
Wallin, Courtney, 74, 81, 85–86, 117, 162, 234
Wangers, Jim, 206
Ward's Auto magazine, 192, 210, 218, 348
Ward's Dealer Business magazine, 127, 249, 328, 355
Wareham MA, 277
Warren MI, 21, 373
Washington Area Dealers Association, 222
Washington Area New Automobile Dealers Association, 382
Washington Post, 45, 46, 48, 254, 334
Watkins, Scott, 50
Waxahachie TX, 3, 176, 177
Way, Ramsey (Bub), 175
Weaver, David, 36–37, 96, 106–107, 119, 135–136, 223, 244, 274, 275
Welch, Jack, 24, 330
Wentzville MO, 217, 371, 381
"What's Going On?" (song), 67
Whitacre, Ed, 24, 40, 204, 265, 279, 298, 311–313, 330–332, 353, 376
White, Maureen, 17
Wilcox, Amy, 201
Wilde, Oscar, 220
Williams, Brian, 373
Williams, Greg, 193
Wilson, Harry, 20, 25
Windsor, Ontario, 26

"The Wind Beneath My Wings" (song), 246
Winfrey, Oprah, 373
Wyckoff NJ, 164

Y

Yahoo, 323
yes-men and women, 172, 200, 253, 364
Young, Debbie, 121, 132–133
Youngstown OH, 214
YouTube videos, 162

Z

Zanetti, Rick, 91
Zanville, Harry, 358

CPSIA information can be obtained at www.ICGtesting.com
Printed in the USA
LVOW080017131011

250292LV00002B/27/P